ESTHER CARLS DODGEN

GLIMPSES OF GOD
Through the Ages

A Collection of Personal Expressions
of Faith from the Bible to the Present

Glimpses of God Through the Ages

Copyright © 2003 Esther Carls Dodgen

Hendrickson Publishers, Inc.
P.O. Box 3473
Peabody, MA 01961-3473

ISBN 1-56563-717-8

Manufactured in the United States of America

First printing November 2003

Book & Cover Design:
Kevin van der Leek Design Inc.

Cover art:
God the Father by Pompeo Batoni (1708-1787)
© National Trust / Art Resource, NY

CONTENTS

PREFACE

"Some people seem not to know that there is any other world but this. They live only amid material things and do not dream there are things that are spiritual. Then some happy day they have a vision of Christ. Some experience lifts the veil and shows them a glimpse of his beauty. After that, life is never the same to them. We go back again to our common place tasks. Our work is not easier, our paths are not smoother, but there is something new in our hearts which transfigures all our experiences."

J. R. MILLER: THE INNER LIFE, 1893

IT IS WITH A GRATEFUL HEART that I put this manuscript aside— grateful for the opportunity now of sharing God's love through it. Working on this project has deepened my own spiritual awareness and made me feel a closeness to all those who have gone before and to those who continue to live, who have experienced God's presence in their lives. It is hoped that as you, the reader, read these expressions of faith, you also will feel this closeness and interconnectedness of Christians throughout the ages.

There is one pathway to God, but individuals find it in various ways. To some the pathway just seems to miraculously open up before them. Others struggle for years to find it. Some have to go through difficulties to catch a glimpse. Still others refuse to even look. Throughout all recorded history God has revealed himself to people in many different ways, each way appropriate to the individual's interests, background, personality, and God-given talents.

Generally speaking, writers have been placed according to the period of time in which they lived most of their lives, or at least most of their writing lives. We are limited, of course, to only those Christians who have left written evidence of their thoughts or who are still alive to verbally communicate it. This collection represents only a sampling of that great "cloud of witnesses" over the past 2000 years. The number of quotations given from each person is not an indication of the importance of that person's testimony. It simply means his personal reflections were more available and stood out to the compiler. No judgment concerning the individual beliefs and lives of the writers has been made. All are taken at their word of witness to God's presence in their lives.

May God use this effort of devotion to bring glory to His matchless name. As you read the following expressions of God's love and goodness in other people's lives, may your own experience be enlarged and enriched and may there be echoed in your own heart a song of praise that spontaneously exclaims, "Thanks be to God for His Unspeakable Gift!"

"A spiritual kingdom lies all about us, enclosing us, embracing us, altogether within reach of our inner selves, waiting for us to recognize it. He is waiting for our response to His presence."

A. W. TOZER, THE PURSUIT OF GOD, 1949

INTRODUCTION

My ears had heard of you, but now my eyes have seen you.

(JOB 42:5)

IN THIS BOOK YOU WILL find hundreds of first-hand expressions of God's presence in individual lives. Some are conversion accounts; others are day-by-day dealings of God in their personal lives. Still other revelations are simply testimonies to God's goodness and faithfulness. These "glimpses of God" have been gathered from various books, diaries, journals and personal recollections. Some of these witnesses are well-known and others are ordinary citizens. Included are testimonies of men and women, widely separated socially, economically, vocationally, denominationally and geographically throughout the ages, who have discovered the love of God and have known His presence in their lives. These voices in the wilderness point our souls to the living Christ, encouraging and inspiring us to greater faith, love and service. All, no matter of what era, unitedly testify to finding the abundant life of which Jesus spoke. Their manner of travel may have varied, but the pathway was always the same.

The only explanation that will account for the spread of Christianity and its endurance through the fire of persecution is the transformation brought about in the inner life of believers. That is the miracle and the proof—changed lives of those who have given up everything to follow God. There exists in us a spiritual reality, attested to by millions who have possessed it, by which God can be known and felt as the most real thing in human existence. Religion is so important, so spontaneous and innate to an individual that one cannot escape it. Our need for God hounds us and holds us even against our will. The following sampling of recorded accounts gives testimony to this miracle and this proof.

Why do some experience God and others do not? Why do some people seem to go through life with blinders on and never see God's goodness all around, never experience the tap on their heart's door? Only God knows the answer to the puzzle. To some God gives a marked sensitivity to the divine stirrings of the heart. Some have hardly thought about Him, yet He comes to them in splendor and glory. Some sail smoothly along without hardly ever a turbulent wave. Others travel over a rough, rutted road with seemingly constant darkness. Each person has his own unique story. Unquestionably, it is a single, straight and narrow path that God calls upon us to follow, but God reveals Himself to each one in a special way. Everything is a gift—grace. We do not do anything to earn it, and sometimes before we are even aware there is more to life, we are "granted this gifted awakening." We are unprepared for such an happening and have not even been thinking of God. He has been seeking us out and bringing us home, out of darkness into His wonderful light" (I Peter 2:9).

The call of God may come in countless ways. To some God's call comes in the exquisite beauty, orderliness and unity of the universe. Perhaps it comes simply, in a gentle, quiet moment of inexpressible elation; under the clear evening violet sky, during a calm, peaceful sunrise, or in the quietness of God's house in a moment of silent devotion,—changing one's perception of oneself and one's place in the world. Perhaps it comes quickly, like a burst of fire or flash of lightning, when one suddenly knows that he is in the presence of a great mystery. It sweeps over one, bringing with it a feeling of deep reverence, engulfing one's soul with God's love. For others it may be an intellectual awakening without any emotional impact—simply recognizing the truth of the Gospel. And for still others it involves a recognition of ones sinfulness and a need to surrender to the power of God's grace, through His Son, Jesus Christ. But more often it happens through a gradual succession of events. It takes place "gently and slowly as the opening of a rosebud to the sun." It is almost unnoticed until one day, everything is seen as different. There has been a slow realization of God's presence that marked no time or place. However it may happen, we open ourselves to God, and His Presence enters and takes possession of our hearts. We and He become One.

Something has to happen to release us from our absorption in self. Sometimes events will do it. Perhaps we sense God's presence in the death or struggle of a loved one or other crises that bring us to a realization of what is really important in life. When sadness comes, those who see God's hand at work will have peace. They will see God in the storm clouds as well as in the rainbow, in the wayside flower as well as in the stately rose, in the sunset as well as in the sunrise. This realization of God's presence may come to us also in the ordinary, daily routine, when we least expect it. It may have been but a word read in a book or a brief conversation with a stranger, or a moment of profound insight in the midst of a walk in the woods or the birth of a precious child....and in passing, left us touched with an unknown power. We then knew that we were in the presence of the Lord.

Spiritual awakening may happen at anytime from childhood to old age. As we look back to the first hint of the beginning of our spiritual journey we begin to see special moments of spiritual awakening and insight—those moments so soft and gentle, yet so forceful, which make the heart thrill and reveal to it suddenly a world of peace, joy and devotion. These experiences are unforgettable and life-changing. They become a hidden and inexhaustible source of strength and comfort. For a moment the veil seems to be suddenly drawn aside and our eyes are opened and we see for ourselves. From time to time we may become discouraged and lose our way, and even dismiss the significance of the experiences, but they will always be there to motivate and inspire us, for we have "seen the city," and it can no longer be hidden. God's plan for our lives was taking shape during all this time and He has been waiting for our wholehearted embrace. We see the fingerprints of God on these events and are convinced of God's touch upon our lives. " 'I know the plans I have for you,' declares the Lord" (Jeremiah 29:11).

When we let the sounds of the world die out in our soul, then we can hear the songs of God's "whispering winds." He is always speaking to us, but we do not always hear because our minds are so preoccupied with other interests and demands upon our lives that we have become deaf to His voice calling us, guiding us day by day. "Blessed are they that have eyes to see, They shall find God everywhere. They shall see him where others see stones" (John Oxenham).

Having this abundant life is so simple—all we have to do is believe. Yet so many strive for all the trappings of this world and never seem to realize that it all leads to a dead end. The gate is too narrow to allow us to carry our possessions with us. If we seek something of our own, we do not seek God only, and we will never find Him. We will find God when we seek Him with our whole heart. We begin our journey of faith seeing only a glimpse of His majesty. As we learn and grow and travel along our life's journey, the "rising light will shine brighter and brighter" and we will catch more and more "glimpses of God." The joy experienced—as expressed by these witnesses throughout recorded history—will continue to flow as a deep, abiding current and our lives will become a "continual discovery of God in new places," for He is the same yesterday, today and forever.

Religious faith, when it comes to its true power, does just that miraculous thing for us all. It turns water to wine. It brings prodigals home. It sets men on their feet. It raises life out of death. It turns sunsets to sunrises. It makes the impossible become possible.

RUFUS M. JONES

As soon as He finds us ready, God is bound to act, bound to pour Himself into our being, just as, when the air is pure and clear, the sun must pour into it without holding back.

MEISTER ECKHART

Abandon yourself to His care and guidance, as a sheep in the care of a shepherd, and trust Him utterly. No matter if you may seem to yourself to be in the very midst of a desert, with nothing green about you inwardly or outwardly, and may think you will have to make a long journey before you can get into the green pastures. Our shepherd will turn that very place where you are into green pastures, for He has power to make the desert rejoice and blossom as a rose.

HANNAH WHITALL SMITH

All who call on God in true faith, earnestly from the heart will certainly be heard, and will receive what they have asked and desired.

MARTIN LUTHER

He may not be gotten by thought, nor concluded by understanding, but He may be loved and chosen with the true lovely will of thine heart.

AN EPISTLE OF DISCRETION

Conversions are like the dawn of morning; they come and irradiate the very dewdrops and change them to jewels; they wake all the birds; they wake all the hearts and melodies.

PHILLIPS BROOKS

This experience of God is the only thing which is certain and self-evident. Before his heart has been moved in this manner, a man is deaf and blind towards everything, even towards miracles. But once this interior sense of God has come to him, he needs no other miracle than that which has been accomplished within his own soul.

ALEXANDER YELCHANINOV

Because of your new sensitiveness, anthems will be heard of you from every gutter, poems of intolerable loveliness will bud for you on every weed. Best and greatest your fellowmen will shine for you with new significance and light. Humility and awe will be evoked in you by the beautiful and patient figures of the poor. All the various members of the human group, the little children and the aged, those who stand for energy, those dedicated to skill,

to thought, to plainest service, or to prayer, will have for you fresh vivid significance, be felt as part of your own wider being.
EVELYN UNDERHILL

Whoever finds it, has found all that he can desire. Here is the height and the depth; here is the breadth and length thereof manifested, as fully as ever the capacity of the soul can contain.
JAKOB BOEHM

This whole experience is a gift from God and is unexplainable and incomprehensible to one who has not experienced it. Windows open to a whole new universe. Life takes on a new significance because you become aware of something greater than yourself. Simplicity sets in. There is an increased, tender concern for all of God's creatures, the poor and those who suffer. You go steadily and quietly on without fretting about the future or looking back to see what you have done. When you fail, you learn to humble yourself, to get up and to one with renewed enthusiasm. You have a long way to go, but you are confident of the direction in which you are headed. You realize that the only thing that really matters, that is absolutely necessary, is this new life in Christ. You have met God and know that life will never be the same again.
CLARA M. MATHESON

Those who hope in the Lord will renew their strength, they will soar on wings like eagles; They will run and not grow weary, they will walk and not faint.
ISAIAH 40:31

✍ PART I ✍

Glimpses from B.C. Through The 1000's
The Early Ages through the Dark Ages

Biblical characters, martyrs, church fathers, and other dedicated Christians keep Christianity alive through the Early Ages and continue through the Dark Ages. The ages which form the prelude to medieval history are dark when compared with the time which followed, but the foundations of medieval civilization were laid in these obscure centuries.

You will seek me and find me when you seek me with all your heart.

JEREMIAH 29:13

Old Testament Writers

⚜ DAVID ⚜

(1085 B.C.)

King of Israel. The victory over Goliath while still a shepherd was a turning point in his life. Saul took him to court and later he became king.

OUT OF THE SLIMY PIT

I waited patiently on the Lord, he turned to me and heard my cry. He lifted me out of the slimy pit, out of the mud and mire; He set my feet on a rock and gave me a firm place to stand. He put a new song in my mouth, a hymn of praise to our God.

(Psalm 40:1)

A SIMPLE DOORKEEPER

Better is one day in your courts than a thousand elsewhere; I would rather be a doorkeeper in the house of my God than dwell in the tents of the wicked.

(Psalm 84:10)

IT WAS GOOD FOR ME THAT I WAS AFFLICTED

It was good for me that I was afflicted so that I might learn your decrees.

(Psalm 119-17)

⇜ HABAKKUK ⇝

(7TH CENTURY B.C.)

Prophet of deeply tender nature and spiritual character. He manifested a great love for his people as he watched over them. The Old Testament book of his name traces his journey from perplexity to faith.

EVEN THOUGH THE FIG TREE DOES NOT BUD

Though the fig tree does not bud
And there are no grapes on the vines,
Though there are no sheep in the pen
And no cattle in the stalls,
Yet I will rejoice in the Lord,
I will be joyful in God my Savior.

(Habakkuk 3:17–18)

⇜ DANIEL ⇝

(6TH CENTURY B.C.)

Born a Hebrew, Daniel was taken in his youth to Babylon in the first de-portation under Nebuchadnezzar. He excelled in wisdom and ultimately rose to become the highest officer of the Medo-Persian Empire. His life in Babylon extended to at least 530 B.C. He lived all his adult life in exile, but never gave up his faith in God.

HOW MIGHTY HIS WONDERS

Our God whom we serve is able to deliver us from the burning fiery furnace, and He will deliver us from your hand. (Daniel and his three friends, Shadrack, Meschach and Abed-Nego before being put in the fiery furnace by King Nebuchadnezzar. After God delivered these four faithful men, the king said,) "Blessed be the God of Shadrack, Meschach and Abed-Nego who sent His Angel and delivered His servants...there is no other God who can deliver like this." (And then he declared to the whole nation,) "I thought it good to declare the signs

and wonders that the Most High God has worked for me. How great
are His signs, and how mighty His wonders."

(Daniel 3:17–4:3)

New Testament Writers

✍ PAUL ✍

(BORN BETWEEN A.D. 0 AND A.D. 5, DIED C. A.D. 67)

**Roman citizen who persecuted the Christians until his conversion on
the road to Damascus in A.D. 37 while he was carrying lists of suspected
Christians. Although Paul never met Jesus during his earthly ministry, he
encountered the earliest believers in the risen Christ. He took three missionary journeys spreading the gospel before he was beheaded at Rome
by Nero in the great persecution of the Christians, A.D. 67–68. Some were
covered with the skins of wild beasts, mauled and torn to pieces by dogs.
Others were nailed to crosses and set on fire.**

THE GRACE OF OUR LORD WAS POURED OUT ON ME

I thank Christ Jesus our Lord, who has given me strength, that he
considered me faithful, appointing me to his service. Even though
I was once a blasphemer and a persecutor and a violent man, I was
shown mercy because I acted in ignorance and unbelief. The grace of
our Lord was poured out on me abundantly, along with the faith and
love that are in Christ Jesus.

Here is a trustworthy saying that deserves full acceptance. Christ
Jesus came into the world to save sinners—of whom I am the worst.
But for that reason I was shown mercy so that in me, the worst of
sinners, Christ Jesus might display his unlimited patience as an
example for those who would believe on him and receive eternal life.
Now to the King eternal, immortal, invisible, the only God, be honor
and glory for ever and ever. Amen.

(I Timothy 1:12–13)

ALL ELSE IS RUBBISH

I consider everything a loss compared to the surpassing greatness of knowing Christ Jesus my Lord, for whose sake I have lost all things. I consider them rubbish, that I may gain Christ and be found in him, not having righteousness of my own that comes from the law, but that which is through faith in Christ—the righteousness that comes from God and is by faith. I want to know Christ and the power of his resurrection and the fellowship of sharing in his sufferings, becoming like him in his death, and so, somehow, to attain to the resurrection from the dead.

(Philippians 3:8-14)

I AM NOT ASHAMED OF THE GOSPEL

I am not ashamed of the gospel, because I know whom I have believed, and am convinced that he is able to guard what I have entrusted to him for that day.

(II Timothy 1:12)

STRENGTH IN WEAKNESS

To keep me from becoming conceited because of these surpassingly great revelations, there was given me a thorn in my flesh, a messenger of Satan, to torment me. Three times I pleaded with the Lord to take it away from me. But he said to me, "My grace is sufficient for you, for my power is made perfect in weakness." Therefore I will boast all the more gladly about my weaknesses, so that Christ's power may rest on me. That is why, for Christ's sake, I delight in weaknesses, in insults, in hardships, in persecutions, in difficulties. For when I am weak, then I am strong.

(II Corinthians 12:10)

ENCOURAGEMENT THROUGH CHAINS

Because of my chains, most of the brothers in the Lord have been encouraged to speak the word of God more courageously and fearlessly.

(Philippians 1:14)

THE TIME HAS COME FOR MY DEPARTURE

I am already being poured out like a drink offering, and the time has come for my departure. I have fought the good fight. I have finished the race. I have kept the faith. Now there is in store for me the crown of righteousness, which the Lord, the righteous Judge, will award to me on that day—and not only to me, but also to all who have longed for his appearing.

(II Timothy 4:6-8)

✍ ZACCHAEUS ✍

A wealthy chief tax collector. He was a short man who wanted to see Jesus, who was coming that way. He could not because of the crowd, so he climbed a sycamore-fig tree to see Him.

"TODAY SALVATION HAS COME TO THIS HOUSE"

When Jesus reached the spot, he looked up and said to him, "Zacchaeus, come down immediately. I must stay at your house today. So he came down at once and welcomed him gladly.

All the people saw this and began to mutter, "He has gone to be the guest of a 'sinner.'"

But Zacchaeus stood up and said to the Lord, "Lord, Lord! Here and now I give half of my possessions to the poor, and if I have cheated anybody out of anything, I will pay back four times the amount."

Jesus said to him, "Today salvation has come to this house, because this man, too, is a son of Abraham. For the son of Man came to seek and to save what was lost".

(Luke 19:1-8)

⚜ LYDIA ⚜

A Dealer in purple cloth from the city of Thyatira.

THE LORD OPENED HER HEART

One of those listening was Lydia, ...who was a worshiper of God. The Lord opened her heart to respond to Paul's message. When she and the members of her household were baptized, she invited us to her home. "If you consider me a believer in the Lord," she said, "come and stay at my house." And she persuaded us.

(Acts 16:14–15)

⚜ PETER ⚜

One of Jesus' twelve apostles. Simon, named Peter by Jesus, was a fisherman. He was fearless under persecution and laid the foundations of the Judean Church.

NEW BIRTH INTO A LIVING HOPE

Praise be to the God and Father of our Lord Jesus Christ! In his great mercy he has given us new birth into a living hope through the resurrection of Jesus Christ from the dead, and into an inheritance that can never perish, spoil or fade.

(I Peter 1:3)

⚜ JOHN ⚜

Jesus' beloved disciple who was one of five partners in a fishing business. He was the most intimate earthly friend of Jesus.

SO THAT WE MAY KNOW HIM WHO IS TRUE

We know also that the Son of God has come and has given us understanding, so that we may know him who is true. And we are in him who is true—even in his Son Jesus Christ. He is the true God and eternal life.

(I John 5:20)

Other New Testament Writers

"I HAVE NOT FOUND ANYONE WITH SUCH GREAT FAITH"

When Jesus had entered Capernaum, a centurian came to him, asking for help. "Lord," he said, "my servant lies at home paralyzed and in terrible suffering."

Jesus said to him, "I will go and heal him."

The centurian replied, "Lord, I do not deserve to have you come under my roof. But just say the word, and my servant will be healed."...

When Jesus heard him, he was astonished and said to those following him, "I tell you the truth, I have not found anyone in Israel with such great faith....

Then Jesus said to the centurian, "Go! It will be done just as you believed it would." And his servant was healed at that very hour.

(Matthew 8:5–13)

HE LEFT EVERYTHING AND FOLLOWED

As Jesus went on from there, he saw a man named Matthew sitting at the tax collector's booth. "Follow me," he told him, and Matthew got up and left everything and followed him.

(Matthew 9:9)

YOUR FAITH HAS HEALED YOU

Just then a woman who had been subject to bleeding for twelve years came up behind him and touched the edge of his cloak. She said to herself, "If I only touch his cloak, I will be healed."

Jesus turned and saw her. "Take heart, daughter," he said, "your faith has healed you." And the woman was healed from that moment.

(Matthew 9:20–22)

JESUS SAW THEIR FAITH

Some men came, bringing to him a paralytic, carried by four of them. Since they could not get him to Jesus because of the crowd, they made an opening in the roof above Jesus and, after digging through it, lowered the mat the paralyzed man was lying on. When Jesus saw their faith, he said to the paralytic, "Son, your sins are forgiven."

(Mark 2:3–5)

GIVE ME THIS LIVING WATER

The Samaritan woman said to him, "You are a Jew and I am a Samaritan woman. How can you ask me for a drink?" (For Jews did not associate with Samaritans.)

Jesus answered her, "If you knew the gift of God and who it is that asks you for a drink, you would have asked him and he would have given you living water."

"Sir," the woman said, "you have nothing to draw with and the well is deep. Where can you get this living water? Are you greater than our father Jacob, who gave us the well and drank from it himself, as did also his sons and his flocks and herds?"

Jesus answered, "Everyone who drinks this water will be thirsty again, but whoever drinks the water I give him will never thirst. Indeed, the water I give him will become in him a spring of water welling up to eternal life."

The woman said to him, "Sir, give me this water so that I won't get thirsty and have to keep coming here to draw water". *(John 4:9–15)*

3,000 SOULS WERE ADDED IN ONE DAY

Those who accepted his message were baptized, and about three thousand were added to their number that day. They devoted themselves to the apostles' teaching and to the fellowship, to the breaking of bread and to prayer....And the Lord added to their number daily those who were being saved. *(Acts 2:41–47)*

THE JAILER IS CONVERTED

The crowd joined in the attack against Paul and Silas, and the magistrates ordered them to be stripped and beaten. After they had been severely flogged, they were thrown into prison, and the jailer was commanded to guard them carefully. Upon receiving such orders, he put them in the inner cell and fastened their feet in the stocks.

About midnight Paul and Silas were praying and singing hymns to God, and the other prisoners were listening to them. Suddenly there was such a violent earthquake that the foundations of the prison were shaken. At once all the prison doors flew open, and everybody's chains came loose. The jailer woke up and when he saw the prison doors open, he drew his sword and was about to kill himself because he thought the prisoners had escaped. But Paul shouted, "Don't harm yourself! We are all here!"

The jailer called for lights, rushed in and fell trembling before Paul and Silas. He then brought them out and asked, "Men, what must I do to be saved?"

They replied, "Believe in the Lord Jesus, and you will be saved— you and your household." Then they spoke the word of the Lord to him and to all the others in his house. At that hour of the night the jailer took them and washed their wounds; then immediately he and all his family were baptized. The jailer brought them into his house and set a meal before them, and the whole family was filled with joy, because they had come to believe in God.

(Acts 16:25-34)

Church Fathers, Martyrs, and Other Christians

✣ IGNATIUS OF ANTIOCH ✣
(C.35–C.107)

Bishop of Antioch. He was tried and condemned to death in his own city, but was taken to Rome to be thrown to the wild beasts in the amphitheater. During the long journey under guard through Asia Minor, Christians from throughout the province came to meet him. He in turn wrote letters of encouragement for them to take to their churches. He was called "Theophorus" (the God-bearer), "because I bore the Christ in my heart."

A SLAVE TO GOD

I write to you not as someone who is superior to you, because, although I am now a slave of God, I am not yet perfect to Jesus Christ. I am learning to be a true disciple, and I look upon you as fellow learners.

(Epistle of Ignatius to the Ephesians)

I DESIRE TO SUFFER FOR CHRIST'S SAKE

I am tempted sometimes to boast about my own knowledge of God and to take pride in my position. But I know to give way to such temptations would prove that in truth I had nothing to boast about. It is better for me to be timid and diffident in what I say, and to ignore those whose admiring words puff me up. I desire to suffer for Christ's sake, but I do not know whether I am worthy to suffer. The devil is constantly at my heels, even though other people imagine me free from temptation.

(Epistle of Ignatius to the Tralliens)

NOT ONLY TO BE CALLED A CHRISTIAN, BUT LIVE LIKE ONE

You have never envied anyone, but only taught people the way of Christ. I desire only that I may stay firmly on that way. Please pray for me, that I may have both spiritual and physical strength to perform my duties, that I may not only speak the truth, but become the truth, that I may not only be called a Christian, but also live like a Christian.

(Epistle of Ignatius to the Romans)

To die for the One who died for me

I am traveling from Syria to Rome, by land and sea, by night and day, guarded by ten soldiers whom I call leopards. The more kindly I speak to these leopards, the more cruelly they treat me; and by their cruelty I am becoming a more devoted disciple of Christ... Grant me this favor; pray that nothing will stand in the way of my suffering for Christ. I shall happily have my skin cut to shreds by the beast's teeth, my limbs torn from my body, my bones mangled in their jaws, my whole body crushed under their feet, that I may come to know Jesus. The wealth of this world counts for nothing; to be king of every nation on earth is worth no more than a few specks of dust. All that I desire is to die for the sake of the one who died for our sake.

(Epistle of Ignatius to the Romans)

Jesus is so deeply written in my heart

My dear Jesus, my Savior, is so deeply written in my heart; that I feel confident, that if my heart were to be cut open and chopped to pieces, the name of Jesus would be found written on every piece.

❧ Barnabas ❧

(lived during the first and second century)

Probably a Christian living in Alexandria. He was known by many in the early Church to be the apostle Barnabas. The epistle may have been written as early as A.D. 70 or as late as 130.

I feel the Lord has traveled with me

Since I was with you I feel the Lord has traveled with me on my journeys, guiding my feet in the way of righteousness. And as I have come to know the Lord a little better, I have grown to love you even more dearly, cherishing you above my own life. And out of that love I want to share with you some of the insights that I have received—hence this short letter. It is a privilege for me to be able to minister to such noble spirits as yours.

(The Epistle of Barnabas)

✦ CALCONIS ✦
(DIED C. 108)

A pagan who was so struck with admiration during the martyrdom of two Christian brothers, who suffered patiently under terrible sufferings, that he cried in faith and was immediately put to death.

A PAGAN'S LAST WORDS
Great is the God of the Christians!

✦ EPICTETUS ✦
(C.50–C.130)

Greek philosopher who was born a slave, given freedom, and then moved to France. He is remembered for the religious tone of his teachings.

WHAT GOD CHOOSES
I am always content with what happens, for I know what God chooses is better than what I choose.

(Discourses)

◈ POLYCARP ◈

(C.69–155)

Greek bishop of Smyrna, now part of Turkey. He became a Christian at nine years of age. He did not wish to defy the authorities and made little effort to avoid arrest. At his trial he was direct in his answers, and in death he was serene and dignified. Refusing to deny Christ, he was burned in the city stadium. His behavior came to be regarded as a model for Christians facing persecution.

FOR EIGHTY-SIX YEARS I HAVE BEEN HIS SERVANT

For eighty-and-six years have I served my Saviour, and he hath never done me any harm. How can I blaspheme my Saviour King who saved Me? *(In response to the military officer's demand to revile Christ)* If you imagine I will swear allegiance to the emperor, then you are ignorant of who I am. Listen plainly: I am a Christian. And if you wish to learn the doctrines of Christianity, let us arrange a day, and I will teach you....You threaten me with fire that burns for a few minutes or hours and is then quenched, but you do not know the everlasting fire that awaits the wicked. Why are you waiting? Do what you will, and quickly. *(They were about to nail him to the stake so that he could not escape the flames. He pleaded with them not to do so.)* Leave me like this because he who gives me power to endure the fire will give me strength to remain here unmoved. So I do not need the security of your rope and nails. *(Polycarp finished his final prayer with a loud "Amen.")*

ᴇᴋ JUSTIN MARTYR ᴋᴈ
(C.100–165)

One of the most important Greek philosopher-apologists in the early Christian church. He spent his early life studying philosophy, then, in his middle years, after studying the new Christian religion, he quickly realized that it answered his deepest questions. Soon after his conversion in 132 he began wandering from place to place, hoping to convert educated pagans to Christianity.

THE NAME CHRISTIAN IS BEAUTIFUL TO US

We are accused of being Christian. To us, that name is beautiful, implying grace and love; the true Christian is incapable of acting dishonestly or hatefully. To others, the name is evil; and if someone confesses to being a Christian, that itself is taken as grounds for punishment. But this puts us in an impossible position. If we deny being Christians, then we are denying the faith that fills us with divine grace; but if we confess to being Christians, we are punished for crimes that we could not possibly have committed. We ask you to ignore the name, and look instead at the lives of those to whom that name is ascribed.

(Justin's Apology).

ᴇᴋ SANCTUS ᴋᴈ
(MARTYRED 177 A.D.)

Early martyr. Red-hot plates of brass were repeatedly placed upon his body. He was thrown into prison and compelled to sit upon red-hot chains until his flesh broiled. Soon after, he was beheaded.

HIS ONLY COMMENT

I am a Christian!

✺ ATHENAGORAS ✺

(2ND CENTURY)

Man of wealth and position, who was loyal to the empire, and after much reflection, came to the conclusion that the teachings of Christ were true. In his *Apology,* written to the emperor in about A.D. 180, he argued that the spread of Christianity was helping to promote peace and harmony.

WE OFFER THE OTHER CHEEK AS WELL

To Marcus Aurelius Anthonius, emperor

The injury we suffer from our persecution does not concern our property or our civil rights or any such matters. We hold these things in contempt, although they appear important to the crowd. We do not return blow for blow, nor do we sue those who rob and plunder us. But to those who hit us on one cheek, we offer the other cheek; and to those who steal our coats, we offer our shirts as well. Yet when we have given up our property, they plot against our souls and bodies, pouring upon us a multitude of accusations without the slightest foundation.

✺ THECLA ✺

(C.150–200)

Early Christian convert and coworker of Paul.

HE ALONE IS THE END OF SALVATION

I am indeed a servant of the living God, and as to what there is about me, I have believed in the Son of God, in whom he is well pleased... For he alone is the end of salvation, and the basis of immortal life: for he is a refuge to the tempest-tossed, a solace to the afflicted, a shelter to the despairing; and once for all, whoever shall not believe on him, shall not live for ever.

༨ CLEMENT OF ALEXANDRIA ༩

(C.150–220)

Christian philosopher, theologian, and scholar. He lived in a dark time and in a very wicked city, but he was a wise man who shone in the darkness.

THE REALLY TRUE WISDOM

We who have become disciples of God, have entered into the really true wisdom which leaders of philosophy only hinted at, but which the disciples of the Christ have both comprehended and proclaimed abroad.

I urge thee to be saved. This is the wish of Christ; in one word, He freely grants thee life. And who is He? Understand briefly: the Word of truth; the Word of incorruption; He who regenerates man by bringing him back to the truth; the goal of salvation; He who banishes corruption and expels death; He who has built His temple in men, that in men He may set up the shrine of God.

(Exhortations to the Greeks)

༨ PERPETUA ༩

(MARTYRED 202 A.D.)

Young, beautiful, and educated woman of noble birth and wealth, from Carthage, North Africa. None of these attributes, even the love of her baby, compared to her love of Jesus.

FINAL WORDS TO HER FAMILY

Do not be ashamed of my death. I think it is the greatest honor of my life and I thank God for calling me to give my life for His sake and in His cause. He gave the same honor to the holy prophets, His dearly beloved apostles, and His blessed chosen martyrs. I have no doubt that I am dying for God's cause and the cause of truth.

⪫ GENESIUS OF ROME ⪪
(MARTYRED C.205)

Early Christian martyr.

WERE I TO BE KILLED A THOUSAND TIMES

There is no King but him whom I have seen; he it is that I worship and adore. Were I to be killed a thousand times for my allegiance to him, I should still go on as I have begun. I should still be his man. Christ is on my lips, Christ is in my heart; no torments can take him from me.

⪫ TERTULLIAN ⪪
(BORN C.155–160, DIED AFTER 220)

Well-educated teacher and lawyer born in Carthage in North Africa, who wrote in defense of the faith. He was converted in the year 193 after witnessing the courage of Christians facing torture and death for their faith. He said that he and most of the converts who came out of paganism were won to Christ, not by books or sermons, but by observing how Christians lived and died. He learned much of the Bible by heart.

ONLY IN CHRIST DO WE KNOW GOD AS OUR LOVING FATHER

We remember the extraordinary privilege we enjoy in being able to speak to God as Father. Others, such as Moses, have yearned to know his name. But only in Christ do we come to know him as our living parent, and can enjoy speaking to him in prayer with the same intimacy that a child speaks to his father and mother.

✣ CYPRIAN ✣

(C.200–258)

Bishop of Carthage, Christian writer, and martyr. When the sentence of death was read to him he said, "I heartily thank Almighty God who is pleased to set me free from the chains of this body."

DOORS THAT HAD BEEN CLOSED TO ME OPENED

When I had drunk the spirit from heaven, and the second birth had restored me so as to make a new man of me, then at once in an amazing way my doubts began to be resolved, doors that had been closed to me opened, dark places became light, and what before had seemed difficult now seemed easy to me.

A JOY WHICH IS A THOUSAND TIMES BETTER

This is a cheerful world as I see it from my garden, under the shadow of my vines. But if I could ascend some high mountain and look out over the wide lands, you know very well what I would see—brigands on the highways; pirates on the seas; armies fighting, cities burning; in the amphitheatres men murdered to please applauding crowds; selfishness and cruelty, misery and despair under all roofs. It is a bad world.

But I have discovered in the midst of it a quiet and holy people who have learned a great secret. They have found a joy which is a thousand times better than any of the pleasures of our sinful life. They are despised and persecuted, but they care not. They are masters of their own souls. They have overcome the world. These people, Donatus, are the Christians—and I am one of them.

SUDDENLY I BREATHED THE BREATH OF HEAVEN

I floated on the stormy sea, a stranger to the light and uncertain where to plant my feet. How can a man be born again? The very idea seemed hard and impossible. But suddenly I breathed the breath of heaven. That lay open which before was shut, that was light which before was darkness, that became easy which before was impracticable.

ᘛ ANDRONICUS ᘚ

(MARTYRED 303 A.D.)

A Roman who had been thrown into prison because he was unwilling to deny the Christian faith. Then he was whipped, and his bleeding wounds were rubbed with salt. He was brought out from prison and tortured again, thrown to the wild beasts, and finally killed with a sword.

I AM NOT TO BE SHAKEN FROM MY RESOLUTION

Do your worst, I am a Christian. Christ is my help and supporter, and thus armed I will never serve your gods nor do I fear your authority or that of your master, the Emperor. Commence your torments as soon as you please, and make use of every means that your malignity can invent, and you shall find in the end that I am not to be shaken from my resolution.

ᘛ EUSEBIUS OF CAESAREA ᘚ

(C.260–C.340)

Historian who was known as the 'Father of Church History.'

RECEIVING THE FINAL SENTENCE

We ourselves have observed crowded together in one day, some suffering decapitation, some the torments of flames; so that the murderous weapon was completely blunted, and the executioners themselves, wearied with slaughter, were obliged to relieve one another. Then we were witnesses of the truly divine energy of those that believed in the Christ of God. They received the final sentence of death with gladness and exultation, so far as even to sing and to send up hymns of praise and thanksgiving until they breathed their last.

⚜ AMBROSE ⚜

(340–397)

Bishop of Milan and one of the church fathers. He introduced congregational singing into his church, wrote many beautiful hymns, and became powerful in winning souls to Christ.

I WILLINGLY GIVE IT ALL UP

If you want my estate, you may have it; if you want my body, I willingly give it up. If you want to put me in irons or kill me, I am content. I will not flee to the people for protection, or cling to the altar. Rather I choose to be sacrificed for the sake of the altar.

WE HAVE A GOOD LORD

I have not so lived among you as to be ashamed to live yet longer; but neither do I fear death, for we have a good Lord.

(Talking to a friend)

TO SERVE IS REAL FREEDOM

The Apostle Paul has taught me something even beyond freedom itself, namely that to serve is real freedom. Though I be free from all, he says, yet have I made myself servant unto all, that I might gain the more. What is that which surpasses liberty but to have the spirit of grace, to have charity? Liberty renders us free to men, but charity renders us beloved by God.

⚜ JEROME ⚜

(C.340–420)

Italian Bible scholar, translator, and hermit.

WORTHY TO BE ONE WHOM THE WORLD HATES

I give thanks to my God that I am worthy to be one whom the world hates.

(Epistle 99)

⊰ JOHN CHRYSOSTOM ⊱

(347–407)

Greek-Syrian Biblical expositor and Bishop of Constantinople.

MY LIFE IS HID WITH CHRIST IN GOD

"You cannot take anything. My treasure is in heaven."

> *(In response to the emperor's demand that he deny Christ*
> *or have his money and property taken, for he was a wealthy man.)*

" God is my friend. You cannot separate me from Him."

> *(In response to the emperor's "You shall live on an island.")*

"My life is hid with Christ in God. I shall live forever."

> *(In response to the emperor's "I shall take away your life."*
> *The soldiers were so cruel that Chrysostom died on the way into exile.)*

WHEN I WAS DRIVEN FROM THE CITY

When I was driven from the city, I felt no anxiety, but said to myself, 'If the empress wishes to banish me, let her do so; the earth is the Lord's. If she wants to have me sawn asunder, I have Isaiah for an example. If she wants me to be drowned in the ocean, I think of Jonah. If I am to be thrown into the fire, the three men in the furnace suffered the same. If cast before wild beasts, I remember Daniel in the lions' den. If she wants me to be stoned, I have before me Stephen, the first martyr. If she demands my head, let her do so; John the Baptist shines before me. Naked I came from my mother's womb; naked shall I leave this world.'

> *(Writing to a friend when he was*
> *driven from the city into exile.)*

BOTH GOD AND MAN

I do not think of Christ as God alone, or man alone, but both together. For I know He was hungry, and I know that with five loaves He fed five thousand. I know He was thirsty, and I know that He turned the water into wine. I know he was carried in a ship, and I know that He walked on the sea. I know that He died, and I know that He raised the dead. I know that He was set before Pilate, and I know that He sits with the Father on His throne. I know that He was worshipped by angels, and I know that He was stoned by the Jews. And truly some of these I ascribe to the human, and others to the divine nature. For by reason of this He is said to have been both God and man.

Persecution is an honor

If any one would give me the choice of all heaven, or the chain of St. Paul, I would instantly prefer St. Paul's chain to all heaven. If any one would give me a place among the angels above the heavens, or put me in the bottom of an obscure dungeon, prisoner with St. Paul, I would choose the prison and the chains. For, in fine, nothing is better than to suffer for Christ. I think St. Paul was not so happy in being caught up to the third heaven as in being loaded with chains. I had rather a thousand times be persecuted for Christ than to be honoured for him. Persecution is an honour that surpasses and eclipses all other.

ᴁ AUGUSTINE ᴂ

(354–430)

Staunch defender of the Christian faith who inspired millions through his *Confessions* and other writings, and has had a lasting influence on the theology of the Christian church. While teaching in Milan, he came under the influence of Ambrose and began to search for God. "I was led to him unknowingly by God, that I might knowingly be led to God by him." He came to know Christ after the fervent prayers of his mother and a long inner struggle. When once accosted by a heathen who showed him his idol and said, "Here is my god; where is thine?" Augustine replied, "I cannot show you my God; not because there is no God to show, but because you have no eyes to see Him."

To know thee is life

God, our true Life, in whom and by whom all things live. Thou commandest us to seek Thee, and are ready to be found; Thou bidest us knock, and openest when we do so. To know Thee is life, to serve Thee is freedom, to enjoy Thee is a kingdom, to praise Thee is the joy and happiness of the soul. I praise, and bless, and adore Thee, I worship Thee, I glorify Thee, I give thanks to Thee for Thy great glory. I humbly beseech Thee to abide with me, to reign in me, to make this heart of mine a holy temple, a fit habitation for Thy divine majesty. Amen.

(Confessions of St. Augustine)

GOD SHOUTED TO ME

I was wandering like a lost sheep searching for You, O God... How I was running hither and thither to seek You. My life was a burden to me... I was poor in riches, and ready to perish with hunger, near a table plentifully spread, and a continual feast. You have called to me, and have cried out, and have shattered my deafness. You have blazed forth with light, and have shone upon me, and You have put my blindness to flight!

(Confessions of St. Augustine)

THE LIGHT OF CONFIDENCE FLOODED INTO MY HEART

I probed the hidden depths of my soul and wrung its pitiful secrets from it, and when I mustered them all before the eyes of my heart, a great storm broke within me. Somehow I flung myself down beneath a fig tree and gave way to the tears which now streamed from my eyes. For I felt that I was still the captive of my sins, and in misery I kept crying, "How long shall I go on saying "Tomorrow, tomorrow'? Why not now? Why not make an end of my ugly sins at this moment?"

I was asking myself these questions, weeping all the while with the most bitter sorrow in my heart, when all at once I heard the singing of a child in a nearby house. Whether it was the voice of a boy or girl, I cannot say, but again and again it repeated the refrain, "Take it and read, take it and read." At this I looked up, thinking hard whether there was any kind of game in which children used to chant words like these, but I could not remember ever hearing them before.

I stemmed my flood of tears and stood up, telling myself that this could only be a divine command to open my book of Scripture and read the first passage on which my eyes should fall. So I hurried back to the place where I had put the book containing Paul's epistles. I seized it and opened it, and in silence I read the first passage on which my eyes fell: "Not in reveling and drunkenness, not in lust and wantomness, not in quarrels and rivalries. Rather, arm yourselves with the Lord Jesus Christ; spend no more thought on nature and nature's appetites."

I had no wish to read more and no need to do so. For in an instant, as I came to the end of the sentence, it was as though the light of confidence flooded into my heart and all the darkness of doubt was dispelled. I marked the place with my finger and closed the book. "You converted me to yourself, so that I no longer placed any hope in this world but stood firmly upon the rule of faith."

(Confessions of St. Augustine)

LATE HAVE I LOVED YOU

Late have I loved you, O beauty so ancient and so new. Late have I loved you! You were within me while I have gone outside to seek you. Unlovely myself, I rushed towards all those lovely things you had made. And always you were with me, and I was not with you.

All these beauties kept me far from you—although they would not have existed at all unless they had their being in you.

You called, you cried, you shattered my deafness.

You sparkled, you blazed, you drove away my blindness.

You shed your fragrance, and I drew in my breath, and I pant for you. I tasted and now I hunger and thirst. You touched me, and now I burn with longing for your peace.

(Confessions of St. Augustine)

I COMMIT MYSELF UNTO YOU

Father, you are full of compassion, I commit and commend myself unto you, in whom I am, and live, and know. Be the Goal of my pilgrimage, and my Rest by the way. Let my soul take refuge from the crowding turmoil of worldly thoughts beneath the shadow of your wings; let my heart, this sea of restless waves, find peace in you, O God. Amen.

✍ PAULINUS OF NOLA ✎
(D. 431)

Italian bishop and poet.

I KNOW THAT I HAVE BEEN ACCEPTED

I bowed my neck, then, to the yoke of Christ, and now I see myself engaged in tasks that are greater than I deserve or can understand. I know that I have been admitted and accepted into the mysteries of the most high God, that I partake of heavenly life, and that I have been brought nearer to God so as to dwell in the very spirit, body and light of Christ.... I pray that we may be found worthy to be cursed, censured and ground down, even put to death in the name of Jesus Christ, so long as Christ himself is not put to death in us.

✍ PATRICK ✎
(C.389–461)

Known as 'The Apostle of the Irish'. Of Romano-British heritage, he was first enslaved in Ireland at age sixteen. The Irish farmer who bought him put him to tending sheep, and somehow through all this, Patrick found Christ. He escaped at twenty-two, but went back as a missionary. A man of deep Christian devotion, he faced danger and opposition with calmness.

HE WATCHED OVER ME BEFORE I KNEW HIM

I was then about sixteen years of age. I did not know the true God. I was taken into captivity to Ireland with many thousands of people— and deservedly so, because we turned away from God, and did not keep His commandments.....And there the Lord opened the sense of my unbelief that I might at last remember my sins and be converted

with all my heart to the Lord my God, who had regard for my abjec-
tion, and mercy on my youth and ignorance, and watched over me
before I knew Him, and before I was able to distinguish between
good and evil, and guarded me, and comforted me as would a father
his son.

Hence I cannot be silent—nor, indeed, is it expedient—about
the great benefits and the great grace which the Lord has deigned to
bestow upon me in the land of my captivity; for this we can give to
God in return after having been chastened by Him, to exalt and praise
His wonders before every nation that is anywhere under the heaven.

HE PLACED ME ON TOP OF THE WALL

I was like a stone lying deep in mud, but he that is mighty lifted me
up and placed me on top of the wall.

THE UNSPEAKABLE GLORY OF ETERNAL LIFE

I was a free man in a good position, and I bargained away my noble
status—and I am not ashamed of this or regretful about it—for the
sake of others. In short, I am a slave of Christ in a remote country
because of the unspeakable glory of eternal life which is in Christ
Jesus our Lord.

ONE OF THE LEAST AMONG HIS SERVANTS

I commend my soul to God for whom I am an ambassador because
he chose me for this task, despite my obscurity, to be one of the least
among his servants.

I AM GREATLY A DEBTOR TO GOD

I am greatly a debtor to God, who has bestowed his grace so largely
upon me, that multitudes were born again to God through me. The
Irish, who had never had the knowledge of God and worshipped only
idols and unclean things, have lately become the people of the Lord,
and are called sons of God.

PATRICK'S BREASTPLATE PRAYER

Christ to protect me to-day
against poison, against burning,
against drowning, against wounding,
so that there may come abundance of reward,
Christ with me, Christ before me, Christ behind me,
Christ in me, Christ beneath me, Christ above me
Christ on my right, Christ on my left,
Christ where I lie, Christ where I sit, Christ where I arise,
Christ in the heart of every man who thinks of me,
Christ in the mouth of every man who speaks of me,
Christ in every eye that sees me,
Christ in every ear that hears me.

⚜ CLOSING THOUGHT ⚜

Lord, you have examined my heart and know everything about me.
You know when I sit or stand. When far away you know my every
thought. You chart the path ahead of me, and tell me where to stop
and rest. Every moment, you know where I am. You know what I am
going to say before I even say it. You both precede and follow me,
and place your hand of blessing on my head.

This is too glorious, too wonderful to believe! I can never be lost
to your spirit! I can never get away from my God! If I go up to heaven,
you are there, if I go down to the place of the dead, you are there. If I
ride the morning winds to the farthest oceans, even there your hand
will guide me, your strength will support me. If I try to hide in the
darkness, the night becomes light around me, for even darkness cannot hide from God; to you the night shines as bright as day. Darkness
and light are both alike to you.

You made all the delicate, inner parts of my body, and knit them
together in my mother's womb. Thank you for making me so wonderfully complex! It is amazing to think about. Your workmanship

is marvelous—and how well I know it. You were there while I was being formed in utter seclusion! You saw me before I was born and scheduled each day of my life before I began to breathe. Every day was recorded in your Book!

How precious it is, Lord, to realize that you are thinking about me constantly! I can't even count how many times a day your thoughts turn towards me. And when I waken in the morning, you are still thinking of me!

(Psalm 139:1–18 TLB)

 Part II

Glimpses From The 1100's Through The 1500's
The Middle Ages

After the Dark Ages, there was a revival of the Christian fellowship. The Golden Age of Mysticism reigned. By the twelfth century life had gone out of the church. Francis of Assisi and Dominic recognized the corruption, but thought the church was not beyond redemption. From the 1100's to the 1400's, the blows against corruption gradually increased, but it was not until the sixteenth century that the reformers accomplished their purpose—a return to the teachings of the Nazarene. The printing press, which was developed in 1450, provided a new means to spread Christianity.

Come, all you who are thirsty, come to the waters, and you who have no money, come, buy and eat! Come, buy wine and milk without money and without cost. Why spend money on what is not bread and your labor on what does not satisfy? Listen, listen to me, and eat what is good, and your soul will delight in the richest fare.

ISAIAH 55:1,2

✺ ANSELM ✺

(1033–1109)

Church leader and writer who was influenced by a godly mother from an early age. His *Proslogium* is an argument for the existence of God.

I BELIEVE AND LOVE THY TRUTH

I do not try to penetrate Thy mystery, O Lord, for in no way is my intelligence commensurate with it. But I desire to find Thy Truth which I believe and love in my heart. I do not seek to understand in order to believe; I believe in order to understand. For I believe that I cannot understand unless I believe.

✺ BERNARD OF CLAIRVAUX ✺

(1090–1153)

Considered the most influential individual in twelfth century Western Christianity. He had a great influence on Martin Luther and John Calvin and ushered in the "golden age of medieval spirituality." His treatise *On the Love of God* has remained his most important work. Some of his hymns include, 'Jesus, the Very Thought is Sweet' and 'O Jesus, King Most Wonderful.'

FILLED WITH WONDER

I want to tell you how these things took place in me....You ask, then, since his ways are thus beyond all searching out, how did I know the Word was present? Because He is living, and powerful to act and to do, and as soon as He came within He roused my sleeping soul. He stirred and softened and wounded my heart, for it was hard and stony and poor in health. He began, too, to pluck out and to destroy, to build up and to plant, to water the dry places, to lighten the dark corners, to throw open the closed doors, to enkindle the chilled regions, to make the crooked straight and the rough places plain, so that my soul blessed the Lord, and all that was within me praised His Holy Name....I was aware of the power of His might; and from the discovery and conviction of my secret faults I came to wonder at the depth of His wisdom, and from the amendment (small though it were) of my life and conversion I learned of His goodness and loving kindness, and through the renewing and refashioning of the spirit of my mind, that is, of my inner man, I perceived in some measure His excellent beauty, and from gazing upon all these things together I was filled with wonder at his abundant greatness.

(Sermons on the Song of Songs)

᚛ HILDEGARD OF BINGEN ᚜
(1098–1179)

German nun, scholar, artist, and visionary who learned medicine, wrote books of science and made evangelistic tours even into her 70's. Her counsel was sought by many of the leaders of her day.

IN MY SEVENTIETH YEAR

From my infancy until now, in the seventieth year of my age, my soul has always beheld this sight... The brightness which I see is not limited by space and is more brilliant than the radiance around the sun... Sometimes when I see it, all sadness and pain is lifted from me, and I seem a simple girl again, and an old woman no more.

᚛ HUGH OF ST. VICTOR ᚜
(1110–1141)

Philospher, theologian, and mystical writer who was known for his spiritual treatises and expositions of Scripture.

THE THOUGHT OF GOD

What is that sweet thing that comes sometimes to touch me at the thought of God? It affects me with such vehemence and sweetness that I begin wholly to go out of myself and to be lifted up, whither I know not. Suddenly, I am renewed and changed; it is a state of inexpressible well-being. My consciousness rejoices. I lose the memory of my former trials, my soul rejoices, my mind becomes clearer, my heart is enflamed, my desires are satisfied. I feel myself transported into a new place, I know not where.

⚘ THOMAS A BECKET ⚘
(1118–1170)

Chancellor of England and later Archbishop of Canterbury. He was murdered in the Canterbury Cathedral.

I AM NOT MOVED BY THREATS
I have committed my cause to the great judge of all mankind, so I am not moved by threats, nor are your swords more ready to strike than is my soul for martyrdom.

⚘ ALIGHIERI DANTE ⚘
(1265–1321)

Italian poet and prose writer. The following excerpt is taken from *The Divine Comedy*, which showed a profound Christian vision of man's temporal and eternal destiny, and which drew from the poet's own experience.

GOD'S BOOK
I raised my eyes aloft, and I beheld
The scattered chapters of the Universe
Gathered and bound into a single book
By the austere and tender hand of God.

❧ RICHARD ROLLE ❧

(1290–1349)

A great spiritual leader of England who was highly revered as "St. Richard the Hermit." *The Mending of Life* and *The Fire of Love* were his most important works.

GUIDED BY A GRACIOUS AND A MIGHTY HAND

A retrospect of my whole life, from the earliest period of my recollection down to the present hour, leaves me with this impression, that I have been, and am being, guided by a gracious and a mighty Hand, which has made, and is making, that possible to me which otherwise to me had been impossible. Oh that I had at all times unhesitatingly trusted and yielded myself to its guidance!

UNKNOWN BISHOP ❧ OF THE EARLY CHURCH ❧

When asked the secret of his contentment, this was his response.

WHERE TRUE HAPPINESS IS

It consists in nothing more than making a right use of my eyes. In whatever state I am, I first of all look up to heaven, and remember that my principal business here is to get there; I then look down upon the earth, and call to mind how small a place I shall occupy in it when I die and am buried; I then look abroad in the world, and observe what multitudes there are who are in all respects more unhappy than myself: thus I learn where true happiness is placed, where all our cares must end, and what little reason I have to repine or complain.

The 1300's and the 1400's
— The Renaissance

∝ MARGARET EBNER ∝
(1291–1351)

German Dominican nun. She had a deep personal relationship with Jesus Christ and lived and prayed with a profound awareness of the presence of God.

THE SWEETEST THING IN THE WORLD

I became ill. While I was having chills and fevers, the sweet name of Jesus filled me so that I could not lie quiet. Everything I said began with "Jesus Christ." For me, this name is the sweetest thing in the world and I can suffer lovingly with my Lord. This name fills me with great joy and makes me become stronger.... There is something about it that goes beyond the ordinary....there is no rational explanation for this kind of spiritual experience. Love and faith are given to me in a powerful way. There is no doubt that God is present with me.

(Revelations)

⚜ THEOLOGIA GERMANICA ⚜

(C.1350)

An anonymous work by a group called the "Friends of God," which grew out of the 14th century German renewal movement. It stressed intimacy with God, piety of life and complete obedience to the commands of Christ. Luther said that next to the Bible and Augustine, he had never read anything as helpful as this.

IT IS UNSPEAKABLE

Now, it may be asked, what is the state of a man who followeth the true Light to the utmost of his power? I answer truly, it will never be declared aright, for he who is not such a man, can neither understand nor know it, and he who is, knoweth it indeed; but he cannot utter it, for it is unspeakable. Therefore let him who would know it, give his whole diligence that he may enter therein; then will he see and find what hath never been uttered by man's lips.

⚜ JOHN WYCLIFFE ⚜

(1330-1384)

English theologian, religious reformer, and forerunner of the Protestant Reformation who insisted upon a direct relationship between God and man. His translation of the Scriptures to make it available to ordinary people was much opposed by the Church, which passed a decree prohibiting the translation of God's Word. Thirty years after his death, he was declared a heretic. It was ordered that his writings be burned and his bones be exhumed, burned, and cast into a river.

THE GOSPEL OF CHRIST

I suppose over this that the gospel of Christ be the heart of the corpus of God's law, for I believe that Jesus Christ, that gave in His own person this gospel, is very God and very man, and by this heart passes all other laws.

THE SCRIPTURES IN THEIR OWN LANGUAGE
Christ and His Apostles taught the people in the language but known to them....As doctrines of our faith are in the Scriptures, believers should have the Scriptures in a language which they fully understand.

✍ JOHN HUSS ❧
(1369–1415)

Teacher at the university in Prague and preacher against the immorality of the clergy, indulgences, and pilgrimages. He was greatly influenced by John Wycliffe. The Emperor summoned him to appear before a council and demanded he recant. He refused and was burned at the stake.

I NOW JOYFULLY DIE
God is my witness that the great purpose of my preaching and writing was to convert men from sin. In the truth of that Gospel which I hitherto have written, taught, and preached, I now joyfully die.

✍ GIROLAMO SAVANAROLA ❧
(MARTYRED 1498)

Italian martyr.

OUT OF LOVE TO HIM
My Lord was pleased to die for my sins; why should I not be glad to give up my poor life out of love to Him?

❧ CATHERINE OF GENOA ❧
(1447–1510)

Born into a prominent religious Italian family. After living a life of worldly vanity, she was converted to Christ. She then led a very spiritual life, dedicating herself to the care of the sick and poor. Her *Life and Teachings* remain an important literary contribution.

I WISH ALL TO BE IN GOD

When I eat or drink, move or stand still, speak or keep silent, sleep or wake, see, hear, or think, whether I am in church, at home, or in the street, in bad health or good, dying or not dying, at every hour and moment of my life, I wish all to be in God. I wish to be unable to wish or do or think or speak anything that is not completely God's will; and the part of me which would oppose this I would wish to be turned into dust and scattered in the wind.

NO LONGER MY OWN

I am no longer my own. Whether I live or whether I die, I belong to my Saviour. I have nothing of my own. God is my all, and my whole being is His.

❧ SIR THOMAS MORE ❧
(1478–1535)

English statesman, author, and close friend of Henry VIII. He refused to forswear obedience to the pope and accept royal supremacy in religious matters. This led to imprisonment in the Tower of London (during which he wrote *A Dialogue of Comfort against Tribulation*) and execution.

SPIRITUAL PROFIT THROUGH IMPRISONMENT

God's grace has given the king a gracious frame of mind toward me, so that as yet he has taken from me nothing but my liberty. In doing this His Majesty has done me such great good with respect to spiritual profit that I trust that among all the great benefits he has heaped so abundantly upon me I count my imprisonment the very greatest. I cannot, therefore, mistrust the grace of God.

(A Dialogue of Comfort Against Tribulation)

WE THANK HIM FOR ADVERSITY AS FOR PROSPERITY

And whereas I am informed by my son Heron of the loss of our barns by fire, with all the corn that was therein; albeit, saving God's pleasure, it is great pity of so much good corn lost, yet since it hath liked him to send us such a chance, we must and are bounden not only to be content but also to be glad of his visitation. He sent us all that we have lost, and since he hath by such a chance taken it away again, his pleasure be fulfilled. Let us never grieve thereat, but take it in good worth and heartily thank him as well for adversity as for prosperity. And peradventure we have more cause to thank him for our loss than for our winning. For his wisdom better seeth what is good for us than we do ourselves. Therefore I pray you be of good cheer, and take all the household with you to church and there thank God for that he hath given us and for that he hath taken away from us and for that he hath left us.

(Letter written after part of his house and barns had been destroyed through a neighbor's carelessness, quoted in Thomas Stapleton's Life of Sir Thomas More*)*

⚛ MICHAEL SATTLER ⚛
(1495–1527)

Swiss reformer and martyr. After becoming an Anabaptist, he was arrested, imprisoned in the tower of Binsdorf for his beliefs, and executed.

TO DIE FOR HIS SAKE

The brethren have doubtless informed you that some of us are in prison. Numerous accusations were proffered against us by our adversaries; at one time they threatened us with the gallows; at another with fire and sword. In this extremity, I surrendered myself entirely to the Lord's will, and prepared myself, together with all brethren and wife, to die for his testimony's sake.

(After being imprisoned, he wrote this letter to his flock.)

I WILL TESTIFY TO THE TRUTH

Almighty, eternal God, thou art the way, the truth: because I have not been shown to be in error, I will, with thy help to this day, testify to the truth and seal it with my blood.

(After being tortured with his tongue sliced and chunks of flesh torn from his body with red-hot tongs, he was still able to speak and asked the people to repent and be converted. His wife was executed by drowning eight days later.)

MARTIN LUTHER

(1483–1546)

German leader of the Reformation who criticized the medieval church's abuses and insisted upon justification by grace through faith. His conversion took place in 1511 on a pilgrimage to Rome. He was ascending the 'holy stairs' on hands and knees while saying his prayers and hoping to find favor with God, when suddenly he remembered the words from the Bible, 'The just shall live by faith'. One of his great achievements was translating the Bible into German.

IN GOD'S HANDS

I have held many things in my hands and lost them all; but whatever I placed in God's hands, that I still possess.

THROUGH THE STORM

If I did not see that the Lord kept watch over the ship, I should long since have abandoned the helm. But I see Him! Through the storm, strengthening the tackling, handling the yards, spreading the sails—aye more, commanding the very winds! Should I not be a coward if I abandoned my post? Let Him govern, let Him carry us forward, let Him hasten or delay, we will fear nothing!

TRIALS AS OPPORTUNITIES
Before every opportunity God gave me a great trial.

I WAS BORN AGAIN
Finally, after days and nights of wrestling with the difficulty, God had mercy on me, and I saw the connection between the righteousness of God and the statement "the just shall live by his faith." Then I understood that the righteousness of God is that righteousness by which, through grace and sheer mercy, God justifies us through faith. Then I felt myself absolutely born again. The gates of Paradise had been flung open and I had entered.

NO ENEMIES
My soul is too glad and too great to be at heart the enemy of any man.

I WOULD STILL PLANT MY APPLE TREE
Even if I knew that tomorrow the world would go to pieces, I would still plant my apple tree.

MY LAST WILL AND TESTAMENT
Lord God, I thank Thee, for that Thou hast been pleased to make me a poor and indigent man upon earth. I have neither house, nor land, nor money to leave behind me. Thou hast given me wife and children, whom I now restore to Thee. Lord, nourish, teach, and preserve them, as Thou hast me.

❧ WILLIAM TYNDALE ❧

(C.1492–1536)

English religious reformer and writer whose life's obsession became to translate the Scriptures into English in order to combat corruption in the English church and extend scriptural knowledge to the common people of England, as "a light to them that walk in darkness, where they cannot stumble." Henry VIII was firmly set against any English version of the Scripture, so Tyndale fled to Germany and then traveled from city to city, in exile, poverty, persecution, and constant danger. He wrote eloquently that salvation is a gift of God, freely bestowed. He completed his translation of the New Testament, and it was printed in Worms and smuggled into England. While working on the Old Testament, he was captured, tried for heresy, strangled, and burned at the stake. His last words were, "Lord, open the King of England's eyes."

I SHALL BE PATIENT

I entreat and beseech your clemency to be urgent with the Procurer that he may kindly permit me to have my Hebrew Bible, Hebrew Grammar, and Hebrew dictionary, that I may spend my time with that study. And in return, may you obtain your dearest wish, provided always to be consistent with the salvation of your soul. But if any other resolution have been come to concerning me, before the conclusion of the winter, I shall be patient, abiding the will of God to the glory of the grace of my Lord Jesus Christ, whose spirit, I pray, may ever direct your heart. Amen.

(While in prison, he suffered from the extreme cold for one and a half years. He converted his keeper and others of his household.)

THOU CANST NOT BUT UNDERSTAND

These things, I say, to know is to have all the scripture unlocked and opened before thee, so that if thou wilt go in, and read, thou cannst not but understand.

(Prologue from Pathway to the Holy Scriptures)

⚜ HANS DENCK ⚜

(C.1495–1527)

**A profoundly spiritual German writer who was one of the "lesser reform-
ers" and a path breaker of "undogmatic Christianity."**

THEY STOP THEIR EARS AND CLAIM THEY CANNOT HEAR

Oh, my God, how does it happen in this poor old world, that Thou
art so great and yet nobody feels Thee, that Thou givest Thyself to
everybody and nobody knows Thy name! Men flee from Thee and say
they cannot find Thee; they turn their backs and say they cannot see
Thee; they stop their ears and say they cannot hear Thee.

(On the Law of God)

⚜ THOMAS BILNEY ⚜

(D. 1537)

English Protestant martyr.

AS IF THE DAY SUDDENLY BROKE ON A DARK NIGHT

When I read that Christ Jesus came into the world to save sinners, it
was as if day suddenly broke on a dark night.

⚜ NICOLAS CAREN ⚜

(D. 1539)

English martyr.

MY IMPRISONMENT

I bless God for my imprisonment, for I then began to relish His life
and the sweetness of God's Holy Word.

❧ ANNE ASKEW ❧

(D. 1546)

Attendant to England's Queen Catherine Parr. She was kicked out of the house by her husband and lost her two children. On the day of her execution she was carried to the stake on a chair, her bones being so dislocated that she could not walk. After being fastened to the stake with a chain, a letter was brought offering pardon from the King if she would recant her faith in Christ. She died praying for her murderers in the midst of the flames, and her last recorded words, an answer to the King's offer of pardon was: "I came not thither to deny my Lord and Master."

I WOULD RATHER DIE THAN BREAK MY FAITH

I was put on the rack for a long time because I would not reveal the names of others who share my faith. They kept me on it a long time. Because I lay still and did not cry, both my lord chancellor and master struck me with their own hands until I was nearly dead.

Then the lieutenant released me from the rack. I immediately fainted. They helped me recover consciousness. For two long hours I sat upon the bare floor, talking with the lord chancellor. With many flattering words, he tried to persuade me to give the answers they wanted. God gave me the grace to persevere.

I was taken to a house and put in bed. My bones were weary and painful. A message came from the lord chancellor that if I would recant, I would be given every comfort. If I would not, I would be taken to Newgate and burned. I sent him word that I would rather die than break my faith.

(Latter Apprehension and Examination)

MORE ENEMIES THAN CAN BE COUNTED

O Lord! I have more enemies now than hairs on my head; yet, Lord, let them never overcome me with vain words, but fight Thou, Lord, in my stead; for on Thee I cast my care. With all the spite they can imagine, they fall upon me, who am Thy poor creature. Yet, sweet Lord, I heartily desire of Thee, that Thou wilt of Thy merciful goodness forgive them that violence they do. Open also their blind hearts, that they may hearafter do that thing in Thy sight which is only acceptable before Thee. So be it, Lord.

✑ IGNATIUS OF LOYOLA ✐
(1491–1556)

Spanish founder of the Society of Jesus. After being wounded as a soldier, he was sent home to recover. He began reading about the life of Christ and idle curiosity soon changed to intense interest. He realized that he was forced with the choice of continuing his old life or serving a new master, Jesus Christ. He chose to follow Christ and tell others about him.

A FOOL FOR CHRIST

I desire and choose poverty with Christ; poor, rather than riches; insults with Christ loaded with them, rather than honours; I desire to be accounted as worthless and a fool for Christ rather than to be esteemed as wise and prudent in this world. So Christ was treated before me.

✑ KATHERINE VON BORA ✐
(1499–1552)

German nun who later became the wife of Martin Luther. She was a skilled nurse, who often had a house full of invalids when the plague raged.

I THANK THEE FOR ALL THE TRIALS

Dear Lord, I thank thee for all the trials, through which thou didst lead me, and by which thou didst prepare me to behold thy Glory. Thou hast never forsaken nor forgotten me.

❧ NICHOLAS RIDLEY ❧

(D. 1555)

Bishop who was burned at the stake in Oxford, England.

GOD HAS CALLED ME TO THIS HONOR

I tell you this so you won't be ashamed by my death. If you love me, you will rejoice that God has called me to this honor, which is greater than any earthly honor I could ever attain. Who couldn't be happy to die for this cause? I trust my Lord God, who put His mind, will and affection in my heart, and choose to lose all my worldly substance, and my life, too, rather than deny His known truth. He will comfort me, aid me, and strengthen me forever, even to the yielding of my spirit and soul into His hands.

❧ FRANCIS BORGIA ❧

(1510–1572)

Spanish Jesuit.

ALTOGETHER THINE

Thou alone knowest best what is for my good. As I am now not my own but altogether thine, so neither do I desire that my will be done, but thine, nor will I have any will but thine.

✦ LADY JANE GREY ✦
(1537–1554)

A remarkably intelligent, young British woman who was queen for ten days. A victim of her time and circumstances, she was imprisoned in the Tower of London and beheaded at age seventeen. From the platform she committed herself to God, saying "Lord, unto Thy hands I commend my spirit."

I SHALL PUT ON INCORRUPTION

Regarding my death, rejoice as I do, good sister. I shall be delivered of this corruption and put on incorruption.

(Found on the last page of her Greek New Testament,
which she sent to her sister the night before she herself was martyred.)

✦ CHRISTOPHER BURTON ✦
(D. 1588)

Christian martyr.

IF I HAD A HUNDRED LIVES

I will not purchase corruptible life at so dear a rate; and indeed, if I had a hundred lives, I would willingly lay down all in defense of my faith.

✦ TERESA OF AVILA ✦
(1515–1582)

Spanish Carmelite nun who founded sixteen convents. She was one of the great contemplative spirits in history. In 1555 she had a mystical experience of God which transformed her life. Her books combine a practical approach to the religious life with a deep love of God.

CALLED BY GOD

....For often when a person is quite unprepared for such a thing, and is not even thinking of God, he is awakened by His Majesty, as though by a rushing comet or a thunderclap. Although no sound is heard, the soul is very well aware that it has been called by God.

✋ WILLIAM SHAKESPEARE ✍

(1564–1616)

Generally acknowledged as not only England's, but also the world's, greatest poet and playwright of all time. He had the quality of universality, "not of an age, but for all time." (Ben Jonson)

LANTERN TO MY FEET

God shall be my hope,
My stay, my guide and lantern to my feet.

LAST WILL AND TESTAMENT

I, William Shakespeare, of Stratford-upon-Avon, in the county of Warrick, gentleman in perfect health and memory, God be praised, do make and ordain this my last will and testament in manner and form following that is to say, first, I commend my soul into the hand of God, my Creator, hoping and assuredly believing, through the only merits of Jesus Christ, my Saviour to be made partaker of life everlasting, and my body to the earth whereof it is made.

✐ CLOSING THOUGHT ✐

God reveals Himself to all, throughout all eras. God's ways are not mechanical, or automatic. They do not come mass-produced as from a factory, but are individually hand-fashioned. No two snowflakes are alike, as no two people are alike. Therefore no conversion is like any other, nor should it be. "He may not be gotten by thought, nor concluded by understanding, but He may be loved and chosen with the true lovely will of thine heart."

(From An Epistle of Discretion)

PART III

Glimpses From the 1600's
From the End of the Renaissance Forward

More Protestants joined the fellowship of believers. Religion was in a state of decline in the first decade of the seventeenth century. War and unstable conditions loosened religious and community ties, and a weakening of the church's influence throughout Europe brought about a decline of morals by the second half of the seventeenth century. In America it was a period of slavery and witch trials. The Quietistic trend left its imprint.

Put God to the test and see how kind he is! See for yourself the way his mercies shower down on all who trust in him. If you belong to the Lord, reverence him; for everyone who does this has everything he needs.

PSALM 34:8,9

✑ GALILEO GALILEI ✒
(1564–1642)

Italian philosopher, astronomer, and mathematician who, in face of being forced to recant and say that the earth did not revolve around the sun, maintained that he was a staunch Christian. He made the first practical use of the telescope and wrote a book showing that science and faith were compatible. When questioned by the Roman Inquisition as to his belief in the existence of God, he replied, pointing to a straw on the floor of his dungeon, "From the structure of that object alone I would infer with certainty the existence of an intelligent Creator."

WHY SHOULD I DOUBT?

The sun, with all those planets moving round it, can ripen the smallest bunch of grapes as if it had nothing else to do. Why then should I doubt His power?

GREAT MYSTERIES

When I consider how many and how great mysteries men have understood, discovered, and contrived, I very plainly know and understand the mind of man to be one of the works of God, yea, one of the most excellent.

✑ JOHANNES KEPLER ✒
(1571–1630)

German astronomer who formulated 'Kepler's Laws' to describe the movements of the planets in the solar system. He determined to discover the truth to the glory of God.

NOW NOTHING CAN KEEP ME BACK

Eighteen months ago the first dawn rose for me; three months ago the bright day; and a few days ago the full sun of a most wonderful vision; now nothing can keep me back. I have stolen the golden vessels of the Egyptians to make out of them a holy tabernacle for God. I am writing this book for my contemporaries or—what does it matter—for posterity. Has not God waited six thousand years for someone to contemplate his work with understanding?

∞ JOHN DONNE ∞
(1573–1631)

Well-known English poet and preacher.

COMMUNION WITH GOD

I count all that part of my life lost which I spent not in communion with God, or in doing good.

∞ THOMAS HEYWOOD ∞
(1574–1631)

English dramatist and poet.

THE SEARCH FOR GOD

I have wander'd like a sheep that's lost,
To find Thee out in every coast.
Without I have long seeking been,
Whilst Thou the while abid'st within.
Through every broad street and strait lane
Of this world's city, but in vain.
I have enquir'd the reason why?
I sought Thee ill, for how could I
Find Thee abroad, when Thou, mean space,
Had'st made within Thy dwelling-place?

(From "The Search for God")

✺ JAKOB BOEHM ✺
(1575–1624)

German mystic who profoundly influenced many of the great thinkers since, including the Quaker, Rufus Jones, who said, "His life was one long story of persecution and hate, beautifully borne. He overcame the world and triumphed over the treatment meted out to him. His life rang true to his message. He breathed a spirit of love, and in him the lily came to blossom with its new smell."

SUDDENLY....I KNEW GOD

Suddenly my spirit did break through the gate, not without the assistance of the Holy Spirit. I knew God—who He is, how He is, and what His Will is.

TRUE UNDERSTANDING

Now while I was wrestling and battling, being aided by God, a wonderful light arose in my soul. It was a light entirely foreign to my unruly nature, but in it I recognized the true nature of God and man, and the relation existing between them, a thing which heretofore I had never understood.

HIS DYING WORDS

Do you hear the music? Now I go home.

✺ THOMAS WENTWORTH ✺
(D. 1641)

Earl of Stafford and English statesman, who was executed for his faith in Christ.

WITHOUT ANY APPREHENSION

I look upon the approach of death without any apprehension, and now lay my head on the block with the same tranquillity as I have laid it on my pillow.

⇜ EDWARD HERBERT ⇝
(1584–1654)

Lord of Cherbury.

THE GREATEST MIRACLE OF NATURE

Whoever considers the study of anatomy, I believe will never be an atheist; the frame of man's body, and coherence of his parts, being so strange and paradoxical, that I hold it to be the greatest miracle of nature.

⇜ JOHN SELDEN ⇝
(1584–1654)

Dedicated English scholar, philosopher, researcher, prolific writer and historian. He was twice imprisoned for going against King Charles I of England.

TO THIS I CLEAVE

I have surveyed most of the learning found among the sons of men; but I can stay my soul on none of them but the Bible…I have endeavored to know everything that is esteemed worth knowing amongst men; but with all my reading, nothing now remains to comfort me at the close of this life but this passage of St. Paul: "It is a faithful saying, worthy of all acceptation, that Jesus Christ came into the world to save sinners, of whom I am chief." To this I cleave and herein do I find rest.

❧ Izaak Walton ❧
(1593–1683)

Deeply religious English writer who presented the Christian point of view in everything he wrote. He wrote biographies of John Donne and George Herbert, but he is best known for his book about fishing, *The Compleat Angler,* a treatise on fishing and life, which has had over 300 editions.

I THEREFORE WILL TRUST IN HIM

When I would beget content and increase confidence in the power and wisdom and providence of Almighty God, I will walk the meadows by some gliding stream, and there contemplate the lilies that take no care, and those very many other little living creatures that are not only created, but fed (man knows not how) by the goodness of the God of Nature, and therefore trust in Him.

❧ Oliver Cromwell ❧
(1599–1658)

English revolutionary military leader and statesman. In 1623, after thinking, "The world needs a man, a good man, a great man, a strong man," he seemed to hear a voice saying, "Thou art the man." Cromwell later became leader of the Puritan Commonwealth Government.

I DREW WATER OUT OF THE WELLS OF SALVATION

I came to the thirteenth verse of the fourth chapter of Philippians where Paul said, "I can do all things through Christ which strengtheneth me." The faith began to work in my heart to find comfort and support, and I said to myself, 'He that was Paul's Christ is my Christ too,' and so I drew water out of the wells of salvation.

⚘ CHARLES I OF ENGLAND ⚘

(1600–1649)

King of England (1625–1649).

AN INCORRUPTIBLE CROWN

I go from a corruptible to an incorruptible crown, where no distur-
bance can have place.

(While he was on the scaffold)

⚘ SAMUEL RUTHERFORD ⚘

(C. 1600–1661)

**Scottish clergyman and writer who lived a careless life as a youth, but after
graduating from the university, became serious about following Christ. He
was forbidden to preach after the appearance of his book, *An Apology for
Divine Grace,* in which he attacked the clergy. He was exiled to Aberdeen
where he wrote heartfelt letters, which were published after his death.**

MOONLIGHT AND DEWS ARE ALSO NECESSARY

I know that, as night and shadows are good for flowers, and moonlight and dews are better than a continual sun, so is Christ's absence
of special use, and that it hath some nourishing virtue in it, and
giveth sap to humility, and putteth an edge on hunger, and fur-
nisheth a fair field to faith to put forth itself, and to exercise its
fingers in gripping it seeth not what......The cross of Christ is the
sweetest burden that I ever bore; it is such a burden as wings are
to a bird, or sails to a ship, to carry me forward to my harbor. Fool
that I was, not to know that the messages of God are not to be read
through the envelope in which they are enclosed......

*(Rutherford was comforted in his deep distress after the death
of his wife and two children and began to see the purpose of it. It was then
he wrote that it takes time for God's purpose to be made clear to us.)*

THE HAPPIEST PASS

I am in the happiest pass to which man ever came. Christ is mine, and I am His; and there is nothing now between me and resurrection, except—Paradise.

(Words uttered when he was dying.)

✍ JEAN EUDES ✍

(1601–1680)

French Missionary.

TO BELONG WHOLLY TO HIM

I no longer wish to find happiness in myself or in created and perishable things, but in Jesus my Saviour. He is my All, and I desire to belong wholly to Him. It is the most extreme folly and delusion to look elsewhere for any true happiness.

✍ ROGER WILLIAMS ✍

(1604–1683)

English colonist who insisted that his fellow Christians return land that had simply been taken from the Indians. He heard that plans were being made to send him back to England. He fled into Indian country, purchased land from the Indians, and there he founded a settlement, naming it Providence, where all could worship in freedom. There he also established the first Baptist church in America and the colony of Rhode Island.

GOD MAKES A PATH

God makes a path, provides a guide,
And feeds a wilderness;
His glorious name, while breath remains,
O that I may confess.
Lost many a time, I have had no guide,
No house but a hallow tree!
In stormy winter night no fire,

No food, no company;
In Him I found a house, a bed,
A table, company;
No cup so bitter but's made sweet,
Where God shall sweetening be.

✑ SIR THOMAS BROWNE ✎
(1605–1682)

British physician and writer. His personal confession of faith is expressed in *Religio Medici*, 1635, written to defend physicians against accusations of skepticism and atheism.

THE FIRST COMPOSER

Music strikes in me a deep fit of devotion and a profound contemplation of the first Composer. There is something in it of divinity more than the ear discovers.

(Speaking of religious music of the great composers.)

✑ OBADIAH HOLMES ✎
(1606–1682)

Minister who was arrested for preaching Baptist doctrine in Lynn, Massachusetts in 1651. He was taken to Boston Commons, stripped to the waist, and tied to a whipping post.

GOD WILL NOT FAIL

As the man began to lay the strokes upon my back, I said to the people, "Though my flesh should fail, yet God would not fail." So it pleased the Lord to come in and fill my heart and tongue, and with an audible voice I broke forth praying unto the Lord not to lay this sin to their charge. In truth, as the strokes fell upon me, I had such a manifestation of God's presence as the like thereof I never had nor felt, nor can with fleshy tongue express; and the outward pain was so removed from me, that indeed I am not able to declare it to you. It was so easy to me that I could well bear it, yea, and in a manner felt it not although it was grievous, the man striking with all his strength (spitting on his hands three times as many affirmed) with a three corded whip, giving me therewith thirty strokes. When he loosed me from the post, having joyfulness in my heart and cheerfulness in my countenance, I told the magistrates, "You have struck me with roses."

(The whipping of Obadiah Holmes deeply impacted Henry Duster, president of Harvard, and led to the organization of Boston's first Baptist church. Taken from Robert J. Morgan's On This Day)

⪕ JOSEPH ELIOT ⪖

(WRITTEN IN 1664)

A man of God whose deep spirituality pervaded his life.

SOONER OR LATER I SEE THE PURPOSE

I have learned to see a need of everything God gives me, and with nothing He denies me. Whether it be taken from or not given me, sooner or later God quiets me in Himself without it. I cast all my concerns on the Lord, and live securely on the care and wisdom of my heavenly Father.

I AM AT REST

I find that while faith is steady nothing can disquiet me, and when faith totters nothing can establish me. If I ramble out among means and creatures, I am presently lost, and can come to no end. But if I stay myself on God and leave Him to work in His own way and time, I am at rest, and can lie down and sleep in a promise, though a thousand rise up against me. Therefore my way is not to cast beforehand, but to walk with God by the day.

⊰ JOHN MILTON ⊱

(1608–1674)

English poet, often regarded as the finest English writer after Shakespeare. He is said to have read every book ever printed in English in his day.

SONNET ON HIS BLINDNESS

When I consider how my light is spent
Ere half my days in this dark world and wide,
And that one talent which is death to hide,
Lodged with me useless, though my soul more bent
To serve therewith my Maker, and present
My true account, lest he returning chide;
"Doth God exact day-labor, light denied?"
I fondly ask. But Patience, to prevent
That murmur, soon replies, "God doth not need
Either man's work or his own gifts; who best
Bear his mild yoke, they serve him best; his state
Is kingly: thousands at his bidding speed,
And post o'er land and ocean without rest;
They also serve who only stand and wait."

⊰ ROBERT LEIGHTON ⊱

(1611–1684)

Scottish theologian.

ILLNESS BRINGS KNOWLEDGE

I have learned more of God since I came to this bed than in all my life before.

(Written while very sick)

❧ BROTHER LAWRENCE ❧ (NICHOLAS HERMAN)
(1611–1691)

A monk who was converted at the age of eighteen, in the winter, after seeing a tree stripped of its leaves, and realizing that within a little time the leaves would be renewed, and then the flowers and fruit would appear. Brother Lawrence's thoughts on the joy of living a simple life and seeking to live continuously in the presence of God are found in *The Practice of the Presence of God*.

IN THE NOISE AND CLATTER OF MY KITCHEN

The time of business does not with me differ from the time of prayer, and in the noise and clatter of my kitchen, while several persons are at the same time calling for different things, I possess God in as great tranquillity as if I were upon my knees….I know not how God will dispose of me. I am always happy. All the world suffers; and I, who deserve the severest discipline feel joys so continual and so great that I can scarce contain them.

TO REMAIN IN THE PRESENCE OF GOD

The world appears very little to a soul that contemplates the greatness of God. My business is to remain in the presence of God.

⊰ JEREMY TAYLOR ⊱
(1613–1667)

English Anglican clergyman, bishop, theologian and devotional writer who strongly objected to religious intolerance and the ruthless persecution of heretics. He preached in St. Paul's Cathedral at age eighteen. He is especially remembered for *Rules and Exercises of Holy Living and Dying.*

THEY LEFT ME ALL I NEED

I praise God they left me the sun and the moon, a loving wife, many friends to pity and relieve, the providence of God, all the promises of the gospel, my religion, my hope of heaven, and my charity towards my enemies.

(Comments when his house had been plundered and all his worldly possessions squandered, and his family turned out of doors)

⊰ HENRY MORE ⊱
(1614–1687)

English poet and philosopher.

AS A FRIEND

God doth not ride me as a horse, and guide me I know no whither myself; but converseth with me as a Friend; and speaketh to me in such a dialect as I understand fully, and can make others understand.

⊰ ISAAC PENINGTON ⊱
(1617–1680)

Zealous follower of Christ who was filled with such faith that he was jailed six times for proclaiming his unshakable convictions. He was jailed five times for worshipping in silence, as opposed to using liturgy, sacraments and sermons, as prescribed by the established church.

THE RIVER OF LIFE

I saw and felt the pure life of the Son made manifest in me; and the Father drew me to Him as to a living stone, and hath built my soul upon Him, and brought me to Mount Zion, and the holy city of our God; where the river of life sends forth its streams, which refresh and make glad the holy city, and all the tabernacles that are built on God's holy hill.

(Letters)

⊰ JOHN BULWER ⊱
(FL. 1654)

American physician who devoted much attention to the discovery of methods for communicating knowledge to those who cannot hear or speak.

WHERE THE RAINBOW NEVER FADES

I cannot believe that earth is man's abiding-place. It can't be that our life is cast up by the ocean of eternity to float a moment upon its waves, and then sink into nothingness; else why is it that the glorious aspirations which leap like angels from the temple of our heart are forever wandering about unsatisfied? Why is it that the rainbow and clouds come over with a beauty that is not of earth, and then pass off, and leave us to muse upon their favored loveliness? Why is it that the stars, who hold their festival around the midnight throne, are set above the grasp of our limited faculties, forever mocking us with their unapproachable glory? And, finally, why is it that bright forms of human beauty are presented to our view, and then taken from us, leaving the thousand streams of our affection to glow back in Alpine torrents upon our heart? We are born for a higher destiny than that of Earth; there is a realm where the rainbow never fades, where the stars will be spread before us like islands that slumber on the ocean; and where the beings that pass before us like shadows will stay in our presence forever.

❧ WILLIAM DEWSBURY ❧
(1621–1688)

English Quaker.

THE BOLTS AND LOCKS WERE AS JEWELS

In the prison house I sang praises to my God, and esteemed the bolts and locks put upon me as jewels.

❧ JAMES GUTHRIE ❧
(D. 1661)

Teacher of philosophy at the University of St. Andrews in Scotland for years before becoming a preacher. He went to the scaffold for his faith.

I WOULD NOT EXCHANGE THE SCAFFOLD

Very well. This is the day that the Lord hath made, let us rejoice and be glad in it. I could not exchange the scaffold for the palace.

(On his execution day he rose at four in the morning for personal worship. This was his reply when asked how he felt.)

IT IS A GOOD CAUSE

William, the day will come when they will cast up to you that your father was hanged. But be not thou ashamed for it is a good cause.

(After speaking thus to his son, he soon mounted the scaffold and preached for an hour to the assembled multitude.)

❧ BLAISE PASCAL ❧

(1623–1662)

French philosopher and mathematician who was often ill and lived only until he was thirty-nine. He personally encountered Jesus Christ while reading John 17. His life changed and he began giving much of his money to the poor. His scientific studies, world famous to this day, became second to his spiritual pursuits. He discovered the principal of the hydraulic jack (Pascal's Law), and built the first calculator. But he was best known for *Pensees,* his scattered thoughts on spiritual matters which he jotted down, but did not have time to revise or set in order.

BY HIS GRACE

I love poverty because He loved it. I love riches because they afford me the means of helping the very poor. I keep faith with everybody; I do not render evil to those who wrong me, but I wish them a lot like mine, in which I receive neither evil nor good from men. I try to be just, true, sincere, and faithful to all men; I have a tender heart for those to whom God has more closely united me; and whether I am alone, or seen of men, I do all my actions in the sight of God, who must judge of them, and to whom I have consecrated them all. These are my sentiments; and every day of my life I bless my Redeemer, who has implanted them in me.

I KNOW! I KNOW! I FEEL! JOY! PEACE!

From about half-past ten in the evening to about half-past twelve.

FIRE!

"God of Abraham, God of Isaac, God of Jacob

Not the God of philosophers and scholars

I know! I know! I feel! Joy! Peace!"

Forgetfulness of the world and everything but God.

The world has not known Thee,

but I have known Thee,

Joy! Joy! Joy! Tears of joy!

This is eternal life, that they might know Thee, the only true God,

and the one whom Thou has sent, Jesus Christ.

(During the night of November 23, 1654 Pascal had a strange and wonderful vision of God. He was told to renounce the world and surrender to Jesus Christ. These words were found after his death on a parchment stitched into the lining of his coat. Above the quote was a cross surrounded by the rays of the rising sun, the year, the day, and the hour of his conversion.)

IN HOLY CONFIDENCE

O Lord, let me not henceforth desire health or life except to spend them for you, with you and in you. You alone know what is good for me; do therefore what seems best to you. Give to me or take from me; conform my will to yours; and grant that with humble and perfect submission and in holy confidence I may receive the orders of your eternal providence, and may equally adore all that comes to me from you.

✧ GEORGE FOX ✧

(1624–1691)

British spiritual leader whose ministry was the origin of Quakerism. He was an itinerant preacher who suffered imprisonment and beatings for his faith. He was also a loving pastor who believed in guidance by the Holy Spirit within and who wrote over three thousand letters. A biographer has said, "The secret of George Fox's life is easily told. He was completely master of himself because he was completely a servant of God."

AN INFINITE OCEAN OF LIGHT

I knew God experientially. I was as one who has the key that opens. I was taken up into the love of God. I saw that there was an ocean of darkness and death. But I saw that there was an infinite ocean of light and life and love which flows over the ocean of darkness, and in that I saw the infinite love of God....The Lord has opened to me by His invisible power how that every man was enlightened by the divine Light of Christ and I saw it shine through all; and they that believed in it came out of condemnation and came to the Light of Life, and became children of it.

ALL THESE TROUBLES WERE GOOD FOR ME

The eternal God, who hath, in and by his eternal powerful arm, preserved me through all my troubles, trials, temptations, and afflictions, persecutions, reproaches, and imprisonments, and carried me over them all, hath sanctified all these things to me, so that I can say, all things work together for good to them that love God, and are beloved of him....I saw clearly that all these troubles were good for me, and temptations for the trial of my faith which Christ had given me.

(Journal)

✥ JOHN BUNYAN ✥

(1628–1688)

English Puritan writer and minister who was bound with chains and imprisoned for twelve years for holding meetings separate from the established Church of England. He wrote much of his *Pilgrim's Progress,* an allegory, during his last stay in Bedford jail. After his release he preached in many places.

CONVERSION FROM OVERHEARING THE TALK OF OTHERS

They were far above, out of my reach, their talk was about new birth, the work of God on their hearts, and of their own righteousness, as filthy and insufficient to do them any good. And methought they spake, as if joy did make them speak; they spoke with such pleasantness of Scripture language. I was so taken with the love of God that I knew not how to contain myself till I got home. I thought I could have spoken of his love to the very crows that sat upon the ploughed lands before me.

(Speaking here of the day of his conversion because of the talk of three or four poor women, sitting at the door in the sun.)

BEYOND THE RIVER THAT HAS NO BRIDGE

I have resolved...to run when I can, to go when I cannot run, and to creep where I cannot go. I thank Him who loves me. I am fixed; my way is before me; my mind is beyond the River that has no bridge...I have loved to hear my Lord spoken of, and wherever I have seen the print of His shoe in the earth, there have I coveted to put mine also.

(Mr. Steadfast, speaking in Pilgrim's Progress)

THOSE YEARS IN JAIL

I never knew all there was in the Bible until I spent those years in jail. I was constantly finding new treasures.

⊰ THOMAS TRAHERNE ⊱
(C.1637–1674)

English poet and clergyman. His best known writings in *Centuries of Meditation* were lost for over two hundred years after his death.

I CANNOT DO OTHERWISE

This estate wherein I am placed is the best for me, though encompassed with difficulties. It is my duty to think so, and I cannot do otherwise. I cannot do otherwise without reproaching my Maker, that is, without suspecting, and in that offending His goodness and Wisdom. Riches are but tarnish and gilded vanities, honors are airy and empty bubbles, affections are but winds, perhaps too great for such a ship as mine, of too light a ballast: pleasures, yea, all them, are but witches that draw and steal us away from God; dangerous allurements, interposing screens, unseasonable companions, counterfeit realities, honied poison, cumbersome distractions, I have found them so. At least they lull us into lethargies and we need to be quickened. Sometimes they puff us up with vainglory and we need to be humbled. Always they delude us if we place any confidence in them and therefore it is as good always to be without them. But it is as good also, were it not for our weakness, sometimes to have them, because a good use may be made out of them.

⊰ ISAAC NEWTON ⊱
(1642–1727)

English physicist and mathematician who was the culminating figure of the scientific revolution of the 17th century. His science was motivated by his Christian thought.

THE SPIRITUAL WORLD ALL BEFORE ME

I seem to have been like a boy playing on the seashore while the great ocean of truth lay all undiscovered before me.

(Testimony after one of his epoch-making discoveries)

I HAVE TRIED IT AND KNOW IT TO BE TRUE

Halley, when you speak of astronomy and mathematics, I will listen to you; but not when you talk of Christianity, for you have never tried it. But I have tried it and know it to be true.

(After hearing the astronomer Halley denounce Christianity)

CLOSER TO GOD

I can take my telescope and look millions and millions of miles into space, but I can lay it aside and go into my room, shut the door, get down on my knees in earnest prayer, and see more of heaven and get closer to God than I can assisted by all the telescopes and material agencies on earth.

❧ MARIE GUYON ❧
(1648–1717)

French writer and thinker who greatly influenced Francois Fenelon, John Wesley, Andrew Murray and countless others. The revelation of Christ that transformed her entire life was the simple discovery that Christ was in her. She suffered greatly and lost everything that was dearest in this world, but saw the hand of God so clearly in them.

NOT MERELY PEACE, BUT THE GOD OF PEACE

In a wonderful manner, difficult to explain, all that which had been taken from me was not only restored but restored with increase and with new advantages. In Thee, my God, I found it all, and more than all! The peace which I now possess is all holy, heavenly, inexpressible. What I had possessed some years before, in the period of my spiritual enjoyment, was consolation and peace—the gift rather than the Giver. I might now be said to possess not merely consolation, but the God of consolation, not merely peace, but the God of peace.

THERE WAS JOY IN MY HEART WHILE I WAS IN THAT PRISON

It sometimes seemed to me as if I were a little bird whom the Lord had placed in a cage; and that I had nothing now to do but sing. The joy of my heart gave a brightness to the objects around me. The stones of my prison looked in my eyes like rubies. I esteemed them more than all the gaudy brilliancies of a vain world. My heart was full of that joy which thou givest to them that love thee in the midst of their greatest crosses.

(While imprisoned in the Castle of Vincennes, in 1695,

she not only sang, but wrote songs of praise to God.)

ᘒ ROBERT BARCLAY ᘓ

(1648–1719)

Scottish Quaker theologian who led a much traveled life with many ups and downs, ranging from friendship with royalty to imprisonment.

A SECRET POWER

Many are the blessed experiences which I could relate of this silence and manner of worship...For, when I came into the silent assemblies of God's people, I felt a secret power among them which touched my heart; and as I gave way unto it, I found the evil weakening in me and the good raised up; and so I became thus knit and united among them, hungering more and more after the increase of this power and life.

⋞ FRANÇOIS FENELON ⋟
(1651–1715)

French Archbishop and devotional and philosophical writer whose main theme was the love of God and joy in the spiritual life. For example, he wrote, "God is so good that he only awaits our desire to overwhelm us with this gift which is himself. If we fill ourselves with Jesus Christ and his Word, we shall be like a vessel in full sail with a fair wind." After his palace burned down in 1697, destroying his precious library and the manuscripts he was working on, he said to a friend, "I had rather the fire had seized my house than a poor man's cottage."

ONLY HE KNOWS WHAT I NEED

I do not know what to ask of God; only He knows what I need. I simply present myself to Him; I open my heart to Him. I have no other desire than to accomplish His will.

THE LIGHT SHINES IN DARKNESS

I cannot open my eyes without admiring the art that shines through all nature; the least cast suffices to make me perceive the Hand of God that made everything....O my God, if many men do not discover you in this great spectacle you give them of all nature, it is not because you are far from any of us. Everyone feels you, as it were, with his hand, but the senses take up all the attention of the mind. Your light shines in darkness, but darkness is so thick and gloomy that it does not admit the beams of your light....How happy he who searches, sighs, and thirsts after you! But fully happy he on whom is reflected the beams of your countenance, and whose desires your love has already completed.

DONALD CARGILL, WALTER SMITH, JAMES BOIG, WILLIAM CUTHILL ✍ AND WILLIAM THOMSON ❧

(1681)

On July 10, 1681 Scottish troops burst into the house where Cargill, Smith and Boig were sleeping. The men were rousted from bed, tied to barebacked horses, and taken to prison. Soon Cuthill and Thomson joined them. All were condemned for being Presbyterians, which was outlawed.

AS I GO UP THIS LADDER

The Lord knows I go up this ladder with less fear, confusion or perturbation of mind than ever I entered a pulpit to preach.

> *(Cargill, speaking after putting his foot on the ladder,*
> *turning and blessing the Lord with uplifted hands)*

WORDS SHORTLY BEFORE BEING HANGED

I have one more word to say, and that is that all who love God and his righteous cause would set time apart and sing a song of praise to the Lord for what he has done for my soul. To him be praise.

> *(Smith ascended the executioner's block, lifted the hood and praised God.*
> *His head fell. Boig, Cuthill and Thomson were next.*
> *"The hangman hashed and hagged off all their heads with an axe.")*

❧ CLOSING THOUGHT ❧

Abandon yourself to his care and guidance, as a sheep in the care of a shepherd, and trust him utterly. No matter if you may seem to yourself to be in the very midst of a desert, with nothing green about you inwardly or outwardly, and may think you will have to make a long journey before you can get into the green pastures. Our shepherd will turn that very place where you are into green pastures, for he has power to make the desert rejoice and blossom as a rose.

—*Hannah Whitall Smith*

PART IV

Glimpses from the 1700's
The Great Awakening and the Enlightenment Period

The Great Awakening set the stage for the next century's revival and mission input. A series of revivals in the 30s and 40s had a profound impact on almost every region and many aspects of colonial religious life. It encouraged people to devote their practical, daily life to loving God and serving their neighbor and stimulated a concern for higher education. The Enlightenment was a religious spirit which inspired a human-centered moral philosophy more than a God-centered life of dependence upon Him.

He will be like a tree planted by the water that sends out its roots by the stream. It does not fear when heat comes; its leaves are always green. It has no worries in a year of drought and never fails to bear fruit.

JEREMIAH 17:18

✃ AUGUST HERMANN FRANCKE ✄
(1663–1727)

German Lutheran leader, educator, and social reformer who, in his teachings, emphasized Christian living, in contrast to rites and ceremonies. He had as a rule never to preach a sermon without including in it so much of the gospel that if his hearers heard but that one sermon, they might be led to accept salvation.

HE GRASPED ME ONCE AGAIN

God did not cast me aside because of my deep corruption in which I stood fast, but He had patience with me and helped me in my weakness, since I could not find the courage but only always hoped that I might break through into a true light which is from God. I experienced in myself that one does not have cause to complain about God, but that He always opens door and gate where He finds a heart that honestly looks to Him and seeks his presence earnestly. God always went before me and lifted the blocks and difficulties out of the way so that I was convinced that my conversion was not mine but His work. God took me at the same time by His hand and led me as a mother leads her weak child, and so great and overpowering was His love that He always grasped me once again when I tore loose from His hand, and allowed me to sense the rod of His discipline. Finally, He heard my prayer and set me in a free and unbound state...

(The Autobiography, 1692)

❧ JOSEPH ADDISON ❧

(1672–1719)

English essayist, poet, and dramatist.

THAT GREAT DAY WHEN ALL OF US SHALL BE CONTEMPORARIES

When I look upon the tombs of the great, every emotion of envy dies in me; when I read the epitaphs of the beautiful, every inordinate desire goes out; when I meet with the grief of parents upon a tomb-stone, my heart melts with compassion; when I see the tomb of the parents themselves, I consider the vanity of grieving for these whom we must quickly follow; when I see kings lying by those who deposed them, or holy men who divided the world with their disputes, I reflect with sorrow on the little competitions and factions of man-kind. When I read the several dates of the tombs, of some that died yesterday and some six hundred years ago, I consider that Great Day when we shall all of us be contemporaries, and make our appearance together.

❧ JOHANN SEBASTIAN BACH ❧

(1685–1750)

Generally regarded as one of the greatest composers of all time. He was an outstanding harpsichordist, organist and expert on organ building. He combined his love of music and Scriptures, writing in the margin of I Chronicles 25, the chapter in which King David commissioned the temple musicians: "This chapter is the true foundation for all God-pleasing music."

TO GOD'S GLORY

(I will create) well-regulated church music to the glory of God.... God writes my music.

(He often scribbled J.J. on his blank pages:
Jesu Juva—Help me Jesus. At the manuscript's end,
he jotted S.D.G.—Soli Deo Gloria—to God alone, the glory.)

✧ GEORGE FREDERICK HANDEL ✧

(1685–1759)

German-born composer who settled in England in 1712. He wrote opera, orchestral works and oratorios, the most famous of which is the Messiah, taken from all parts of the Bible and all telling of Jesus, *The Messiah*. It was written after his right side was paralyzed, his money gone, and his creditors had threatened to imprison him. His faith prevailed. Audiences everywhere have stood in reverence during the stirring words: "Hallelujah! For He shall reign forever and ever."

WHILE COMPOSING THE "HALLELUJAH CHORUS"

I did think I did see all heaven before me, and the great God himself.

> *(Sitting at a table with tears streaming down his face, he commented to a servant after composing the 'Hallelujah Chorus' from the Messiah. He had been working on it for 24 days without leaving his house.)*

✧ COUNT NICHOLAUS ZINZENDORF ✧

(1700–1760)

Religious and social reformer who was born into one of Europe's leading families and grew up in an atmosphere of prayer, Bible-reading, and hymn-singing. He excelled in school and seemed destined for national leadership. While visiting the art museum at Dusseldorf, he had a deeply moving experience that stayed with him the rest of his life. He gave his life to Christ and oversaw the sending of the first missionaries in Protestant history.

WHATEVER HE LEADS ME TO DO

I have loved Him for a long time, but I have never actually done anything for Him. From now on, I will do whatever He leads me to do....I have but one passion—it is Christ. (Comments after seeing Domenico Feti's "Ecce Homo" ("Behold the Man"), a portrait of the thorn-crowned Jesus, and reading the inscription below it—"I Did This For Thee! What Hast Thou Done For Me?" His life was never again the same, and he went on to found a spiritual community on his property, Herrnhut, which provided hundreds of missionaries and sparked the modern missionary movement.)

IN MY FOURTH YEAR

In my fourth year, I began to seek God with such earnestness as accorded with my childish notions. From that time, especially, it was my steadfast resolve to become a true servant of the crucified Jesus.

(At age four, he signed his name to this covenant: Do Thou be mine and I will be Thine. As a child, he wrote tender letters to the Savior, and threw them out of the window, confident that the Lord would receive and read them.)

✑ PHILLIP DODDRIDGE ✑

(1702–1751)

English minister whose writings have been translated into many languages. Even though he had lost his earthly parents when he was eight, he wrote in his diary, "God is an immortal father, my soul rejoices in Him; He hath hitherto helped me and provided for me; may it be my study to approve myself a more affectionate, grateful and dutiful child." He began his ministry at $60 a year. He is remembered for the hymn, "O, Happy Day."

LIKE LIGHTNING FROM HEAVEN

I have known those of distinguished genius, polite manners, and great experience in human affairs, who, after having outgrown all the impressions of a religious education; after having been hardened, rather than subdued, by the most singular mercies, even various, repeated, and astonishing deliverances, which have appeared to themselves no less than miraculous; after having lived for years without God in the world, notoriously corrupt themselves, and labouring to the utmost to corrupt others, have been stopped on a sudden in the full career of their sin, and have felt such rays of the divine presence, and of redeeming love, darting in upon their minds, almost like lightning from heaven.

⋙ JONATHAN EDWARDS ⋘

(1703–1758)

American Presbyterian pastor, college president, missionary, theologian, and a key figure in the eighteenth century's "Great Awakening." He graduated from Yale at age fifteen, was ordained at age nineteen and taught at Yale by age twenty. He had a special love of God from the age of seven, and traced his conversion to age twenty. "I made a solemn declaration of myself to God and wrote it down; giving up myself and all that I had to God; to be for the future in no respect my own."

QUITE DIFFERENT FROM ANYTHING ELSE

The first instance I remember of that sort of inward sweet delight in God and divine things, which I have lived much in since, was on reading those words in I Timothy 1:17, "Now unto the King eternal, immortal, invisible, the only wise God, be honor and glory forever and ever. Amen." As I read the words, there came into my soul and was, as it were, diffused throughout it, a sense of the glory of the Divine Being. It was a new sense, quite different from anything I had ever experienced. Never any words of Scripture seemed to me as these words did. I thought to myself, how excellent a Being that was and how happy I should be if I might enjoy that God, be rapt up to Him in heaven, and be swallowed up in Him forever!

(Describing his conversion at age 20.)

THE GLORIOUS MAJESTY AND GRACE OF GOD

And as I was walking there and looked up on the sky and clouds, there came into my mind, so sweet a sense of the glorious majesty and grace of God, that I know not how to express.....It was a sweet and gentle, and holy majesty...After this my sense of divine things gradually increased, and became more and more lively, and had more of that inward sweetness. The appearance of every thing was altered, there seemed to be, as it were a calm, sweet cast, or appearance of divine glory, in almost everything. God's excellency, his wisdom, his purity and love, seemed to appear in every thing...And scarce any thing, among all the works of nature, was so sweet to me as thunder and lightning: formerly, nothing had been so terrible to me. I used to be a person uncommonly terrified with thunder, and it used to strike me with terror when I saw a thunderstorm rising. But now, on the contrary, it rejoiced me. I felt God at the first appearance of a thunderstorm; and used to take the opportunity, at such times, to fix myself to view the clouds, and see the lightnings play, and hear the majestic and awful voice of God's thunder.

(From The Works of Jonathan Edwards, vol. I, S. Converse, 1829)

RESOLVED AS AN EIGHTEEN YEAR OLD

Resolved that all men should live to the glory of God. Resolved, secondly, that whether or not anyone else does, I will.

(Written in his diary at age 18.)

⚜ JOHN WESLEY ⚜

(1703–1791)

English pastor who began his life's work at eleven years of age and at seventeen initiated the beginnings of what was later known as Methodism. He was an itinerant preacher who traveled on horseback 250,000 miles after he was thirty-six years of age and preached over 40,000 sermons, some of them to congregations of 20,000 or even 30,000 people. He rose at four in the morning, and preached until five nearly every day. The gospel message which he preached changed lives and changed England in the 18th century. His influence indeed was worldwide.

ABOUT A QUARTER BEFORE NINE

I went very unwillingly to a society of Aldersgate Street, where one was reading Luther's *Preface to the Epistle to the Romans*. About a quarter before nine, while he was describing the change God works in the heart through faith in Christ, I felt my heart strangely warmed. I felt I did trust in Christ, Christ alone, for salvation; and an assurance was given me that He had taken away my sins, even mine and saved me from the law of sin and death. I began to pray with all my might for those who had in a more especial manner despitefully used me and persecuted me. I then testified openly to all there what I now first felt in my heart.

(Journal, 1758)

WE PRAISE THEE, O GOD

Monday, January 1, 1739. Mr. Hall, Kinchin, Ingham, Whitefeild, Hutchins, and my brother Charles were present at our lovefeast in Fetterslane, with about sixty of our brethren. About three in the morning, as we were continuing instant in prayer, the power of God came mightily upon us, insomuch that many cried out for exceeding joy and many fell to the ground. As soon as we recovered a little from the awe and amazement at the presence of His majesty, we broke out with one voice, 'We praise Thee, O God, we acknowledge Thee to be the Lord.'

(Journal, 1758)

THE CONFIDENCE IN WHICH I SLEEP BY NIGHT AND WORK BY DAY

I trust myself upon His love. It is not knowledge, now, of what will come or how it can be met; it is only the sympathetic apprehension of His love and care who is all-strong, all-wise. This is what I rest upon. This is the confidence in which I sleep by night and work by day. It is a peace which passeth understanding and fulfills itself in love.

(Journal, 1758)

I DO NOT WANT IT TO FIND A WAY INTO MY HEART

When I have any money, I get rid of it as quickly as possible, lest it should find a way into my heart.

(After necessities, he gave away the rest of the meager salary he received.)

LIKE AN ARROW THROUGH THE NIGHT

I am a creature of a day, passing through life as an arrow through the air. I am a spirit come from God and returning to God; just hovering over the great gulf; till, a few moments hence, I am no more seen; I drop into an unchangeable eternity! I want to know one thing—the way to heaven; how to land soft on that happy shore. God Himself has condescended to teach the way; for this very end He came from heaven.

(Journal, 1738)

IF I KNEW I WERE GOING TO DIE TOMORROW

I should preach this evening at Loucester, and again at five tomorrow morning, after that, I should ride to Tewkesbury, preach in the afternoon, and meet the societies in the evening. I should then repair to friend Martin's house, who expects to entertain me; converse and pray with the family as usual; retire to my room at ten o'clock; commend myself to my heavenly father; lie down to rest; and wake up in glory.

(When asked how he would spend the intervening time
if he knew he were to die at twelve o'clock tomorrow night.)

✎ BENJAMIN FRANKLIN ✐
(1706–1790)

American statesman, diplomat, scientist, philosopher, and writer.

THAT PRAYERS BE HELD IN THIS ASSEMBLY

Mr. President, in the beginning of the contest with Great Britain, when we were sensible of danger, we had daily prayer in this room for divine protection. Our prayers were heard and answered. I have lived a long time. And the longer I live, the more convincing proofs I see of this truth—that God governs in the affairs of men. And if a sparrow cannot fall on the ground without his notice, is it probable that an empire can rise without his aid? I therefore beg leave to move that henceforth prayers, imploring the assistance of heaven and blessings upon our deliberations, be held in this assembly every morning.

(A motion made by Franklin when the Federal Constitutional Convention
opened its session in Philadelphia, June 28, 1787. The motion carried.)

✄ JOHN NELSON ✄

(1707–1774)

One of John Wesley's helpers who was thrown into a dungeon underneath a slaughterhouse because of his beliefs.

MY DUNGEON WAS A PARADISE TO ME

The dungeon stank worse than a hogsty by reason of the blood and filth that flowed into it from above… My soul was so filled with the love of God that it was a paradise to me.

✄ CHARLES WESLEY ✄

(1707–1788)

English clergyman, poet, and hymn writer. During the winter of 1728–9, he underwent a spiritual awakening. He became an eloquent preacher and translated the gospel message into hymns. He published more than 4,500 hymns and left some 3,000 in manuscript. George Frederic Handel wrote music specifically for some of them. A couple of his most well-known hymns are: "Love Divine, All Love Excelling," "Hark the Herald Angels Sing," and "Christ the Lord is Ris'n Today."

I ROSE, WENT FORTH AND FOLLOWED THEE

Long my imprisoned spirit lay
First bound in sin and nature's night;
Thine eye diffused a quickening ray—
I woke, the dungeon flamed with light;
My chains fell off, my heart was free,
I rose, went forth, and followed Thee.

(Hymn describing an event on Whitsunday, May 21, 1738,
when both he and his bother John found themselves "at peace with God")

❧ LUDWIG VON BEETHOVEN ❧
(1712–1773)

Recognized by many as one of the greatest composers who ever lived. Referring to his deafness, he said, "I shall hear in heaven."

AN ECHO OF THE HEAVENLY MUSIC

My ninth symphony is but an empty echo of the heavenly music I heard in my dream.

❧ GEORGE WHITEFIELD ❧
(1714–1770)

English evangelist of the Church of England who became a Christian while attending Oxford in 1735. At age twenty-one he was a famous pulpit orator. He was a pioneer in open air preaching who covered vast distances, including fourteen visits to Scotland and seven tours of the colonies, each of which lasted more than a year. It is estimated that he preached at least 18,000 sermons, or an average of ten times a week for thirty-four years. Once he preached four hours amidst the noise of 20,000–30,000 people at Bartholomew Fair and received a thousand notes from persons who had heard him.

A LIVING FAITH

I must bear testimony to my old friend Mr. Charles Wesley. He put a book into my hands called *The Life of God in the Soul of Man*, through which God showed me that I must be born again.… I know the exact place…Whenever I go to Oxford, I cannot help running to the spot where Jesus Christ first revealed himself to me and gave me a new birth. I learned that a man may go to church, say his prayers, and receive the sacrament, and yet not be a Christian. How my heart did rise and shudder like a poor man who is most reluctant to look into his ledger for fear that he would find himself bankrupt.….O what a ray of divine life did then break in upon my soul!

(In a sermon of 1769)

⚘ DAVID BRAINERD ⚘

(1718–1747)

Missionary who overcame many years of doubt. He was converted on July 12, 1739. His short life of twenty-nine years was brought on by hardship and exposure in bringing the gospel to the American Indians. He claimed the promise in John 7: "Have faith in me, and you will have life-giving waters flowing from deep inside you." His story moved his generation—Henry Martyn, William Cary, Jonathan Edwards, Adoniram Judson, John Wesley—toward missions. Oswald J. Smith was so influenced by his life that he named his youngest son after him.

MY SOUL REJOICED WITH JOY UNSPEAKABLE

As I was walking in a dark, thick grove, unspeakable glory seemed to open to the view and apprehension of my soul. I do not mean any external brightness, for I saw no such thing, but it was a new inward apprehension or view that I had of God, such as I never had before. I stood still, wondered, and admired. It was widely different from all conceptions that ever I had of God or things divine. My soul rejoiced with joy unspeakable to see such a God, such a glorious Divine Being.

HIS INSTRUMENT

It was raining and the roads were muddy; but this desire grew so strong that I kneeled down by the side of the road and told God all about it. While I was praying, I told Him that my hands should work for Him, my tongue speak for Him, if He would only use me as His instrument—when suddenly the darkness of the night lit up, and I knew that God had heard and answered my prayer, and I felt and I was accepted into the inner circle of God's loved ones."

(Writing of his experience one Sunday night as he totally dedicated his life into God's service)

EVEN TO DEATH

Here am I, send me; send me to the ends of the earth; send me to the rough, the savage pagans of the wilderness; send me from all that is called comfort on earth; send me even to death itself, if it be in Thy service and to promote Thy kingdom.

(His diary became one of the most powerful Christian books in early American history, containing such entries as this one.)

APPOINTMENTS WITH GOD

In the silences I make in the midst of the turmoil of life I have appointments with God. From these silences I come forth with spirit refreshed, and with a renewed sense of power. I hear a voice in the silences, and become increasingly aware that it is the voice of God.

A SOUL THAT LOVES GOD

This I saw, that when a soul loves God with a supreme love, God's interests and his are become one. It is no matter when nor where nor how Christ should send me, nor what trials He should exercise me with, if I may be prepared for His work and will....Oh that I were a flame of fire in my Master's cause!...I cared not where or how I lived, or what hardships I went through, so that I could but gain souls to Christ. While I was asleep, I dreamed of these things, and when I awoke the first thing I thought of was this great work. All my desire was for the conversion of the heathen, and all my hope was in God.

HIS DYING WORDS

I am almost in eternity. I long to be there. My work is done. The Watcher is with me; why tarry the wheels of the chariot?

⚜ JOHN WOOLMAN ⚜

(1720–1772)

Quaker born during a difficult time in America with the impending revolt against England, the slave trade, the war with the Indians, and spreading poverty. He demonstrated his love of God through his love of the Indians and slaves, and promoted their freedom. He had accepted slavery until the day his employer asked him to make out a bill-of-sale for a female slave. He lived what he preached, a life lived in rigorous integrity, witnessing to God's love.

INEXPRESSIBLE, YET UNDERSTOOD

While I silently ponder on that change wrought in me, I find no language equal to it, nor any means to convey to another a clear idea of it. I looked on the works of God in this visible creation, and an awfulness covered me; my heart was tender and often contrite, and universal love to my fellow-creatures increased in me. This will be understood by such as have trodden the same path.

(Journal)

⚜ JOHN NEWTON ⚜

(1725–1807)

English writer of the beloved hymn, "Amazing Grace" which tells of his conversion in 1748 after a terrifying voyage at sea. He wrote over 240 books and booklets published in fifteen languages, and engaged in many evangelistic tours even late in life. He established and directed schools, seminaries, and training institutions for the underprivileged, and became friends with John Wesley and George Whitefield, who guided him into the ministry.

THE 10TH OF MARCH IS A DAY MUCH TO BE REMEMBERED

The 10th of March is a day much to be remembered by me, and I have never suffered it to pass wholly unnoticed; on that day the Lord sent from on high and delivered me out of deep waters....I began to think of my former religious professions, the extraordinary turns in my

life, the calls, warnings I had met with; the licentious course of my
conversation, particularly my unparalleled effrontery in making
the gospel history the constant subject of profane ridicule...When
I heard in the evening that the ship was freed from water, there
arose a gleam of hope; I thought I saw the hand of God displayed in
our favor: I began to pray. I began to think of that Jesus that I had
so often derided;.... I began to know there is a God that hears and
answers prayer.... I was sincerely touched with a sense of undeserved
mercy I had received. Thus to all appearance, I was a new man.

GOD'S PLAN FOR ME

I can hardly recollect a single plan of mine, of which I have not since
seen reason to be satisfied that, had it taken place in season and
circumstance just as I proposed, it would, humanly speaking, have
proved my ruin; or at least it would have deprived me of the greater
good the Lord had designed for me.

TWO LESSONS

When I was young, I was sure of many things; now that my memory
is nearly gone, there are only two things of which I am sure; one is,
that I am a great sinner; and the other, that Christ is my all-sufficient
Saviour....He is well taught who learns these two lessons.

JOHN NEWTON'S SELF-WRITTEN EPITAPH

John Newton, clerk, once an infidel and libertine, a servant of slaves
in Africa, was, by the rich mercy of our Lord and Savior, Jesus Christ,
preserved, restored, pardoned, and appointed to preach the faith he
had long labored to destroy.

LIKE THE LIONS IN THE TOWER

I was once a wild thing on the coast of Africa, but the Lord caught
me, and tamed me: and now people come to see me like the lions in
the Tower. Doubt if the Lord can convert the heathen? Look at me!"

⚜ WILLIAM COWPER ⚜

(1731–1800)

English poet and hymn writer who was influenced by John Newton's sermons about man's personal relationship with God. He struggled with depression throughout his life and tried to take his life several times. Then one morning, in a moment of cheerfulness, he took up his Bible and read a verse in Romans. He believed and rejoiced in the forgiving power of God. Cowper summed up his faith in God's dealings with him, in a hymn, stating, "God moves in a mysterious way His wonders to perform;/ He plants his footsteps in the sea, and rides upon the storm."

I WAS STRICKEN LIKE A DEER

I was a stricken deer, that left the herd
Long since. With many an arrow deep infixt
My panting side was charged, when I withdrew
To seek a tranquil death in distant shades.
There I was found by One who had Himself
Been hurt by th' archers. In his side He bore,
And in his hands and feet, the cruel scars.
With gentle force soliciting the darts,
He drew them forth, and healed, and bade me live.

I, TOO, HAVE BEEN WITH JESUS

And thankfully we say—
Though none but God may hear:
"Rejoice! Rejoice!
For He is guiding me—
I, too,
Have been with Jesus."

☙ FRANZ JOSEPH HAYDN ❧

(1732–1809)

Austrian composer who was one of the most important figures in the development of the classical style in music. Served as chorister at St. Stephen's Cathedral in Vienna at age eight.

DANCING AND LEAPING NOTES

I cannot make my music otherwise. I write according to the thoughts I feel. When I think upon my God, my heart is so full of joy that the notes dance and leap from my pen; and since God has given me a cheerful heart, it will be pardoned me that I serve Him with a cheerful spirit.

(Response when asked by Caprani why his music was so full of gladness.)

FROM HEAVEN ABOVE COMES ALL!

No, no! not from me, but (pointing to heaven) from thence—from heaven above—comes all.

(In 1808, rising to his feet at the intense applause and standing ovation of the audience after the grand performance of the "Creation" at Vienna—as the chorus and orchestra burst in full power upon the passages, "And there was light.")

A SURE AND CONFIDENT JOY

I prayed to God—calmly, slowly. In this I felt that an infinite God would surely have mercy on his finite creature, pardoning dust for being dust. These thoughts cheered me up. I experienced a sure joy so confident that as I wished to express the words of the prayer, I could not express my joy, but gave vent to my happy spirits and wrote above the Miserere, 'Allegro.'

≈ JOHN ADAMS ≈
(1735–1826)

Second President of the United States.

BETTER THAN ALL THE LIBRARIES OF THE WORLD

I have examined all, as well as my narrow sphere, my straitened means, and my busy life would allow me, and the result is that the Bible is the best book in the world. It contains more of my little philosophy than all the libraries of the world....I believe in God and in His wisdom and benevolence.

≈ PATRICK HENRY ≈
(1736–1799)

American statesman.

REGRETS ABOUT NOT BEING MORE FORTHCOMING

I have heard it said that Deists claimed me. The thought pained me more than the appellation of Tory; for I consider religion of infinitely higher importance than politics, and I find much cause to reproach myself, that I have lived so long, and given no decided proof of my being a Christian.

THEY WOULD BE RICH

I have now disposed of all my property to my family. There is one thing more I wish I could give them, and that is the Christian religion.—If they had that, and I had not given them one shilling, they would have been rich, and if they had not that, and I had given them all the world, they would be poor.

⨀ SIR WILLIAM JONES ⨀

(1748–1794)

British philologist and linguist who studied ancient Sanskrit texts and who determined in 1786 its link to classical Greek and Latin.

THESE HOLY SCRIPTURES

I have carefully and regularly perused these Holy Scriptures, and am of opinion that the volume, independently of its divine origin, contains more sublimity, purer morality, more important history, and finer strains of eloquence, than can be collected from all other books, in whatever language they may have been written.

⨀ RICHARD CECIL ⨀

(1748–1810)

Minister of the Church of England who was one of the leaders of the evangelical revival. He was an infidel who was brought to faith by the prayers and example of his mother. On his conversion he resolved to devote himself to the work of the Christian ministry. His sermons "riveted the attention of his congregation by the originality of his conceptions, the plain, straightforward force of his language, the firm grasp of his subject, and by a happy power of illustration which gave freshness and novelty to the most familiar subjects." (Jerram, *Memoir,* p. 267).

I STAND HERE A LIVING WITNESS

I tried when I was a boy to be an infidel, but there was one thing I could never get over. I never could answer my mother's love and character. My father was an intemperate man, and my mother, when made miserable by his brutal treatment, would lead my little brother and myself to a spot under a hillside, and kneeling there, would commend us to God. Hardship and her husband's harshness brought her to her grave. At the age of twenty-one I was vicious, hardened, utterly impenitent. Once I found myself near the home of my boyhood, and felt irresistibly moved to take another look at the little hollow under the hill. There it was as I left it; the very grass looked as if no foot had ever trod it since the guide of my infant years was laid in her early grave. I sat down. I heard again the voice pleading for me. All my bad habits and my refusals of Christ came over me and crushed me down. I did not leave the spot till I had confidence in my Saviour. My mother's prayers came back in answers of converting grace, and I stand to-day the living witness of a mother's faithfulness, and of a prayer-hearing God.

THE BOOKS OF GOD

I cannot look around me without being struck with the analogy observable in the works of God. I find the Bible written in the style of His other books of creation and providence. The pen seems in the same hand. I see it, indeed, write at times mysteriously in each of these books; but I know that mystery in the works of God is only another name for my ignorance. The moment, therefore, that I become humble, all becomes right.

෨ JOHANN WOLFGANG VON GOETHE ෪
(1749–1832)

German philosopher, poet, novelist, dramatist, and scientist. In "Easter Hymn" in *Faust*, he proclaims, "Christ is arisen, Joy to thee, mortal! Christ is risen. Seek Him not here."

THE BIBLE STANDS ALONE

I consider the Gospels to be thoroughly genuine; for in them there is effective reflection of a sublimity which emanated from the person of Christ; and this is as divine as ever the divine appeared on earth....I read all kinds of books, including sacred books, but the Bible stands alone because it reads me...It is belief in the Bible, the fruits of deep meditation, which has served me as the guide of my moral and literary life.

THE SOUL IS LIKE THE SUN WHICH SHINES ON

When a man is as old as I am, he is bound occasionally to think about death. In my case this thought leaves me in perfect peace, for I am fully convinced that our soul is indestructible. Its activity will continue through eternity; it is like a sun which only seems to set, but in truth never sets but shines on unceasingly.

(Comments made one day as he stood with his friend Johann Peter Eckermann,
together gazing in rapt attention at the majestic setting sun.)

I BOW BEFORE HIM

There is in the four Gospels, which are thoroughly genuine, the reflection of a greatness which emanated from the person of Jesus, and which was of as divine a kind as ever was seen upon earth. If I am asked whether it is in my nature to pay Him devout reverence, I say—certainly! I bow before Him as the divine manifestation of the highest principle of morality.

(Conversation between Goethe and his
friend, Johann Peter Eckermann.)

❧ THOMAS ERSKINE ❧
(1750–1823)

American educator and novelist.

THE BASIS ON WHICH HE WILL BUILD BLESSINGS

I believe that love reigns, and that love will prevail. I believe that He says to me every morning. "Begin again thy journey and thy life; thy sins, which are many, are not only forgiven, but they shall be made, by the wisdom of God, the basis on which He will build blessings."

UNFAILING WISDOM

I feel that goodness, and truth, and righteousness are realities, eternal realities, and that they cannot be abstractions, or vapors floating in a spiritual atmosphere, but that they necessarily imply a living, personal Will, a good, loving, righteous God, in whose hands we are perfectly safe, and who is guiding us by unfailing wisdom.

❧ OTHER WRITERS OF THE 1700'S ❧

IF YOU TAKE JESUS OUT OF MY LIFE, I HAVE NOTHING LEFT

I am unemployed and I am very poor, and I have a wife and three children, but if you take Jesus Christ out of my life, I have nothing left. He is greater than my poverty and I love him.

(Unknown Christian at an open-air meeting in Bristol, England in July, 1727, in response to a heckler who shouted out that economic laws govern the situation of the world and Christ has nothing to do with it, as recorded by Leslie D. Weatherhead)

JOY IN SIMPLICITY

I do not know when I have had happier times in my soul, than when I have been sitting at work, with nothing before me but a candle and a white cloth, and hearing no sound but that of my own breath, with God in my soul and heaven in my heart.... I rejoice in being exactly what I am,—a creature capable of loving God, and who, as long as God lives must be happy. I get up and look for a while out of the window, and gaze at the moon and stars, the work of an Almighty hand. I think of the grandeur of the universe, and then sit down, and think myself one of the happiest beings in it.

(Comments by a poor Methodist woman of the 18th century)

I WAS ACCEPTED

I heard no outward voices; I saw no external light or vision of any kind; there was no text of scripture brought to my mind; neither did I feel any exterior joy. I received a conviction or evidence in my soul whereby I was assured that my sins were forgiven, for Christ's sake, and that I was accepted of God in the Beloved.

(Thomas Rutherford, 1752–1806)

✑ CLOSING THOUGHT ✎

There must be some kind of earthquake within us, something that must rend and shake us to the bottom, before we can be sensible enough either of the state of death we are in or enough desirous of that Saviour, who alone can raise us from it.

(—William Law)

PART V

Glimpses from 1801–1850
The Spirit of Revival and the Foundations for Missions

The nineteenth century became known as "The Great Century of Christianity." From 1800 to the Civil War, revivalism broke out in many areas and was responsible for initiating the great missionary crusades. It was truly a second "Great Awakening." The church became a defender of social reform and human rights. Reform societies sprang up in areas of antislavery, temperance, peace, women's rights, missions, education and penal reform. Approximately 150 church colleges were founded between 1820 and 1860.

The winter is past; the rains are over and gone. Flowers appear on the earth: the season of singing has come, the cooing of doves is heard in our land. The fig tree forms its early fruit; the blossoming vines spread their fragrance.

Song of Songs 2:11–13

❧ WILLIAM BLAKE ❧

(1757–1827)

Visionary English artist and poet of mystical symbolism.

As a man is so he sees

I feel that a man may be happy in this world and I know that this world is a world of imagination and vision. I see everything I paint in this world but everybody does not see alike. To the eye of a miser a guinea is far more beautiful than the sun and a bag worn with the use of money has more beautiful proportions than a vine filled with grapes. The tree which moves some to tears of joy is in the eyes of others only a green thing which stands in the way. As a man is so he sees.

When the sun rises, do you not see a round disk of fire something like a gold piece? O, no, no, I see an innumerable company of the Heavenly host crying, 'Holy, Holy, Holy is the Lord God Almighty.' I do not question my bodily eye any more than I would question a window concerning sight. I look through it and not with it.

❧ WILLIAM CAREY ❧

(1761–1834)

Lifelong British missionary to India who, after making a commitment to Christ as a result of the influence of a young fellow cobbler and reading Captain Cook's *Voyage Around the World,* was inspired to carry the Gospel to distant lands. Everything seemed against him during his first years in India, including family problems, loss of money, opposition of local authorities, and no fruit to show for his work.

I have God and His Word is sure

When I first left England, my hope of the conversion of the heathen was very strong, but among so many obstacles, it would entirely die away, unless upheld by God. Nothing to exercise it, but plenty to obstruct it, for now a year and nineteen days, which is the space since I left my dear charge (church) at Leicester. Since that I have had hurrying up and down; a five months' imprisonment with carnal men on board the ship; five more learning the language; my colleague separated from me; long delays and few opportunities; no earthly thing to depend on, or earthly comfort, except food and raiment. Well, I have God, and His word is sure.

(Written in his diary as recorded in Mary Drewery's,
William Carey: A Biography. Grand Rapids, MI: Zondervan, 1979, p. 74)

WE WILL GO ON FOR CHRIST

The work of years—gone in a moment. The loss is heavy, but as traveling a road the second time is usually done with greater ease and certainty than the first time, so I trust the work will lose nothing of real value. We are not discouraged; indeed the work is already begun again in every language. We are cast down, but not in despair... There are grave difficulties on every hand, and more are looming ahead. Therefore we must go forward.

(Carey's print shop burned down in Calcutta and with it his massive polyglot dictionary,
two grammar books, whole versions of the Bible, and his entire library— "years of work
gone in a moment." But what happened from that is astounding. Thousands of pounds
were raised for the work and volunteers offered to come help. The enterprise was
rebuilt and enlarged. By 1832 complete Bibles, New Testaments, or separate books
of Scripture had issued from the printing press in 44 languages and dialects.)

A SANCTUARY OF PRAYER

It was through the grace of God. As to courage, let me show you the path to my strength. Here now you see my sanctuary of prayer and meditations. Without this I could not carry on through all the hindrances and hardships. I come here at five o'clock in the morning to pray aloud, talking to God and listening to him and amid these flowers that he created in all their beauty. I leave the garden about six o'clock for my breakfast and to begin my work for the day. After supper, I come again for prayer and meditation with my Bible in my hand.

(In response to Ann Judson's question of how he could get so much courage and faith after three attempts to murder Carey, the governmental restriction on his mission work, and the calamitous fire that had destroyed his printing house and his manuscripts and translations. He then led the Judsons along a path in his walled garden to a quiet bower.)

✄ CHRISTMAS EVANS ✄

(1766–1838)

Great preacher of Wales. He was born on Christmas day, 1766. His father died when he was six, and he was raised by a cruel uncle. He could not read a word at age seventeen. Many misfortunes befell him, including being stabbed, nearly drowning, and falling from a tree with an open knife in his hand. After his conversion some of his former companions beat him so unmercifully that he lost one eye. But God mercifully preserved him through all these trials.

THE MOUNTAINS OF SNOW WERE MELTING WITHIN ME

After I had commenced praying in the name of Jesus, I soon felt as if the shackles were falling off, and as if the mountains of snow and ice were melting within me. This engendered confidence in my mind for the promise of the Holy Ghost. I felt my whole spirit relieved of some great bondage, and as if it were rising up from the grave of a severe winter. My tears flowed copiously, and I was constrained to cry aloud and pray for the gracious visits of God, for the joy of his salvation, and that He would visit again the churches in Anglesea that were under my care....Thus I gave myself up wholly to Christ, body and soul, talents and labors—all my life—every day, and every hour that remained to me, and all my cares I entrusted in the hands of Christ. The road was mountainous and lonely, so that I was alone, and suffered no interruption in my wrestling with God. This even caused me to expect a new revelation of God's goodness to myself and the churches.

⚝ John Quincy Adams ⚝

(1767–1848)

Sixth President of the United States. He was chosen by the House of Representatives when the electoral college could not determine a clear winner of the 1824 election. Andrew Jackson received more popular votes, but he did not gain enough electoral votes to win outright. He is quoted, "I have for many years made it a practice to read through the Bible once a year…It is an invaluable and inexhaustible mine of knowledge and virtue."

A DIVINE REVELATION

The combination of these qualities, justice and fidelity, so essential to the heroic character; with those of meekness, lowliness of heart, and brotherly love, is what constitutes that moral perfection of which Christ gave an example in his own life, and to which he commended his disciples to aspire…

Jesus Christ came into the world to preach repentance and remission of sins, to proclaim glory to God in the highest, and on earth, peace, good will to man; and finally, to bring life and immortality to light in the gospel; and all this is clear, if we consider the Bible as a divine revelation.

ADVICE TO MY CHILDREN

So great is my veneration for the Bible that the earlier my children begin to read it, the more confident will be my hope that they will prove useful citizens to their country, and respectable members of society.

⊰ WILLIAM WORDSWORTH ⊱

(1770–1850)

English nature poet.

THE JOY OF ELEVATED THOUGHTS

I have felt
A presence that disturbs me with the joy
Of elevated thoughts, a sense sublime
Of something far more deeply interfused.
Whose dwelling is the light of setting suns,
And the round ocean and the living air,
And the blue sky, and in the mind of man;
A motion and a spirit, that impels
All thinking things, all objects of all thought
And rolls through all things....

THE MUSIC CONTINUES

I listened, motionless and still;
And as I mounted up the hill,
The music in my heart I bore,
Long after it was heard no more.

⊰ SAMUEL TAYLOR COLERIDGE ⊱

(1772–1834)

English poet, critic, and philosopher, who was greatly influenced by George Fox and Jakob Boehm. He struggled with his faith, but by the end of his life he was expressing his Christian beliefs: "God's child in Christ adopted,— Christ my all: In Christ I live! in Christ I draw the breath of the true life!"

IN CHRIST I LIVE

In what way, or by what manner of working, God changes a soul from evil to good—how he impregnates the barren rock with priceless gems and gold—is, to the human mind, an impenetrable mystery.

THE EVE OF MY DEPARTURE

I have known what the enjoyments and advantages of this life are,
and what are the more refined pleasures which learning and intellectual power can bestow; and with all the experience that more than
three-score years can give, I now, on the eve of my departure declare
to you, that health is a great blessing, competence obtained by honorable industry is a great blessing, and a great blessing it is to have
kind, faithful and loving friends and relatives, but that the greatest
blessing, as it is the most ennobling of all privileges, is to be indeed
a Christian.

SONGS FOR MY JOY

I have found in the Bible words for my inmost thoughts, songs for
my joy, utterance for hidden griefs and pleadings for my shame and
feebleness.

✣ SIR HUMPHREY DAVEY ✣

(1778–1829)

**English chemist who discovered laughing gas, calcium, and sodium. He
also invented the miner's safety lamp.**

NO OTHER BLESSING AS GREAT

I envy no quality of mind or intellect in others—not genius, power,
wit, or fancy; but if I could choose what would be most delightful,
and, I believe, most useful to me, I should prefer a firm religious
belief to every other blessing; for it makes life a discipline of goodness, creates new hopes when all earthly hopes vanish, and throws
over the decay, the destruction of existence the most gorgeous of
all lights; awakens life even in death, and from the corruption and
decay calls up beauty and divinity; makes an instrument of torture
and shame the ladder of ascent to paradise; and far above all combination of earthly hopes, calls up the most delightful visions, palms
and amaranths, the gardens of the blessed, the security of everlast-

ing joys, where the sensualist and the skeptic view only gloom, decay, and annihilation.

ᴁ WILLIAM ELLERY CHANNING ᴂ
(1780–1842)

Minister of Boston's Federal St. Church for forty years. He had a great influence on Emerson, Bryant and Longfellow.

IT WAS REAL

This Jesus lived with men: with the consciousness of unutterable majesty, he joined a lowliness, gentleness, humanity, and sympathy which have no example in human history. I ask you to contemplate this wonderful union. In proportion to the superiority of Jesus to all around him, was the intimacy, the brotherly love, which he bound himself to them. I maintain that this is a character wholly remote from human conception. To imagine it to be the production of imposture or enthusiasms, shows a strange unsoundness of mind. I contemplate it with a veneration second only to the profound awe with which I look up to God. It bears no mark of human invention. It was real. It belonged to, and it manifested, the beloved son of God...

Here I pause; and indeed I know not what can be added to heighten the wonder, reverence, and love which are due to Jesus. When I consider him, not only as possessed with the consciousness of an unexampled and unbounded majesty, but as recognizing a kindred nature in human beings, and living and dying to raise them to a participation of his divine glories; and when I see him, under these views, allying himself to men by the tenderest ties, embracing them with a spirit of humanity, which no insult, injury, or pain could for a moment repel or overpower, —I am filled with wonder as well as reverence and love. I feel that this character is not of human invention; that it was not assumed through fraud, or struck out by enthusiasm; for it is infinitely above their reach. When I add this character of Jesus to the other evidence of his religion, it gives, to what before seemed so strong, a new and a vast accession of strength: I feel as if I could not be deceived. The Gospels must be true: they were drawn from a living original; they were founded on reality. The character of Jesus is not a fiction: he was what he claimed to be, and what his followers attested. Nor is this all. Jesus not only was, he is still, the Son of God, the Saviour of the world. He exists now; he has entered that heaven to which he always looked forward on earth. There he lives and reigns. With a clear, calm faith, I see him in that state of glory; and I confidently expect, at no distant period, to see him face to face.

(From his sermon "Character of Christ" in his Works, Boston Edition, 1848, vol. IV)

⚜ ELIZABETH FRY ⚜
(1780–1845)

English Victorian prison reformer who began her great work by making baby clothes for the unclothed babies of Newgate Prison. It was her moment of outrage and inspiration.

MY HEART WAS TOUCHED AT 17

Since my heart was touched at 17, I believe I have never awakened from sleep, in sickness or in health, by day or by night, without my first waking thought being how best I might serve my Lord.

⚜ HENRY MARTYN ⚜
(1781–1812)

Missionary to India who fought consumption of the lungs while carrying on evangelistic work in incredibly difficult circumstances. He had translated the Bible into three Indian dialects.

NEW IMPRESSIONS

Since I have known God in a saving manner, painting, poetry and music have had charms unknown to me before. I have either received what I suppose is a taste for them, or religion has refined my mind and made it susceptible of new impressions from the sublime and beautiful....Oh, how religion secures the heightened enjoyment of those pleasures which keep so many from God by their being a source of pride.

A DESIRE TO SERVE GOD

Let me forget the world and be swallowed up in a desire to glorify God...I see no business in life but the work of Christ.

(Written as a young man after deciding to become a missionary)

✍ DANIEL WEBSTER ✍

(1782–1852)

U. S. Senator, Representative, and Secretary of State, who was known for his oratorical skills.

I BELIEVE

I believe Jesus Christ to be the Son of God. The miracles which He wrought establish in my mind His personal authority, and render it proper for me to believe whatever He asserts. I believe, therefore, all His declarations, as well when He declares Himself to be the Son of God as when He declares any other proposition. And I believe there is no other way of salvation than through the merits of his atonement.

I CANNOT COMPREHEND IT

No, sir, I cannot comprehend it. If I could comprehend Him, He would be no greater than myself. I feel that I need a superhuman Saviour.

(During a conversation with literary men in Boston, he was asked if he could comprehend how Christ could be both God and man. This was his response.)

❧ JOHN JAMES AUDUBON ❧

(1785–1851)

American naturalist known for his keen interest in birds. He spent part of his early life in Kentucky, in the area of and at the time of Abraham Lincoln. He passed through hardships and discouragements, but in it all he realized God's presence.

AT THE SOUND OF THE WOOD THRUSH'S MELODIES

Through those dark days I was being led to the development of the talents I love. One of the most extraordinary things among all these adverse circumstances was that I never for a day gave up listening to the song of our birds, or watching their peculiar habits, or delineating them in the best way that I could; nay, during my deepest troubles I frequently would wrench myself away from the persons around me and return to some secluded part of our noble forests, and many a time at the sound of the wood thrush's melodies have I fallen on my knees, and there earnestly prayed to God. This never failed to bring me the most valued thoughts, and always comforted me.

❧ PETER CARTWRIGHT ❧

(1785–1872)

Circuit rider. After his conversion at age nineteen during the famous Cumberland Revival, Cartwright began a life-long career traveling from the Appalachians to the Mississippi, preaching, organizing, and watching over the preachers under his charge. He was instrumental in spreading the revival that was sweeping through Kentucky and many other states.

SATURDAY EVENING IN A CAMP MEETING

On Saturday evening of a great camp-meeting, I went with weeping multitudes, and bowed before the stand, and earnestly prayed for mercy. In the midst of a solemn struggle of soul, an impression was made on my mind, as though a voice said to me, 'Thy sins are all forgiven thee.' Divine light flashed all around me, unspeakable joy sprung up in my soul. I rose to my feet, opened my eyes, and it really seemed as if I was in heaven; the trees, the leaves on them, and everything seemed, and I really thought were praising God... And though I have been since then, in many instances, unfaithful, yet I have never, for one moment, doubted that the Lord did, then and there, forgive my sins and give me religion.

(Describing his conversion experience)

⊰ ADONIRON JUDSON ⊱
(1788–1850)

Baptist missionary to Burma who translated the Bible into the Burmese language. During the war between Burma and England, he was put in prison, suspected of being a spy for England. He was bound for 19 months with 3 sets of fetters. His dark, dank cell was filled with vermin. Every night he was hung upside down with only his head and shoulders resting on the ground..

BECAUSE OF MY SUFFERINGS

This awes me. This is good news. When I was a young man I prayed for the Lord to send me to the Jews in Jerusalem as a missionary. But He sent me to Burma to preach and to suffer the tortures of imprisonment. Now, because of my sufferings, God had brought some Jews in Turkey to repentance!"

(When he was dying, news came to him that some Jews in Turkey had been converted through reading the account of his sufferings in Burma.)

LIKE A SCHOOLBOY BOUNDING AWAY FROM SCHOOL

I am not tired of my work, neither am I tired of the world. Yet, when Christ calls me home, I shall go with the gladness of a schoolboy bounding away from school!....Death will never take me by surprise. I feel strong in Christ. He has not led me so tenderly thus far to forsake me at the very gate of heaven.

➴ ANN HESSELTINE JUDSON ➶

(1789–1826)

**Wife of Adoniron Judson, a missionary pioneer in Burma, who had trans-
lated the Bible into the Burmese language. Her husband was in prison and
she knew that the manuscript would be found and seized in her home, so
she buried it; and then, fearing that it would decay, she wrapped it about
with cotton and made it into a pillow for her husband in his cell. Once the
pillow was stolen by the soldiers, but Ann redeemed it by giving them a
better one. Then one night Dr. Judson was hurried off to another prison and
his pillow was thrown out into the prison yard. There one of his faithful
converts found it and took it home. It was found long afterwards.**

WE WERE NEVER HAPPIER

Exposed to robbers by night and invaders by day, we both unite in
saying that we were never happier.

(In her journal in Rangoon, Burma)

GOD HAS GIVEN ME AN OPPORTUNITY

We have found by experience since we left our native land, that the
Lord is indeed a covenant-keeping God, and takes care of those who
confide in him. I have ever considered it a singular favour that God
has given me an opportunity to spend my days in a heathen land....If
I may be instrumental of leading some infant female to lisp the
praise of God, I shall rejoice in the sacrifice of country, reputation,
and friends.

*(Ann, at age 16, made a covenant with God. That covenant guided her life to its
early end as a missionary in Burma in 1826 at the age of 36; Nancy Judson, "Letter to
Mrs. Carleton," Massachusetts Baptist Missionary Magazine, May 1990, p. 166–67.)*

⚛ MICHAEL FARADAY ⚛

(1791–1867)

English chemist who proposed field theory, discovered the generator and the transformer, and made electricity useful. He was a man of Christian faith. Love and humility governed his life.

BEYOND OUR LANGUAGE TO EXPRESS

When I consider the multitude of associated forces which are diffused through nature—when I think of that calm balancing of their energies which enables those most powerful in themselves, most destructive to the world's creatures and economy, to dwell associated together and be made subservient to the wants of creation, I rise from the contemplation more than ever impressed with the wisdom, the beneficence, and grandeur, beyond our language to express, of the Great Disposer of us all.

I AM RESTING ON CERTAINTIES

Speculations! I know nothing about speculations. I am resting on certainties. 'I know that my Redeemer liveth,' and because He lives, I shall live also.

(When he was dying, some journalists asked him
as to his speculations for a life after death.)

❧ CHARLES G. FINNEY ❧

(1792–1872)

American Methodist circuit rider evangelist who, in 1821 while praying secretly in the woods, found Christ and received "a retainer from the Lord to plead His cause." He was a part of the great revival of 1858–1859, in which around 600,000 were brought to Christ. Between 1,500 and 2,000 persons were converted in one day in Finney's meetings that were held all over England and the U. S. In 1831 after a six month series of meetings in New York, 100,000 were reportedly converted. Probably a half million were converted during his lifetime. He said about the outpouring, "Unless I had the spirit of prayer, I could do nothing."

YOU SHALL SEEK ME AND FIND ME

Just at that point this passage of Scripture seemed to drop into my mind with a flood of light: "Then shall ye go and pray unto me, and I will hearken unto you. Then shall ye seek me and find me, when ye shall search for me with all your heart." I instantly seized hold of this with my heart. I had intellectually believed the Bible before; but never had the truth been in my mind that faith was voluntary trust instead of an intellectual state. I was as conscious as I was of my existence, of trusting at that moment in God's veracity. Somehow I knew that that was a passage of Scripture, though I do not think I had ever read it. I knew that it was God's word, and God's voice, as it were, that spoke to me. I cried to Him, "Lord, I take thee at thy word. Now thou knowest that I do search for thee with all my heart, and that I have come here to pray in thee; and thou hast promised to hear me."

(Charles Finney first began reading the Bible because he noticed how often his law books referred to it. Taken from Memoirs of Rev. Charles G. Finney, *1876)*

A POWERFUL EXPERIENCE THAT REDIRECTED MY ENTIRE LIFE

There was no fire and no light in the room; nevertheless, it appeared to me as if it were perfectly light. As I went in and shut the door after me, it seemed as if I met the Lord Jesus Christ face to face....He said nothing, but looked at me in such a manner as to break me right down at his feet. I have always since regarded this as a most remarkable state of mind; for it seemed to me a reality that he stood before me, and I fell down at his feet and poured out my soul to him. I wept aloud like a child and made such confessions as I could with my choked utterance. It seemed to me that I bathed his feet with my tears....Without any expectation of it, without ever having the thought in my mind that there was any such thing for me, without any recollection that I had ever heard the thing mentioned by any person in the world, the Holy Spirit descended upon me in a manner that seemed to go through me, body and soul. I could feel the impression, like a wave of electricity, going through and through me. Indeed it seemed to come in waves and waves of liquid love; for I could not express it in any other way. It seemed like the very breath of God. I can recollect distinctly that it seemed to fan me, like immense wings......No words can express the wonderful love that was shed abroad in my heart. I wept aloud with joy and love; and I do not know but I should say, I literally bellowed out the unutterable gushings of my heart.

> (This experience took place while alone in his law office on October 10, 1821.
> After three days of spiritual struggle, "All at once the glory of God shone upon and
> round about me in a manner most marvelous." He traced all of his later religious
> work to this single experience. Taken from Memoirs of Rev. Charles G. Finney)

ALLEN GARDINER

(1794–1851)

English missionary martyr who attempted to preach the Gospel in Tierra del Fuego, but was driven back by the unfriendly inhabitants. He returned to his home and pleaded with his people to outfit him once more. When he landed a second time, the natives killed his companions and drove Gardiner to his boat.

I DRINK AT THE KING'S WELL

My little boat is a Bethel to my soul. Asleep or awake, I am happier than tongue can tell. I am starving, yet I feel neither hunger nor thirst. I feed on hidden manna and drink at the King's well. I am not disappointed, for I remember that one soweth and another reapeth.

(He eventually died of starvation without seeing a single soul saved, but the missionary society he founded has been sending missionaries and saving souls for over 150 years.)

MERLE D'AUBIGNÉ

(1794–1873)

Swiss historian and writer of the Reformation. "But do you see it in your own heart?" was the penetrating question which led to D'Aubigne's conversion. He had seen the doctrine of salvation theologically, and then, while at the University in Geneva, he "experienced the joys of the new birth."

THE LORD HATH DEALT BOUNTIFULLY WITH ME

We were studying the epistle to the Ephesians, and had got to the end of the third chapter, where we read the last two verses— 'Now unto him who is able to do exceeding abundantly above all that we ask or think, according to the power that worketh in us, unto him be glory, etc.' This expression fell upon my soul as a revelation from God. 'He can do by his power,' I said to myself, 'above all that we ask, above all even that we think; nay, exceeding abundantly above all.' A full trust in Christ for the work to be done within my poor heart now filled my soul. We all three knelt down, and, although I had never fully confided my inward struggles to my friends, the prayer of Kiel was filled with such admirable faith as he would have uttered had he known all my wants. When I arose, in that inn room at Kiel, I felt as if my 'wings were renewed as the wings of eagles.' From that time forward I comprehended that all my own efforts were of no avail; that Christ was able to do all by his 'power that worketh in us.'... Then I was able to say, 'Return unto thy rest, O my soul! for the Lord hath dealt bountifully with thee.'

WILLIAM CULLEN BRYANT

(1794–1878)

Beloved American poet. One bleak autumn day Bryant, lonely and homesick, was making his way westward—leaving home, starting out in life, facing the world. Just then he happened to see a waterfowl winging its way southward. That waterfowl, guided by its wonderful instinct, preserved and upheld by its Creator, made young William Cullen Bryant think of God's care for his own life, and so he wrote the magnificent poem, "To a Waterfowl."

HE WILL LEAD MY STEPS ARIGHT
He who, from zone to zone,
Guides through the boundless sky thy certain flight,
In the long way that I must trod alone,
Will lead my steps aright.

(Taken from "To a Waterfowl")

A FOREST HYMN
My heart is awed within me when I think
Of the great miracle which still goes on,
In silence, round me—the perpetual work
Of thy creation, finished, yet renewed
Forever. Written on thy works I read
The lesson of thy own eternity.

(Taken from "A Forest Hymn")

❧ THOMAS ARNOLD ❧

(1795–1842)

English historian, classical scholar, and headmaster of Rugby.

THE GREAT SIGN WHICH GOD HAS GIVEN

I know of no one fact in the history of mankind which is proved by better evidence of every sort, to the understanding of a fair enquirer, than the great sign which God has given us that Christ died and rose from the dead.

❧ THOMAS CARLYLE ❧

(1795–1881)

Scottish writer and historian. He struggled to find his role in life, until he turned to writing, and then felt he had found his life's work and his life's happiness. He exhibited a truly generous soul and magnanimity when he forgave his friend whose maid had used his manuscript, his only copy, entrusted to him for reading, for starting a fire.

STANDING ON THE BRINK OF ETERNITY

The older I grow, and now stand on the brink of eternity—the more comes back to me that sentence in the Catechism I learned when a child, and the fuller and deeper its meaning becomes: "What is the chief end of man? To glorify God and to enjoy him forever.

NOTHING BUT FAITH

I am now an old man, and done with the world. Looking around me, before and behind, and weighing all as wisely as I can, it seems to me there is nothing solid to rest on but the faith which I learned in my old home, and from my mother's lips.

(In a conversation with Dr. John Brown.)

⚜ ROBERT MOFFAT ⚜

(1795–1883)

Scottish missionary to Africa for fifty years, evangelist, translator, educator, diplomat, explorer and writer. He was known as the "venerable father of the missionary world."

CAN IT BE THAT I NEVER UNDERSTOOD WHAT I HAD BEEN READING?
Living alone in an extensive garden, my leisure was my own. While poring over the epistle to the Romans, I could not help wondering over a number of passages which I had read many times before. They appeared altogether different. I exclaimed with a heart nearly broken, 'Can it be possible that I have never understood what I had been reading?' turning from one passage to another, each sending light into my darkened soul. The Book of God seemed to be laid open, and I saw at once what God had done for the sinner. I felt that, being justified by faith, I had peace with God through the Lord Jesus Christ.

(Written at age 20)

⚜ SØREN KIERKEGAARD ⚜

(1813–1855)

Danish theologian and philosopher whose writings were a judgment against a church that minimized the distance between the human and the divine. He believed that Jesus Christ was the only bridge between God and man. "Christ came in through locked doors," was how he described his conversion.

THROUGH AN UNHAPPY CHILDHOOD
O my God, my God, unhappy and tormented was my childhood, full of torments my youth. I have lamented, I have sighed, and I have wept. Yet I thank Thee, not as the wise sovereign; no, no, I thank Thee, the one who is infinite love for having acted thus! Man has before him a life of thirty, forty, perhaps seventy years; in Thy love Thou hast prevented me from buying for this sum just the little

sweets of the kind for which I would even recall for my eternal torment—as having bought the worthless.

(Prayers of Kierkegaard.

University of Chicago Press, 1956)

MY HUMBLE WORK

My very humble work is to make people aware....to make room that
God may come.

⊰ EMILY BRONTE ⊱

(1818–1848)

**English novelist whose career was cut short by death. When the family
opened her desk after her death, they found the poem, "Last Lines," which
is a fit tribute to her heroic spirit.**

AND FIRST AN HOUR OF MOURNFUL MUSING

And first an hour of mournful musing,
And then a gush of bitter tears,
And then a dreary calm diffusing
Its deadly mist o'er joys and cares;
And then a breathing from above,
And then a star in heaven brightening—
The star, the glorious star of love.

LAST LINES

No coward soul is mine,
No trembler in the world's storm-troubled sphere.
I see Heaven's glories shine,
And faith shines equal, arming me from fear.

OTHER WRITERS OF THE
∂Ꙅ FIRST HALF OF THE 19TH CENTURY ꙅ∂

MY CALLING

Since I attained to a clear consciousness, by inward experience; that there is no way of satisfying the needs of the soul, or tranquilizing the heart's longing, but by the inner life of Christ, I am aware of an increase of power for the work of my calling, whatever it be, and of joy and spirit in performing it.

(Christian Karl von Bunsen, 1791-1860)

I AM GOIN' HOME

I've got a home out yonder,
Few days, few days
I've got a home out yonder;
I am goin' home.

(The Negro Singer's Own Book, 1841

FREE AT LAST

Free at last, free at last.
I thank God I'm free at last;
Some of these mornings bright and fair,
I thank God I'm free at last,
Going to meet King Jesus in the air,
I thank God I'm free at last.

(The Negro Singer's Own Book, 1841)

AT LAST I FOUND MERCY

Five and forty years I wandered up and down in the darkness of this world, knowing nothing and caring for nothing, so great a sinner I was. When I was about forty-five the blessed Lord opened my eyes, and showed me what I was,—a poor, wretched, guilty sinner. At last I found mercy, and there was given to me a good hope through Christ Jesus.

(Sarah Wood, born a slave, lived close to 100 years, died in 1863)

GOD HAS COME IN

God has been depriving me of one blessing after another; but, as every one was removed, he has come in, and filled up its place; and now, when I am a cripple, and not able to move, I am happier than ever I was in my life before, or ever expected to be. And, if I had believed this twenty years ago, I might have been spared much anxiety.

(*Edward Payson, fl. 1808*)

✑ CLOSING THOUGHT ✐

In what way, or by what manner of working, God changes a soul from evil to good—how he impregnates the barren rock with priceless gems and gold—is, to the human mind an impenetrable mystery.

(*Samuel Taylor Coleridge*)

 PART VI

Glimpses from 1851–1900
A Remarkable Acceleration of Conversions and Missions

By the mid-1800's conversions and missions grew in number and spirit. After the Civil War, Americans entered the "Gilded Age." They saw the assassinations of two presidents, the impeachment of another, a stolen election, and a reign of rampant political and business corruption and greed. Turmoil was brought about by migration to cities and massive immigrations, which continued through the 1920s and brought immense growth and a large ethnic diversity. Intellectual challenges, including Darwin's theory of evolution, were eroding faith. In the late 80's volunteer organizations, crusades and rescue missions were organized by all major denominations for Christian missions and service.

The kingdom of God is like a mustard seed, which is the smallest seed you plant in the ground. Yet when planted, it grows and becomes the largest of all garden plants, with such big branches that the birds of the air can perch in its shade.

MARK 4:30–32

❧ JOHN TODD ❧

(1800–1873)

American minister who was six years old when both parents died. He went to live with a kindly aunt until he left to study for the ministry. Later when his aunt became seriously ill and feared she would die, she wrote her nephew with questions about death. This was his reply.

AT THE END OF THE ROAD

It is now thirty-five years since I, as a little boy of six, was left quite alone in the world. You sent me word that you would give me a home and be a kind mother to me. I will never forget the day when I made the long journey of ten miles to your house in North Killingworth. I can still remember my disappointment when instead of coming for me yourself, you sent Caesar to fetch me.

I well remember my tears and anxiety as, perched high on your horse and clinging tight to Caesar, I rode off to my new home. Night fell before we finished the journey, and, as it grew dark, I became lonely and afraid. "Do you think she'll go to bed before we get there?" I asked Caesar anxiously. "Oh, no," he said reassuringly. "She'll stay up for you. When we get out of this here woods, you'll see her candle shinin' in the window."

Presently we did ride out into the clearing, and there, sure enough, was your candle. I remember you were waiting at the door, that you put your arms close about me and that you lifted me—a tired and bewildered little boy—down from the horse. You had a fire burning on the hearth, a hot supper waiting on the stove. After supper you took me to my room, heard me say my prayers and then sat beside me till I fell asleep.

You probably realize why I am recalling all of this to your memory. Someday soon God will send for you to take you to a new home. Don't fear the summons, the strange journey or the dark messenger of death. God can be trusted to do as much for you as you were kind enough to do for me so many years ago. At the end of the road you will find love and a welcome awaiting, and you will be safe in God's care. I shall watch you and pray for you till you are out of sight and then wait for the day when I shall make the journey myself and find my Savior and you waiting at the end of the road to greet me.

A MINE RICH IN GOLD

Some look upon the Bible as a garden of spices, in which you may walk, and at your leisure pluck the flowers and gather the fruits of the Eden of God. But this does not accord with my experience. I have found it more like a mine, in which you must dig and labor, the wealth of which is not obtained without labor—a mine rich in gold and precious things, but it must be worked day and night in order to produce them.

⊰ JOHN HENRY NEWMAN ⊱

(1801–1890)

American Catholic scholar noted for his sincerity and devotion in his religious writings. At the age of fifteen he felt a strong call to religion. His conversion made him change from the study of law to divinity. He wrote the hymn, "Lead, Kindly Light" after weeks of ill health and anguish.

LIKE COMING INTO PORT

I have been in perfect peace and contentment; I never had one doubt. I was not conscious to myself, on my conversion, of any change, intellectual or moral, wrought in my mind. I was not conscious of firmer faith in the fundamental truths of revelation, or of more self-command; I had not more fervor; but it was like coming into port after a rough sea; and my happiness on that score remains to this day without interruption.

A PART IN A GREAT WORK

God has created me to do Him some definite service; He has committed some work to me which He has not committed to another. I have my mission....I have a part in a great work; I am a link in a chain, a bond of connection between persons. He has not created me for naught. I shall be an angel of peace, a preacher of commandments and serve Him in my calling.

Therefore I will trust Him. Whatever, wherever I am, I can never be thrown away. If I am in sickness, my sickness may serve Him; in perplexity, my perplexity may serve Him; if I am in sorrow, my sorrow may serve Him. My sickness, or perplexity, or sorrow may be necessary causes of some great end, which is quite beyond us. He does nothing in vain; He may prolong my life, He may shorten it; He knows what He is about. He may take away my friends, He may throw me among strangers, He may make me feel desolate, make my spirits sink, hide the future from me—still He knows what He is about.

(Meditations and Devotions)

INCOMPREHENSIBLE

O my God....I adore Thee because Thou art so mysterious, so incomprehensible. Unless thou wert incomprehensible, thou wouldst not be God. For how can the Infinite be other than incomprehensible to me.

✺ VICTOR HUGO ✺
(1802–1885)

French literary genius who, when fifteen was honorably mentioned by the French Academy. He is known for his novels, *The Hunchback of Notre Dame* and *Les Miserables.*

THE SOUND OF IMMORTAL SYMPHONIES

The nearer my approach to the end, the plainer is the sound of immortal symphonies of worlds which invite me. It is wonderful, yet simple. It is a fairy tale; it is history.

I feel in myself the future life. I am like a forest cut down; the new shoots are stronger and livelier than ever. I am rising, I know, toward the sky. The sunshine is on my head. The earth gives me its generous say, but heaven lifts me with the reflection of unknown worlds.... For half a century I have been translating my thoughts into prose and verse; history, philosophy, romance, tradition, satire, ode, and song; all of them have I tried, but I feel that I haven't given utterance to the thousandth part of what lies within me. When I go to the grave I can say as others have said, "My day's work is done." But I cannot say, "My life is done." My day's work will recommence the next morning. The tomb is not a blind alley; it is a thoroughfare. It closes upon the twilight, but opens upon the dawn.

☙ HORACE BUSHNELL ❧

(1802–1896)

American Congregational pastor and teacher at Yale who underwent a profound conversion experience. His influence through writing and lecturing became world-wide. The death of his little boy and infant daughter influenced his whole life and character. From this experience he said he learned more of experiential religion than from all his life before. Along with this was a life-long struggle with ill-health, including a cough from chronic bronchitis which prevented any continued sleep. He carried on voluminous correspondence with people who were in trouble.

I HAVE PUT GOD TO THE TEST

My men, I have a wonderful thing to tell you. I laughed to scorn all that this man preached, and all the rest of them, and the churches. I have found out that I was in the darkness, and they were in the light. Oh, I have put God to the test, and I know that He is the Saviour, and I am henceforth His disciple and friend forever.

(A preacher had come to Yale and for days there was no response to his preaching. The preacher challenged Bushnell to put God to the test. He knelt in his dormitory room and asked God to "take the dimness of my soul away. Reveal Thyself to me." He arose from his knees and felt as if he had received wings. Three days later he came back and stood on the rostrum of the old chapel and spoke to his students the above words.)

I SEE IT, I SEE IT.

I see it, I see it. The Gospel. It is not the submitting of one's thought in assent to any proposition, but the trusting of one's being there to be tested, kept, guided, molded, governed, and possessed forever.

(After laboring for years in his Hartford parish, Bushnell awoke one morning at the age of forty-six, crying out these words. He was one of those who by faith at last discovered what it was to be admitted into the presence of God.)

⋐ RALPH WALDO EMERSON ⋑
(1803–1882)

American clergyman, and leader of Transcendentalism, who was influenced by many, including Plotinus, Goethe, the Methodists and the Quakers.

A NEW MOMENT

As I went to church I thought how seldom the present hour is seized upon as a new moment. To a soul alive to God every moment is a new world. A new audience, and new Sabbath, affords an opportunity of communicating thought and moral excitement that shall surpass all previous experience, that shall constitute an epoch, a revolution, in the minds on whom you act and in your own. The awakened soul, the man of genius, makes every day such a day, by looking forward only.

THANK YOU, GOD

When I first open my eyes upon the morning meadows and look out upon the beautiful world, I thank God I am alive.

I HEAR HIS VOICE

Henceforth, please God, forever I forego
The yoke of men's opinions, I will be
Light-hearted as a bird, and live with God.
I find Him in the bottom of my heart,
I hear continually His voice therein.

All I have seen teaches me to trust the Creator for all I have not seen.

⨮ GEORGE MUELLER ⨭
(1805–1898)

Prussian-born member of the Open Brethren. With fifty cents in his pocket and faith in God, he started an orphanage in Bristol, England, where he housed more than 121,000 orphans in his lifetime. At the age of seventy, he began to make great evangelistic tours, including three in the U. S., and continued until the age of ninety. He traveled 200,000 miles, going around the world and preaching in many lands and several different languages, frequently speaking to as many as 4,500 or 5,000 persons. At the time of his death he had a congregation of 2,000 persons.

THE TURNING POINT OF MY LIFE

One Saturday afternoon, about the middle of November, 1825, I had taken a walk with my friend Beta. On our return he said to me that he was in the habit of going on Saturday evenings to the house of a Christian, where there was a meeting....We went together in the evening. As I did not know the manners of the brethren, and the joy they have in seeing poor sinners, even in any measure caring about the things of God, I made an apology for coming. The kind answer of this dear brother I shall never forget. He said: 'Come as often as you please; house and heart are open to you.' After a hymn was sung they fell upon their knees, and a brother, named Kayser, who afterwards became a missionary to Africa, asked God's blessing on the meeting. This kneeling down made a deep impression upon me, for I had never either seen anyone on his knees, nor had I ever myself prayed on my knees. He then read a chapter and a printed sermon; for no regular meetings for expounding the Scriptures were allowed in Prussia, except an ordained clergyman was present. At the close of the meeting we sang another hymn, and then the master of the house prayed.... I was happy, though if I had been asked why I was happy, I could not clearly have explained it.

When we walked home, I said to Beta, all we have seen on our journey to Switzerland, and all our former pleasures, are as nothing in comparison with this evening. Whether I fell on my knees when I returned home I do not remember, but this I know, that I lay peaceful and happy in my bed. This shows that the Lord may begin his work in different ways. For I have not the least doubt that on that evening He began a work of grace in me, though I obtained joy without any deep sorrow of heart, and with scarcely any knowledge. But that evening was the turning point in my life. The next day, and Monday, and once or twice besides, I went again to the house of this brother, where I read the Scriptures with him and another brother; for it was too long for me to wait until Saturday came again.

(Deeper Experiences of Famous Christians)

I HAVE LEARNED MY FAITH BY STANDING FIRM

The only way to learn strong faith is to endure great trials. I have learned my faith by standing firm amid severe testings.

I DIED TO GEORGE MUELLER

There was a day when I died, utterly died; died to George Mueller, his opinions, preferences, tastes, and will—died to the world, its approval or censure—died to the approval or blame even of my brethren and friends—and since then I have studied only to show myself approved unto God.

(When asked the secret of his victorious Christian life.)

THIS WAS MY GREATEST TRIAL

My beloved daughter and only child, and a believer since 1848, was taken ill on June 20, 1853. This illness, at first a low fever, turned to typhus. On July 3rd there seemed no hope of her recovery. Now was the trial of faith, but faith triumphed. My beloved wife and I were enabled to give her up into the hands of the Lord. He sustained us both exceedingly. Though my only and beloved child was brought near the grave, yet was my soul in perfect peace, satisfied with the will of my Heavenly Father, being assured that he would only do that for her and her parents, which in the end would be best. She continued very ill till about July 20th, when restoration began.

Parents know what an only child, a beloved child, is. Well, the Father in Heaven said, as it were, "Art thou willing to give up this child to me?" My heart responded, "As it seems good to Thee, my Heavenly Father, Thy will be done." Just as our hearts were made willing to give back our child to Him, so He was ready to leave her to us, and she lived.

Of all the trials of faith that as yet I have had to pass through, this was the greatest; and by God's abundant mercy, I owe it to His praise, I was enabled to delight myself in the will of God; for I felt perfectly sure, that, if the Lord took this beloved daughter, it would be best for her parents, best for herself, and more for the glory of God than if she lived. This better part I was satisfied with, and thus my heart had peace, perfect peace.

IN GOD'S GOOD TIME AND MANNER

God has answered thousands of specific prayers. Often He answered them immediately. At other times He delayed the answer. I knew that the answer would come in God's good time and manner.

(Writing in his 70s. All necessary money for the building and maintenance of his orphan homes in Bristol and later for his evangelistic tours was sent in answer to the prayer of faith.)

ELIZABETH BARRETT BROWNING
(1806–1861)

Beloved and famous English Victorian poet who married against the wishes of her father to the love of her life, Robert Browning. She said, "We want the touch of Christ's hand upon our literature." At death's door, she said, "It is beautiful!"

ROUND OUR RESTLESSNESS
And I smiled to think God's greatness flowed around
Our incompleteness,
Round our restlessness, His rest.

DE PROFUNDIS
I praise Thee while my days go on;
I love Thee while my days go on:
Through dark and dearth, through fire and frost,
With emptied arms and treasure lost,
I thank Thee while my days go on.

⚜ LOUIS AGASSIZ ⚜
(1807–1873)

Swiss-American naturalist and one of the great scientists of his day, who was one of the founders of ichthyology. He was a Harvard professor who defined a species as "a thought of God."

UNFOLDING GOD'S SECRETS
I will frankly tell you that my experience in prolonged scientific investigations convinces me that a belief in God—a God who is behind and within the chaos of vanishing points of human knowledge—adds a wonderful stimulus to the man who attempts to penetrate into the regions of the unknown. Of myself I may say, that I never make the preparations for penetrating into some small province of nature hitherto undiscovered without breathing a prayer to the Being who hides his secrets from me only to allure me graciously on to the unfolding of them.

❧ ANTHONY MARY CLARET ❧
(1807–1870)

Spanish missionary, founder of an order and archbishop.

JESUS IS MY CENTER

I will imagine that my soul and body are like the two hands of a compass, and that my soul, like the stationary hand, is fixed in Jesus, who is my centre, and that my body, like the moving hand, is describing a circle of assignments and obligations.

❧ HENRY WADSWORTH LONGFELLOW ❧
(1807–1882)

A most beloved American poet of the 19th century.

HIM EVERMORE I BEHOLD

Him evermore I behold
Walking in Galilee,
Through the cornfield's waving gold;
In hamlet or grassy wold,
By the shores of the Beautiful Sea.
He toucheth the sightless eyes;
Before Him the demons flee.
To the living: follow me!
And that voice still soundeth on
From the centuries that are gone,
To the centuries that shall be!

I WILL LEAVE THE ERRING SOUL OF MY FELLOWMAN TO HIM

The little I have seen of the world teaches me to look upon the errors of others in sorrow, not in anger. When I take the history of one poor heart that has sinned and suffered, and think of the struggles and temptations it has passed through, the brief pulsations of joy, the feverish inquietude of hope and fear, the pressure of want, the desertion of friends, I would fain leave the erring soul of my fellowman with Him from whose hands it came.

⊰ JOHN GREENLEAF WHITTIER ⊱
(1807–1892)

American Quaker poet of rural New England who was a voice of calm and sincere religious faith.

THE ETERNAL GOODNESS

Yet, in the maddening maze of things,
And tossed by storm and flood,
To one fixed trust my spirit clings;
I know that God is good;
I know not where His islands lift
Their fronded palms in air;
I only know I cannot drift
Beyond His love and care.

THE MEETING

And so I find it well to come
For deeper rest to this still room,
For here the habits of the soul
Feel less the outer world's control;
And from the silence multiplied
By these still forms on either side
The world that time and sense have known
Falls off and leaves us God alone.

BARCLAY OF URY

Through the dark and stormy night
Faith beholds a feeble light
Up the blackness streaking;
Knowing God's own time is best,
In patient hope I rest
For the full day-breaking!

⚞ GEORGE OSBORN ⚟

(1808–1891)

English Wesleyan Methodist pastor.

IT STOOD THERE FOR FOURTEEN HUNDRED YEARS

One Sunday I went to worship in the little church that stands by the shore at Aberdaron. It has stood there for fourteen hundred years. The sand has drifted all round it, the wintry storms have beaten upon it, but it is set firm on the rock underneath. The church has been altered and enlarged during the centuries, but the walls of the old church are built into it. As I worshipped there, I tried to imagine the sort of people who came there fourteen centuries ago and prayed to the same God and loved Jesus as I do. Almost everything has altered since then, but God hasn't changed, and Jesus Christ is "the same yesterday, and today, and for ever"! On the shore by the old church the children play, making castles and houses in the sand. They look fine, but the next high tide will sweep them away. But love and truth and goodness and God will last forever. His "words shall not pass away." The firm "foundation of God standeth sure."

✍ ABRAHAM LINCOLN ✍

(1809–1865)

Sixteenth President of the United States. There is evidence of a conversion in 1862, as related by those close to him. He said, "I think I can safely say that I know something of that change". From this time on he was seen often with the Bible in his hands, and he was known to have prayed often. His personal relationship to God occupied his mind much and deepened over time.

WITH HIS ASSISTANCE, I CANNOT FAIL

Here I have lived a quarter of a century and have passed from a young to an old man. Here my children have been born, and one is buried. I now leave, not knowing when or ever I may return, with a task before me greater than that which rested upon Washington. Without the assistance of that Divine Being, who ever attended him, I cannot succeed. With that assistance, I cannot fail. Trusting in Him who can go with me, and remain with you, and be everywhere for good—let us confidently hope that all will yet be well. To His care commending you, as I hope in your prayers you will commend me, I bid you an affectionate farewell.

> *(Expressing an affectionate good-bye to his neighbors and friends, and at the same time, revealing a humble, but eloquent faith in God, in a speech of less than 200 words at Springfield, IL, Feb. 11, 1861, when he was about to leave for Washington to be inaugurated.)*

ON GOD'S SIDE

My concern is not whether God is on our side; my great concern is to be on God's side, for God is always right.

> *(Lincoln's response during the Civil War to a cabinet member who tried to console him with: "Mr. President, the Lord surely is on our side.")*

I GOT DOWN ON MY KNEES

I went to my room and got down on my knees in prayer. Never before had I prayed with so much earnestness. I wish I could repeat my prayer. I felt that I must put all my trust in Almighty God. He gave

our people the best country ever given to men. He alone could save it
from destruction.

(In a letter to Major General Daniel V. Sickles

after the Battle of Gettysburg)

I THEN AND THERE CONSECRATED MYSELF TO CHRIST

When I left Springfield I asked the people to pray for me. I was not a
Christian. When I buried my son, the severest trial of my life, I was
not a Christian. But when I went to Gettysburg and saw the graves
of thousands of our soldiers, I then and there consecrated myself to
Christ.

AN OVERWHELMING CONVICTION

I have been driven many times to my knees by the overwhelming
conviction that I had nowhere else to go. My own wisdom and that
of all about me seemed insufficient for the day. If the Lord did not
answer prayer, I could not stand it. And if I did not believe in a God
who works his will with nations, I should despair of the republic.

HIS PLANS WILL BE THE BEST

I am confident that the Almighty has His plans and will work them
out; and, whether we see it or not, they will be the wisest and best
for us. I have always taken counsel of Him, and referred to him my
plans, and have never adopted a course of proceeding without being
assured, as far as I could be, of his approbation. I should be the most
presumptuous blockhead upon this footstool if I for one day thought
that I could discharge the duties which have come upon me since I
came into this place, without the aid and enlightenment of One who
is wiser and stronger than all others.

⚯ ALFRED, LORD TENNYSON ⚮

(1809–1892)

English poet, Poet Laureat for forty years, and humble believer in Christ. He started writing poems at age six with blank verse scribbled on a slate and ended seventy-five years later with the much quoted "Crossing the Bar." Someone has said his poetry "glides with the grace and beauty of swans, moving slowly across an unruffled lake."

THE SUN OF MY SOUL

What the sunshine is to those flowers, the Lord Jesus Christ is to my soul. He is the sun of my soul.

(Commenting while walking in the poet's garden
with a friend, who asked him what he thought of Jesus Christ)

Christ is walking with us now, just as truly as He was with the two disciples on the road to Emmaus long ago. To feel that He is by my side now as much as you are, fills my heart with joy! There is not a flower beside our pathway that owes as much to the sun as I do to Jesus Christ.

(Commenting one day while out walking with his niece.)

CROSSING THE BAR

Sunset and evening star,
Are one clear call for me!
And may there be no moaning of the bar,
When I put out to sea.
But such a tide as moving seems asleep,
Too full for sound and foam,
When that which drew from out the boundless deep
Turns again home.
Twilight and evening bell,
And after that the dark!
And may there be no sadness of farewell,
When I have crossed the bar.

(Written when his friend Arthur Hallam died. The poet's son, to whom this poem was shown,
said, "It is the crown of your life's work." Tennyson answered, "It came in a moment.")

✍ WILLIAM E. GLADSTONE ✍

(1809–1898)

British statesman and Prime Minister.

THE ONE CENTRAL JOY

All that I think, all that I hope, all that I write, and all that I live for is based on the divinity of Jesus Christ, the one central joy of my poor, wayward life.

(Letter written to Rev. Dr. Tupper of Philadelphia, May 22, 1893
in response to a query as to his religious belief.)

THE GREATEST GIFT EVER GIVEN TO MANKIND

If I am asked, what is the remedy for the deeper sorrows of the human heart: what a man should chiefly look for in his progress through life, as the power that is to sustain him under trials, and enable him manfully to confront his afflictions, I must point to something very different—which in a well-known hymn is called— the old, old story, told in an old, old Book, and taught in an old, old teaching, which is the greatest gift ever given to mankind.

✍ THEODORE PARKER ✍

(1810–1860)

American Congregational pastor, teacher, writer, and advocate of the anti-slavery movement.

CONSCIOUS OF ETERNAL LIFE

The dust goes to its place, and man to his own. I look through the grave into heaven. I ask no miracle, no proof, no reasoning, for me. I ask no risen dust to teach me immortality. I am conscious of eternal life.

⚜ JAMES F. CLARKE ⚜

(1810–1880)

American minister and theologian, whose influence helped elect Grover Cleveland President of the U. S. in 1884.

THE DAY SEEMS TO DAWN IN MY HEART

I am sitting on a summer's day in the shadow of a great New England elm. Its long branches hang motionless; there is not breeze enough to move them. All at once there comes a faint murmur; around my head the leaves are moved by a gentle current of air; then the branches begin to sway to and fro, the leaves are all in motion, and a soft, rushing sound fills my ear. So with every one that is born of the Spirit.... I am heart-empty, and there comes, I know not where or whence, a sound of the divine presence. I am inwardly moved with new comfort and hope, the day seems to dawn in my heart, sunshine comes around my path, and I am able to go to my duties with patience. I am walking in the spirit, I am helped by the help of God, and comforted with the comfort of God. And yet this is all in accordance with law. There is no violation of law when the breezes come, stirring the tops of the trees; and there is no violation of law when God moves in the depths of our souls, and rouses us to love and desire of holiness.

⚜ SIR JAMES SIMPSON ⚜

(1811–1870)

Scottish obstetrician, scientist, and professor of obstetrics at the University of Edinburgh, who discovered the anesthetic properties of chloroform. On the headstone of his beloved daughter he put, "Nevertheless, I live."

MY GREATEST DISCOVERY

The greatest discovery I ever made was the discovery I had a Saviour.

(His quick reply when asked to name the most wonderful discovery he had ever made.)

❧ HARRIET BEECHER STOWE ❧
(1811(2)-1896)

American poet, essayist and author of *Uncle Tom's Cabin* which became a phenomenal best-seller. Within a matter of months, the book was translated and sold in some twenty languages. For many months, it took three power presses running twenty-four hours a day, a hundred bookbinders, and three paper mills to keep up with the demand. Her powerful stories, taken from first-hand knowledge, encouraged readers to share the guilt of a nation that condoned slavery.

WITHIN SIGHT OF THE RIVER OF DEATH

I have thought much lately of the possibility of my leaving you all and going home. I am come to that stage of my pilgrimage that is within sight of the River of Death, and I feel that now I must have all in readiness day and night for the messenger of the King. I have had sometimes in my sleep strange perceptions of a vivid spiritual life near to and with Christ, and multitudes of holy ones, and the joy of it is like no other joy—it cannot be told in the language of the world. What I have then I know with absolute certainty, yet it is so unlike and above anything we conceive of in this world that it is difficult to put into words. The inconceivable loveliness of Christ! It seems that about him there is a sphere where the enthusiasm of love is the calm habit of the soul, that without words, without the necessity of demonstrations of affection heart beats to heart, soul answers soul, we respond to the infinite Love, and we feel his answer in us, and there is not need of words.......This was but a glimpse; but it has left a strange sweetness in my mind.

ROBERT BROWNING

(1812–1889)

Victorian English poet whose mother's evangelical piety and love of music was a great influence on him. His main theme was a chronicling of souls in growth or crisis.

PARACELSUS

I am a wanderer: I remember well
One journey, how I feared the track was missed,
So long the city I desired to reach
Lay hid; when suddenly its spires afar
Flashed through the circling clouds; you may conceive
My transport. Soon the vapors closed again,
But I had seen the city....

A DEATH IN THE DESERT

I say, the acknowledgment of God in Christ
Accepted by the reason, solves for thee
All questions in the earth and out of it.

PARACELSUS

If I stoop
Into a dark tremendous sea of cloud,
It is but for a time; I press God's lamp
Close to my breast; its splendour, soon or late,
Will pierce the gloom; I shall emerge one day.

⚜ ROBERT M. MCCHEYNE ⚜

(1813–1843)

Scottish Presbyterian minister who went out of his way to minister to the poor, the needy, and children. He began to think of his soul at age 18, when an older brother died. His conversion was not sudden, but a slow painful development. He looked upon his fragile health as a means of sanctification, to teach him to feel the weakness and sorrows of others similarly afflicted and to learn to hold on to God, and God alone. He was much influenced by reading the works of great men of God.

A MILLION ENEMIES

If I could hear Christ praying for me in the next room, I would not fear a million enemies. Yet distance makes no difference. He is praying for me.

⚜ DAVID LIVINGSTONE ⚜

(1813–1873)

British physician, scientist, missionary and diplomat of warring tribes who lived a life of courage and hardship for more than thirty years. He was above all a sincere and humble Christian, who was challenged to go to Africa after hearing the words of Robert Moffat, "There is a vast plain to the north, where I have sometimes seen, in the morning sun, the smoke of a thousand villages where no Christian has ever gone." After a sixteen year sojourn in Africa, twenty-seven attacks of African fever, one arm having been rendered useless by the teeth of a lion, he nevertheless went back.

I WILL DEVOTE MY LIFE TO HIS SERVICE

Great pains had been taken by my parents to instill the doctrines of Christianity into my mind, and I had no difficulty in understanding the theory of a free salvation by the atonement of our Savior; but it was only about this time that I began to feel the necessity and value of a personal application of the provision of that atonement to my own case.

(He then came upon Dick's Philosophy of a Future State, *which made clear to him the need for a personal relationship with Christ.)*

....it is my desire to show my attachment to the cause of Him who died for me by devoting my life to His service....I am a missionary, heart and soul. God had an only Son, and He was a missionary, and a physician. A poor, poor imitation of Him I am, or wish to be. In this Service I hope to live; in it I wish to die.

THE KINGDOM OF GOD
I place no value on anything I possess, except in relation to the Kingdom of God. If anything I have will advance that kingdom it shall be given or kept, as by giving or keeping it I shall best promote the glory of Him to whom I owe all my hopes both for time and eternity... All that I am I owe to Jesus Christ revealed to me in His divine Book.

YEARS OF EXILE
Shall I tell you what supported me through all these years of exile among a people whose language I could not understand, and whose attitude toward me was always uncertain and often hostile? It was this, "Lo, I am with you always even unto the end of the world." On these words I staked everything, and they never failed.

(Words spoken at the University of Glasgow while he was home on furlough.)

IT IS A PRIVILEGE
People talk of the sacrifice I have made in spending so much of my life in Africa. Can that be called a sacrifice which is simply paid back as a small part of a great debt owing to our God, which we can never repay? Is that a sacrifice which brings its own best reward in healthful activity, the consciousness of doing good, peace of mind, and a bright hope of a glorious destiny hereafter? Away with the word in such a view, and with such a thought! It was emphatically no sacrifice. Say rather it is a privilege.

I cannot do it alone! The waves dash fast and high; the fog comes chill around, and the light goes out in the sky. But I know that we two shall win in the end—Jesus and I. Coward and wayward and weak, I change with the changing sky, today so strong and brave, tomorrow too weak to fly. But He never gives up, so we two shall win—Jesus and I!"

(At the time of Dan Crawford's death, this note in his New Testament was found in the pocket of his jacket.)

⊰ HENRY WARD BEECHER ⊱
(1813–1887)

Pastor of the Plymouth (Congregational) Church of Brooklyn for forty years. He held a prayer meeting every Friday evening which lasted one hour, but after the meeting he would stay in front of the room to answer questions or to converse with those who were seeking counsel. He had a "combination of sympathy and strength" that drew the troubled and distraught to him.

WHEN CHRIST FIRST APPEARED TO ME
I remember full well the time Christ first appeared to me to be the Chief among ten thousand and altogether lovely. I had procrastinated; I had excused myself, sometimes through ignorance and sometimes through reluctance; but there came a day, a morning, when there rose up in my mind a sense of a saving God who not only poured out his life once, but was pouring it out eternally, to make his goodness and wisdom the medicine of wounded hearts. The thought came to me that it was God's nature to love his children for the sake of curing them. Not that he was by Christ doing it as a special favor, but that it was his nature to love sinful creatures like me, to heal them, and to use the infinite stores of his goodness and the marvels of his grace as medicine for sin-sick souls. It was a thought that neither time nor death nor eternity can ever efface.

(Autobiographical Reminiscences)

I HAVE FOUND GOD

I was walking near Lane Seminary (where I studied theology without a hope), and was working over a lesson that I was to hear recited. The idea dawned upon me, not that there had been a covenant formed between God and his son, but that Christ revealed the nature of God whose very soul was curative, and who brought himself and his living holiness to me, because I needed so much, and not because I was so deserving. That instant the clouds rose, and the whole heaven was radiant, and I exclaimed, "I have found God."

(Autobiographical Reminiscences)

THE LAST AND BEST REVELATION OF GOD'S SPIRIT

It pleased God to reveal to my wandering soul the idea that it was His nature to love a man in his sins for the sake of helping him out of them; that he did not do it out of compliment to Christ, or to a "law" or a "plan of salvation," but from the fullness of His great heart. Time went on, and next came the disclosure of a Christ ever present with me—a Christ that never was far from me, but was always near me, as a companion and friend, to uphold and sustain me. This was the last and the best revelation of God's Spirit to my soul.

(Autobiographical Reminiscences)

I CANNOT FOR A MOMENT DOUBT THAT I AM A CHILD OF GOD

My education and surroundings have always been religious. The precise time of my conversion I cannot tell. I never felt that burden of sin which Bunyan describes, and probably never shall. And yet, I cannot for a moment doubt that I am a child of God.

Let every man come to God in his own way. God made you on purpose, and me on purpose, and He does not say to you, "Repent, and feel as Deacon A. feels," or, "Repent, and feel as your minister feels," but "Come just as you are, with your mind and heart and education and circumstances." You are too apt to feel that your religious experience must be the same as others; but where will you find analogies for this? Certainly not in nature. God's works do not come from His hand like coins from the mint. It seems as if it were a necessity that each one should be in some sort distinct from every other. No two leaves on the same tree are precisely alike; no two buds on the same bush have the same unfolding, nor do they seek to have.

THAT COMMUNION WITH GOD THAT LIFTS THE SOUL

It seems but yesterday when my face was as young and fresh as yours. It seems but as yesterday when I began my race. I am near the end of it; and I bear witness that with a heart as open, and on as many sides, to pleasure and joy as any man's can be here, and having been on the whole under favorable circumstances in life, and tasted of almost all the lawful things that are permitted to mankind in a respectable ambition, I testify that there is nothing in all the earth that is not rendered more sweet and bright by having that communion with God that lifts and refines and strengthens the soul itself.

SONG IN THE NIGHT

Ice breaks many a branch, and so I see a great many persons bowed down and crushed by their afflictions. But now and then I meet one that sings in affliction, and then I thank God for my own sake as well as his. There is not such sweet singing as a song in the night. You recollect the story of the woman who, when her only child died, in rapture looking up, as with the face of an angel, said, "I give you joy, my darling." That single sentence has gone with me years and years down through my life, quickening and comforting me.

I WALKED WITH GOD

When I walked one day on the top of Mount Washington,—glorious day of memory! Such another day I think I shall not experience till I stand on the battlements of the new Jerusalem—how I was discharged of all imperfection! The wide far-spreading country which lay beneath me in beauteous light, how heavenly it looked, and I communed with God. I had sweet tokens that he loved me. My very being rose right up into his nature. I walked with him, and the cities far and near of New York, and all the cities and villages which lay between it and me, with their thunder, the wrangling of human passions below me, were to me as if they were not.

THE MUSIC OF MY LIFE

If a man says there never was a Christ, or that He was only a man, I answer that I have found Him of whom Moses and the prophets spoke. I have asked Him, "What wilt Thou?" and He has told me. I have put my soul and my heart, as He has commanded me, into His hand. Will any man now undertake to reason me out of result? I know in whom I have trusted, and know what He has done for me. Is the music of my life, the inspiration of every faculty, the transformation of my views, the regeneration of my hopes—are these nothing? Am I to go back eighteen hundred years, with a sceptical philosopher, to reason about Jerusalem, and about the Lord Jesus Christ, and not reason upon my own actual daily positive experience?

I LOVE THAT HYMN

I would rather have written that hymn of Wesley's, 'Jesus, Lover of My Soul,' than to have the fame of all the kings that ever sat on the earth. It is more glorious. It has more power in it. That hymn will go on singing until the last trumpet brings forth the angel band; and then, I think it will mount up on some lip to the very presence of God.

✍ JAMES CALVERT ✍

(1813–1892)

Missionary to the cannibals of the Fiji Islands. The captain of the ship sought to turn him back saying, "You will lose your life and the lives of those with you if you go among such savages." Calvert only replied, "We died before we came here."

I BURIED THE BODIES AND LATER A MIRACLE

When I arrived at the Fiji group, my first duty was to bury the hands, arms, feet and heads of eighty victims whose bodies had been roasted and eaten in a cannibal feast. I lived to see those cannibals who had taken part in that inhumane feast gathered about the Lord's table.

✍ THOMAS H. HILL ✍

(1818–1891)

American minister, scientist and college professor.

FOR FIFTY YEARS

A personal experience of fifty years gives me an absolute knowledge of the saving, uplifting power of Jesus. His word has a power to rebuke, to cleanse, to uphold, to enlighten me, incomparably greater than that of any word which has ever reached me. The nearer I keep to him, and the more unreservedly I trust in him, so much the more tenderly do I feel the love of God redeeming, guiding and sanctifying me.

(Christ as Saviour)

⊰ LUCY STONE ⊱
(1818–1893)

American teacher and speaker for the suffrage cause. She was chosen to write a speech for Oberlin's Commencement in 1843 so that a man might read it. She thus resigned. Thirty-six years later she spoke at Oberlin's Semi-centennial.

HE GAVE US YEARNINGS AND LONGINGS

I know not what you believe of God, but I believe He gave yearnings and longings to be filled, and that He did not mean all our time should be devoted to feeding and clothing the body.

⊰ GEORGE ELIOT, ⊱
PSEUDONYM OF MARY ANN EVANS
(1819–1880)

English novelist, whose works brilliantly illustrate the religious sensibility of her time.

THE DIVINE VOICE WITHIN US

We can't choose happiness either for ourselves or for another, we can't tell where that will lie. We can only choose whether we will indulge ourselves in the present moment, or whether we will renounce that, for the sake of obeying the divine voice within us, for the sake of being true to all the motives that sanctify our lives. I know this belief is hard; it has slipped away from me again and again; but I have felt that if I let it go forever, I should have no light through the darkness of this life.

⚜ JAMES RUSSELL LOWELL ⚜
(1819–1891)

American poet, critic, essayist, editor, and diplomat.

THE SAIL'S HORIZON

God is in all that liberates and lifts;
    In all that humbles, sweetens, and consoles.
    A mystery of purpose gleaming through the secular confusions
of the world,
    Whose will we darkly accomplish, doing ours.
    Sometimes at waking, in the street sometimes, or on the hillside,
always unforewarned,
    Man sees a grace of being finer than himself, that beckons and is
gone.
    Power, more near than life itself,
    Or what seems life to us in sense immured.
    When as the roots, shut in the darksome earth, share in the tree-
top's joyance, and
    Conceive of sunshine and wide air and winged things, by sympa-
thy of nature,
    So do I have evidence of Thee so far above, yet in and of me.

⚜ WALT WHITMAN ⚜
(1819–1892)

**American poet, journalist, and essayist whose verse collection, *Leaves of
Grass,* is a landmark in the history of American literature.**

SONG OF MYSELF

I find letters from God drop't in the street,
and every one is signed by God's name,
And I leave them where they are, for I know
that whereso'er I go,
Others will punctually come for ever and ever.

⚜ JOHN RUSKIN ⚜

(1819–1900)

English writer, poet, art historian, and critic, who went through difficulties in life but triumphed in the end.

A PEACE NEVER KNOWN BEFORE

One day last week I began thinking over my past life, and what fruit I have had, and the joy of it which had passed away, and of the hard work of it, and I felt nothing but discomfort, for I saw that I have been always working for myself in one way or another. Then I thought of my investigations of the Bible, and found no comfort in that either. This was about ten o'clock in the morning, so I considered that I had now neither pleasure in looking to my past life nor any hope, such as would be my comfort on a sick bed, of a future one, and I made up my mind that this would never do. So, after thinking, I resolved that at any rate I would act as if the Bible were true—that if it were not I would be at all events no worse off than I was before; that I should believe in Christ and take Him for my Master in whatever I did; that to disbelieve the Bible was quite as difficult as to believe it; and when I had done this I fell asleep. When I rose in the morning, though I was still unwell, I felt a peace and spirit in me that I had never known before.

IT WAS ALL DUE TO MY MOTHER

All that I have taught of art, everything that I have written, whatever greatness there has been in any thought of mine, whatever I have done in my life, has simply been due to the fact that, when I was a child, my mother daily read with me a part of the Bible and daily made me learn a part of it by heart.

⚜ QUEEN VICTORIA ⚜

(1819–1901)

Queen of the United Kingdom of Great Britain and Ireland (1837–1901) beginning at age eighteen. She left her name on an era, the Victorian Age.

To lay my crown at his feet

Oh, that Jesus would come in my lifetime so that I could, with my own hands, take my crown and lay it at his feet.

⚜ FLORENCE NIGHTINGALE ⚜

(1820–1910)

Nurse in the Crimean War. In 1842 at age twenty-two Florence Nightingale knew what she wanted to do. She would be a nurse. Seven years earlier at age fifteen she had received God's call. She never forgot that occasion and kept the anniversary to her dying day. She had waited, and wondered what God had called her to do. She founded trained nursing as a profession for women.

God's work for me

My mind is absorbed with the sufferings of man. Since I was 24 there never has been any vagueness in my plans or ideas as to what God's work was for me.

This great desire

Oh God, you put into my heart this great desire to devote myself to the sick and sorrowful, I offer it to you. Do with it what is for your service.

✥ FANNY CROSBY ✥
(1820–1915)

Writer of more than 9,000 hymns, beginning at age thirty-four. She became blind at six weeks of age by a doctors tragic mistake. Often in her hymns she referred to sight as seeing the light of God's salvation, as in "Blessed Assurance," when she exclaimed, "Visions of rapture now burst on my sight."

LOSS IS NO LOSS

I believe that the greatest blessing the Creator ever bestowed on me was when He permitted my external vision to be closed. He consecrated me for the work which He created me. I have never known what it was to see, and therefore I cannot realize my personal loss. But I have had the most remarkable dream. I have seen the prettiest eyes, the most beautiful faces, the most remarkable landscapes. The loss had been no loss to me.

I SHALL SEE HIM FACE TO FACE

There is one hymn I have written which has never been published. I call it my soul's poem. Sometimes when I am troubled, I repeat it to myself, for it brings comfort to my heart: "Someday the silver cord will break, and I no more as now shall sing; but O the joy when I shall wake within the palace of the King! And I shall see Him face to face, and tell the story—saved by grace!"

(Spoken at a Bible conference when D. L. Moody asked her to give a personal testimony)

✥ JOHN CAIRD ✥
(1820–1898)

British Presbyterian theologian and preacher.

WHY GOD MADE THE WORLD SO BEAUTIFUL

If we try to conceive why it is that this strange, indefinable thing we call beauty exists, or why the hand of God has scattered it with infinite prodigality over the face of the visible world,—why it is

that beyond mere material form and ordered sequence of material phenomena, and adaptation to the uses of man, far and wide
over heaven and earth, over mountain and forest and stream and
sea, suffusing, insinuating into all processes of nature, the dawn
and the sunset, the spring, the summer glory, the fading splendor
of autumn woods and fields, the softened play of light and shadow,
the infinitely varied wealth and harmony of color and form, into
all fair scenes and sweet sounds—if we ask why God has so made
the world that this strange element of beauty is everywhere added
to use, and what is the secret of its power over us—its power not
merely to awaken admiration, to charm and thrill us, but at least in
some minds, to stir in them inexpressible longings and aspirations
that transcend the range of experience—if we ask such questions as
these, I think the answer must be that the highest end and use of all
this material glory of God's world lies in its power to carry us beyond
itself, to be the suggestive type and symbol of a beauty which eye
hath not seen, nor ear heard, nor imagination conceived.

(University Sermons, *presented before the University of Glasgow*)

⚶ B. F. CRARY ⚶

(PUB. 1868)

American Methodist minister.

I AWOKE IN A NEW WORLD

My conversion was a wonderful change, affecting my whole nature,
and new-creating my heart. I awoke in a new world, filled with new
ideas, hopes, fears, and ambitions. The work was instantaneous,
overwhelming, convincing, giving me peace with God through our
Lord Jesus Christ.

(*Reported in* Pioneer Experiences, *ed. W. C. Palmer, Jr., NY, 1868*)

❧ FEODOR MIKHAYLOVICH DOSTOEVSKY ❧
(1821–1881)

Russian novelist who was condemned to death for revolutionary activities. He was reprieved at the last moment and did four years of forced labor in Siberia with only a Bible as reading material. This led to his conversion. In *The Brothers Karamazov*, described by some as the greatest Christian novel ever written, he expresses faith in the ultimate triumph of spiritual values and of Christianity. The author states, "Much on earth is hidden from us, but to make up for that we have been given a precious mystic sense of our living bond with the heavenly world."

MOMENTS OF PERFECT PEACE

God gives me sometimes moments of perfect peace; in such moments I love, and believe that I am loved; in such moments I have formulated my creed, wherein all is clear and holy to me. This creed is extremely simple; here it is: I believe that there is nothing lovelier, deeper, more sympathetic, more rational; more manly and more perfect than the Saviour; I say to myself with jealous love that not only is there no one else like Him, but that there could be no one....There is in the world only one figure of absolute beauty: Christ. That infinitely lovely figure is as a matter of course an infinite marvel. I have never been able to conceive of mankind without Him.

(In a letter written from exile in Siberia).

THE GREAT MYSTERY

It is the great mystery of human life that old grief gradually passes into quiet tender joy. The mild serenity of age takes the place of the riotous blood of youth. I bless the rising sun each day, and, as before, my heart sings to meet it, but now I love even more its setting, its long slanting rays and the soft, tender, gentle memories that come with them, the dear images from the whole of my long, happy life— and over all the Divine Truth, softening, reconciling, forgiving! My life is ending. I know that well, but every day that is left me I feel how my earthly life is in touch with a new infinite, unknown, but approaching life, the nearness of which sets my soul quivering with rapture, my mind glowing and my heart weeping with joy.

⚔ HENRI-FREDERIC AMIEL ⚙

(1821–1881)

Swiss philosopher, poet, and critic. The following excerpts are taken from his fascinating diary which captures the essence of ordinary life in a Swiss village in the 1800's. His *Journal* was published after his death.

TO LOSE ONE'S LIFE THAT ONE MAY GAIN IT

I thank Thee, my God, for the hour that I have just passed in Thy presence. Thy will was clear to me: I measured my faults, counted my griefs, and felt Thy goodness towards me. I realized my own nothingness—Thou gavest me Thy peace. In bitterness there is sweetness; in affliction, joy, in submission, strength, in the God who punishes, the God who loves. To lose one's life that one may gain it, to offer it that one may receive it, to possess nothing that one may conquer all, to renounce self that God may give Himself to us.—How impossible a problem, and how sublime a reality! No one truly knows happiness who has not suffered....

GOD'S GUEST

For nearly two hours have I been lost in the contemplation of this magnificent spectacle. I felt myself in the temple of the infinite, in the presence of the world, God's guest in this vast nature. The stars wandering in the pale ether drew me far away from earth. What peace beyond the power of words, what dews of life eternal they shed on the adoring soul! I felt the earth floating like a boat in its blue ocean. Such deep and tranquil delight nourishes the whole man—it purifies and ennobles. I surrendered myself. I was all gratitude and docility.

NOTES IN THE GREAT CONCERT

Magnificent weather. The morning seems bathed in happy peace, and a heavenly fragrance rises from mountain and shore; it is as though a benediction were laid upon us...One might believe oneself in a church—a vast temple in which every being and every natural beauty has its place. I dare not breathe for fear of putting the dream to flight—a dream traversed by angels.

In these heavenly moments the cry of Pauline rises to one's lips. 'I feel! I believe! I see!' All the miseries, cares, the vexations of life, are forgotten; the universal joy absorbs us; we enter into the divine order, and into the blessedness of the Lord. Labor and tears, sin, pain, and death have passed away. To exist is to bless; life is happiness. In this sublime pause of things all dissonances have disappeared; It is as though creation were but one vast symphony, glorifying the God of goodness with an inexhaustible wealth of praise and harmony. We question no longer whether it is so or not. We have ourselves become notes in the great concert; and the soul breaks the silence of ecstasy only to vibrate in unison with the eternal joy.

⚶ FRIEDRICH MAX MUELLER ⚶

(1823–1900)

English Orientalist, scholar, and professor at Oxford.

THE KEY TO ALL SEEMING CONTRADICTIONS

How shall I describe to you what I found in the New Testament? I had not read it for many years, and was prejudiced against it before I took it in hand. The light which struck Paul with blindness on the way to Damascus was not more strange than that which fell on me when I suddenly discovered the fulfillment of all hopes, the highest perfection of philosophy, the key to all the seeming contradictions of the physical and moral world. The whole world seemed to me to be ordered for the sole purpose of furthering the religion of the Redeemer, and if this religion is not divine, I understand nothing at all.

(Late in life, in a letter to a friend.)

THOMAS JONATHAN
(STONEWALL) JACKSON
(1824–1863)

American soldier and Confederate commander. He earned his nickname at the First Battle of Bull Run where his troops stood against the Union force "like a stone wall."

ACCORDING TO GOD'S HOLY WILL

You see me wounded, but not depressed, not unhappy. I believe it has been according to God's holy will, and I resign entirely to it. You may think it strange, but you never saw me more perfectly contented than I am today, for I am sure my Heavenly Father designs this affliction for my good. I am perfectly satisfied that either this life or in that which is to come I shall discover that what is now regarded as a calamity is a blessing. I can wait until God, in His own time, shall make known to me the object He has in thus afflicting me. But why should I not rather rejoice in it as a blessing and not look on it as a calamity at all? If it were in my power to replace my arm, I would not dare to do it unless I could know it was the will of my Heavenly Father.

(Jackson lost his left arm in battle.)

I LIVE IN THE SPIRIT OF PRAYER

I live in the spirit of prayer. I pray as I walk, when I lie down, and when I arise. When I am persuaded that a desired thing is right, I continue to pray for it until the answer comes. I never seal a letter without putting a word of prayer under the seal. I never receive a dispatch from the post without a brief sending of my thoughts upward. I never meet my troops without a moment's petition on those who go out and those who come in. Everything calls me to prayer.

∂∽ GEORGE MacDONALD ∾∂

(1824–1905)

Scottish clergyman, novelist, and poet.

THE FACE OF GOD

When I look like this into the blue sky, it seems so deep, so peaceful, so full of a mysterious tenderness, that I could lie for centuries and wait for the drawing of the face of God out of the awful loving-kindness.

IT IS GOD

A Voice in the wind I do not know;
A meaning on the face of the high hills
Whose utterance I cannot comprehend.
A something is behind them: that is God.

(From "Within and Without")

NO GAPS

I came from God, and I'm going back to God, and I won't have any gaps of death in the middle of my life.

(From Mary Marston, ch. 57)

NO TIME FOR DISPUTING

I find that doing the will of God leaves me no time for disputing about his plans.

WHAT AM I

My prayers, my God, flow from what I am not; I think thy answers make me what I am.

✺ ANNIE KEARY ✺

(1825–1879)

English devotional writer.

INTERRUPTIONS MAY BE THE MOST IMPORTANT WORK OF THE DAY

I think I find most help in trying to look on all interruptions and hindrances to work that one has planned out for oneself as discipline, trials sent by God to help one against getting selfish over one's work. Then one can feel that perhaps one's true work—one's work for God—consists in doing some trifling hap-hazard thing that has been thrown into one's day,—the part one can best offer to God.

✺ EDWARD H. BICKERSTETH ✺

(1825–1906)

Writer on religious themes. On the last morning of his life he said, "I have no other ground of confidence than the blood of Jesus. Christ first, Christ last, Christ all in all."

FRAGMENTS OF BEAUTY WHICH GOD HAS SCATTERED SO WIDELY

All beauty is a gleam from the fountain of beauty. No work of beauty can be more beautiful than the mind which designed it. I do not think a sculptor can possibly chisel a marble so as to make it more beautiful than his own ideal conception. I do not think a painter can produce a painting more beautiful than the thought of his mind which led up to it; I do not think a musician can express in sound, or a poet on paper, anything beyond the thought within him. I know, indeed, that the conception of either may grow with the process by which it is presented to others, and that the man may, as he proceeds, have a fairer and nobler view of what he is trying to express; but, after all, the mind of the sculptor is more beautiful than the marble which he has sculptured; and the mind of the painter is a more beautiful thing than the work of art which he has painted; and the mind of the musician is better and higher and nobler than the most exquisite symphony which he has composed and reduced to writing; and the mind of the poet is better than his most beautiful piece of poetry. And so we must rise from all the fragments of beauty which God has scattered so widely over His world to say with Milton—

"Then this universal frame
Thus wondrous fair; Thyself how wondrous then!"

❧ THEOPHANE VENARD ❧
(1829–1861)

French missionary, priest, and martyr.

WITHIN A FEW SHORT HOURS MY EXILE WILL BE OVER
I shall be beheaded. Within a few short hours my soul will quit this earth, exile over, and battle won. I shall mount upwards and enter into our true home. There among God's elect I shall gaze upon what eye of man cannot imagine, hear undreamed of harmonies, enjoy a happiness the heart cannot comprehend.

❧ MRS. JOHN MASON TURNER ❧
(PUB. 1886)

Pastor's wife. This excerpt is taken from "The Congregationalist", a prominent church paper in the 1880's.

A WAY OF PRIVILEGE AND BLESSING
Comfort—no other word expresses so well the ministry of Christ's truth to my life. To be uncomforted is to be filled with despair. The soul trusting in itself may be brave, but only the soul that finds itself in God is comforted...No longer baffled by a sense of the futility of life, but comforted with a great and abiding faith, knowing that I can never "drift beyond His love and care," I am still following the path that once seemed so dark. It has been a way of privilege and blessing.

THAT VOICE IN THE DARK

From a happy childhood and a care-free girlhood I came to the stern responsibilities and cares of more mature life, only to find myself unprepared to meet them.

Life had been to me a lovely dream-filled thing, and when I found myself face to face with Reality, I cried out in bitterness and rebellion. This hard, rough path was surely not for me; my path had been a beautiful shining path. I had started out with glowing purpose to follow the Gleam, and in the path at my feet every ray of light had darkened. If I had been called to a great sacrifice I could have risen to its heights; it was the very common character of my lot that humiliated me and robbed me of my strength.

At this time there came to me a dark period of doubt. I did not want to be a doubter and struggled against its unhappy influence. With doubt came a distrust of God's care of my life. It seemed as if it were of no concern to the Heavenly Father that I suffered. I was a constant prey to the sense of the futility of life.

There remained of my wreck of faith and dreams a sense of God and a great desire to find the light. This sense of God comforted me even when I was unconscious of it, and always in the darkness I could hear His voice saying, "This way, my child, this way toward the Light," even as I had heard my mother's voice when as a little child I lost my way in the darkness of my room.

That voice in the dark—what infinite tenderness and patience in its call! Following it I found light and the comforting enfolding sense of eternal love and care. Amid the feeling that life was unkind and that my obvious duties were unworthy, my best effort was lost. Strength and courage came as I learned to accept all as the fulfillment of God's purpose in my life.

LIFE TRIUMPHANT

Not only do those who suffer a great bereavement need the consolations of the assurance of immortality. In my own life, in the hard daily duty, the truth symbolized by Easter floods my way with light.

Life triumphant in all the universe—this is the larger faith that banished my sense of the shortness and vanity of life.

⚖ GENERAL LEW WALLACE ⚖
(1827–1905)

Agnostic who had set out to write a novel that would prove all of Christ's claims fraudulent. However, in his research of the life of Christ he became a Christian, and his novel, *Ben-Hur,* portrayed that faith.

My own personal Savior

After six years given to the impartial investigation of Christianity, as to its truth or falsity, I have come to the deliberate conclusion that Jesus Christ was the Messiah of the Jews, the Savior of the world, and my own personal Savior.

(Converted while doing research for Ben Hur, *a novel set during the life and times of Christ; New York: Dodd, Mead & Company, 1953)*

⚖ ELIZABETH RUNDLE CHARLES ⚖
(1828–1896)

Gifted English poet, musician, painter, author, and hymn writer.

Receiving from God the free gift

From a weary laborer, worn with slavish and ineffectual toil, I had become as a little child receiving from God the free gift of eternal life and of daily sustenance; and prayer, from a weary spiritual exercise, had become the simple asking from the Heavenly Father of daily bread and thanking Him.

To feel God's love

What inexpressible joy for me to look up through the apple blossoms and the fluttering leaves and to see God's love there; to listen to the thrush that has built his nest among them and to feel God's love, who cares for the birds, in every note that swells his little throat; to look beyond to the bright blue depths of the sky and to feel they are a canopy of blessing—the roof of the house of my Father; that if the clouds pass over it, it is the unchangeable light they veil; that, even when the day itself passes, I shall see that the night itself only unveils new worlds of light; and to know that if I could unwrap fold after fold of God's universe, I should only unfold more and more blessing, and see deeper and deeper into the love which is at the heart of all.

⁊ LEO TOLSTOI ⁊

(1828–1910)

Russian author and philosopher. He is probably best known for *War and Peace*, which is recognized by many as one of the greatest novels ever written. It became one of the great moral forces of his time. Even in Russia he was allowed to say what he liked without any fear of censorship.

LIKE THE THIEF ON THE CROSS

Five years ago I came to believe in Christ's teaching, and my life suddenly changed; I ceased to desire what I had previously desired, and began to desire what I formerly did not want. What had previously seemed to me good seemed evil, and what had seemed evil seemed good. It happened to me as it happens to a man who goes out on some business and on the way suddenly decides that the business is unnecessary and returns home. All that was on his right is now on his left, and all that was on his left is now on his right; his former wish to get as far as possible from home has changed into a wish to be as near as possible to it. The directions of my life and my desires became different, and good and evil changed places....

I, like that thief on the cross, have believed Christ's teaching and been saved. And this is no far-fetched comparison, but the closest expression of the condition of spiritual despair and horror at the problem of life and death in which I lived formerly, and of the condition of peace and happiness in which I am now. I, like the thief, knew that I had lived and was living badly.... I, like the thief, knew that I was unhappy and suffering.... I, like the thief to the cross, was nailed by some force to that life of suffering and evil. And as, after the meaningless sufferings and evils of life, the thief awaited the terrible darkness of death, so did I await the same thing.

In all this I was exactly like the thief, but the difference was that the thief was already dying, while I was still living. The thief might believe that his salvation lay there beyond the grave, but I could not be satisfied with that, because besides a life beyond the grave life still awaited me here. But I did not understand that life. It seemed to me terrible. And suddenly I heard the words of Christ and understood them, and life and death ceased to seem to me evil, and instead of despair I experienced happiness and the joy of life undisturbed by death.

("What I Believe", Introduction, translated by Aylmer Maude,
in a Diary of Readings, ed. John Baillie, Collier Books, 1955)

A FIRM, QUIET ASSURANCE

I have been thinking much about God, about the essence of my life, and, as it seemed, only to feel doubtful as to both the one and the other, and I questioned the evidence of His existence. And then, not long ago, I simply felt the desire to lean myself upon faith in God, and in the imperishableness of my soul; and to my astonishment I felt such a firm, quiet assurance as I had never felt before, so that all the doubts and testings evidently not only did not weaken, but to an enormous extent confirmed, my faith.

THAT LIGHT NEVER LEFT ME

One day in the early spring, seeking after God in my thoughts, a flash of joy illumined my soul. I realized that the conception of God was not God himself. I felt that I had only truly lived when I believed in God. God is life. Live to seek God, and life will not be without him. The light that then shone never left me.... I came to know that God is all we need.

ANDREW MURRAY

(1828–1917)

South African pastor and writer of many books on important aspects of the Christian life. He was converted at age seventeen, as a result of "the blessing of praying parents" and the deep spiritual impressions he received from godly men and women who impacted his life during the years of his formal education in Scotland and Holland.

THE MOST EVENTFUL YEAR IN MY LIFE

Tomorrow will close a year which is certainly the most eventful in my life, a year in which I have been made to experience most abundantly that God is good to the soul that seeketh him.

(Written on the eve of his 18th birthday about his conversion)

My justification was clear as the noonday; I knew the hour in which I received from God the joy of pardon.

(Written many days after his conversion)

A VESSEL TO BE FILLED

I have learned to place myself before God every day as a vessel to be filled with His Holy Spirit. He has filled me with the blessed assurance that He, as the everlasting God, has guaranteed His work in me.

THE DEEP SEA OF CALMNESS

Humility is perfect quietness of heart. It is to have no trouble. It is never to be fretted or irritated or sore or disappointed. It is to expect nothing, to wonder at nothing that is done to me. It is to be at rest when nobody praises me and when I am blamed or despised. It is to have a blessed home in the Lord, where I can go in and shut the door and kneel to my Father in secret, and am at peace as in the deep sea of calmness when all around and above is trouble.

ᴁ WILLIAM BOOTH ᴂ

(1829–1912)

A combination English evangelist, philanthropist, reformer, and counselor who wanted to spend his life in "publishing the Savior to a lost world." After working twelve hours, he would spend the entire evening speaking at street or cottage meetings, visiting the sick, and comforting the dying, often as late as midnight. He went into the slums of London to start his organization, the Salvation Army, in 1878. On one Christmas greeting to all the Salvation Army workers around the world, he wrote one word, "Others." He drew all who needed him, regardless of color, creed, station, or condition of life.

THE SECRET OF MY SUCCESS

I will tell you the secret of my success. God has had all there was of me. There have been men with greater brains than I, men with greater opportunities. But from the day I got the poor of London on my heart and caught a vision of what Jesus Christ could do with them, I made up my mind that God should have all of William Booth there was. And if any thing has been achieved, it is because God has had all the adoration of my heart, all the power of my will, and all the influence of my life.

(As told to Wilbur Chapman when asked the secret of his success in the Salvation Army)

ᴁ JOHN PATON ᴂ

(FL. LATTER 1800'S)

Scottish missionary to the South Pacific. He left home in 1858 and found himself among cannibals with his life endangered. After he dug a well for the islanders, opposition to his mission work ceased.

TILL MY MASTER'S WORK WITH ME WAS DONE

They encircled us in a deadly ring, and one kept urging another to strike the first blow. My heart rose up to the Lord Jesus; I saw him watching all the scene. My peace came back to me like a wave from

God. I realized that my life was immortal till my Master's work with me was done.

(Meeting the cannibals for the first time)

As I put the bread and wine into those hands once stained with the blood of cannibalism, now stretched out to receive and partake the emblems of the Redeemer's love, I had a foretaste of the joy of Glory that well nigh broke my heart to pieces.

(In 1869, nearly 11 years after his arrival)

THE MOST INTIMATE GLIMPSES OF THE PRESENCE OF MY LORD

Without the abiding consciousness of the presence and power of my Lord and Savior, nothing in the world would have preserved me from losing my reason and perishing miserably. His words, "Lo, I am with you always, even unto the end," became to me so real that it would not have startled me to behold him, as Stephen did, gazing down upon the scene. It is the sober truth that I had my nearest and most intimate glimpses of the presence of my Lord in those dread moments when musket, club, or spear was being leveled at my life.

✍ SHANG-MO HSI ✍

(D. 1896)

Confucian scholar, lawyer, and drug addict who was converted to Christianity and was received with great kindness by Christian friends. He later became a pastor.

ALL FEAR WAS GONE

All sense of fear was gone; my mind was at rest. Pride broke with tears that flowed and could not cease. He loved me and gave himself for me. He has redeemed me. I am forever His.

ROBERT ARTHUR
✍ TALBOT GASCOYNE-CECIL ✍
(1830–1902)

Third Marquess of Salisbury and British statesman.

THE CENTRAL POINT IS THE RESURRECTION

To me, the central point is the Resurrection of Christ, which I believe. Firstly, because it is testified by men who had every opportunity of seeing and knowing, and whose veracity was tested by the most tremendous trails, both of energy and endurance, during long lives. Secondly, because of the marvelous effect it had upon the world. As a moral phenomenon, the spread and mastery of Christianity is without a parallel. I can no more believe that colossal moral effects lasting for two thousand years can be without a cause than I can believe that the various motions of the magnet are without a cause, though I cannot wholly explain them. To anyone who believes the Resurrection of Christ, the rest presents little difficulty. No one who has that belief will doubt that those who were commissioned by him to speak—Paul, Peter, Mark, John—carried a Divine message.

✍ JOSEPH PARKER ✍
(1830–1902)

American minister and writer.

ONCE I WAS BLIND, BUT NOW I SEE

When He touched my heart into life, I did not say, "Hand me down the Greek grammar and the Hebrew lexicon, and three volumes of the encyclopedia, to see how this really stands." I did not say, "Let me see what the 'Fathers' have said about this." I knew it to be a fact. Nobody ever did for me what He has done. Once I was blind, now I see. I go to other men—writers, speakers, teachers—hear what they have to say, and behold, they are broken cisterns that can hold no water. I go to the Son of God, whose teaching is written in the

New Testament, and gets into the deep places of my life; it redeems me; it goes further than any other influence and does more for me than any other attempt that ever was made to recover and bless my life. It is, therefore, in this great sweep of His, in this reply to every demand that is made upon His resources, this infinite sufficiency of His grace, that I find the exposition and the defense of His God-head. Some things must be felt; some things must be laid hold of by sympathy, affection, sensibility. The heart is in some cases a greater interpreter than the understanding.

BREAD AND WATER

Man needs Jesus Christ as a necessity and not as a luxury. You may be pleased to have flowers, but you must have bread...Jesus is not a phenomenon, He is bread: Christ is not a curiosity, He is water. As surely as we cannot live without bread we cannot live truly without Christ; if we know not Christ we are not living, our movement is a mechanical flutter, our pulse is but the stirring of an animal life... I would call Him the water of life; I would speak of Him as the true bread sent down from heaven; I would tell men that it is impossible to live without him; I would say, with heightening passion, with glowing and ineffable love, that He only, even the holy Christ of God, can satisfy the hunger and the thirst of the soul of man.

(The Inner Life of Christ, vol. II, pp. 320-321)

⁂ JAMES A. GARFIELD ⁂
(1831–1881)

Twentieth President of the U. S. He was killed by an assassin's bullet only four months after he took office. He was fatherless at two and later drove canal boat teams, somehow earning enough money for an education. He attended seminary and later was a classics professor and college president before becoming the "dark horse" Republican candidate for President. He defeated his opponent by only 10,000 votes.

MY CONVERSION

I injured my foot in chopping a piece of wood. The blue dye in my homemade socks poisoned the wound, and I was kept at home. Just then, a remarkable Revival began in our neighbourhood, and being unable to go from home, I went to the meetings, and was converted. New desires then possessed me, and I determined to seek an education that I might live more usefully for Christ.

THE OLDER I GROW

I suppose that seasons of religious doubt come to every man. But I have noticed this in my own internal experience, that the older I grow the less do I care about the dogmas and theories, and the more do I care for the beauty and force that are a part of Jesus Christ. There is no possible means by which any man or any number of men could have created in fiction a character like this. It is the very highest type of manhood, and the high ideal which any man feels he has the right to imitate, even when he knows he cannot reach it.

⊰ Thomas DeWitt Talmage ⊱

(1832–1902)

American Dutch Reformed and Presbyterian pastor who became a Christian at the age of eighteen and viewed himself as a conservative defender of the faith. He was a lawyer until at the age of twenty-one he felt the call to the ministry. The leading dailies of Great Britain, Canada, the U. S., Australia, France, Germany, Sweden and Russia printed his sermons for years in full. It was said that when he was nearing the silver jubilee of his service in Brooklyn that his congregation each week including radio and newspaper was never less than twenty million.

FRIENDSHIP

I have found a great many kind friends, but Jesus is the best. He understands me so well, and has such a way of putting up with my frailties, and has promised to do so much for me, when all other loved ones swim away from my vision, and I can no more laugh with them over their joys or cry with them over their sorrows. Oh! When a man has trouble, he needs friends. When a man loses property, he needs all these of his acquaintances who have lost property to come in with their sympathy. When bereavement comes to a household, it is a comfort to have others who have been bereaved come in and sympathize. God is a sympathetic Friend.

AT MIDDLE AGE

I have learned, having come up one side of the hill, and before I go down on the other side, that nothing is accomplished without work, hard work, continuous work, all-absorbing work, everlasting work.

I have learned also in coming up this steep hill of life, that all events are connected. I look back and now see events which were isolated and alone, but I find now they were adjoined to everything that went before, and everything that came after. The chain of life is made up of a great many links—large links, small links, silver links, iron links, beautiful links, ugly links, mirthful links, solemn links—but they are all parts of one great chain of destiny. Each minute is made up of sixty links, and each day is made up of twenty-four links, and each year is made up of three hundred and sixty-five links; but they are all parts of one endless chain which plays and works through the hand of an all-governing God. No event ever stands alone. Sometimes you say, "This is my day off." You will never have a day off. Nothing is off.

(The Authentic Life of T. DeWitt Talmage, *by John Rusk, 1902, L. G. Stahl*)

I MUST HAVE IT OR I CANNOT LIVE

And I came to understand also that this grace of God is an absolute necessity. I hear people talk of it as though this religion were a mere adornment, a shoulder-strap decorating a soldier, a frothy, light dessert after the chief banquet has passed, something to be tried after calomels and mustard plasters have failed, but in ordinary circumstances of no especial importance—only the jingling of the bells on the horse's neck while he draws the load, but in no way helping him to draw it. Now, I denounce that style of religion. Religion, while it is an adornment, is the first and the last necessity of an immortal nature. I must have it, you must have it, or we cannot live.

(The Authentic Life of T. DeWitt Talmage, *by John Rusk, 1902 by L. G. Stahl*)

⪍ J. HUDSON TAYLOR ⪏

(1832–1905)

Missionary of extraordinary faith who endured hardship and suffering. He opened China for the Gospel and had a great impact on missions. When his supporting organization failed, Taylor simply accepted the ways and dress of the Chinese and became one of them. In 1860, broken in health, he returned to England; but his sympathies for the Chinese were so strong that five years later he returned without financial support of any kind and organized the China Inland Mission on an interdenominational basis.

DOING HIS WORK THROUGH ME

I used to ask God to help me. Then I asked if I might help him. I ended up by asking him to do his work through me.

GOD WAS FAITHFUL

I will give you the motto of my life, "Have faith in God." Reckon on God's faith to you. All my life has been so fickle; sometimes I could trust and sometimes I could not; but when I could not trust, then I reckoned that God would be faithful.

THE SWEETEST PART

The sweetest part, if one may speak of one part being sweeter than another, is the rest which full identification with Christ brings. I am no longer anxious about anything, as I realize the Lord is able to carry out His will, and His will is mine. It makes no matter where He places me, or how. That is rather for Him to consider than for me; for in the easiest positions He must give me His grace, and in the most difficult, His grace is sufficient.

❧ HANNAH WHITALL SMITH ❧
(1832–1911)

American Quaker whose well-known devotional classic, *The Christian's Secret of a Happy Life*, has sold millions of copies. Her writings deal directly with the day-to-day struggles of ordinary people, encouraging them to a more consecrated life-style. Her personal discovery of God came after a process of searching that began with what she called "the aching void in my heart."

SEPTEMBER 13, 1858

It was in the year 1858 and I was twenty-six year old. I had just lost a precious little daughter, five years old, and my heart was aching with sorrow. I could not endure to think that my darling had gone out alone into a Godless universe, and yet, no matter on which side I turned, there seemed no ray of light...

(At a noonday meeting in Philadelphia)

Then suddenly something happened to me. What it was or how it came I had no idea, but somehow an inner eye seemed to be opened in my soul, and I seemed to see that, after all, God was a fact—the bottom fact of all facts—and that the only thing to do was to find out all about Him. It was not a pious feeling, such as I had been looking for, but it was a conviction—just such a conviction as comes to one when a mathematical problem is suddenly solved. One does not feel it is solved, but one knows it, and there can be no further question. I do not remember anything that was said. I do not even know that I heard anything. A tremendous revolution was going on within me that was of far profounder interest than anything the most eloquent preacher could have uttered. God was making Himself manifest as an actual existence, and my soul leaped up in an irresistible cry to know Him.

(From her diary, recorded in The Unselfishness
of God, *Barbour Publishing, Inc. 1993)*

NOTHING MORE TO BE SAID

From that moment the matter was settled, and not a doubt as to my being a child of God and the possessor of eternal life has ever had the slightest power over me since. I rushed to my Bible to make myself sure there was no mistake, and I found it brimming over with this teaching. "He that believes has, " "He that believes is." There seemed to be nothing more to be said about it...... There were the things about Christ, written in the Bible, as clear as daylight, and I believed what was written with all my heart and soul, and therefore I could not doubt that I was one of those who had "life through His name." The question was settled without any further argument. It had nothing to do with how I felt, but only with what God had said. The logic seemed to me irresistible; and it not only convinced me then, but it has carried me triumphantly through every form of doubt as to my relations with God which has ever assailed me since.

(The Unselfishness of God, Barbour Publishing, Inc., 1993)

WHY HAD NOBODY EVER TOLD ME?

The thing that amazed me was how I could have lived so long in a world that contained the Bible, and never have found all this before.

Why had nobody ever told me? How could people, who had found it out, have kept such a marvelous piece of good news to themselves? Certainly I could not keep it to myself, and I determined that no one whom I could reach should be left a day longer in ignorance, as far as I could help it.

(The Unselfishness of God, *Barbour Publishing, Inc., 1993*)

IT IS DELIGHTFUL GROWING OLD

We are in 1903 and I am nearly seventy-one years old. I always thought I should love to grow old, and I find it is even more delightful than I thought. It is so delicious to be done with things, and to feel no need any longer to concern myself much about earthly affairs. I seem on the verge of a most delightful journey to a place of unknown joys and pleasures, and things here seem of so little importance compared to things there, that they have lost most of their interest for me.

I cannot describe the sort of done-with-the-world feeling I have. It is not that I feel as if I was going to die at all, but simply that the world seems to me nothing but a passage way to the real life beyond; and passage ways are very unimportant places. It is of very little account what sort of things they contain, or how they are furnished. One just hurries through them to get to the place beyond.

My wants seem to be gradually narrowing down, my personal wants, I mean, and I often think I could be quite content in the Poorhouse! I don't know whether this is piety or old age, or a little of each mixed together, but honestly the world and our life in it does seem of too little account to be worth making the least fuss over, when one has such a magnificent prospect close at hand ahead of one; and I am tremendously content to let one activity after another go, and to await quietly and happily the opening of the door at the end of the passage way, that will let me in to my real abiding place. So you may think of me as happy and contented, surrounded with unnumbered blessings, and delighted to be seventy-one years old.

A FEW FAINT GLIMPSES OF GLORY

Everything is safe when an unselfish love is guiding and controlling, and therefore my old heart is at rest, and I can lay down my arms with a happy confidence that, since God is in His heaven, all must necessarily be right with His world. And I can peacefully wait to understand what seems mysterious now, until the glorious day of revelation to which every hour brings me nearer.

Therefore with an easy mind I can look forward to death, and the prospect of leaving this life and of entering into the larger and grander life beyond is pure bliss to me. It is like having a new country, full of unknown marvels, to explore; and the knowledge that no one and nothing can hinder my going there is a secret spring of joy at the bottom of my heart.

I am like the butterfly just preparing to slip out of its old cocoon; panting for the life outside, but with no experience to tell it what kind of life that outside life will be. But I believe with all my heart that the apostle told the truth when he declared that, "Eye hath not seen, nor ear heard, neither hath it entered into the heart of man the things which God hath prepared for them that love him" (I Cor. 2:9). And what better prospect could the soul have!

Then will be fulfilled the prayer of our Lord, "Father, I will that they, also, whom thou hast given me, be with me where I am; that they may behold my glory which thou hast given me." (John 17: 24). That glory is not the glory of dazzling light but it is the glory of unselfish love. I have had a few faint glimpses of this glory now and here, and it has been enough to ravish my heart. But there I shall see him as He is, in all the glory of an infinite unselfishness which no heart of man has even been able to conceive; I await the moment with joy.

❧ CHARLES HADDEN SPURGEON ❧

(1834–1892)

English Baptist preacher who was respected by all. He was a famous preacher at age sixteen. At age nineteen he preached to 27,000 persons on a British hillside, and at twenty he was pastor of the great Metropolitan Tabernacle in London. He preached powerful Biblical sermons to audiences of 10,000 in London and in the United States. He published 2,000 sermons (his collection of sermons stands as the largest set of books by a single author in the history of the church), and wrote 135 books (which is more than any other Christian author of his time). He founded orphanages, a Bible Society, and a pastor's college.

FROM DEATH TO LIFE

I sometimes think I might have been in darkness and despair until now had it not been for the goodness of God in sending a snowstorm one Sunday morning while I was going to a certain place of worship. When I could go no further, I turned down a side street, and came to a little Primitive Methodist chapel. In that chapel there may have been a dozen or fifteen people....The minister did not come that morning; he was snowed up, I suppose. At last, a very thin-looking man, a shoemaker, or tailor or something of that sort, went up into the pulpit to preach. Now, it is well that preachers should be instructed; but this man was really stupid. He was obliged to stick to his text, for the simple reason that he had little else to say. The text was—"Look unto me, and be ye saved, all the ends of the earth! (Isaiah 45:22)" He did not even pronounce the words rightly, but that did not matter. There was, I thought, a glimpse of hope for me in that text.......When he had gone to about that length, and managed to spin out ten minutes or so, he was at the end of his tether. Then he looked at me....and said, "Young man, look to Jesus Christ. Look! Look! You have nothin' to do but to look and live."

I saw at once the way of salvation......I had been waiting to do fifty things, but when I head that word, "Look!" what a charming word it seemed to me! Oh! I looked until I could almost have looked my eyes away. There and then the cloud was gone, the darkness had rolled away, and that moment I saw the sun; and I could have risen that instant and sung with the most enthusiastic of them, of the precious blood of Christ, and the simple faith which looks alone to Him. Oh, that somebody had told me this before....

It is not everyone who can remember the very day and hour of his deliverance; but, as Richard Knill said, "At such a time of the day, clang went every harp in heaven, for Richard Knill was born again," it was e'en so with me. The clock of mercy struck in Heaven the hour and moment of my emancipation, for the time had come. Between half-past ten o'clock, when I entered that chapel, and half-past twelve o'clock, when I was back again at home, what a change had taken place in me! I had passed from darkness into marvelous light, from death to life. Simply by looking to Jesus, I had been delivered from despair, and I was brought into such a joyous state of mind that when they saw me at home, they said to me, 'Something wonderful has happened to you'; and I was eager to tell them all about it. Oh, that somebody had told me that before.

(The faithfulness of a poor deacon, who had walked thirteen miles to church in the snow and was called upon to bring the message, was God's instrument in spreading God's message to millions through that thirteen-year-old boy, who later became a dedicated preacher.)

TELLING THE STONES OF MY DELIVERANCE

When the Lord first pardoned my sin, I was so joyous that I could scarce refrain from dancing. I thought on my road home from the house where I had been set at liberty, that I must tell the stones in the street the story of my deliverance. So full was my soul of joy, that I wanted to tell every snow-flake that was falling from heaven of the wondrous love of Jesus, who had blotted out the sins of one of the chief of rebels.

(On the way home from that little Primitive Methodist church, mentioned above, at age 13.)

FIRE OF LIVING COAL

Give me the comforts of God and I can well bear the taunts of men. Let me lay my head on the bosom of Jesus, and I fear not the distraction of care and trouble. If my God will give me ever the light of his smile, and glance of his benediction, it is enough. Come on, foes, persecutors, fiends, aye, Apollyon himself; for "The Lord God is my sun and shield." Gather, ye clouds, and environ me, I carry a sun within; blow winds of the frozen north, I have a fire of living coal within; yea, death, slay me, but I have another life—a life in the light of God's countenance.

CAN I BE SILENT?

Doth not all nature around me praise God? If I were silent, I should be an exception to the universe. Doth not the thunder praise Him as it rolls like drums in the march of the God of armies? Do not the mountains praise Him when the woods upon their summits wave in adoration? Does not the lightning write His name in letters of fires? Hath not the whole earth a voice? And shall I, can I, be silent?

ANSWERING PRAYER

To believe that the Lord will hear my prayer is honor to His truthfulness. He has said that He will, and I believe that He will keep His word. It is honorable to His power. I believe that He can make the word of His mouth stand fast and steadfast. It is honorable to His love. The larger things I ask the more do I honor the liberality, grace and love of God in asking such great things. It is honorable to His wisdom; for if I ask what He has told me to ask, and expect Him to answer me, I believe that His word is wise, and may safely be kept....I have sought God's aid, and assistance, and help, in all my manifold undertakings, and though I cannot here tell the story of my private life in God's work, yet if it were written it would be a standing proof that there is a God that answers prayer. He has heard my prayers, not now and then, nor once nor twice, but so many times, that it has grown into a habit with me to spread my case before God with the absolute certainty that whatsoever I ask of God, He will give to me...

In all labor there is profit, but most of all in the work of intercession: I am sure of this for I have reaped it.

I HAVE LOST NOTHING

The Christian knows no change with regard to God. He may be rich today and poor tomorrow, he may be distressed; but there is no change with regard to his relationship to God. If he loved me yesterday he loves me today. I am neither better nor worse in God than I ever was. Let prospects be blighted, let hopes be blasted, let joy be withered, let mildews destroy everything. I have lost nothing of what I have in God.

(Sermons)

✍ PHILLIPS BROOKS ✍

(1835–1893)

American Episcopal pastor, and writer of essays and poems, one of which is the much beloved "O Little Town of Bethlehem". He integrated modern thought and Christianity into an optimistic, though socially and politically conservative, "American message." He had a great love for humanity, "a genius for friendship" and a great gift for inspiring people. He spent his mornings in his study and his afternoons, calling on his parishioners and the sick. He was open at any and all hours to "friends, parishioners, and seekers for advice, help, jobs or the truth, or inspiration and comfort."

AFLAME WITH POETRY

I saw God write a gorgeous poem this very morning. With the fresh sunbeam for a pencil, on the broad sheet of level snow, the diamond letters were spelled out one by one, till the whole was aflame with poetry.

THE RICHNESS AND JOY OF LIFE

The great danger facing all of us is not that we shall make an absolute failure of life, nor that we shall fall into outright viciousness, nor that we shall feel that life has no meaning at all—not these things. The danger is that we may fail to perceive life's greatest meaning, fall short of its highest good, miss its deepest and most abiding happiness, be unable to render the most needed service, be unconscious of life ablaze with the light of the Presence of God—and be content to have it so—that is the danger. That some day we may wake up and find that always we have been busy with the husks and trappings of life—and have really missed life itself. For life without God to one who has known the richness and joy of life with Him, is unthinkable, impossible. That is what one prays one's friends may be spared—satisfaction with a life that falls short of the best, that has in it no tingle and thrill which comes from a friendship with the Father.

NO CHOICE
As soon as I believed there was a God, I understood I could not do otherwise than to love Him alone.

(The Influence of Jesus, 1903)

✦ GEORGE CONGREVE ✦
(1835–1918)

Member of the Anglican Society of St. John the Evangelist.

THE NEXT STAGE OF OUR JOURNEY
I find growing old something quite new and a surprise... I feel it is a sort of undressing of the soul for the next and better stage of our journey. I am so sure of the purpose of God for us, an increasing purpose from good to better, that I determine not to notice even in my thoughts (if I can help it) the inconveniences and absurdities, mortifications that come with the years. We are not at home in them, only pushing on through them on the way home.

⚜ LYMAN ABBOTT ⚜

(1835–1922)

Henry Ward Beecher's successor as pastor of the Plymouth Congregational Church in Brooklyn, editor, and author.

WHEN I WAS EIGHTEEN

It was not until at about eighteen years of age when I came under the influence of Henry Ward Beecher's preaching that I began to understand that Jesus Christ is not a lawgiver but a lifegiver, and that one is not a Christian because he obeys the laws of God, but he obeys the laws of God because he is a Christian.

(What Christianity Means to Me,

written when he was eighty-five)

A GRADUATION

I neither know nor wish to know what the future has for me. I would not, if I could, stand at the open window and peer into the unknown beyond. I am sure that He whose mercies are new every epoch of my morning and fresh every evening, who brings into every epoch of my life a new surprise, and makes in every experience a new disclosure of His love, who sweetens gladness with gratitude, and sorrow with comfort, who gives the lark for the morning and the nightingale for the twilight, who makes every year better than the year preceding, and every new experience an experience of His marvelous skill in gift-giving, has formed some future of glad surprise which I would not forecast if I could.

❧ FRANCES RIDLEY HAVERGAL ❧

(1836–1879)

English linguist, musician, hymn writer, poet, and student of the Word of God, who at the age of twenty-two knew most of the New Testament and several books of the Old Testament by heart. Even though she suffered much from poor health, she sang in churches and hospitals and other places and sent many letters of comfort and consolation to all parts of the earth.

SUCH REST

It is such rest and peace to know that He hath ordered and appointed all, and will yet order and appoint my lot.

THAT IS HOW MY HYMNS COME TO ME.

I believe my King suggests a thought, and whispers me a musical line or two, and then I look up and thank Him delightedly and go on with it. That is how my hymns come.

❧ JOHN CLIFFORD ❧

(1836–1923)

British evangelical Baptist minister and social reformer active in the labor movement.

LOOKING BACK

Looking back upon my past, upon these sixty years spent in Christ's school, I see many lessons badly learned, many blunders, innumerable faults, yet, scientifically interpreting the whole of the past, I say, with the full assurance of understanding, that all that there is in me, and has been in me, throughout these years, of any good, is due to Jesus Christ...whatsoever of value there has been in my life is due entirely to Him, whatsoever of service I have been able to perform for my generation owes all its inspiration, all its strength, to His indwelling. All the conceptions I have formed of God, the answers I am able to give for myself as to what is religion, human duty, human destiny, all that man may hope for, I get from Him who is the Way, the Truth, and the Life.

("Looking Back," from his diary, in Anthology of Jesus)

⚹ DWIGHT L. MOODY ⚹
(1837–1899)

One of the great evangelists of all time who was converted through the influence of a Sunday school teacher. He went to a little mission Sunday school in Chicago that had twelve members. With his influence, and by the time he was twenty-three, the school soon numbered 15,000. Parents were brought in, and meetings were held almost every night in the week. He knew every boy and girl by name, visited them in their homes and knew most of their personal problems. He made several great evangelistic tours of the British Isles and America. During his lifetime he is said to have covered a million miles on preaching tours and spoken to 100 million people.

FAITH HAS BEEN GROWING EVER SINCE

I suppose that if all the times I have prayed for faith were put together, it would amount to months. I used to say, "What we want is faith; if we only have faith we can turn Chicago upside down, or rather right side up." I thought that some day faith would come down and strike me like lightning. But faith did not seem to come. One day I read in the tenth chapter of Romans, "Faith cometh by hearing, and hearing by the Word of God." I had closed my Bible and prayed for faith. I now opened my Bible and began to study, and faith has been growing ever since.

I REMEMBER THAT MORNING WELL

I remember the morning on which I came out of my room after I had first trusted Christ. I thought the old sun shone a good deal brighter than it ever had before—I thought that it was just smiling upon me; and as I walked out upon Boston Common and heard the birds singing in the trees, I thought they were all singing a song to me... Do you know, I fell in love with the birds. I had never cared for them

before. It seemed to me that I was in love with all creation. I had not
a bitter feeling against any man, and I was ready to take all men to
my heart.

(Describing the effect of his conversion upon his
life after 40 years, when preaching in Boston.)

THE SWEETEST LESSON I HAVE LEARNED

The sweetest lesson I have learned in God's school is to let the Lord
choose for me.

GOD REVEALED HIMSELF TO ME

One day in New York, oh, what a day, I cannot describe it, I seldom
refer to it, it is almost too sacred an experience to name; I can only
say God revealed Himself to me. I had such an experience of His love
that I had to ask Him to stay His hand. I went to preaching again; the
sermons were no different. I did not present any new truth, yet hundreds were converted, and I would not be placed back where I was
before that blessed experience if you would give me all Glasgow.

(From Deeper Expressions of Famous Christians, The Warner Press, 1911)

I WAS BORN OF THE SPIRIT IN 1858

Some day you will read in the papers that D. L. Moody of East North-
field, is dead. Don't you believe a word of it! At that moment I shall
be more alive than I am now; I shall have gone up higher—that is
all—out of this old clay tenement into a house that is immortal, a
body that death cannot touch, that sin cannot taint, a body fashioned like unto His glorious body....I was born of the flesh in 1837;
I was born of the Spirit in 1856. That which is born of the flesh may
die, but that which is born of the Spirit will live forever!

(His last words were: "This is my triumph; this is my coronation day! I have been looking
forward to it for years. Earth is receding; heaven is approaching; God is calling me.")

THE BEST FRIEND I EVER HAD

I have come to Him as the best friend I have ever found, and I can trust Him in that relationship. I have believed He is Savior; I have believed He is God; I have believed His atonement on the cross is mine, and I have come to Him and submitted myself on my knees, surrendered everything to Him, and gotten up and stood by His side as my friend, and there isn't any problem in my life, there isn't any uncertainty in my work, but I turn and speak to Him as naturally as to someone in the same room, and I have done it these years because I can trust Jesus.

(When asked how he managed to remain
so intimate in his relationship with Christ.)

I NEVER BEFORE REALIZED WHAT HE HAD DONE FOR ME

Oh, until I came to read all about what Christ suffered, I never before realized what he had done for us. I never knew until I came to read all about the Roman custom of scourging, what it meant by Christ being scourged for me. When I first read about that I threw myself on the floor and wept, and asked him to forgive me for not having loved him more. Let us imagine the scene where he is taken by the Roman soldiers to be scourged. The orders were to put forty stripes, one after another, upon his bared back. Sometimes it took fifteen minutes, and the man died in the process of being scourged. See him stooping while the sins of the world are laid upon him, and the whips come down upon his bare back, cutting clear through the skin and flesh to the bone. And, after they had scourged him, instead of bringing oil and pouring it into the wounds, he who came to bind up the broken heart and pour oil into its wounds—instead of doing this they dressed him up again, and someone reached out to him a crown of thorns, which was placed upon his brow.

✑ JOHN PIERPONT MORGAN ✑

(1837–1913)

American financier and philanthropist who made his fortune in railroads, steel, and financing.

MY LAST WILL AND TESTAMENT

I commit my soul into the hands of my Saviour, in full confidence that having redeemed it and washed it in his most precious blood, he will present it faultless before the throne of my heavenly father, and I entreat my children to maintain and defend at all hazard and at any cost of personal sacrifice the blessed doctrine of the complete atonement for sin through the blood of Jesus Christ, once offered, and through that alone.

✑ J. R. MILLER ✑

(1840–1912)

American devotional writer.

JESUS AND I ARE FRIENDS

To me religion means just one thing: Jesus and I are friends

SPRINGTIME IN THE AIR

I thought the winter was here;
That the earth was cold and bare;
But I feel the coming of birds,
And the springtime in the air.

GLIMPSES OF THE INFINITE SWEEP OF LIFE BEYOND

Once I went up the winding staircase of Bunker Hill monument. Its great walls shut in the view on all sides. I could see only the bit of dusty floor at my feet and the cheerless walls that surrounded me but as I climbed up the staircase there were windows here and there, and through these I looked out and caught glimpses of a very beautiful world outside,—green fields, rich gardens, picturesque landscapes, streams flashing like silver in the sunshine, the sea yonder, and far away; on the other hand, the shadowy forms of great mountains. How little, how dark and gloomy, seemed the close, narrow limits of the staircase as I looked out upon the illimitable view that stretched from the windows!

This earthly life, hemmed in as it is by its limitations and its narrows horizons, is like that tower—a little patch of dusty floor, with cheerless walls around it. But while we climb heavily and wearily up its steep, dark stairway, there lies outside the thick walls a glorious world, reaching away into eternity, filled with the rarest things of God's love. And through the windows of revelation we get glimpses of the infinite sweep and stretch of life beyond this hampered, broken, fragmentary existence of earth.

⊰ JAMES CHALMERS ⊱
(1841–1901)

English missionary to New Guinea.

I WOULD DO IT ALL AGAIN

Recall the twenty-one years, give me back all its experiences, give me its shipwrecks, give me its standing in the face of death, give me back my surroundment of savages with spears and clubs, give me back again the spears flying about me with the club knocking me to the ground—give it all back to me, and I will still be Your missionary!

❦ HENRY M. STANLEY ❧

(1841–1904)

British explorer and adventurer whose efforts led to an influx of missionaries in East Africa. His effort to find David Livingstone, whose whereabouts were unknown, resulted in his living with him for four months and being greatly influenced by him, resulting in his conversion.

I WAS CONVERTED BY LIVINGSTONE'S LIFE

I went to Africa prejudiced as the biggest atheist in London. But there came for me a long time for reflection. I saw this solitary old man there and asked myself, 'How on earth does he stop here—is he cracked, or what? What is it that inspires him? For months after we met I found myself wondering at the old man carrying out all that was said in the Bible—'Leave all things and follow Me.' But little by little his sympathy for others became contagious; my sympathy was aroused; seeing his piety, his gentleness, his zeal, his earnestness, and how he went about his business. I was converted by him, although he had not tried to do it.

IN THE SILENCE OF THE WILDS

The Bible, with its noble and simple language, I continued to read with a higher and truer understanding than I had ever before conceived. Its powerful verses had a different meaning, a more penetrating influence, in the silence of the wilds. I came to feel a strange glow while absorbed in its pages.

❧ HANDLEY C. G. MOULE ❧

(1841–1920)

Teacher, principal, and minister in the Church of England. He was converted to Christ at Christmas time, 1866. He referred to 1884 as a new departure in his life, a date when a deeper spiritual life became real to him.

INNER HARMONY

I am an instrument for His use; perhaps to bear burdens, as a pain, sorrow, or shame; perhaps to convey messages, writing, speaking, conversing; perhaps simply to reflect light, showing his mind in the commonest of all daily rounds. In only one way can I truly do anything of these; in the way of inner harmony with Him, and peace and joy in Him....This Jesus Christ has, somehow, touched, and changed, and set free my soul, my being. He, and only He—His Name, His Person—has had a power over me which is like nothing else.

(Jesus and the Resurrection, *Seely*, 1905)

❧ SIDNEY LANIER ❧

(1842–1881)

Beloved American poet who had a lifelong struggle with ill health, a lack of financial means, and a continual misunderstanding on the part of the public and even of his friends. Yet he learned obedience by the things which he suffered. These words reveal a sublime faith in God.

I WILL BUILD MY A NEST ON THE GREATNESS OF GOD
As the marsh-hen secretly builds on the watery sod,
Behold I will build me a nest on the greatness of God;
I will fly in the greatness of God as the marsh-hen flies
In the freedom that fills all the space 'twixt the marsh and the skies.

(From "The Marshes of Glynn")

ᴊᴏʜɴ Fɪꜱᴋᴇ

(1842–1901)

American philosopher and historian.

ᴛʜᴇ ꜰɪᴛ ᴄʟɪᴍᴀx ᴛᴏ ᴀ ʙᴇᴀᴜᴛɪꜰᴜʟ ᴄʀᴇᴀᴛɪᴠᴇ ᴡᴏʀᴋ
For my own part I believe in the immortality of the soul, not in the sense that I accept the demonstrable truths of science, but in the supreme act of faith in the reasonableness of God's work. Such a crown of wonder seems to me no more than the fit climax to a creative work that has been ineffably beautiful and marvelous in all its myriad stages.

Hᴇɪɴʀɪᴄʜ Hᴏꜰᴍᴀɴɴ

(1842–1902)

Musician, artist, and painter of the likeness of Christ.

ꜰʀᴏᴍ ᴛʜᴇ ᴠᴀʟʟᴇʏ ᴛᴏ ᴛʜᴇ ʙʀᴏᴀᴅ ᴛᴀʙʟᴇʟᴀɴᴅ
When I read again the story of his life and contemplate his teachings it is as though I were lifted from the valley to the broad tableland, and from thence to successive mountain heights, until I stand at last upon the highest peak above the clouds, where all is clear and radiant with sunlight; and it has been during these mountaintop experiences that I have seemed to behold his face and have attempted to paint his likeness.

Gᴇᴏʀɢᴇ Mᴀᴛʜᴇꜱᴏɴ

(1842–1906)

Scottish clergyman and poet who was blind.

ꜱᴇᴛ ꜰʀᴇᴇ ᴛʜʀᴏᴜɢʜ ꜱᴜꜰꜰᴇʀɪɴɢ
This is one of the grandest testimonies ever given by man to the moral government of God. It is not a man's thanksgiving that he has

been set free from suffering. It is a thanksgiving that he has been set free through suffering: "Thou has enlarged me when I was in distress." He declares the sorrows of life to have been themselves the source of life's enlargement. And have not you and I a thousand times felt this to be true?

(My Aspirations)

I NEVER THOUGHT TO THANK THEE FOR MY THORN

My God, I have never thanked Thee for my thorn. I have thanked Thee a thousand times for my roses, but not once for my thorn. I have been looking forward to a world where I shall get compensation for my cross, but I have never thought of my cross as itself a present glory.

(Talking about his blindness.)

A LIGHT WITHIN MY SOUL

There are patterns hung up in my heart to which I can find nothing outside that answers. The light within my soul is a light that never shone on sea or land. All attempts to copy it are vain. There are spots in every sunbeam, there are thorns in every rose, there are crosses in every life. I have never seen the perfect landscape, I have never beheld the cloudless day. I have never looked upon the faultless human soul. Never till I found Thee.

(From Voices of the Spirit, *J. Nisbit, 1988)*

⊰ SAMUEL H. HADLY ⊱
(1842–1906)

American worker with the Water Street Mission who preached and found homes for the outcast.

IT HAPPENED ONE TUESDAY

One Tuesday I was sitting in Harlem, a homeless, friendless, dying drunkard. I had pawned or sold everything that would bring a drink. I had not eaten for days, and for four nights I had suffered with delirium tremors from midnight till morning. I had often said, 'I will never be a tramp. I well never be cornered. When the time comes, I will find a home in the bottom of the river.' But when the time did come, I was not able to walk a quarter of the way there.

Along toward evening it came into my head to go to the Jerry McAuley Mission. The place was packed, and it was with difficulty that I made my way to the space near the platform. McAuley arose and told his experience. I found myself saying, 'I wonder if God can save me?' Then I listened to the testimony of twenty or thirty others, everyone of them saved from rum. I made up my mind that I would be saved too, or die right there. When the invitation was given I knelt down with a crowd of drunkards. What a conflict was going on for my poor soul! Something within me said, 'Come.' Something else said, 'Be careful.' I hesitated for a moment, and then with a raking heart I cried, 'Dear God, can you save me?' Never can I describe what happened.

Up to that moment I had been filled with utter darkness. Now the brightness of noonday seemed to stream around me. I was a free man again.

THE ONLY THING I KNOW NOW

When I was a young man I knew everything; when I got to be thirty-five years of age, in my ministry I had only a hundred doctrines of religion; when I got to be forty years of age I had only fifty doctrines of religion; when I got to be sixty years of age I had only ten doctrines of religion; and now I am dying at seventy-five years of age, and there is only one thing I know, and that is, that Christ Jesus came into the world to save sinners.

≈ ISABELLA GILMORE ≈

(1842–1923)

Reformer of the Anglican Deaconess Order.

A TRUMPET CALL

I went to church service alone, and to the 11 o'clock with the children. The preacher was a stranger; he gave out his text, 'God worked for me today in my vineyard.' To me it was a trumpet call; I never heard any of the sermon. I could hardly keep from off my knees until it was finished; it was just as if God's voice had called me, and the intense rest and joy were beyond words.

⚜ WILLIAM MCKINLEY ⚜
(1843–1901)

Twenty-fifth President of the United States and an ardent Christian. During one of his campaigns he was followed around by a reporter who continually misrepresented him. During a rainy night the reporter was riding with the driver in the exposed seat. McKinley, in genuine kindness, offered him his coat and put him in the carriage. His dying words were, "It is God's way. His will be done."

THE MIGHTIEST FACTOR

My belief embraces the divinity of Christ and a recognition of Christianity as the mightiest factor in the world's civilization.

⚜ NEWMAN SMYTH ⚜
(1843–1902)

American writer.

A ROSE GROWING IN THE DESERT

When I can see a rose growing in the desert, and forming its depths of pure color out of the yellow grains of sand, when I can see a wheat-field ripening in the furrows of the salt waves; when I can believe that the villagers among the hills of New Hampshire, with their wagons and pickaxes, gathered the stones and heaped up the massive peak of Mt. Washington; then, but not till then, can I believe that the thoughts of the disciples invented the deeds and the glory of Jesus the Christ—whose beatitudes shed the fragrance of a new spirit over the wastes of Pharisaism; whose fruitful life, in the midst of sin and raging passion, grew in grace and favor with God and man; the Christ whose glorious majesty, still unequaled and inimitable, looks down upon our low estate, and proclaims itself to be the mighty work of God.

(The Religious Feeling)

⚜ ALBERT BENJAMIN SIMPSON ⚜
(1843–1919)

Gifted Presbyterian pastor who, with a simple faith, resigned to embark upon an independent ministry among the poor—The Christian and Missionary Alliance. Hundreds of missions-oriented groups of Christians from various Protestant denominations support hundreds of missionaries and their spiritual and social ministries.

AN OLD MUSTY BOOK OPENED MY EYES

My whole religious training had left me without any conception of the sweet and simple gospel of Jesus Christ....There was no voice to tell me that simple way of believing in the promise and accepting the salvation fully provided and freely offered. My life seemed to hang upon a thread, for I had the hope that God would spare me long enough to find salvation.... One day in the library of my old minister and teacher, I stumbled upon an old musty volume called *Marshall's Gospel Mystery of Sanctification.* As I turned the pages, my eyes fell upon a sentence which opened for me the gates of life eternal. It is this in substance: 'The first good work you will ever perform is to believe on the Lord Jesus Christ. Until you do this, all your works, prayers, tears, and good resolutions are in vain.'...

To my poor bewildered soul this was like the light from heaven that fell upon Saul of Tarsus on his way to Damascus. I immediately fell upon my knees, and looking up to the Lord, I said, "Lord Jesus, You have said, 'Him that comes to me I will in no wise cast out.' You know how long and earnestly I have tried to come, but I did not know how. Now I come the best I can, and I dare to believe that You do receive me and save me, and that I am now Your child, forgiven and saved simply because I have taken You at Your word."

The months that followed my conversion were full of spiritual blessing. The promises of God burst upon my soul with a new and marvelous light, and words that had been empty before became divine revelations and seemed especially meant for me.

(A. E. Thompson, The Life of A. B. Simpson
Harrisburg, Pa; The Christian Alliance Publishing Co., 1920)

⚐ RUSSELL H. CONWELL ⚐
(1843–1925)

Baptist preacher for forty-three years, who is most well-known for *Acres of Diamonds,* a text which he delivered more than 6,000 times throughout America. He was the author of forty books and many hymns and founded Temple University.

A SILENT WITNESS BROUGHT ME TO CHRIST

The faithful and silent witnessing of John Ring saved me from a life of folly to a life of faith in Christ. He was my orderly during the Civil War. On his first night in my tent he read the Bible and knelt and prayed. I was an agnostic and ridiculed him. Thereafter he went outside to read his Bible and pray. One day he was mortally wounded. Twas then I surrendered myself to Jesus Christ.

⚐ JOSEPH ESTLIN CARPENTER ⚐
(1843–1927)

British theologian.

GOD HAD FOUND ME

I went out one afternoon for a walk alone. I was in the empty unthinking state in which one saunters along country lanes, simply yielding oneself to the casual sights around which give a town-bred lad with country yearning such intense delight. Suddenly I became conscious of the presence of someone else. I cannot describe it, but I felt that I had as direct perception of the being of God all around me as I have of you when we are together. It was no longer a matter of inference, it was an immediate act of spiritual apprehension. It came unsought, absolutely unexpectedly. I remember the wonderful transfiguration of the far-off woods and hills as they seemed to blend in the infinite being with which I was thus brought into relation. This experience did not last long. But it sufficed to change all my feeling. I had not found God because I had never looked for him. But he had found me.

✑ HENRY J. HEINZ ✑
(1845–1919)

American businessman who, with his brother and cousin, founded the firm F & J Heinz to make and sell pickles and other prepared food in 1876.

THE BEGINNING OF MY WILL

Looking forward to the time when my earthly career will end, I desire to set forth at the very beginning of this will, as the most important item in it, a confession of my faith in Jesus Christ as my Saviour. I also desire to bear witness to the fact that throughout my life, in which were the usual joys and sorrows, I have been wonderfully sustained by my faith in God through Jesus Christ. This legacy was left me by my consecrated mother, a woman of strong faith, and to it I attribute any success I have attained.

✒ JAMES HANNINGTON ✒

(1847–1885)

English missionary to Africa and bishop. His small diary, written with tiny handwriting, is among the most moving missionary documents ever written.

UNDER THE SHADOW OF HIS WINGS

(A friend's letter) led to my conversion. I sprang out of bed and leaped about the room, rejoicing and praising God that Jesus died for me. From that day to this I have lived under the shadow of His wings.

✒ FREDERICK B. MEYER ✒

(1847–1929)

English Baptist preacher for more than sixty years and author of over seventy books in English, twenty in Swedish and many pamphlets, translated into many languages. He was converted at age six. His theme was, "If we link ourselves to the eternal power of God, nothing will be impossible to us." He called himself, "Just God's errand boy."

THE ANSWER TO MY QUESTIONINGS

From an early age I had desired to become a minister of Christ's Gospel, but was perpetually haunted by a fear that I should not be able to speak. At sixteen, the secret locked in my breast, I had been pleading with tears that God would show me His will, and especially that He would give me some assurance as to my powers of speech. Again that room at Streatham, near London, to which we had moved, is before me, with its window toward the sun, and the leather-covered chair at which I kneeled. Turning to my Bible, it fell open at this passage, which I had never seen before: "But the Lord said unto me, Say not, I am a child: for thou shalt go to all that I shall send thee, and whatsoever I command thee, thou shalt speak" (Jer. 1:7). With indescribable feelings I read it again and again, and even now never come on it without a thrill of emotion. It was the answer to all my perplexed questionings. Yes, I was the child; I was to go to those to whom He would send me; and He would be with me, and send me, and He would be with me, and touch my lips.

ON MY SEVENTIETH BIRTHDAY

I knew Him as a boy. I trusted Him because of the testimony of my parents and my minister. Since then I have wintered and summered with Him, and spent days and nights with Him. I know what He can be when a man sins and fails, and when the heart is hard and loveless. I know Him whom once I simply believed, and on my seventieth birthday this is my assurance—that He is able to keep that which I have committed to him.

WE SHALL MEET IN THE MORNING

I have just heard to my surprise, that I have only a few days to live. It may be before this reaches you, I shall have entered the palace. Don't trouble yourself to write. We shall meet in the morning. With much love, Yours Affectionately.

(In his 80s, writing to a friend)

THOMAS A. EDISON
(1847–1931)

American inventor.

I AM CONVINCED

I tell you no person can be brought into close contact with the mysteries of nature, or make a study of chemistry, without being convinced that, behind all, there is a supreme Intelligence.

⊰ SIR WILLIAM OSLER ⊱
(1848–1919)

Canadian physician.

BEGINNING EACH DAY IN HIS PRESENCE

I begin each day with Christ and his prayer. At night as I lay off my clothes, I undress my soul, too, and lay aside its sin. In the presence of God I lie down to rest and to waken free and with a new life.

⊰ ROBERT LOUIS STEVENSON ⊱
(1850–1894)

Scottish poet and novelist. He believed that "No man can achieve success in life until he writes in the journal of his life the words, 'Enter God.'"

GOD AND I

The stars shall last for a million years,
a million years and a day,
But God and I will live and love
when the stars have passed away.

⊰ HENRY DRUMMOND ⊱
(1851–1897)

Scottish writer, theologian and student of Dwight L. Moody. He was converted at age nine.

THE MOMENTS THAT STAND OUT

I have seen almost all the beautiful things God has made; I have enjoyed almost every pleasure that He has planned for me; and yet as I look back I see standing out above all the life that has gone, four or five short experiences when the love of God reflected itself in some poor imitation, some small act of love of mine, and these seem to be the things which alone of all one's life abide. Everything else in all our lives is transitory. Every other good is visionary. But the acts of love which no man knows about, or can ever know about—they never fail.

(The Greatest Thing in the World)

LIFTED THROUGH FAITH

I believe in miracles because I see them every day in the changed lives of men and of women who are saved and lifted through faith in the power of the loving Christ.

(The Greatest Thing in the World)

⚜ FORBES ROBINSON ⚜

(1867–1904)

English university Anglican chaplain and theological lecturer.

THE NEXT PIECE OF ROAD

I delight in the feeling that I am in eternity, that I can serve God now fully and effectively, that the next piece of road will come in sight when I am ready to walk in it.

(Letters to His Friends)

OTHER WRITERS OF THE LAST HALF ⚜ OF THE 19TH CENTURY ⚜

THE SWEET AND THE BITTER

If there are hindrances in the way to-day, if I stumble and fall, if the heart grows weary and the feet move with faint and longing tread, possessed by the invincible determination that I am here to do the will of God, that He is guiding me through life's sweet and through its bitter, I can lean upon that strong arm, I can drink from the fountain of peace that flows from the heart divine.

(F. E. Marsten)

THE BEST TRANSLATION

I like my mother's translation of the Bible the best. She translated it into life and it was the most convincing translation I ever saw.

(Author Unknown, when asked what translation of the Bible he liked best.)

HOW I FOUND GOD

When I was a boy of 14 years of age, in the old church at the North End, I heard Lyman Beecher preach on the theme, "You belong to God." I went home after that service, threw myself on the floor in my room with locked doors, and prayed: "O God, I belong to thee. Take what is thine own. I ask this, that whenever a thing is wrong, it may have no power of temptation over me, and whenever a thing is right, it may take no courage to do it."

(Wendell Phillips, 1811–1884, when asked how he found God.
"That very day I accepted my mission.")

NO LONGER A DUTY

The time when I was converted was when religion became no longer a mere duty, but a pleasure.
(John L. Lincoln, 1817–1891, American author)

I WAS SEEKING WHERE HE COULD NOT BE FOUND

I searched for it in the poetic nights of glorious climate, in the clear waters of the Swiss lakes, in the most magnificent scenery. I have also sought it in fashionable drawing rooms, in splendid dinners, balls, and festivities. I have been looking for it in riches, in the excitement of gambling, in romance, in an adventurous life and in the satisfaction of an unmeasured ambition. I have sought happiness in artistic fame and in all the pleasures of the senses and the mind. Indeed, where, O my God, did I not seek it, this happiness, the dream of all human hearts?

What is this happiness? God alone can satisfy the longing of the human heart. And God has descended into the world in the Person of His Son Jesus Christ; He has become the companion of our pilgrimage, the Bread of our souls. But, someone may say, I do not believe in Jesus Christ. I can only answer: nor did I. And for this reason I was unhappy.... Let us love Jesus. There is only one happiness, to love Jesus and to be loved by him.

(Herman Cohen, 1821–1871)

THE GREAT GARDENER

I stood there in a lovely garden one night.—
And marveled at the enchanting sight!
When lo! There in the Cathedral-like hush
I heard the swish of a painter's brush.
I saw the flowers and the trees in prayer.
And knew the Great Gardener was working there!

(Frances Angermayer)

I AM FILLED WITH AWE

Each day I am filled with awe at the magnificent beauty of God: a sunrise, a sunset, a season's change, a breeze, a stream—and yet of what worth am I that I should be given these gifts from him?

(Herbert Shipman, 1869–1930)

THOUGHTS UPON REACHIHG THE AGE OF EIGHTY-TWO

Though youth and beauty have departed, the well springs of love and imagination are, in my nature, too deep to be touched by the frost of age. Nourished by the dews of the heart and the intellect, they will grow sweeter and deeper and more refreshing to the end of my life; for the things of the soul and the heart are eternal.

(Amelia Barr, 1831–1919)

ONE MOMENTARY GLIMPSE

The supreme moment itself, may prove a revelation to our souls of the Highest and bring us into the very presence of the Infinite Love and Tenderness. For myself I cannot doubt that this was my own experience. To speak of it is to profane it. I am unworthy to so much as hint at it. But it has been the comfort of my life ever since.

Alas, for the years that have followed! One momentary glimpse into the ineffable brightness, followed by gathering clouds and darkness, painful stumblings and wide errors, unsupported by any

recognizable spiritual aid or presence, the heavens, deaf and careless to my most earnest prayers and agonizings, nay, even slighting
them, so far as appeared. But through it all, like the steadfast shining
of a clear star, the memory of that sacred time has remained deep
in my heart, and I have never really doubted for a moment that an
Infinite Wisdom and Love does encircle all our lives—tender, pity-
ing and sympathizing. We may pass our lives without ever realizing
it, doubting it, flatly denying it, but it is there; and he to whom the
vision has ever come at all, though in the briefest transient flash of
momentary consciousness, can never again forget it, though his
whole after path may be enveloped in darkness and he himself may
fall into gross error and backsliding.

(*Author Unknown, brought up in the church with family worship and a mother whose spirituality influenced him deeply, reported in Richard M. Bucke's* Cosmic Cosnsciousness, *1901*)

SUCH AS I HAD NEVER SEEN BEFORE

I suddenly felt the love of God wrap me about as though a visible
presence enfolded me and a joy filled me such as I had never known
before.
(*John Wilhelm Rowntree, 1868–1905, after being told he was going blind.*)

IN A MOMENT'S TIME

Suddenly there flashed upon my mind, like a light from heaven, this
Scripture. 'Come unto me, all ye that labor and are heavy laden, and I
will give you rest.' I seemed to see Jesus standing before me, looking
reproachfully and tenderly and pleadingly, seeming to rebuke me for
having gone to all other sources for rest but the right one, and now
inviting me to come to Him. In a moment I went, once and forever,
casting myself unreservedly and for all time at Christ's feet, and in
a moment the rest came, indescribably and unspeakably, and it has
remained from that day until now, brighter than the sunlight and
sweeter than the songs of birds. Now, for the first time, I understood
the Scripture which I had often heard.

(*B. H. Carroll, infidel turned Bible teacher and scholar, who was converted after he
returned home wounded from the Civil War. Taken from a book of his messages, 1898*)

MY CONVERSION TOOK PLACE QUIETLY

I had just turned into my twentieth year. Hundreds of miles from home, I was a stranger in a strange city. I had taken a good position in a clothing store and started in to make my way in the world. I was stricken with typhoid fever and taken to a hospital where I lay for nine weeks.

One Sabbath afternoon, discouraged beyond description, I lay homesick and ready to give up the fight, as the doctors had held out little hope. A young man approached my bed and spoke. He opened his Bible and read to me from various Scriptures. At last he turned to the 121st Psalm and read it. It struck home to my heart in all its graciousness; hope revived. That night the doctor noted a change. My conversion took place quietly: the way opened to the ministry. The Scripture has always been precious to me.

(David T. Robertson, b. 1875, speaking as he lay dying of typhoid fever)

✑ CLOSING THOUGHT ✒

Men come into the kingdom in as many ways as plants come to flower. Some come right up out of the earth to blossom, some come up and grow the whole summer, and then blossom; some grow a year; some grow up like trees, and do not bloom until they are three or six years old; some put the leaves out first; some put the blossoms first and the leaves afterward. There is every possible flourescence.

(H. W. Beecher)

PART VII

Glimpses from 1900–1950
A Time of Two World Wars and Increasing Complexities of Life

In the early 1900s missions and the Sunday school movement reached new peaks. The social gospel movement grew to counter the social ills caused by rapid industrialization and urbanization. There was continued social concern and movement towards reunification. By the beginning of World War I there was a decline in religious fervor and awareness. In the late 40's and early 50's church attendance reached an all time high in the United States. World War II, the atom bomb and fear of total destruction, and the growth of atheistic communism seemed to accelerate religious awareness in the United States.

If anyone would come after me, he must deny himself and take up his cross and follow me, for whoever wants to save his life will lose it, but whoever loses his life for me will find it. What good will it be for a man if he gains the whole world, yet forfeits his soul.
MATTHEW 1:24, 25

✍ SIR OLIVER LODGE ✎

(1851–1940)

English physicist.

THE GREATEST LESSON

The greatest lesson life has taught me is the reality of the spiritual world.

✍ HENRY VAN DYKE ✎

(1852–1933)

American Presbyterian minister and poet.

IT IS LIFE

Heaven is like the woman sinner from the streets who bathed the feet of Jesus in her tears, and wiped them with her hair. I do not want to know more than that. It is peace, joy, victory, triumph—it is life. It is love; it is tireless work—faithful and unselfish service going on forever.

✍ EDWIN MARKHAM ✎

(1852–1940)

American poet. When asked which of his poems he valued the highest, he answered, "How can you choose between your own children?" He did say that his four lines called, "Outwitted" might have lasting qualities because love lasts. "He drew a circle that shut me out/ Heretic, rebel, a thing to flout./ But Love and I had the wit to win:/ We drew a circle that took him in!"

LIFE ITSELF IS INCREDIBLE

That we should survive death is not to me incredible. The thing that is incredible is life itself.

Why should there be any life at all? Why should this world of stars have ever come into existence? Why should you be here and

why I here? Why should we be here in this sun-illumined universe?
Why should there be green beneath our feet: How did all this happen?

This wonder that we know this is the incredible thing. What
power projected it all into existence? This challenges my faith,
excites my astonishment, lifts me to the ineffable.

Some power has called us here out of the unknown. We did not
come here of our own wills. Some Higher Power has evolved it all.
And the Power that has caused this revelation of wonder and mystery
can easily have prepared for us another surprise beyond the shadows
of death. I believe that this stupendous Power we call God has created a world beyond this world, a world of spirit for the spirit of man.

THE PLACE OF PEACE
At the heart of the cyclone tearing the sky
And flinging the clouds and the towers by,
Is a place of central calm:
So here is the roar of mortal things.
I have a place where my spirit sings,
In the hollow of God's palm

⊰ JOHN TREVOR ⊱
(1855-1930)

**Writer who had many spiritual experiences, including this one during his
walk one Sunday morning with his wife and children on the way to chapel.**

GOD IS HERE
The spiritual life justifies itself to those who live it; but what can
we say to those who do not understand? This, at least, we can say,
that it is a life whose experiences are proved real to their possessor,
because they remain with him when brought closest into contact
with the objective realities of life. Dreams cannot stand this test. We
wake from them to find that they are but dreams. Wanderings of an
overwrought brain do not stand this test. These highest experiences
that I have had of God's presence have been rare and brief—flashes

of consciousness which have compelled me to exclaim with surprise—God is here—or conditions of exaltation and insight, less
intense, and only gradually passing away. I have severely questioned
the worth of these moments. To no soul have I named them, lest I
should be building my life and work on mere phantasies of the brain.
But I find that after questioning and test, they stand out to-day as
the most real experiences of my life, and experiences which have
explained and justified and unified all past experiences and all past
growth. Indeed, their reality and their far-reaching significance are
ever becoming more clear and evident. When they came, I was living the fullest strongest, sanest, deepest life. I was not seeking them.
What I was seeking, with resolute determination, was to live more
intensely my own life, as against what I knew would be the adverse
judgment of the world. It was in the most real seasons that the Real
Presence came, and I was aware that I was immersed in the infinite
ocean of God.

(My Quest for God)

ஜை CHARLES M. SHELDON ൪ை
(1857–1946)

**American novelist. His 1896 novel, *In His Steps,* a moving story of how
a congregation awakened by taking seriously the question, "What would
Jesus do?", sold millions of copies.**

THE BEGINNING AND END OF ALL ARGUMENT

I believe in immortality because Jesus taught it and believed it. This
is all the proof I need. That is the basis of my knowledge and the
beginning and end of all argument.

⚜ CHARLES DE FOUCAULD ⚜

(1858–1916)

French explorer known as "the hermit of the Sahara."

NO OTHER CHOICE

The moment I realized that God existed, I knew that I could not do otherwise than to love Him alone... Faith strips the mask from the world and reveals God in everything. It makes nothing impossible and renders meaningless such words as anxiety, danger, and fear, so that the believer goes through life calmly and peacefully, with profound joy—like a child hand in hand with his mother.

⚜ THEODORE ROOSEVELT ⚜

(1858–1919)

Twenty-sixth President of the U. S. (1901–1909) who won the Nobel Peace Prize for mediating the Russo-Japanese War.

HOLY, HOLY, HOLY, LORD GOD ALMIGHTY

After a week of perplexing problems and heated contests, it does so rest my soul to come into the house of the Lord and worship, and to sing, and mean it, "Holy, Holy, Holy, Lord God Almighty," and to know that He is my Father and takes me up into His life and plans, and to commune personally with Christ. I am sure I get a wisdom not my own, and a superhuman strength for fighting the moral evils I am called to confront.

MICHAEL PUPIN

(1858–1935)

American teacher of mathematical physics, physicist, and inventor who came to this country as an orphan farm lad from Serbia with only five cents to his name. Wishing to prevent his becoming a public charge, the immigration examiners asked him if he knew any people in this country. "Oh, yes," he answered, "Benjamin Franklin, Abraham Lincoln, Harriet Beecher Stowe." Unusual as it was, they decided to admit him for they were convinced that anybody with such friends was sure to get on in the world.

MESSAGES TO THE SOUL

Fifty years ago, instructed by David's psalms, I found in the light of the stars a heavenly language which proclaims the glory of God, but I did not know how that language reached me, and I hoped that some day I might find out. That hope was in my soul when I landed at Castle Garden. Today science tells me that the stars themselves bring it to me. Each burning star is a focus of energy, of life-giving activity, which it pours out lavishly into every direction of the energy-hungry space; it pours out the life of its own heart, in order to beget new life. Oh, what a beautiful vista that opens to our imagination, and what new beauties are disclosed by science in the meaning of the words in Genesis: "He breathed into his nostrils the breath of life, and man became a living soul." The light of the stars is a part of the life-giving breath of God. I never look now upon the starlit vault of the heaven without feeling this divine breath and its quickening action.

(From Immigrant to Inventor)

⨎ WILLIAM JENNINGS BRYAN ⨍

(1860-1925)

Crusader, public servant, member of Congress who had devoted, godly Christian parents. Bryan was an eloquent Christian spokesman who combined conservative evangelicalism with progressive politics. He became famous for being the lawyer who took the creationist position in the famous Scopes Monkey Trial.

THE MOST IMPORTANT DAY OF MY LIFE

At the age of fourteen I reached one of the turning points in my life. I attended a revival that was being conducted in a Presbyterian church and was converted. I look back at that day as the most important in my life. It has had far more to do with my life than any other day, and the book to which I swore allegiance on that day has been more to me than any party platform."

(Bryan fought for many platforms in national conventions.)

THE MYSTERY OF GOD

I have observed the power of the watermelon seed. It has the power of drawing from the ground and through itself 200,000 times its weight. When you can tell me how it takes this material and out of it colors an outside surface beyond the imitation of art, and then forms inside of it a white rind and within that again a red heart, thickly inlaid with black seeds, each one of which in turn is capable of drawing through itself 200,000 times its weight—when you can explain to me the mystery of a watermelon, you can ask me to explain the mystery of God.

LIKE A ROYAL GUEST

If the Father deigns to touch with divine power the cold and pulseless heart of the buried acorn and to make it burst from its prison walls, will He leave neglected in the earth the...man made in the image of his Creator? If matter, mute and inanimate, though changed by the forces of nature into a multitude of forms can never die, will the spirit of man suffer annihilation when it has paid a brief visit like a royal guest to this tenement of clay? No, I am as sure that there is another life as I am that I live today!

⚜ WILLIAM A. QUAYLE ⚜

(1860–1925)

American Methodist Episcopal clergyman and bishop.

CHANGING WINTER INTO SPRING

Christ is come and has changed my Winter into laughing Spring. I am less December now than June. My flowers are children's smiling faces and my birds' singing is the Christmas laughter of such hearts as have heard that in Bethlehem a child is born and the angels sing and I, December of the frozen heart, have caught the angels' tune. "Praise! Praise!"

LIFE IS GOOD

All's well with my soul, if not with my body. It is beautiful to have God and the Church and Christian friends and a loving home. Life is good all the way through, and I think the crossing to Life Eternal will be good.

(Writing to a friend from his sick bed.)

⚜ SAMUEL CHADWICK ⚜

(1860–1932)

English Wesleyan Methodist clergyman.

IT WAS AS WHEN JESUS STEPPED INTO THE BOAT

There came into my soul a deep peace, a thrilling joy and a new sense of power. My mind was quickened. Every power was alert. Either illumination took the place of logic, or reason became intuitive. My bodily powers also were quickened. There was a new sense of spring and vitality, a new power of endurance, and a strong man's exhilaration in big things. Things began to happen. What we had failed to do by strenuous endeavor came to pass without labor. It was as when the Lord Jesus stepped into the boat that they with all their rowing had made no progress, immediately the ship was at the land whither they went. It was gloriously wonderful.

⊰ SAMUEL LOGAN BRENGLE ⊱
(1860–1936)

Author, counselor, teacher and Methodist preacher who served with the Salvation Army for 46 years. He lived the life of a devoted servant of Christ, "going about doing good."

WHEN INTRODUCED AS "THE GREAT DR. BRENGLE"

If I appear great in their eyes, the Lord is most graciously helping me to see how absolutely nothing I am without Him, and helping me to keep little in my own eyes. He does use me. But I am so concerned that He uses me and that it is not of me the work is done. The axe cannot boast of the trees it has cut down. It could do nothing but for the woodsman. He made it, he sharpened it, and he used it. The moment he throws it aside, it becomes only old iron. O that I may never lose sight of this.

(Writing in his diary after being introduced as "the great Dr. Brengle.")

⨳ RODNEY (GIPSY) SMITH ⨲
(1860–1947)

Independent evangelist, whose mother died when he was a young boy. He remembered her last words, "I have a Father in the promised land; my God calls me, I must go to meet him…" After visiting John Bunyan's house in Bedford, he said, "I stood and wept and longed to find the same Jesus that made Bunyan what he was."

BY THE GRACE OF GOD

I remember one evening sitting on the trunk of an old tree not far from my father's tent and wagon. Around the fallen trunk grass had grown about as tall as myself. I had gone there to think and, because I was under the deepest conviction, had an earnest longing to love the Savior and to be a good lad. I thought of my mother in Heaven, and I thought of the beautiful life my father, brother, and sisters were living, and said to myself, "Rodney, are you going to wander about as a gypsy boy and a gypsy man without hope, or will you be a Christian and have some definite object to live for?" Everything was still, and I could almost hear the beating of my heart. For an answer to my question, I found myself startling myself by my own voice; "By the grace of God, I will be a Christian and I will meet my mother in Heaven!" My decision was made. I believe I was as much accepted by the Lord Jesus that day as I am now, for with all my heart I had decided to live for Him. My choice was made forever.

MY GREAT DESIRE IS TO LIVE FOR CHRIST

I am only a gypsy boy. I do not know what you know about many things, but I know Jesus. I know that He has saved me. I cannot read as you do; I do not live in a house as you do; I live in a tent. But I have got a great house up yonder, and some day I am going to live in it. My great desire is to live for Christ.

(He went forward at age 16 in a Methodist church and someone whispered, "Oh, it's only a gypsy boy." William Booth later recognized him at one of his meetings and asked him to sing a solo. He did and after the solo he spoke the above words. He then set about teaching himself to read from the Bible and began preaching. Thus began 70 years of evangelistic work.)

≈ WILLIAM R. INGE ≈

(1860–1954)

English clergyman, scholar, and writer.

THE CANDLE IS STILL LIT

I have no fear that the candle lighted in Palestine years ago will ever be put out.

≈ WALTER RAUSCHENBUSCH ≈

(1861–1918)

Pastor of a little German-speaking Baptist church on the edge of Hells's Kitchen in New York, where he worked for eleven years with those who were "out of work, out of clothes, out of shoes, and out of hope." Here he received the social passion that stayed with him all his life. He was a seminary professor from 1897 to his death. He believed that the alliance between the mainline churches and the business interests of the middle class had cut the heart from the gospel. Deeply pious, he insisted that the gravest danger facing the church was complacency.

THE LITTLE GATE TO GOD

In the castle of my soul there is a little postern gate
Where, when I enter, I am in the presence of God.
In a moment, in a turning of a thought, I am where God is.
When I meet God there all life gains a new meaning,
Lowly and despised things are shot through with glory.
My troubles seem but the pebbles on the road,
My joys seem like the everlasting hills,
All my fear is gone in the great peace of God.
So it is when I step through the gate of prayer.

(From "The Postern Gate")

✒ RABINDRANATH TAGORE ✒
(1861–1941)

Indian Christian philosopher, poet, and writer.

HIDDEN HONEY

When I go from hence let this be my parting word, that what I have seen is unsurpassable.

I have tasted of the hidden honey of this lotus that expands on the ocean of light, and thus am I blessed—let this be my parting word.

In this playhouse of infinite forms I have had my play and here have I caught sight of him that is formless.

My whole body and my limbs have thrilled with his touch who is beyond touch; and if the end comes here, let it come—let this be my parting word.

(Gitanjali)

HE COMES, COMES, EVER COMES

Have you not heard his silent steps?

He comes, comes, ever comes.

Every moment and every age, every day and every night he comes, comes, ever comes.

Many a song have I sung in many a mood of mind, but their notes have always proclaimed, "He comes, comes, ever comes."

In the fragrant days of sunny April through the forest path he comes, comes, ever comes.

In the rainy gloom of July nights, on the thundering chariot of clouds he comes, comes, ever comes.

In sorrow after sorrow it is his steps that press upon my heart, and it is the golden touch of his feet that makes my joy to shine.

(Gitanjali)

◈ WALTER B. HINSON ◈

(1862–1926)

Baptist minister and author, born in England. He later had ministries in Canada and the U. S.

GOD'S OWN POETRY TO MY SOUL

I remember a year ago when a man in this city said, "You have got to go to your death." I walked out to where I live, five miles out of this city, and I looked across at that mountain that I love, and I looked at the river in which I rejoice, and I looked at the stately trees that are always God's own poetry to my soul. Then in the evening I looked up into the great sky where God was lighting his lamps, and I said, "I may not see you many more times, but, Mountain, I shall be alive when you are gone; and River, I shall be alive when you cease running toward the sea; and, Stars, I shall be alive when you have fallen from your sockets in the great down-pulling of the material universe!"

(Speaking from the pulpit a year after the beginning
of an illness from which he ultimately died)

William (Billy) Sunday

(1862–1935)

A powerful, impassioned, colorful evangelist. Having been a famous baseball player, great crowds, estimated at over 100,000,000, thronged to hear him after his conversion.

I never go by that street without thanking God

Twenty-nine years ago I walked down a street in Chicago in company with some ball players who were famous in this world, and we went into a saloon. It was Sunday afternoon and we got tanked up and then sat down on a corner. I never go by that street without thanking God for saving me. It was a vacant lot at that time.

We sat down on a curbing. Across the street a company of men and women were playing on instruments—horns, flutes, and slide trombones—and the others were singing the gospel hymns that I used to hear my mother sing back in the old church, where I used to go to Sunday school.

And God painted on the canvas of my recollection and memory a vivid picture of the scenes of other days and other faces. Many have long since turned to dust. I sobbed and sobbed, and a young man stepped out and said, "We are going to the Pacific Garden Mission; won't you come down to the mission? I am sure you will enjoy it. You can hear drunkards tell how they have been saved and girls tell how they have been saved from the red light district."

I arose and said to the boys, "I'm through. I am going to Jesus Christ. We've come to the parting of the ways," and I turned my back on them. Some of them laughed, and some of them mocked me; one of them gave me encouragement; others never said a word.

Twenty-nine years ago I turned and left that little group on the corner of State and Madison Streets and walked to the little mission and fell on my knees and staggered out of sin and into the arms of the Savior.

(From an account in The Boston Herald)

✍ CHARLES R. BROWN ✄

(1862–1950)

American lecturer and author.

A MOST DEFINITE FEELING OF FELLOWSHIP WITH GOD

I was living on the shores of San Francisco Bay on the eighteenth day of April, 1906, when the great earthquake and fire came. Three hundred thousand people turned into the streets, homeless, foodless, with no clothing, save what they wore on their backs! Their homes, their places of business, their places of employment, their schools, churches, hospitals, all swept away by the flames! The fire burned from a quarter past five Wednesday morning until late Friday afternoon. It was finally checked, not by the use of water, for the earthquake had broken the water mains and there was no water to be had, but by the use of dynamite, blowing up whole blocks of buildings to arrest the further progress of the fire.

There was something magnificent about the way those people rose to the occasion. I scarcely ever heard a murmur of complaint. There was something in them which the earthquake had not shaken down, which the fire had not burned up. There came to us a deeper sense of our common humanity, a firmer grasp upon those realities which cannot be shaken, a more definite feeling of fellowship with God. We never could have borne it, we never could have done what we did, but for God. Out of the unseen came strength to keep the will firm and the heart brave.

≈ Charles T. Studd ≈

(1862–1951)

English missionary to China, later to India and then Africa. He was converted in 1883 through D. L. Moody's influence.

JUST COMMON, ORDINARY HONESTY

When I came to see that Jesus Christ had died for me, it didn't seem hard to give up all for him. It seemed just common, ordinary honesty. If Jesus Christ be God and died for me, then no sacrifice can be too great for me to make for him.

(He toiled day and night, 18 hours at a stretch, with no meals except when gulped down while working, and no vacations.)

THE PLEASURES OF THIS WORLD ARE AS NOTHING

I cannot tell you what joy it gave me to bring the first soul to the Lord Jesus Christ. I have tasted almost all the pleasures this world can give. Those pleasures were as nothing compared to the joy that the saving of that one soul gave me.

(When he turned 25 he came into a large inheritance which he gave to the Lord, for he had found a greater wealth.)

Sir Francis ≈ Edward Younghusband ≈

(1863–1942)

British Army officer, explorer, geographer, minister and author.

IT WAS THE LOVE OF GOD

I had been preparing a sermon on the love of God. For a week I had read and thought about the subject. On Sunday morning I went over my sermon notes; and then, for some reason, I decided to walk to church rather than drive, as I usually did.

Upon opening the front door of our house it happened. I walked out into a world I had never seen before. The familiar things were

there as usual, but they were all different—clothed in a radiance and
beauty beyond description. The grass was infinitely greener than
I had ever seen it before. I glanced at the trees, silhouetted against
the deep blue sky, and their beauty was thrilling beyond measure.
I became a part of the whole, embracing it; and it embraced me. I
almost feared to breathe lest the experience dissolve, but the apprehension was only in the back of my mind, for the rest of me was
experiencing an ecstatic joy that came from something other than
visual beauty. Suddenly I knew what it was. It was love! I felt it rather
than thought it. Love, I sense, was at the heart of everything, and
God was in everything, and everything was in God, and God was
inexpressible love.

....Two strangers approached me and I felt a sudden surge
of affection for them. I greeted them warmly, and their obvious
surprise did not matter in the slightest. The rest of the way to the
church I felt something which can only be described as overwhelming love, and warmth, and affection. We were all one, and there was
no barrier between us. They were just parts of God's glorious, wonderful, joyous, loving, universe, and they were beautiful.

(Recorded by Raynor C. Johnson in Watcher on the Hills)

⁂ RUFUS M. JONES ⁂
(1863–1948)

**American Quaker philosopher and writer who studied and wrote about the
inner life and indwelling presence of God. He experienced a deep inner relationship with God and was moved by an intense desire to share the inner
life with his fellow men, regardless of their denominational allegiance. He
did this mainly through his many books.**

FROM MORNING TILL NIGHT

We had very few things, but we were rich in invisible, enduring
wealth. Our home was permeated with the dew of religious devotion
from morning till night. We never ate a meal which did not begin

with a prayer of thanksgiving. We never began a day without a family gathering at which Mother read a chapter from the Bible. There was work waiting to be done. Yet we sat there hushed until someone would talk with God simply and quietly. When I first began to think of God, I thought of Him, not as some far-off being, but as an ever present Friend and Helper. In those simple ways, the roots of my faith in unseen realities reached down far below my childish surface thinking.

I KNEELED DOWN THERE AND THEN

Alone on a solitary walk, near Dieu-le-fit, in the foothills of the Alps, I had felt the walls grow thin between the visible and the invisible and there came a sudden flash of eternity, breaking in on me. I kneeled down then and there, in that forest glade, in sight of the mountains, and dedicated myself in the hush and silence, but in the presence of an invading Life, to the work of interpreting the deeper nature of the soul and its direct mystical relation to God.

THE DEATH OF A YOUNG SON OPENS HIS HEART TO GOD'S LOVE

When my sorrow was at its most acute I was walking along a great city highway, when suddenly I saw a little child come out of a great gate, which swung to and fastened behind her. She wanted to go to her home behind the gate, but it would not open. She pounded in vain with her little fist. She rattled the gate. Then she wailed as though her heart would break. The cry brought the mother. She caught the child in her arms and kissed away the tears. 'Didn't you know I would come? It's all right now.' All of a sudden I saw with my spirit that there was love behind my shut gate...... I know now, as I look back across the years, that nothing has carried me up into the life of God, or done more to open out the infinite meaning of love, than the fact that love can span this break of separation, can pass beyond the visible and hold right on across the chasm. The mystic union has not broken and knows no end. Lowell (his son who died) had here only eleven years of happy, joyous life. The victory that comes through the long years of struggle in a world full of hard choices could not be his. He was not to have the chance, 'with toil of heart and knees and hands, through the long gorge to the far light, to form his character and to do his life work; but who knows what chances there are for transplanted human worth to bloom, to profit in God's other garden: As certainly as God lives there is more to follow after this brief span of preparation ends... Yes, "where there is so much love, there must be more."

(The Luminous Trail, *New York: The Macmillan Co., 1947, p. 165. Here, Jones is writing many years later after losing his beloved 11 year old son. He tells of sailing from America to England in July, 1903, leaving his son Lowell in America. Lowell, ill from diphtheria, seemed to be recovering when he left. A relapse occurred, paralysis set in, and death came. News of this sorrow came by cable when his ship landed at Liverpool.)*

ANOTHER KIND OF WORLD WITHIN

I find the most convincing evidence of him...in the quiet testimony of beauty, truth, love, goodness, peace, joy, self-sacrifice, and consecration, which point to another kind of world within, than one we see and touch.

(*My Idea of God*)

THERE WAS A SENSE OF DIVINE PRESENCE

One of the most powerful influences in shaping my early religious life was my almost constant attendance at Quaker Meeting with our united family. It was three miles from home, through a fascinating woods, full of imaginary animals. The House where we met was very plain, no bell, no pulpit, no organ, no choir, no ritual, no pictures, but the view across the spaces to Mount Blue was a thrilling one in God's outdoor world. We met in complete silence, but it was silence infused with expectation. It was plus and not minus. There was a kind of spell of awe and wonder in it. It was 'luminous,' though I did not know that word then. There was a sense of Divine Presence, which is what the word means and which even a boy felt. Meditation, contemplation, prayer of inward quiet, in a strange way, feeds or fertilizes the subsoil of the soul and leaves a deposit in the deep well below the threshold of consciousness. Anyway the silence "worked";

it did something. One grew confident that there was mutual and reciprocal intercourse with the Beyond, and it was a stabilizing experience for a boy. I wish all American boys had this cult of silence.

⊰ ALFRED C. LANE ⊱
(1863–1948)

American geologist and educator, Vice-President of the American Academy of Arts and Sciences.

FAITH BRINGS HOPES TO FRUITION

I believe that faith keeps one true in the dark and humble in the spotlight. But most important, I believe that faith works, bringing hopes to fruition and ideals to reality. Without faith man is a cold creature, lost in a world of human progress. He has nothing to live for. He fears death. Fear distorts his outlook. He becomes a human shell.

⊰ JOHN H. JOWETT ⊱
(1864–1923)

English Congregational pastor and author of many devotional and spiritual books.

FOLLOWING THE STREAM TO ITS SOURCE

I stood one day in a lovely vale in Switzerland in which flowed a gladsome river, full and forceful, and rejoicing in its liberty. I prayed that my life might be as the river—full of power, clearing obstacles by a nimble leap, and hastening on to the great and eternal sea. To my voiceless prayer came the reply, 'Follow up the stream to its source.' I tracked the buoyant river to the snow line and found in the spreading wastes of virgin snow the river's source. Then I knew that full and forceful Christian lives must have their source in the holiness of God.

⚜ MIGUEL DE UNAMUNO ⚜
(1864–1936)

Spanish educator, philosopher, and author whose essays had considerable influence on early twentieth century Spain.

I FEEL HIS INVISIBLE HAND LEADING ME

If you ask me how I believe in God, how God creates himself in me, my answer may perhaps provoke your smiles and laughter, and even scandalize you. I believe in God as I believe in my friends, because I feel the breath of His affection, feel His invisible and intangible hand, drawing me, leading me, grasping me; because I possess an inner consciousness of a particular providence and of a universal mind that marks out for me the course of my own destiny.

(Prosa Diversa)

⚜ GEORGE WASHINGTON CARVER ⚜
(1864–1943)

American botanist who as an infant was traded for a broken-down race horse. He worked his way through college and became a professor at Tuskegee Institute. He broke the peanut down into 300 usable, salable products.

FINDING HIS WISHES FOR THE DAY

There is literally nothing that I have ever wanted to do, that I asked the blessed Creator to help me do, that I have not been able to accomplish. It is all very simple, if one knows how to talk with the Creator. It is simply seeking the Lord and finding him....I gather specimens of flowers and listen to what God has to say for the day.

(Rising at four, he made it a habit to walk and pray for two hours each morning.)

THE SECRET OF MY SUCCESS

The secret of my success? It is simple. It is found in the Bible: "In all they ways acknowledge Him and He shall direct thy paths."

⚞ WILFRED GRENFELL OF LABRADOR ⚟

(1865–1940)

English physician, missionary, teacher, counselor and preacher who not only helped countless individuals, but almost single-handedly transformed a vast section of Labrador. "To me now any service to the humblest of mankind is Christ-service."

HOW I CAME TO MY DECISION TO FOLLOW CHRIST

It takes real courage to confess Christ. Let me tell you how I came to my decision to receive and serve Christ. I was in a meeting in which the minister urged those who had made a decision for Christ to stand up. There were a number of my friends in the meeting, and also about a hundred sailors who were from a training ship in the harbor. I felt chained through fear to the seat. Suddenly one of the sailors stood. I knew he would be ridiculed when he got back to his ship. His standing gave me the nerve also to stand up and confess Christ as my Saviour. How thankful I am that I did! That act gave new meaning of life to me!

ONE OF MY MOST CHERISHED POSSESSIONS

The privilege of prayer to me is one of my most cherished possessions because faith and experience alike convince me that God himself sees and answers, and his answers I never venture to criticize. It is only my part to ask. It is entirely his to give or withhold, as he knows what is best. If it were otherwise, I would not dare to pray at all. In the quiet of home, in the heat of life and strife, in the face of death, the privilege of speech with God is inestimable. I value it more because it calls for nothing that the wayfaring man, though a fool, cannot give—that is, the simplest expression to his simplest desire. Then I can neither see, nor hear, nor speak, still I can pray so that God can hear. When I finally pass through the valley of the shadow of death, I expect to pass through it in conversation with him.

LIKE THE TRUEST OF TRUE FRIENDS

To me the memorizing of Scripture has been an unfailing help in doubt, anxiety, sorrow, and all the countless vicissitudes and problems of life. I believe in it enough to have devoted many, many hours of stowing away passages where I can neither leave them behind me or be unable to get to them. The Word of God is the Christian's best weapon and must be with him always. Facing death alone on a floating piece of ice on a frozen ocean, the comradship it afforded me supplied all I needed. It stood by me like the truest of true friends that it is.

REMEMBERING A HYMN FROM MY BOYHOOD

Night found me ten miles on my seaward voyage. I had killed three of my dogs, stripped off their skins, and wrapped their fur about me as a coat. Their bodies I piled up to make a windbreak on the ice. At intervals I took off my clothes, wrung them out, swung them in the wind, and then put them on again, hoping that the heat of my body would dry them. Forcing my biggest dog to lie down I cuddled close to him, drew the improvised dogskin rug over me, and eventually dropped to sleep. The hand that was against the dog stayed warm, but the other was soon frozen. About midnight I awoke shivering. The moon was just rising, and the wind and current were sweeping me steadily toward the open sea. But somehow my faith was unshaken. After all, it seemed the natural thing, for a Labrador doctor to be drifting toward the portal of death on a half-frozen stream. And quite unbidden the words of a hymn I had learned in boyhood began running through my mind:

My God and Father, while I stray
Far from my home on life's rough way
O teach me from my heart to say,
Thy will be done!

> (Grenfell was summoned to a village on the Labrador coast to perform an emergency
> operation. He drove his dog team across a river which seemed to be frozen. The ice,
> however, gave way, and the doctor and his dogs were thrown into the freezing water.
> After considerable effort, he succeeded in pulling himself and his dogs onto a huge cake of

drifting ice which immediately began to carry them toward the Atlantic Ocean. He was rescued by fishermen near the mouth of the river. Taken from What Life Means to Me.*)*

❧ WILLIAM LYON PHELPS ❧

(1865–1943)

A most beloved American professor of literature, speaker, pastor of an interdenominational church, and later honorary pastor of a Baptist church. In his youth he was unsure of whether God was calling him to be a teacher, preacher, or journalist—he eventually became all three.

IN THE LAST ANALYSIS

I find daily life not always joyous, but always interesting. I have some sad days and nights, but none that are dull. As I advance deeper into the vale of years, I live with constantly increasing gusto and excitement. I am sure it all means something; in the last analysis, I am an optimist because I believe in God. Those who have no faith are quite naturally pessimists and I do not blame them.

❧ WILLIAM ADAMS BROWN ❧

(1865–1943)

American Presbyterian minister and professor of theology.

FROM EVERLASTING TO EVERLASTING

I cannot dispense with Jesus because he gives me my clearest picture of what God is like. I do not need anyone to prove to me the fact of God. That rests on foundations so deep that I have no fear that any future happening will shake it. My sense of dependence, my consciousness of responsibility, my capacity for reverence—all that is in me that looks up and out and forward makes me aware that I am in direct contact with a reality greater and worthier than I whose nature and purposes continually elude me. But when I ask myself how I am to think of this reality, I find myself involved in insuperable and intellectual difficulties. How can I, a being finite and transient, touching reality only for the briefest moment and in the smallest part, make for myself a picture of the one who is from everlasting to everlasting and with whom are the issues of interpretation the things I instinctively believe. Such a symbol I find in Jesus. He gives me my clearest picture of God, for in him I find united those qualities for which my heart cries out in ultimate reality—supreme love, perfect righteousness, and above all an unwavering patience that no disappointment can discourse and no failure dismay.

EXPERIENCES IN LIFE

We believe in God because there are experiences in life at once so arresting and so significant that, apart from God, it is psychologically impossible for us to account for them.

N. McGee Waters

(1866–1916)

American Congregational minister, lecturer, and after-dinner speaker.

THE SPIRIT RETURNS TO GOD WHO GAVE IT

The other day some lilacs came to us from a southern friend. They were placed in a vase in my bedroom. That night I was awakened by their rich, honey-like fragrance. My memory awoke, too, and then there was no more sleep for me. I thought of the lilac tree that grew by my window in my father's house, and I began to turn over the pages of memory like the pages of a book. On every page there was a picture, and beautiful they were to me. I was out in the fields again picking violets in the springtime with my little flaxen-haired sister. Together we made playhouses on the dark edge of the woods and carpeted them with moss. I saw my first sweetheart with her freckled face and red hair. I stood before the teachers I loved. I went fishing. I felt the plunge in the cool water of the old swimming hole. I bagged my first game, and was so excited that I threw down my gun and ran home to exhibit it. I lived over the sweetly sad day when I left home for college. I stood up to speak on commencement day. I wept again over defeats that hurt, and I shouted anew over victories that were earned. I went over all my life. It was like reading a tale, and I said it is all mine. I am the boy in the story. And then I said. "Am I?" There is not a hair in my head that was on the head of the boy. Not an ounce of blood, or bone, or flesh, not a single muscle or nerve, not a single particle of matter in that boy's body is in my body today. If the body is I, I am not the same fellow. The body of the boy is dead and buried in the vaults of Nature. My body has been buried once every seven years. If a body is life I have had several lives.

I know I am I. I have kept my identity though my body has been dying all the time. I have actual demonstration that the death of the body does not harm the soul. Indeed the soul has grown stronger all the time. Indeed the dying of the body is necessary for the development and largest good of the soul. If all the death we know about deals with the soul, why should we not say of the death we do not know all about, "Dust returns to the earth from which it came, but the spirit returns to God, who gave it" I believe then in the immortality of the soul.

✍ H. G. WELLS ✍
(1866–1946)

One of modern England's most prolific and best-known writers.

THE FIRST THING AND THE LAST THING

Religion is the first thing and the last thing, and until a man has found God, and been found by God, he begins at no beginning, he works at no end. He may have his friendships, his partial loyalties, his scraps of honor, but all these fall into place, and life falls into place, only with God.

The moment may come while we are alone in the darkness under the stars, or while we walk by ourselves or in a crowd. It may come upon the sinking ship or in the tumult of the battle. There is no saying when it may come. For it comes as the dawn comes, through whatever clouds and mists. It comes as the day comes to the ships put to sea. But after it comes our lives are changed. Before the coming of the true King, the inevitable King, the King who is present when just men foregather, this blood-stained rubbish of an ancient world shrivels like paper thrust into a flame. Thereafter one goes about like one who had found a solution. One is assured that there is a Power that fights against the confusion and evil of the world. There comes into the heart an enduring happiness and courage.

(God the Invisible King)

✂ ROBERT E. SPEER ✂
(1867–1947)

Deeply spiritual Christian whose gifted son was cruelly murdered.

A LIVING PRESENCE

During more than forty-three years of incessant struggle, journeying to and fro throughout the world, I have never lost the assurance of Christ's living presence with me. He is not a mere vision: He is no imaginative dream, but a living Presence, who daily inspires me and gives me grace. In him, quite consciously, I find strength in time of need. In all that followed my conversion, Christ and God became one single thought of God in human ways. I could not think of God apart from Christ or Christ apart from God.

(Reported by Christian F. Reisner
in Treasury of the Christian Faith)

WHAT JESUS DOES FOR ME

He gives me a clearer vision and the courage to try to live by that vision. He gives me the desire to work in the world as intensely as he worked. He kindles me, when I grow sluggish or indifferent, to a positive and aggressive antagonism to evil within and without. He gives me confidence in the truth and so helps me to rest, no matter what happens in the world, because I know that God and the truth must prevail. He counterbalances, as I cannot, the variable circumstances and unequal conditions of life and takes care of the excesses that are beyond me. He gives me grace and strength to try, at least, things that I know are impossible, and to attempt, first of all, the things that are hardest to be done. He helps me refuse to do good when I know that something better can be done. He helps me to keep on when I have to, even though I know I cannot. He saves me from the fret and killing of pride and vanity, and helps me to cease to care for the things that make people sick. He helps me to keep the central things clear and not to be fogged and broken down by the accessories and secondary things. He gives me a new and inward living principle. I believe that he is this principle, and that there is another personality inside my personality that would not be there if it had not been for him and if it were not for him today.

(What Jesus Does for Me)

ᷡ AMY WILSON CARMICHAEL ᷢ
(1867–1951)

Missionary born in Ireland who spent fifteen months in Japan, but suffered there physically and emotionally. She found her life's work in India—working with girls whom she rescued from slavery and prostitution. She served fifty-six years in India without a furlough and lived out her life under the vow she made to sacrificial giving of everything she possessed. Her life and forty books have touched thousands. Her suffering, being bedridden the last twenty years of her life, and Romans 8:28 led her to write, "A wise master never wastes his servant's time."

THE JOY BURIED DEEP WITHIN

"Hereby perceive we the love of God, because He laid down His life for us, and we ought to lay down our lives for the brethren." How often I think of that OUGHT. No sugary sentiment there. Just the stern, glorious trumpet call, OUGHT. But can words tell the joy buried deep within? Mine cannot. It laughs at words.

I TURNED TO MY GOD IN DESPERATION

On this day many years ago I went away alone to a cave in the mountain called Arima. I had feelings of fear about the future. That is why I went there—to be alone with God. The devil kept on whispering, "It's all right now, but what about afterwards? You are going to be very lonely." And he painted pictures of loneliness—I can see them still. And I turned to my God in a kind of desperation and said, "Lord, what can I do? How can I go on to the end?" And He said, "None of them that trust in Me shall be desolate" (Psalm 34:22). That word has been with me ever since.

(In a letter written forty years later to one of her "children" that she had worked with and who was going through a similar dilemma.)

MARY AUSTIN

(1868–1934)

Brilliant writer who at the height of her career was told that she had only eight months to live, devoted herself to her "prayer project" trips and returned in a picture of health. "I realized that in the process of achieving complete detachment I had left my pain behind."

GOD, GOD!

It must have been between five and six when this experience happened to me. It was a summer morning, and the child I was had walked down through the orchard alone and come out on the brow of a sloping hill where there was grass and a wind blowing and one tall tree reaching into infinite immensities of blueness. Quite suddenly, after a moment of quietness here, earth and sky and tree and wind-blown grass and the child in the midst of them came alive together with a pulsing light of consciousness. There was a wild foxglove at the child's feet and a bee buzzing about it, and to this day I can recall the swift inclusive awareness of each for the whole—I in them and they in me and all of us enclosed in a warm lucent bubble of living-ness. I remember the child looking everywhere for the source of this happy wonder, and at last she questioned—'God?—because it was the only awesome word she knew. Deep inside, like the murmurous swinging of a bell, she heard the answer, 'God, God....'"

How long this ineffable moment lasted I never knew. It broke like a bubble at the sudden singing of a bird, and the wind blew and the world was the same as ever—only never quite the same. The experience so initiated has been the one abiding reality of my life, unalterable except in the abounding fullness and frequency of its occurrence.

(Experiences Facing Death, *The Bobbs-Merrill Co., 1931*)

⫷ HUGH BLACK ⫸

(1868–1953)

Scottish-born American pastor, author, and professor of theology.

IT IS THE DAY OF OUR MASTER

Each winter I grow daffodil bulbs in my study. I have watched them growing, shooting up their spike-like leaves and flower stalks. And yet, never until the flower naturally expanded have I ever caught any hint of scent. Then, in a flash, it arrives like a benediction and sprays my room with fragrance. This is the hope that I hold out for all of us who are steadily, patiently growing. One day as the flower opens the scent will come. It is the day of our Master. But its secret lies deep in the long, slow, patient growth of the dark winter.

⊱ CHARLES SCOVILLE ⊰

(1869–1946)

American minister of the Church of Christ and evangelist who built the Metropolitan Church of Chicago from 107 members to, a few years later, 600 members and a Sunday School of 500.

CHRIST'S ENEMIES BECAME THE CHARTER MEMBERS OF HIS CHURCH

There are many historical facts in the world that were not attended by one-tenth as many witnesses as was the resurrection of Jesus Christ. Therefore I need not beg anybody's pardon for what I believe. I believe with all my heart that Jesus, the Christ, is risen indeed. I believe that He was seen after His resurrection, by 641 eyewitnesses. During those forty days, Jesus appeared to different men under different circumstances at various places. He ate with them, walked with them, and talked with them. They positively could not have been deceived. Such deception would be without parallel in history and without an analogy in the annals of men. Christ's enemies became the charter members of His church in Jerusalem on the day of Pentecost. Account for that fact if you deny the resurrection.

⊱ MELVIN TROTTER ⊰

(1870–1940)

A humanly hopeless and helpless drunkard until after his conversion, when he became a mighty preacher.

JUST ONE GLIMPSE

There was not anything that I knew about that I had not gone through. I had taken cure after cure. I had taken everything known to science. I had made resolution after resolution. I could no more stay sober than I could fly. When my liberty depended upon it, I would lose my liberty, because I would break my pledge. I have

signed the pledge with my own blood. I promised the judge never
to drink to the last day I lived. I went right out and did it over again.
But just one glimpse of Jesus Christ, and I have never wanted a drink
from that instant to this!

⊰ ALICE HEGAN RICE ⊱
(1870–1942)

**Author of children's books and other books, including *My Pillow Book,* a
little book of devotion, with comments and quotations chronicled during a
lifetime by one seeking to grow in the spiritual life.**

DAILY JOY IN FELLOWSHIP WITH HIM

I believe in a personal God, because my finite mind cannot conceive
of Him in any other way, and because I have experienced a communion with Him, gaining strength in weakness, comfort in sorrow,
and daily joy in fellowship with Him.... I hold that Jesus Christ is
the highest manifestation of God's intention for man, the supreme
example of what He wishes us to be. Love is the Eternal Verity, and
any real love we have given or received in this world, will not pass
out of our lives in the world to come.

(My Pillow Book, 1937)

⊰ DAVID GRAYSON, ⊱
PSEUDONYM OF RAY STANNARD BAKER
(1870–1946)

**American journalist and popular essayist who won the Pulitzer Prize in
1940 for his biography of Woodrow Wilson.**

THE VOICE IN THE FIRE

We cannot remain steadily upon the heights. At least I cannot, and
would not if I could. After I have been out about so long on such an
adventure as this, something lets go inside of me, and I come down

out of the mountain—and yet know deeply that I have been where the bush was burning and have heard the Voice in the Fire.

(Great Possessions)

ALL THINGS BECOME CLEARER

I rarely work in my garden or upon the hills of an evening without thinking of God. It is in my garden that all things become clearer to me.

(Great Possessions)

HIS WORD IS LIKE A FIRE

I don't know much about religion—but I do know that His Word is like a fire, and that a man can live by it, and if once a man has it he has everything else he wants.

(Adventures in Contentment)

✍ MRS. CHARLES E. (LETTIE D.) COWMAN ✍
(1870–1960)

American missionary. She is most well-known for writing *Streams in the Desert,* a daily devotional classic written to sustain her during her years of missionary work in Japan and China—particularly the six years she nursed her husband while he was dying.

A VERY DARK NIGHT IN MY LIFE

On a very dark night in my life these words came to me: "Praise waiteth for thee, O God, in Zion" (Ps. 65:1). I had been waiting in prayer for months. God was waiting for me to take this final step of faith. When I began to praise Him for the answer, He began to answer "exceeding abundantly above all" that I could ask or think!

THE MUSIC OF HEAVEN'S CHOIR

Get up early, go to the mountains and watch God make a morning. The dull gray will give way as God pushes the sun toward the horizon, and there will be tints and hues of every shade as the full-orbed sun bursts into view. And as the king of the day moves forward majestically flooding the earth and every lowly vale, listen to the music of heaven's choir as it sings of the majesty of God and the glory of the morning. In the hush of the earthly dawn, I hear a voice saying, "I am with you all the day. Rejoice! Rejoice!"

⊰ C.F. ANDREWS ⊱
(1871–1940)

English clergyman and writer. In an evening when he was alone in his room and prepared for rest, he kneeled down a few moments for his usual evening prayers. Without warning, a strong conviction of God's presence overcame him.

I HAVE KNOWN THE SECRET

For I have known the secret of His presence, here and now, as a daily reality, at some times more intimately than at other times, but always the same Christ—the same yesterday, today and forever.

Therefore He has become to me the living Christ, and it has not been possible for me to think of Him or speak of Him in any other terms, because my articulate life as a Christian began from that day forward, and all my deepest thoughts are colored with this one impression. This fact has to be taken for granted by anyone who wishes to understand the meaning of Christ in my life, and what I owe to Him. Christ's presence became a daily experience.

There was a new power in my life. There had stolen into my heart from Him a forgiveness, deep as the ocean, wide as the blue sky, unfathomable in its depths of divine love. This had broken me down completely and made a new man of me. There had been a sacrifice on God's part. I could understand it that night so clearly. He had given Himself for me. This brought me close to Him, not in fear, but in boundless love. I began to know the perfect love which casts out all fear. It was the Divine Presence, this spirit of redeeming love, around and about and within me, which had made the real change in me.

There was, it is true, nothing directly outward, visible, and objective. I saw no vision of Christ, as Saul did on his way to Damascus. Nevertheless, the love and the forgiveness that I experienced were made real to me in Christ and through Christ. They had come to me in that way. I understood by an inner experience what St. Paul meant when he said, "God was in Christ reconciling the world to Himself." For at the very time of blessing, God was in Christ forgiving me and healing me and making a new man of me. Apart from Christ, all this would have been impersonal and abstract. In Christ, God Himself had become human and personal and real; His love had become human and personal also.

(Letters to a Friend, *George Allen & Unwin, 1923, pp. 25–26*)

✼ FRANCIS J. McCONNELL ✼
(1871–1953)

American Methodist pastor and bishop.

A MATTER OF INEVITABILITY

I believe in immortality because I believe in the God of Christ. That such a God would call men into existence, mock them with a few draughts of life, and then let them perish is incredible to me. The doctrine of God as Father means nothing to me without the possibility of the immortality of the sons of God. Once accept the Christ ideal of God, and immortality seems to me to follow as a matter of moral inevitability.

ᔆᑢ ELISABETH ELLIOT ᔆᕈ

(1871–1954)

Missionary author whose husband Jim perished at the hands of the Auca Indians he was trying to reach with the Gospel.

I GIVE MYSELF AGAIN TO GOD

I walked out to the hill just now. It is exalting, delicious, to stand embraced by the shadows of a friendly tree with the wind tugging at your coattail and the heavens hailing your heart, to gaze and glory and give oneself again to God—what more could a man ask? Oh, the fullness, pleasure, sheer excitement of knowing God on earth! I care not if I never raise my voice again for him, if only I may love him, please him. Maybe in mercy he will give me a host of children that I may lead them through the vast star fields to explore his delicacies whose finger ends set them to burning. But if not, if only I may see him, touch his garments, and smile into his eyes—ah then, not stars nor children shall matter, only himself.

(From The Dynamics of Religious Conversion*)*

ᔆᑢ PHILIP CABOT ᔆᕈ

(1872–1941)

American author and lecturer.

THE RIDDLE OF LIFE WAS SOLVED

That afternoon I went back to Oppenheim, but, finding him intolerable, took up again *The Meaning of Prayer* with a rather sheepish feeling to be reading such a book. The hours of the afternoon, however vanished as those of the morning, and supper was another unwelcome interruption. After supper I sat down to think. This thing looked serious. Here was I for the first time in my life bored with novels and absorbed in worship. Was this the first stage of conversion or the madness which precedes death?

After a few days of this sort during which I experimented and examined my sensations with scientific coldness, I was convinced that I was not mad. Something different was in process. It seemed that in worship, or prayer, and in my Bible, the solution to the riddle of my universe had been revealed to me; for I was living in a new world of peace, beauty, gladness, such as I had never conceived.

(Except Ye Be Born Again)

⚶ ANNE DOUGLAS SEDGWICK ⚶
(1873–1935)

Novelist, born in America, but lived in England since the age of nine.

A STRUGGLE, YET JOY IN THE MIDST

Now, added to everything else, I can't breathe unless lying down, then my ribs collapse. Yet I can't drink my food sitting up. Life is a queer struggle. Yet it is mine, and beautiful to me. There is joy in knowing I lie in the hands of God. When you wrote, "Your spirit can surmount anything," I felt a strange tremor of response from an indomitable thread of life within me. It is mine, but I felt it communicated from God.

(Writing to a friend from her sickbed about what trust in Christ meant to her.)

⚶ GEORGE MOORE ⚶
(1873–1958)

Irish novelist.

GOD SOMETIMES SHUTS US UP IN A SICK-ROOM

God often reads us the story of our lives. He sometimes shuts us up in a sick-room and reads it to us there. I shall never forget all that I learned this time last year.

(Writing in his diary after a severe attack of pleurisy)

⊰ ROBERT NORWOOD ⊱

(1874–1932)

Canadian Anglican pastor and writer.

LIKE A MARBLE PILLAR IN A DESERT

My early acceptance of Jesus began that moment when I discovered something in myself that natively responded to him and as the years have gone by, I have a conscious oneness with him as I walk through this world. I have often been overwhelmed by this stupendous business of walking through the world. There have been times when I have lost for a while my faith in God, in myself as a son of God; and Jesus has always been my helper. Somehow I could dismiss from my consciousness in such moments of doubt all sense of reality, but I could never dismiss Jesus. At such times I was indifferent to any theory or doctrine concerning him as the Savior of the world. I knew only that he stood out stalwart, straight, and beautiful like a marble pillar in a desert. This had been to me my most precious experience, and though I have often tried to escape the gentle tyranny of Jesus, I have always failed, crying with Julian, "Thou has conquered, O Galilean!"

⊰ GILBERT K. CHESTERTON ⊱

(1874–1936)

English essayist, novelist, poet, and champion of the Christian faith who was converted in 1922. One major aspect of his writing involved the awakening of wonder or of awareness of a thing as being seen for the first time.

THE CONVERT

After one moment I bowed my head
And the whole world turned over and came upright,
And I came out where the old road shone white,
I walked the ways and heard what all men said,

They rattle reason out through many a sieve
That stores the sand and lets the gold go free:

And all these things are less than dust to me
Because my name is Lazarus and I live.

THOUGHTS OF JESUS

There was a Man who dwelt in the East centuries ago and now I cannot look at a sheep or a sparrow, a lily or a cornfield, a raven or a sunset, a vineyard or a mountain without thinking of Him.

✒ JOHANNES ANKER-LARSEN ✑

(1874–1957)

Danish novelist who introduced the quest for a living faith in all his work.

AN EXPERIENCE OF ETERNITY

I left theology (University of Copenhagen) deprived of all belief in Christianity. Still there was that religious feeling that seemed inherent in my nature and not to be eradicated as long as life was within me; so I studied as a layman the other great religions of the world, had even a look into theosophy and occultism, till at last I gave up every attempt to find in religion or "isms" a substitute for the Christianity of my childhood and nourishment for my religious feeling. Then life began to show me a little more of itself. Glimpses of a deeper reality came to me, and led me, in the course of some years, into an experience of eternity, not an ecstatic rapture, but an experience as simple and natural as seeing and feeling the sunshine. Since then I find my ordinary daily life placed in the very middle of eternity: this is not caused by the process of reasoning; it is a simple unquestionable fact, I sense life in that way.

IN THE SERVICE OF THE GREAT FARMER

When God entered into my life, warm and powerful, it was from them (the farm laborers on the great Danish farms he had known as a boy) that I learned my right relationship to Him. "No more, therefore, than Thou wilt, and not for my sake, but for the sake of that which thou intendest for me." In this I saw the crux of my situation.

I resolved to renounce personal aims; I tried to "sell all I possessed" and to enter the service of the Great Farmer, to report to Him merrily in the morning with the question, "What orders have you got for me today?"

(With the Door Open)

ᗓ EMILY HERMAN ᗗ

(1875–1923)

Journalist, minister's wife, and writer who had a striking style and penetrating spiritual insight.

BIRTH INTO A NEW AND WONDERFUL WORLD

Then, perhaps by a sudden sharp invasion of a new life….we become conscious of the birth of the Christ spirit within ourselves, of our own birth into a new and wonderful world….It is the world of which God is the center. We look upon Him, and our life is renewed. We are given a set of new values, a spiritual coinage other than that with which we have hitherto traded. Things that but a little while ago seemed desirable now appear as dross….We discover untold beauties in God; we find in Christ secrets of final restitution that fill us with a deathless hope. Matter is seen to be the storehouse of unguessed spiritual treasure, a hiding-place of holy powers, a laboratory of divine alchemy. Everywhere we see mysteries of healing and regeneration, of individual transfiguration and world renewal that remained hidden while self was our center….It is as though we had developed a new set of faculties of appreciation and distaste, pleasure and pain.

(Creative Prayer)

A PILGRIMAGE FROM SELF TO GOD

Prayer, in most cases, begins with personal petition. We ask benefits for ourselves and for those we love. Then we come to realize that the power of prayer lies not in the external benefit, or even in the mental and spiritual reinforcement, that comes to us through it, but in our communion with God. A new love takes possession of us, a new relationship transfigures life, a new world dawns upon our unsealed eyes. We know that communion with God does not only mean mastery over life, but that it is life itself. And as we humbly press closer to the heart of God and read a little of its secret, it is gradually borne in upon us that it is only as we die to self-love that we shall be able to take our true place within the heart of love. We see that prayer is a long and arduous pilgrimage from self to God, not, indeed, the pilgrimage of those who imagine that God can be reached by human effort, but the progress of souls that have been redeemed by Christ, and now desire to be wholly found in him.

(Creative Prayer)

❧ MARY McLEOD BETHUNE ❧
(1875–1955)

Educator, born to former slaves. She devoted her life to ensuring the right to education and freedom from discrimination for black Americans. She originally hoped to become a missionary to Africa, but realized that "Africans in America needed Christ and school just as much as Negroes in Africa." She had immense faith in God and believed nothing was impossible, including founding a college, Bethune-Cookman College in South Carolina. The following excerpts are taken from a speech by Dr. Bethune. Used with permision of the Bethune-Cookman College Library.

THE SOURCE OF MY POWER

My birth into wisdom and spiritual acceptance is a very real fact to me. Out of the womb of salvation and truth my new life was born, and it is in that life that I live and move and have my being. Continually, I commune with the God Who gave me that birth. He is the Guide of all that I do. I seek Him earnestly for each need. My thanksgiving to Him has been unconsciously spontaneous. I believe that the Thanksgiving which is continually in my heart, and upon my lips is the source of my power and growth in personality development. Any time, any place, I can hear myself saying, "Father, I thank Thee" or "Thank Thee, Father."

GOD OPENED UP OPPORTUNITIES

As I grew I knew what it meant to absorb my will in the will of God, Whom I claimed as my Father. Where He reigned at first, I do not know; I am sure my child mind personalized Him, but when I knew Him to be a great Spirit, His fatherhood increased because His Spirit could dwell in me and go with me and never leave me to my own devices. Part of that learning His will was in the secret of knowing how to hold the faith with the desire, and how to work continually to bring things to pass. When I had my first experiences with people who could read, when I could not, and with seeing fine churches when my people worshipped in shacks, I asked God to open to me the opportunity to do something about that. The idea that I needed gripped me. I found myself endowed with creative power from within. I put all negative thoughts away from me, as I do now, and then and there, I affirmed my needs, my hopes, and my aspirations. That affirmation with God took me from the cotton fields to the little mission school run by the Presbyterian Church, to Scotia College, to Moody Bible Institute, and finally to the planting of Bethune-Cookman College—the real child of my desire.

⊰ CARL G. JUNG ⊱
(1875–1961)

Swiss psychologist who said, "Among all my patients there has not been one whose problem in the last resort was not that of finding a religious outlook on life."

EVEN BEFORE MY BIRTH

From the beginning I had a sense of destiny, as though my life was assigned to me by fate and had to be fulfilled. This gave me an interior security, and though I could never prove it to myself, it proved itself to me. I did not have this certainty, it had me. Nobody could rob me of the conviction that it was enjoined upon me to do what God wanted. That gave me the strength to go on my own way. Often

I had the feeling that in all decisive matters I was no longer among men, but was alone with God. And when I was "there," where I was no longer alone, I was outside time; I belonged to the centuries; and He who then gave answer was He who had always been, who had been before my birth. He who always is was there. These talks with the "Other" were my profoundest experiences: on the one hand a bloody struggle, on the other supreme ecstasy.

(Memories, Dreams, Reflections)

ALBERT SCHWEITZER

(1875–1965)

German-born medical missionary, theologian, and musician who won the Nobel Peace Prize in 1952.

A DECISION MADE TO SERVE GOD

There came to me as I awoke the thought that I must not accept this happiness as a matter of course, but must give something in return for it....You see, I had to do something for Christ.

(Recalling a decision made at Gunsbach when asked why he would leave the comfort and security of Europe to return to live in Africa)

J. C. PENNEY

(1875–1971)

American businessman and founder of J. C. Penney stores.

IT CHANGED ME AS A MAN

I had to pass through fiery ordeals before reaching glimmerings of conviction that it is not enough for men to be upright and moral. When I was brought to humility and the knowledge of dependence on God, sincerely and earnestly seeking God's aid, it was forthcoming, and a light illumined my being. I cannot otherwise describe it than to say that it changed me as a man.

SOMETHING HAPPENED

I was broken nervously and physically, filled with despair, unable to see even a ray of hope. I had nothing to live for. I felt I hadn't a friend left in the world, that even my family turned against me.

> *(Then he entered the little hospital chapel and heard the words of a song, "Be not dismayed whate'er betide, God will take care of you," and listened to the Scripture reading and to the prayer.)*

Suddenly something happened. I can't explain it. I can only call it a miracle. I felt as if I had been instantly lifted out of the darkness of a dungeon into warm, brilliant sunlight.

> *(In 1929 when the Great Depression hit, Penney found himself in crisis. He began to worry about his financial losses and soon he was unable to sleep. He developed shingles and was hospitalized. He expected to die and wrote farewell letters to his wife and sons. He later called those moments in the chapel "the most dramatic and glorious twenty minutes of my life.")*

⚞ HARRY A. IRONSIDE ⚟
(1876–1951)

Pastor of Moody Bible Institute who realized that God had been speaking to him from a very early age.

GOD SPOKE TO ME IN TREMENDOUS POWER

At last, on an evening in 1890, God spoke to me in tremendous power while out at a party with a lot of other young people, mostly older than myself, intent only on an evening's amusement. I remember now that I had withdrawn from the parlor for a few moments to obtain a cooling drink in the next room. Standing alone by the refreshment table, there came home to my inmost soul, in startling clearness, some verses of Scripture I had learned months before. I saw as never before my dreadful guilt in having so long refused to

trust Christ for myself and in having preferred my own willful way
to that of Him who had died for me....I read the words again (John
3:16). There could be no mistake, God loved the world of which I
formed a part. God gave His son to save all believers. I believed in
Him as my Savior. Therefore I must have everlasting life.

≈ ANCILLA, PSEUD. OF GRACE A. WOOD ≈

(-1952)

Writer who found the love of God after years of searching.

SUDDENLY, SIMPLY, SILENTLY

It was positive, and I cannot, by taking thought, repeat it. It had the
stillness of humility shining with surprised joy, the quality of joy
seen sometimes on the face of a very young child when he recog-
nizes, unexpectedly, someone he loves. I had the impression that
it was momentary, the time taken to switch on a light, or to press a
button.

But suddenly, simply, silently, I was not there. And I was there. It
lasted for a moment, yet it was eternal, since there was no time. How
long the experience lasted I had no idea, but I think it was momentary. When it ceased I felt as though I had expended a great deal of
time, and that, equally, there was no time in that moment. That
timelessness was the clearest impression.

It was whole, complete, and not to be analyzed, fussed over, frit-
tered away. It was within me and would grow like the mustard seed
of the parable and fill all my mind, though I did not know that then. I
was realizing that what had happened had happened for always, that
having thus known I should always know, that for me the world was
all new.

Was not all life spiritual, the reality unseen merely because our
peep-hole on it was set at a wrong angle, an angle that could be, and
occasionally was, readjusted?

It was like finding the footprints of some earlier traveler along an unknown and desolate road. It was the beginning of the search in Pascal's sense: "Thou would not have sought Me if thou had not found Me."

⚜ JOHN E. BROWN ⚜
(1877–1944)

American evangelist until his final year at age seventy-six. Records show 400,000 decisions for Christ made in his meetings.

I CANNOT EXPLAIN, NOR DO I UNDERSTAND IT

On the night of May 15, 1896, I made the decision that has wonderfully changed my life. I am lost in wonder, and to this day I cannot explain nor do I understand the wonderful workings of God.

⚜ JOSEPH FORT NEWTON ⚜
(1878–1959)

American clergyman.

FAITH AFFIRMS THAT LIFE HAS VALUE

Why do I believe in personal immortality? Because God is God, a man is man and life is what it is. Once we see what it is that gives dignity, worth, and meaning to life, argument for immortality is not needed. Until we do see it, argument is useless. Faith affirms that life has value. Religion is the realization of the value of life. Faith in immortality is faith in the conservation of the highest values of life. Since these values are personal values, faith in personal immortality is inevitable.

THE HAND OF GOD HEALED MY SPIRIT

Never shall I forget the power of those words: "I am the resurrection and the life; he who believes in me, though he die, yet shall he live, and whoever lives and believes in me shall never die" (John 11:25–26).

It was as if a great, gentle hand, stronger than the hand of man and more tender than the hand of any woman, had been put forth from the Unseen, to caress and heal my spirit—from that day to this, I have loved Jesus beyond the power of words to tell.

> *(As a young boy, too young to comprehend what he had witnessed,*
> *he looked into the grave of his father. As the minister read those words,*
> *"I am the resurrection and the life; he who believes in me, though he die,*
> *yet shall he live," he knew in his heart something powerful had happened.)*

⚜ UPTON SINCLAIR ⚜
(1878–1968)

American novelist, playwright, child prodigy, and advocate for social causes.

A PERSONAL GOD

I believe in a personal God; a power, operating at the center of this universe, which creates, maintains, and comprehends my personality, and all other personalities....a power which causes my being... which sustains my being....which understands my being.

(What God Means to Me)

THE MOST REAL THING IN THE UNIVERSE

My soul is myself, the well-spring or point of consciousness, or center of inner activity...the most real thing in the universe to me; the start for all other knowing, the test by which I judge all other data.

Harry Bisseker

(1878–)

English Wesleyan minister and educator.

Conscious of His Presence

There is a connection between God and stillness. There is a sense in which God never seems so near to me as when everything about me is hushed and I myself am quiet and still. I do not say He is any nearer than when I am pressed by many duties, but it is in those moments I myself am most conscious of His presence. Now and again, when I can get away from all the stir and bustle of life and there comes perfect calm, I seem to know that God is real. If that were only my own isolated experience it would be hardly worthwhile to mention it. I discover, however, that it is the experience of many men, and of men quite different from myself in temperament and outlook. It was in lonely fellowship with nature that Wordsworth felt the presence, the sense sublime, of a being deeper than he. Once there was an experience in his life when his doubt was shaken, and he felt that, after all, God was real. Captain Peary, who discovered the North Pole, once said it was impossible for a man to spend his life amid the mysterious loneliness of miles of unbroken ice without feeling that there is a God. A famous Alpine climber in one of his books tells of a mountaineer who, resting on a height half-way up a mountain, scribbled idly on the rocks, "There is no God", but when he reached the top and saw beneath him range after range of snow-clad peaks, there crept into his soul such a mysterious sense of awe that as he descended he changed what he had previously written into, "The fool hath said in his heart there is to God." In the absolute stillness of that mountain summit, far away from the rush of human life that man's soul had discovered God. We find, then, this interesting and most suggestive fact that men of quite different types, the preacher, the poet, the strong man of action, when they get away from the turmoil of human strife and activity into the great solitudes, find that the reality of God grips them with convincing force. There is a connection of some sort between knowledge and stillness.

⊰ HARRY EMERSON FOSDICK ⊱
(1878–1969)

American Baptist preacher, teacher, author, and lecturer. Perhaps most significant was his personal service to perplexed and needy people in what he calls his "confessional conferences." His understanding of the discouraged came in part from his own experience of passing through a severe physical and nervous breakdown when he was in seminary.

VISIONS OF POSSIBILITY

A young boy once went with his family to church one Sunday morning. He was not trying hard about anything. His will was unharnessed and it did not dawn on him that anything important was afoot. He can now recall nothing about the service until the minister was well on in his sermon concerning the right use of life to meet human needs. The doors began to open in that boy's mind; there came visions of possibility not there before and a new sense of direction and purpose. That was nearly sixty years ago, and the boy has never escaped the influence of those few moments. This is a typical human experience—a single hour of inspiration when we are not trying can determine the meaning of many subsequent years when we are trying.

(On Being a Real Person, *here describing his call to the ministry*)

I STAKE MY LIFE ON CHRIST

I stake my life on Christ that every detour by which man tries to escape his principles will only lead back to him again as the way, the truth, the life. Already one historian has said about Napoleon Bonaparte that, though for years he bestrode Europe, shuffled national boundary lines, made and unmade kings and princes, and left millions slaughtered in his wake, the whole Napoleonic episode was an "enormous irrelevance." But they never will successfully say that about Christ, though he was born in a manger and slain on a cross. I'll bet my life on that.

TOO MANY SUNRISES TO EVER DOUBT

A part of every year I spend among the high mountains. I have seen sunrise on too many mountain peaks ever to doubt the reality of God.

(Told by a member of his congregation)

⊰ CLARENCE E. MCCARTNEY ⊱

(1879–1957)

American Presbyterian minister, writer, and lecturer who was a staunch conservative in a liberal time. He struggled with doubt and suffered serious bouts of shyness, but wrote fifty-seven books and preached wonderful sermons without notes.

I KNOW THAT IT CAME FROM GOD

When I stand on the coast of Cornwall and see those tremendous granite cliffs against which the waves, rolling in clear from Labrador, are flinging themselves in their fury, I know that man's hand did not cut those mighty niches in the rock. When I see the sun setting in the west, as I saw it tonight—a beautiful center of red and about it a border of blue, just fading here and there into grey—I know that the hand of man did not paint it. When I look upon the gospel with its great answer, with its marvelous remedy, with its satisfactions for the whole nature of man, I know that it came from God—"Master, no man can do the work thou doest except God be with him."

⊰ RALPH S. CUSHMAN ⊱

(1879-1960)

American pastor, poet, and writer on religious subjects.

SUNDOWN

Across the evening sky
I sense the dark;
I see the sun
Sink down into the west;
I know that all too soon
Will come the night.
I hear strange voices
Calling me to rest.
And yet I do not fear
The darkness nor its might,
I know that God will bring again
The morning and the light!

WHY?

I wish someone
Would tell me why
My heart leaps up
To see the sky?
The morning light,
The clouds, the blue,
I often wonder—
Yet, 'tis true!
And it is so
At evening too,
When skies take on
Their heavenly hue.
It may be
God is smiling through!
Indeed, I think
That's just the why

My heart leaps up
To see the sky!

✦ HUGH R. L. SHEPPARD ✦
(1880–1937)

English clergyman.

MY SIMPLE FAITH

My deepest conviction is that love is the one thing to cling to in all the darkness. I too...have been disappointed and disillusioned a hundred times. But nothing and no-one has been able to undermine my very simple faith that God is as Jesus Christ.

✦ HELEN KELLER ✦
(1880–1968)

American writer and speaker who was blind, deaf and mute after a serious illness at nineteen months of age. She has inspired millions with her devotion to God.

A FLAME OF FIRE
The word of God came unto me.
Sitting alone among the multitudes;
And my blind eyes were touched with light,
And there was laid upon my lips a flame of fire.

THE VOICE IN MY SILENCE
I believe that life is given us so we may grow in love, and I believe that God is in me, as the sun is in the color and fragrance of a flower—the Light in my darkness, the Voice in my silence.

THE REASON WHY
The reason why God permitted me to lose both sight and hearing seems clear now—that through me He might cleave a rock unbroken

before and let quickening streams flow through other lives desolate as my own once was. I am content.

I THANK GOD FOR MY HANDICAPS

I thank God for my handicaps, for, through them, I have found myself, my work, and my God.

I DIDN'T KNOW HIS NAME, BUT I KNEW HIM

I knew Him! I knew Him! I didn't know His name, but I knew Him! I am so glad you told me His name, for He has often spoken to me.

(Helen, age 10, replied after she was told the story of God's revelation of love in Jesus Christ for the first time)

THE DESERT ALSO LEADS TO GOD

Other feet have traveled that road before me, and I know the desert leads to God as surely as the green, refreshing fields and fruitful orchards.

WHAT LIGHT, COLOR, MUSIC ARE TO THE EYE AND EAR

Gradually I came to see the Bible, which had so baffled me, as an instrument for digging out precious truths, just as I could use my hindered, halting body for the high behests of my spirit....I can only say that the Word of God freed me from the blots and stains of barbarous creeds and has been at once the joy of good of my life, wonderfully linked with my growing appreciation of my teacher's work and my own responsibilities of service, hours of struggle and solitude, hours of deepest joy, harsh truths faced squarely and high dreams held dearer than the pleasant baits of ease and compliance. Those truths have been to my faculties what light, color, music are to the eye and ear. They have lifted my wistful longing for a fuller sense life into a vivid consciousness of the complete being within me. Each day comes to me with both hands full of possibilities, and in its brief course I discern all the verities and realities of my existence, the basis of growth, the glory of action, the spirit of beauty.

WHERE NIGHTINGALES NEST AND SING

Dark as my path may seem to others, I carry a magic light in my heart. Faith, the spiritual, strong searchlight, illumines the way, and although sinister doubts lurk in the shadow, I walk unafraid toward the Enchanted Wood where foliage is always green, where joy abides, where nightingales nest and sing, where life and death are one in the presence of the Lord.

(Midstream: My Later Life)

THE LAMP OF FAITH

For three things I thank God every day of my life—that He has vouchsafed my knowledge of His works, deep thanks that He has set in my darkness the lamp of faith, deep, deepest thanks that I have another life to look forward to—a life joyous with light and flowers and heavenly song.

W. COSBY BELL

(1881–1933)

American seminary professor. Bell, who was dying after a sudden illness of only a few hours, sent this final valedictory to his seminary students.

JUST AN INCIDENT THAT MEANS NOTHING

Tell the boys that I've grown surer of God every year of my life, and I've never been so sure as I am right now. Why, it's all so! It's a fact—it's a dead certainty. I'm so glad to find that I haven't the least shadow of shrinking or uncertainty. I've been preaching and teaching these things all my life, and I'm so interested to find that all we've been believing and hoping is so. I've always thought so, and now that I'm right up against it, I know.... Tell them I say 'goodbye'— they've been a joy to me. I've had more than any man that ever lived, and life owes me nothing. I've had love in its highest form and I've got it forever.... I can see now that death is just the smallest thing, just an incident—that it means nothing. There is no real break, and life, all that really counts in life, goes on.

⊱ ALEXANDER YELCHANINOV ⊰

(1881–1934)

Leader of the Russian Christian Student Movement in exile.

THORNS AND THISTLES

It often seems to me that the thorns and thistles of our life's condition are ordained by God in view of curing precisely our soul. I see this with absolute clearness in my personal life.

(Diary)

⊱ WILLIAM TEMPLE ⊰

(1881–1944)

Archbishop of Canterbury. He was a pioneer of the ecumenical movement and tireless church reformer. "In our dealings with one another let us be more eager to understand those who differ from us than either to refute them or press upon them our own tradition."

COINCIDENCES

When I pray, coincidences happen, and when I don't, they don't.

⊱ WALTER L. WILSON ⊰

(1881–1969)

American writer, Plymouth Brethren pastor, and physician.

TRANSFORMED INTO A BEAUTIFUL GARDEN

A handful of sand is deposited by the Lord in the heart of the earth. Great heat is applied from beneath, and ponderous weight from above, until, when found by man, it has become a beautiful fiery opal. God does the same thing with clay, and man finds a lovely amethyst. He does the same thing with black carbon, and man finds a glorious diamond. How? I don't know. I only know that He can take a life, drab, useless, fruitless, and transform it into a beautiful garden of the sweetest graces for His glory.

❧ RAISSA MARITAIN ❧

(1883–1960)

A French Jew who converted to Catholicism. The following excerpts are taken from Raissa's *Journal*, 1974.

A SPIRITUAL DESTINY

Faced with death, shall I be afraid? Ought I to be afraid? It seems to me, no. Well or ill, I have done what I could to keep on the track of my destiny. My eternal future is in the hands of God. I abandon myself to my heavenly Father. I shall go to Christ, that will be deliverance. I have a peaceful feeling about it. The Lord knows what I have suffered.

A LANDSCAPE OF LIVING WATERS

When everything is at peace around me and I am quiet and alone, silence with God comes and then I find in my heart everything I love on earth and in heaven. And a landscape of living waters, and a light breeze, and savour and rest and enthusiasm.

PEACE WHICH I CANNOT UNDERSTAND

And, as you know, when one can put a name to a few of those who died in Auschwitz, in Belsen or in Dachau, and call up a face among them, the vast sorrow one feels for all the other victims itself assumes a face which haunts you with unspeakable horror and compassion. In spite of all this, God preserves in our souls a weight and stability of peace which I cannot understand; it is thus, no doubt, and much more powerfully still, that he preserved the souls of martyrs against despair.

FROM NOW ON

My Jesus is so much my God that I cannot have any other God but him. I have truly chosen him from my youth. Henceforth he is my life. And any other life I can only call temptation. These temptations are very rare, it is true. But for me they have all the intensity they can have in a human heart. Beyond lies madness or death. Or a way out in sin. But my choice was made long ago and forever; anything rather than offend the immense love of my God who is my much-loved love, from now on.

NOT ENOUGH SIMPLY TO LIVE

It was not enough for me to live, I wanted a reason for living and moral principles which were based on an absolutely certain knowledge; God gives this unrest to those who do not know him in order that they will seek him.

✐ VICTOR F. HESS ✐
(1883–1964)

American professor of physics and Nobel Prize winner in 1936 for the discovery of cosmic rays.

THE GIFT MUST BE DISCOVERED BY EACH ONE

I must confess that in all my years of research in physics and geophysics I have never found one instance in which scientific discovery was in conflict with religious Faith. It is sometimes said that the "necessity" of the "laws" of nature is incompatible with men's free will and, still more, with miracles. This is not so. When scientists formulate the so-called "laws" of physics, they are fully aware, for example, that they can no more predict the actual life history of an atom of radium than they can predict the moral conduct of this or that person.

Real Faith, for me as a scientist, as for anyone else, is often a matter of bitter struggle. The victory must be won—or the gift must be discovered—by each one in his own soul. It often takes the personal experience of grave danger or death to bring conviction and to prepare the way for Faith in Divine Providence. What is certain is that, when Faith comes, there follows a great serenity of soul and a deep peace in the human heart.

ᐱ HUGH WALPOLE ᐳ
(1884–1941)

British novelist, critic, and dramatist.

A MAN LIKE NO OTHER MAN

First the personality and character of Jesus Christ Himself. I had
read that He had never existed. Georg Brandes, whom I had known
once in Denmark, had written a book to prove it. I had been told and
read again that there was nothing new in His doctrine, that He was
a commonplace obscure rebel.....But, I did know that, increasingly
through my life, had I never been told a word about Him and had
chanced upon the Lord's Prayer, the Sermon on the Mount, the say-
ings and the parables, His tenderness to little children and all the
lost, His anger and indignation, the details of the Last Supper and
the Crucifixion, I would have cried out: "Here is a Man like no other
man who has ever been, and in realizing Him I go beyond all earthly
physical things into the world of the spirit. If He is true then the life
of the spirit is true."

ᐱ THOMAS A. LAMBIE ᐳ
(1885–1954)

Missionary with the Sudan Interior Mission.

THE HAND OF CHRIST WAS STRETCHED OUT TO ME

Either I dozed off and had a dream, or I actually had a waking
vision,—I have never known which, but this I saw vividly in that
midnight hour: a map of northeastern Africa, and from the center
of which came a hand and an arm. It was stretched out toward me,
pleading, beckoning,—a hideous leper hand. What! Must I clasp that
hand in mine? I sought to evade it, but, compelled by some power
beyond my comprehending, at last I reluctantly took it in mine. To
my intense surprise I found it was not the hand of a leper but the

hand of Christ, the beautiful hand of my Saviour—the imprint of nails in the palm.

(While home on furlough, his brother-in-law urged him to join him in his large medical practice. Dr. Lambie then attended a missionary conference where he had the above experience.)

✍ OSWALD W. S. McCALL ✺

(1885–1959)

Congregational clergyman who was born and educated in Australia. He came to the U. S. in 1921.

THE PURPLE IS NOT THERE UNTIL THE GRAPES ARE RIPE

The sap does not flow until the spring, and the grapes grow not purple before their season. Neither does a man see until he be ready.

So I recalled the day when first my eyes fell on the Master, and how his words meant nothing to me except weariness, and he no more than a provincial out of Nazareth. Indeed the grapes have ripened since that day!

For I have grown to see that yonder silver crescent, slowly sliding in its amber sea behind the sooty head of Tabor, has in it no heart-holding beauty nor serenity to stand beside the fundamental thing Christ means to men.

Christ is the whisper in the rushes, the spirit in the twilight. Christ, the truth beyond appearance, like the thought within the word, is the mystery which makes the ruby of the wind, the painted peacock's elegance, and all the artist sees and hears of shape and sound and color. You do not realize this? Nay, nor did I.

The purple is not there until the grapes are ripe.

(The Hand of God, 1939)

❧ TEUNIS E. GOUWENS ❧
(1886–)

American Presbyterian minister and writer.

WE CANNOT DO OTHERWISE

You and I can honestly testify that we have had such experiences. And in the light of them we cannot do other than believe in God.

❧ SISTER EVA OF FRIEDENSHORT ❧
(1886–1930)

Eva Tele-Winckler, speaking after long denying Christ.

MY EYES WERE OPENED

He, the King of Heaven, was stronger than my wayward heart. God Himself took me into His school. My eyes were opened to the misery of the world... There was work for me to do in the world. Jesus had sought me and found me. I broke down every bridge behind me; I could never leave Him again.

❧ MARTHA SNELL NICHOLSON ❧
(1886–1957)

American poet, afflicted with intense suffering from arthritis, tuberculosis, an ankylosed spine, Parkinson's disease, and cancer. She was bedridden for most of her twenty-nine years, yet lived with unfailing cheerfulness.

AND SO MY LORD AND I BEGAN OUR WALK TOGETHER

What is life without God? Pointless, fruitless, unfinished, actually not yet begun. I don't know the day nor the way God in His great graciousness and tenderness made Himself known to me. I wish that I could remember. I must have been six or seven when the tremendous event transpired and I became—as well the daughter of Mr. and Mrs. Snell—a child of the living God.

Not only a child of God, but a joint-heir with Christ! All His riches became my riches. My sins were washed away in the precious blood of Christ. I had a great High Priest who would pray for me and present me faultless before the throne of God. I had the promise that nothing could ever touch me without His permission, the absolute certainty of a heavenly Home lovely beyond all my dreams of beauty, where I would dwell forever through eternity.

I only knew that my passionate little heart was flooded with love for God and especially for the Lord Jesus. I loved Him so, that I thought of Him by day and dreamed of Him by night.... A small, lonely soul venturing for the first time into the vast realms of the infinite cannot be satisfied with something dim and distant. The heart's deep cry is for someone near and dear with whom to tread these paths. And so, my Lord and I began to walk together, my hand resting trustingly in His.

⋙ JOHN BAILLIE ⋘

(1886–1960)

Scottish theologian, teacher, and author. His devotional life was at the center of all his academic endeavors, and he was able to find a delicate balance between faith and reason.

MY UPBRINGING

When I think of my own upbringing, the love and care that were lavished on me in my youth, the kind of home in which I was born, the community in which I was reared, the gracious influences that were brought to bear on me, the examples that were held up before me, the kind of teaching I was given, the signposts that awaited me at every turn of the road, the fences that were set to keep me from wandering from the way, the warnings that were given me against every pitfall, the words in season so often spoken to me—when I think of all these things, and in spite of my shame for having so little profited from them, I must indeed prostrate myself in gratitude before the memory of my parents, my teachers, my wonderful friends, and those who wrote the books I was given to read, who rendered me this inestimable service. Yet I know that they themselves had it all from Christ. Nothing of it would have been there if Christ had not come to seek and to save that which was lost.

⊰ CHARLES E. FULLER ⊱

(1887–1968)

American revivalist who brought the Gospel to many through the Old Fashioned Gospel Hour.

I JUST WANTED GOD TO USE ME

Back in 1917 I was a successful young businessman from a Christian home, but I had my faith in God shattered in college. One Sunday in that year....I went, out of curiosity, to hear Paul Rader preach at the Church of the Open Door in Los Angeles. I entered the place a lost sinner; I came out under deep conviction because Paul Rader preached Christ and Him Crucified in such a spirit-empowered message that I saw myself a lost, undone sinner. He preached from Ephesians 1:18,19.

Leaning my head on the seat in front of me I trembled under deep conviction, though I did not then know what was the matter with me. I left the afternoon meeting and drove out to a park in Hollywood, where I got down on my knees in the back of my touring car, and there, in prayer after a real struggle, I asked God to save my soul, which He did—and to use me in some capacity to reach others for Himself.

I became a new creation, then and there, and I went back to the evening meeting to hear Paul preach another sermon, which seemed to me like manna from Heaven. My heart was fairly bursting with joy, and all desire to get ahead in the business world and to make money left me. I just wanted God to use me, if He could, to win souls for Himself.

I AM NOT AFRAID

Next Sunday you are to talk about Heaven. I am interested in that land, because I have held a clear title to a bit of property there for over fifty-five years. I did not buy it. It was given to me without money and without price. But the Donor purchased if for me at tremendous sacrifice. I am not holding it for speculation since the title is not transferable. It is not a vacant lot.

For more than half a century I have been sending material out of which the greatest Architect and Builder of the universe has been building a home for me which will never need to be remodeled nor repaired because it will suit me perfectly, individually, and will never grow old.

There is a valley of deep shadow between the place where I live in California and that to which I shall journey in a very short time. I cannot reach my home in that City of God without passing through this dark valley of shadows. But I am not afraid because the best Friend I ever had went through the same valley long, long ago and drove away all its gloom. He has stuck by me through thick and thin, since we first became acquainted fifty-five years ago, and I hold His promise in printed form, never to forsake me or leave me alone. He will be with me as I walk through the valley of shadows, and I shall not lose my way when He is with me.

(Taken from a letter that Fuller received from an ailing, old man who sent it after hearing that the next sermon would be on "Heaven.")

⚞ TOYOHIKO KAGAWA ⚟
(1888–1960)

Japanese Christian reformer, evangelist, and writer, whose family disinherited him. He went to work in the slums, helping to establish churches, schools, and missions. He was imprisoned during World War II.

EVEN IN THE DARKNESS I FEEL NO SENSE OF LONELINESS

Health is gone. Sight is gone. But as I lie forsaken in this dark room, God still gives light. To me all things are vocal. O wonderful words of love!....God and every inanimate thing speak to me! Thus, even in the darkness, I feel no sense of loneliness....Prayer continues....In the darkness I meet God face to face....I am constantly praising God for the joy of the darkness....I am constantly praising God for the joy of the moments lived with him.

(When he was once threatened with blindness and lay
for months in the dark with scorching pain in his eyes.)

⚞ ROBERT G. LETOURNEAU ⚟
(1888–1964)

American earth-moving machinery manufacturer who founded the LeTourneau Foundation. Ninety percent of the stocks of LeTourneau Corp. went into financing evangelical Christian work world-wide.

IN ABOUT FIVE MINUTES THE PLAN WAS PLAIN

Our young people had been going regularly to a mission to hold a Gospel service, and I had been going with them. One night I had some special work to do. I was operating a small factory at the time, and machinery had to be built the next day for which I had to make the design that night in order that a crew of men on contract could build it the next morning. How could I do my work and attend the meeting at the mission? The Lord and I had quite a struggle while I was trying to decide what to do. Although I could not understand how I was going to get the plan drawn for the next morning, I went with the young people and we had a profitable time. I returned home about ten o'clock. Up to that time I had been unable to make a single plan. I sat down at the drafting board, and in about five minutes the outline and plan was as plain as it could be. What is more, the little piece of machinery designed that night has been the key machine in all that I have been building since.

A BUSINESSMAN JUST AS MUCH AS A PREACHER

For 25 years or more, I've been traveling this land of ours and a few foreign countries trying to teach and preach by word of mouth and example, that a Christian businessman owes as much to God as a preacher does. The rest of the time I build machinery, almost any kind of machinery as long as it is big, and powerful, and can move around to do things no other machine could do before. Some people think I'm all mixed up—that you can't serve the Lord and business, too, but that's just the point. God needs businessmen as partners as well as preachers. When He created the world and everything in it, He didn't mean for us to stop there and say, "God, you've done it all. There's nothing left for us to build." He wanted us to take off from there and really build for His greater glory.

(Mover of Men and Mountains, *Prentice-Hall*, 1960)

⁂ SADHU SUNDAR SINGH ⁂
(1889–1933)

Indian Christian mystic who was raised a Sikh. A mighty conversion to Christ, whom he had ridiculed, took place after great despair from the death of his mother. He cried out, "Oh God, if there be a God reveal yourself to me tonight." If God did not speak to him before morning, he planned to lay his head on the rails and wait for a train. At 4:45 a. m. a bright cloud of light suddenly filled his room and out of the brightness came the face and figure of Jesus who said, "How long are you going to persecute me. For you I gave my life. You were praying to know the right way, why don't you take it? I am the Way." That moment he believed.

HE IS MY LIFE

Christ is my Saviour. He is my life. He is everything to me in heaven and earth. Once while traveling in a sandy region I was tired and thirsty. Standing on the top of a mound I looked for water. The sight of a lake at a distance brought joy to me, for now I hoped to quench my thirst. I walked toward it for a long time, but I could never reach it. Afterwards I found out that it was a mirage, only a mere appearance of water caused by the refracted rays of the sun. In reality there was none. In a like manner I was moving about the world in search of the water of life. The things of this world—wealth, position, honor and luxury—looked like a lake. By drinking of those waters I hoped to quench my spiritual thirst. But I could never find a drop of water to quench the thirst of my heart. I was dying of thirst. When my spiritual eyes were opened, I saw the rivers of living water flowing from His pierced side. I drank of it and was satisfied. Thirst was no more. Ever since I have always drunk of that water of life, and have never been athirst in the sandy desert of this world. My heart is full of praise.

(From The Sadhu, *by B. H. Streeter and A. J. Appasamy)*

THE DEEP EXPERIENCE OF THE INNER LIFE

It is very difficult to explain the deep experience of the inner life. As Goethe has said: "The highest cannot be spoken." But it can be enjoyed and put into action. This is what I mean. One day, during my meditation and prayer, I felt His presence strongly. My heart overflowed with heavenly joy. I saw that in this world of sorrow and suffering there is a hidden and inexhaustible mine of great joy of which the world knows nothing, because even men who experience it are not able to speak of it adequately and convincingly.

(With and Without Christ)

⊰ OSWALD J. SMITH ⊱

(1889–1986)

American writer of many books and hymns. He remembered what his Sunday School teacher said when he was a boy: "Any one of you boys might be a minister." He answered in his heart, "I will be that boy."

I KNEW IT BEYOND A SHADOW OF A DOUBT

Then suddenly it happened. I cannot explain it even to this day. It seems so simple and so ordinary. I just bowed my face in my hands and, suddenly, the tears gushed through my fingers and down on to the chair. And all I know is that Jesus Christ, the Savior of the World, came into this heart of mine. I knew as I dried my tears that the great change had taken place, knew it beyond the shadow of a doubt. That was forty years ago. It has lasted from that day to this, and Jesus Christ means more to me now than He ever did before.

(Recalling a meeting conducted by R. A. Torrey)

⚜ KATHERINE BUTLER HATHAWAY ⚜

(1890–1942)

American writer. In 1895, at age five, she was strapped to a board for ten years to counter the effects of spinal tuberculosis, but the treatment stunted her growth. She nevertheless strove to overcome her physical disabilities.

LIKE THE FLOWERS OF SPRING

It is wonderful never to have read or known anything about the teachings of Christ until you have found that in spite of your proud intellect and your worldly experience and your artistic insight you are defeated and helpless. Then they do seem like the flowers of spring—for freshness and miraculous beauty and so much more besides.

(From her memoir, The Journals and Letters of the
Little Locksmith, *Coward-McCann, Inc., 1942)*

⚜ CHRISTOPHER MORLEY ⚜

(1890–1957)

American writer.

A THOUSAND QUESTIONS

I had a thousand questions to ask God, but when I met him, they all fled and didn't seem to matter.

*(*Inward Ho! *Copyright 1923, 1950 by Christopher Morley, pub. by J. B. Lippincott)*

⊰ DWIGHT D. EISENHOWER ⊱
(1890–1969)

Thirty-fourth President of the United States.

ONE OF THE SIMPLEST NECESSITIES OF LIFE

Personal prayer, it seems to me, is one of the simplest necessities of life, as basic to the individual as sunshine, food and water—and at times, of course, more so. By prayer I believe we mean an effort to get in touch with the Infinite. We know that our prayers are imperfect. Of course they are. We are imperfect human beings. A thousand experiences have convinced me beyond room of doubt that prayer multiples the strength of the individual and brings within the scope of his capabilities almost any conceivable objective.

COURAGE AND CONFIDENCE

This is what I found out about religion: It gives you courage to make decisions you must make in a crisis, and then the confidence to leave the result to a Higher Power. Only by trust in God can a man carrying responsibility find repose.

⊰ EDITH STEIN ⊱
(1891–1942)

German Carmelite nun who died at Auschwitz.

SATISFIED WITH EVERYTHING

I am satisfied with everything. The only way of winning a knowledge of the Cross is by feeling the whole weight of the Cross. I have been convinced of this from the first moment.

ᨏ EDNA ST. VINCENT MILLAY ᨎ

(1892–1950)

American poet and playwright.

A GLAD AWAKENING

O God, I cried, give me new birth
And put me back upon the earth!...
I ceased; and through the breathless hush
That answered me, the far-off rush
Of herald wings came whispering
Like music down the vibrant string
Of my ascending prayer...
I know not how such things can be;
I only know there came to me
A fragrance such as never clings
To aught save happy living things;
A sound as of some joyous elf
Singing sweet songs to please himself,
And, through and over everything,
A sense of glad awakening....

(Taken from "Renascence", a poem of 214 lines written at age sixteen)

ᨏ ARTHUR H. COMPTON ᨎ

(1892–1962)

Physicist, educator, recipient of the Nobel Prize for Physics, 1927, for research on the scattering of x-rays, which he explained by assuming that the rays consist of tiny discrete particles now called photons.

"IN THE BEGINNING GOD CREATED THE HEAVEN AND THE EARTH"
For myself, faith begins with a realization that a supreme intelligence brought the universe into being and created man. It is not difficult for me to have this faith, for it is incontrovertible that where there is a plan there is intelligence. An orderly, unfolding universe

testifies to the truth of the most majestic statement ever uttered: "In the beginning God created the heaven and the earth."

(Knight's Illustrations for Today, Moody)

ᴁ WILLIAM FAULKNER ᴂ
(1897–1962)

Nobel prize winning American novelist and short story writer recognized as one of this century's best. The following excerpt is taken from his acceptance speech, December 10, 1950

A SPIRIT CAPABLE OF COMPASSION

I decline to accept the end of man. ...I believe that man will not merely endure; he will prevail. He is immortal, not because he has an inexhaustible voice, but because he has a soul, a spirit capable of compassion and sacrifice and endurance.

("Chemical and Engineering News", December 24, 2001)

ᴁ A. W. TOZER ᴂ
(1897–1963)

American pastor of deep spirituality who instilled that in his preaching, teaching, and writing. He traced the awakening of his intellect and every other gift to his conversion at age fifteen. It was for him a transforming experience like Saul's on the road to Damascus, but the seed had been planted by his paternal grandmother who often talked to the children about God. His writings reveal a deep thirst for the things of God. He is best known for *The Pursuit of God,* which he wrote on a train trip late at night from Chicago to Texas in the late 1940's.

JESUS CHRIST WAS BECKONING TO ME

I do not mind telling you that I have always found Jesus Christ beckoning to me throughout the Scriptures. I am convinced that it was

God's design that we should find the divine Creator, Redeemer and Lord whenever we search the Scriptures.

(Renewed Day by Day, Vol. 1)

SUNLIT PEAKS

Some will read and will recognize an accurate description of the sunlit peaks where they have been for at least brief periods and to which they long often to return. And such will need no proof.

(The Root of the Righteous)

⚶ C. S. LEWIS ⚵
(1898–1963)

Brilliant British scholar, writer, and poet of religious themes. He was born in Ireland and taught at Oxford and Cambridge. He became a believer after a long period of internal questioning and intellectual struggle. It was in 1931 that he was "surprised by joy," Lewis' own description of his conversion to Christianity and also the title of his autobiography. All his life he had experienced moments of intense and sudden joy. At last he recognized his moments of joy for what they were—pointers or signposts to the perfect joy that awaited him in the presence of God.

IF A GOOD GOD MADE THE WORLD, WHY HAS IT GONE WRONG?

And for many years I simply refused to listen to the Christian answers to this question, because I kept on feeling "Whatever you say, and however clever your arguments are, isn't it much simpler and easier to say that the world was not made by any intelligent power? Aren't all your arguments simply a complicated attempt to avoid the obvious?" But then that threw me back into another difficulty.

My argument against God was that the universe seemed so cruel and unjust. A man does not call a line crooked unless he has some idea of a straight line. What was I comparing this universe with when I called it unjust? If the whole show was bad and senseless from A to Z, so to speak, why did I, who was supposed to be part of the show, find myself in such violent reaction against it? A man feels wet when he falls into water, because man is not a water animal: a fish would not feel wet. Of course I could have given up my idea of justice by saying it was nothing but a private idea of my own. But if I did that, then my argument against God collapsed too—for the argument depended on saying that the world was really unjust, not simply that it did not happen to please my private fancies. Thus in the very act of trying to prove that God did not exist—in other words, that the whole of reality was senseless—I found I was forced to assume that one part of reality—namely my idea of justice—justice was full of sense. Consequently atheism turns out to be too simple. If the whole universe has no meaning, we should never have found out that it has no meaning: just as, if there were no light in the universe and therefore no creatures with eyes, we should never know it was dark. Dark would be without meaning.

(Mere Christianity, a book composed of material taken from talks on various Christian topics delivered through Great Britain and the U. S.)

YOU ARE THE ANSWER

I know now, Lord, why you utter no answer.
You are yourself the answer.
Before your face questions die away.

(Till We Have Faces)

SEEING EVERYTHING ELSE

I believe in Christ like I believe in the sun, not just because I see it, but because by it I can see everything else.

(Weight of Glory, "Is Theology Poetry?")

THE MOST PROBABLE EXPLANATION

If I find in myself a desire which no experience in this world can satisfy, the most probable explanation is that I was made for another world. If none of my earthly pleasures satisfy it, that does not prove that the universe is a fraud. Probably earthly pleasures were never meant to satisfy it, but only to arouse it, to suggest the real thing. If that is so, I must take care, on the one hand, never to despise, or be unthankful for, the earthly blessings, and on the other, never to mistake them for the something else of which they are only a kind of copy, or echo, or mirage. I must keep alive in myself the desire for my true country, which I shall not find till after death; I must never let it get snowed under or turned aside; I must make it the main object of life to press on to that other country and to help others to do the same.

(Mere Christianity)

PRAYER CHANGES ME

I pray all the time these days. If I stopped praying, I think I'd stop living....I pray because I can't help myself. I pray because I'm helpless. I pray because the need flows out of me all the time, waking and sleeping. It doesn't change God, it changes me.

JOY AND PLEASURE

Joy is never in our power, and pleasure is. I doubt whether anyone who has tasted joy would ever, if both were in his power, exchange it for all the pleasure in the world.

SURPRISED BY JOY

I know very well when, but hardly how, the final step was taken. I was driven to Whipsnade one sunny morning. When we set out I did not believe that Jesus Christ is the Son of God, and when we reached the zoo I did. Yet I had not exactly spent the journey in thought. Nor in great emotion. "Emotional" is perhaps the last word we can apply to some of the most important events. It was more like when a man, after long sleep, still lying motionless in bed, becomes aware that he is now awake. And it was, like that moment on top of the bus, ambiguous. Freedom, or necessity? Or do they differ at their maximun? At that maximum a man is what he does; there is nothing of him left over or outside the act. As for what we commonly call Will, and what we commonly call Emotion, I fancy these usually talk too loud, protest too much, to be quite believed, and we have a secret suspicion that the great passion or the iron resolution is partly a put-up job.

(Surprised By Joy, *Lewis' autobiography, describing his conversion*)

⨯ EDWIN P. BOOTH ⨯

(1898–1969)

American actor who tells of his experiences upon hearing the news of his son's death in World War II in April, 1945.

GOD IS WORKING OUT HIS PURPOSES

At first the whole world was shaken beneath my feet. Then slowly a few simplicities came steadily before me. God's existence never wavered in my thought. His nature of Fatherhood stood steadfast. I could not cry out against him for I realized I thought him powerless without us. I seemed to sense his tears as real as my own, and to hear his cry as poignantly as that of the boy's mother. A God who works under law and plays no favorites became the center of the universe. My philosophy of history never faltered...One comes to feel that God is above and in all things, working, with his universe and his people toward the final goal. History lightens up with the glow from spirits who are immortal and into whose company Bray (his son) now has entered. Deep peace comes with the thought of the struggling millions whose lives are lifted a little by the tragedy of war. Moral vigor enters to defeat the continuing selfishness and to urge us to continue in our work. Christ seems in honest truth to be the Elder Brother of our suffering.

(From Experience to Faith, *Association Press, 1951*)

⨯ WHITTIKER CHAMBERS ⨯

(1901–1961)

American, a former Communist and Soviet spy.

THE FINGER OF GOD WAS LAID UPON MY FOREHEAD

My daughter was in her high chair. I was watching her eat. She was the most miraculous thing that had ever happened in my life. I liked to watch her even when she smeared porridge on her face or dropped it meditatively on the floor. My eye came to rest on the delicate convulutions of her ear—those intricate, perfect ears. The thought passed through my mind: "No, those ears were not created by any chance coming together of atoms in nature (the Communist view). They could have been created only by immense design." The thought was involuntary and unwanted. I crowded it out of my mind. But I never wholly forgot it or the occasion I had to crowd it out of my mind. If I had completed it, I should have had to say: Design presupposes God. I did not then know that, at that moment, the finger of God was first laid upon my forehead.

(Witness)

≈ PETER MARSHALL ≈

(1903–1949)

Popular Presbyterian pastor and chaplain of the United States Senate. While out walking one Sunday afternoon in Scotland, where he grew up, three weeks after he prayed fervently for guidance for the direction in life, in his own dramatic phrase, "God tapped me on the shoulder." An opportunity opened for him to come to America.

TAP ON THE SHOULDER
I know that Christ is alive,
and personal
and real, and closer than we think.
I have met Him.
I have felt His presence.

✦ GRETTA PALMER ✦

(1905–1953)

American free-lance journalist who converted from atheism to Christianity. She wrote *God's Underground*, 1949, which narrates the experiences of Father George, a Croat priest who, incognito, spent many months inside Russia, spreading the gospel.

THE FOOTHILLS OF HEAVEN

The new world into which I have entered is flooded with the sunshine of God's love. His divine artistry is mirrored in the running brook, the smiling meadow, and the tall trees which lift verdant fingers in prayer and praise to their Creator. I glimpse His artistry as He paints the wayside flowers and lights the evening star. All nature, tremulous with His presence, is articulate in His homage. Books, people, the experiences of every day also echo Him, so that I can best describe the new world into which I have come as at least the foothills of heaven.

✦ DAWSON TROTMAN ✦

(1905–1956)

Founder of the Navigators, a Bible study and witnessing organization.

A CHALLENGE TO MEMORIZE VERSES LED ME TO CHRIST

God picked out a couple of schoolteachers to have a large part in my coming to Christ. Miss Mills was a general science teacher, and I was one of her problem pupils. She wrote my name down on her prayer list and prayed for me every day for six solid years. On the Friday night when I was arrested, she was home with Miss Thomas, looking up verses in the Bible to find ten on the subject of salvation which they could give to the young people to memorize. Little did she know that the boy for whom she had prayed for six years was going to memorize those verses.

(With a characteristic desire to win the contest, he learned the ten verses by the next Sunday night, and during the next week he learned ten more. And the Word of God transformed him.)

≈ DIETRICH BONHOEFFER ≈
(1906–1945)

Theologian who died a political martyr for speaking out fearlessly against the Nazi regime. In obedience to Jesus Christ, he took up the cross of resistance even when he knew it would probably mean death. He was arrested in 1943, imprisoned at Buchenwald and hanged on April 8, 1945. His last words, a message to a friend, were, "This is the end—for me the beginning of life." His writings live on, inspiring many with his insights into God's grace and living at all cost for Him.

I AM TRAVELING MY APPOINTED ROAD

I'm so sure of God's guiding hand and I hope I shall never lose that certainty. You must never doubt that I am traveling my appointed road with gratitude and cheerfulness. My past life is replete with God's goodness, and my sins are covered by the forgiving love of Christ crucified. I am thankful for all those who have crossed my path, and all I wish is never to cause them sorrow, and that they, like me, will always be thankful for the forgiveness and mercy of God and sure of it. Please don't for a moment get upset by all this, but let it rejoice your heart.

(Letter written while in prison waiting to be hanged.)

GOD CAN USE OUR MISTAKES

I believe that God can and will bring good out of evil, even out of the greatest evil. For that purpose he needs men who make the best use of everything. I believe that God will give us all the strength we need to help us resist in all time of distress. But he even gives it in advance, lest we should rely on ourselves and not on him alone. A faith such as this should allay all our fears for the future. I believe that even our mistakes and shortcomings are turned to good account, and that it is no harder for God to deal with them than with our supposedly good deeds. I believe that God is not timeless fate, but that he waits for and answers sincere prayers and responsible actions.

(Letters and Papers from Prison)

⊰ JOHN STAM ⊱

(1907–1934)

John and his wife, Betty, were called to the mission field in China. Within a few years they had been arrested by hostile Communist soldiers, held for ransom, and then beheaded. Though their mission was brief, their courage led hundreds of other young people to volunteer for missionary service.

AS WE LOOK BACK

Take away anything I have, but do not take away the sweetness of walking and talking with the King of Glory! It is good to let our thoughts run away with us sometimes, concerning the greatness of our God and His marvelous kindness to us. As we look back, what wonderful leadings and providences we see; what encouragement we find for the future.

⊰ ETTY HILLESUM ⊱

(1914–1943)

A young Jewish woman living in Amsterdam in 1942. During that time, the Nazis were arresting Jews and herding them off to concentration camps. As she awaited inevitable arrest, and with a fear of the unknown, she began to read the Bible, and there she met Jesus. She embraced God and found courage and confidence. She died at Auschwitz in 1943 at the age of twenty-nine.

LIFE BECOMES ONE LONG STROLL WITH GOD

From all sides our destruction creeps up on us and soon the ring will be closed and no one at all will be able to come to our aid. But I don't feel that I am in anybody's clutches. I feel safe in God's arms. And whether I am sitting at my beloved old desk in the Jewish district or in a labor camp under SS guards, I shall feel safe in God's arms. For once you have begun to walk with God, you need only keep on walking with Him, and all of life becomes one long stroll—such a marvelous feeling....I hate nobody. I am not embittered. And once the love of mankind has germinated in you, it will grow without measure.

(An Interrupted Life:Diaries of Etty Hillesum, 1941–1943; *written about her internment in a prison in Amsterdam during World War II.*)

OTHER WRITERS OF THE FIRST HALF OF THE TWENTIETH CENTURY

FOR SEVENTY-SIX YEARS I HAVE KNOWN GOD'S LOVE

My experience of seventy-six years includes many more blessings than I am able to recount. From the early date of six years I have been made the recipient of God's love, and the life of the Believer has been beautiful to me.

(*Author unknown, taken from* The Shaker Manifesto XII, 3, 1882)

FACE TO FACE

As for me, the writing on the face of the earth is too clear to leave place for hesitation. I can read nothing but this: a will and intelligence working out a design, a person striving to accomplish some purpose through slowly yielding difficulties, a God.......Only of this I am assured, that some time and in some way, spirit to spirit, face to face, I shall meet the great Lord of life, and falling before Him, tell my gratitude for all He has done, and implore pardon for all that I have left undone.

(*Paul Elmer More, editor, critic and scholar, 1864-1937,* Pages from an Oxford Diary, *Princeton: Princeton University Press, 1937 Chapter XXVIII and XXXIII*)

WHY I BELIEVE IN GOD

The supreme reason I have for trusting God is—God. My religion is not founded upon my ability to understand God nor upon my ability to lay down what I shall recognize as a logical course for this procedure. I trust Him because he is God.

(*Merton S. Rice, 1872-1943*)

THOUGHTS ON GROWING OLDER

They say I am growing old because my hair is silvered, and there are crow's feet on my forehead, and my step is not as firm and elastic as before. But they are mistaken. That is not me. The knees are weak, but the knees are not me. The brow is wrinkled, but the brow is not me. This is the house I live in, but I am young—younger than ever I was before.

(James Guthrie, 1874–1952)

THE ONE WHITE FLOWER

Homer and Plato, Aristotle and Shakespeare were men of great intellectual power and literary genius. Like great mountain peaks, they tower over the heads of the common herd. I am in debt to these men. They have enriched my life, but with all their genius, I am not willing to call any one of them Lord and Master.

But when I come into the presence of Jesus I feel that I am on holy ground. To me He is the one white flower of the human race. I am enthralled by the beauty of His character. All my highest ideals are realized in Him. He is such a person as I would expect God to be if He became incarnate. His life of purity, the compassionate heart that made Him a friend of the poor and the outcast, the heroism that enabled Him to meet slander and hatred and persecution, the love that leaped the barriers of race and social position, the sacrificial spirit that sent Him staggering up the hill of Calvary with a cross on His back, the richness of His grace revealed in His prayer for them who were murdering him, "Father, forgive them, for they know not what they do,"—all command the allegiance of my heart. Such a character is worthy not only of my homage, but of my worship. He and He only is my Master and Lord.

(Perry J. Stackhouse, 1875–)

I CAME BACK TO THE REAL THING

I shall never forget a Sunday morning service on an English liner. I had spent the summer in Europe, my first visit. I had been hungry to see everything. I had rushed through churches and cathedrals, but I had paused to worship in none. Then came this morning service at sea. The ship's orchestra playing, not dance music but the dear old hymns, the Bible being read, the captain leading the worship, reading from the prayer book so reverently. The people worshipping so earnestly, I arose refreshed; it was a blessed experience to worship on that ship. I had needed it so much, having been so long away from worship. And so we come back, after our indifference, after our sins, after our neglect, after our selfishness, after our eager quests—we come back to the real thing, to the Bible, to God.

(John R. Ewers, b. 1877)

THE MAJESTY OF GOD EVERLASTING

I was on the edge of the Libyan Desert. A black Bedouin stood beside the camel on which I sat. The colossal, dim pyramids rose in the background, and the full moon shone on the face of the Sphinx. My camel stood high on the rim of a hill of sand, and I sat on his back like an island in the sky. Yet the sublime face of that monument was lifted so high above me that I had to look far upward to see it. I had known that for ages the riddle of the Sphinx was a byword, yet I gazed on that amazing form in the moonlight so thrilled by its majesty that I never thought of the riddle at all. Even so, while Death stands like a black Bedouin at my knee, I seem to gaze on God, on things unseen which are eternal. Faith never thrives on self-deception. I will acknowledge my stark horror of death; I will own my poor human fears. Nevertheless I do not doubt. I am gazing at a reality so sublime that all these shrivel in its presence. By very contrast they show me the majesty of God Everlasting. Life is a reality so majestic that all its riddles fade. "I know that my Redeemer liveth."

(Arthur Wentworth Hewitt, 1883-)

AS THE AFTERNOON SUN SINKS LOWER

I watch the sunset as I look out over the rim of the blue Pacific, and there is no mystery beyond the horizon line, because I know what there is over there. I have been there. I have journeyed in those lands. Over there where the sun is sinking is Japan. That star is rising over China. In that direction lie the Philippines. I know all that. Well, there is another land that I look forward to as I watch the sunset. I have never seen it. I have never seen anyone who has been there, but it has a more abiding reality than any of these lands which I do know. This land beyond the sunset—this land of immortality, this fair and blessed country of the soul—why, this heaven of ours is the one thing in the world which I know with absolute, unshaken, unchangeable certainty. This I know with a knowledge that is never shadowed by a passing cloud of doubt. I may not always be certain about this world; my geographical locations may sometimes become confused, but the other—that I know. And as the afternoon sun sinks lower, faith shines more clearly, and hope, lifting her voice in a higher key, sings the songs of fruition. My work is about ended, I think. The best of it I have done poorly; any of it I might have done better; but I have done it. And in a fairer land, with finer material and a better working light, I shall do a better work.

(Robert Burdette, 1844-1914, in a letter shortly before his death)

IT'S BEEN A GREAT RUN

As I sit in the study on a beautiful, cool August afternoon, I look back with many thanks. It has been a great run. I wouldn't have missed it for anything. Much could and should have been better, and I have, by no means, done what I should have done with all that I have been given. But the overall experience of being alive has been a thrilling experience. I believe that death is a doorway to more of it... But with Christ's atonement and Him gone on before, I have neither doubt nor fear whether I am left here a brief time or a long one. I believe that I shall see Him and know Him...It is His forgiveness and grace that give confidence and not merits of our own. But again I say, it's been a great run.

(Samuel Moor Shoemaker, 1893-1963, shortly before his death)

WITHOUT KNOWING IT, MY SEARCH WAS FOR GOD

I found myself in finding God. What I was searching for was my own identity, and without knowing it my search was for God.

(D. R. Davies 1889–1958, In Search of Myself)

A JOY THAT NEVER LEAVES ME

God is more real to me than any thought or thing or person. I feel his presence positively, and the more as I live in closer harmony with his laws as written in my body and mind. I feel him in the sunshine or rain; and awe mingled with a delicious restfulness most nearly describes my feelings. I talk to him as to a companion in prayer and praise, and our communion is delightful. He answers me again and again, often in words so clearly spoken that it seems my outer ear must have carried the tone, but generally in strong mental impressions. Usually a text of Scripture, school matters, social problems, financial difficulties, etc. That he is mine and I am his never leaves me. It is an abiding joy. Without it life would be a blank, a desert, a shoreless, trackless waste.

(Author Unknown, age 49, in William James' Varieties of Religious Experiences)

I REMEMBER THE NIGHT I STOOD FACE TO FACE WITH GOD

I remember the night, and almost the very spot on the hillside, where my soul opened out, as it were, into the Infinite, and there was a rushing together of the two worlds, the inner and the outer. It was deep calling unto deep—the deep that my own struggle had opened up within being answered by the unfathomable deep without, reaching beyond the stars. I stood alone with Him who had made me, and all the beauty of the world, and love, and sorrow, and even temptation. I did not seek Him, but felt the perfect union of my spirit with His. The ordinary sense of things around me faded. For the moment nothing but an ineffable joy and exultation remained. It is impossible fully to describe the experience. It was like the effect of some great orchestra when all the separate notes have melted into one swelling harmony that leaves the listener conscious of nothing save that his soul is being wafted upwards, and almost bursting with its own emotion. The perfect stillness of the night was thrilled by a more solemn silence. The darkness held a presence that was all the more felt because it was not seen. I could not any more have doubted that He was there than that I was. Indeed, I felt myself to be, if possible, the less real of the two.

My highest faith in God and truest idea of Him were then born in me. I have stood upon the Mount of Vision since, and felt the Eternal round about me. But never since has there come quite the same stirring of the heart. Then, if ever, I believe, I stood face to face with God, and was born anew of His spirit.

(Author Unknown, from William James, The Varieties of Religious Experience)

SERVING GOD

When I was a girl, I came across a sentence by George William Curtis that I have never forgotten, and that has encouraged me more than any other saying I know. It was that "An engine of one-cat power, running all the time, is more effective than one of forty-horse power standing idle." I realized strongly that I had not a forty-horse power, that my life was narrow in many ways, and my opportunities were likely to be few. But one-cat power I certainly possessed and I determined to run my little engine as hard and as steadily as I could serving God.

(Author unknown)

I PUT MY HAND IN THE HAND OF GOD

And I said to the man who stood at the gate of the year:

"Give me a light, that I may tread safely into the unknown!"

And he replied: "Go out in to the darkness and put your hand into the hand of God.

That shall be to you better than light and safer than a known way."

So, I went forth, and finding the hand of God, trod gladly into the night.

And He led me toward the hills and the breaking of day in the lone East.

(M. Louise Haskins, 1875–1957)

WITHOUT QUESTION

So sure has become my faith in this love of God that I abide in it without question. When my human prayer is not answered the way I would expect, then I am exalted, for I know that I have submitted to a will greater than my own, capable of infinitely more goodness.

(The mother of Glenn Clark [1882–1956] in her parting
message to her son just a few days before her death)

RESURRECTION

If it be all for naught, or nothingness
At last, why does God make the world so fair?
Why spill this golden splendor out across
The western hills, and light the silver lamp
Of eve? Why give me eyes to see, and soul
To love so strong and deep? Then, with a pang
This brightness stabs me through, and wakes within
Rebellious voice to cry against all death?
Why set this hunger for eternity
To gnaw my heartstrings through, if death ends all?
If Christ rose not again.

(Unknown soldier, killed in World War I, poem found after his death)

THE UNSEARCHABLE RICHES OF CHRIST

I shall never forget that night. Not only did I know that I was born again, but I knew that I had received a call even then to preach the unsearchable riches of Jesus Christ. I didn't know anything about the Bible. I did not even know that John 3:16 was in the Scriptures. I had no knowledge of the Word of God at all. But I had a knowledge that Christ was my Savior, and that my sins were gone, and that

I was a new creature in Christ Jesus, and that the old things had passed away and all things had become new. The fear that I had lived in for three years from the drowning experience at fifteen years of age was gone, and I knew that some day I would spend eternity with Christ.

(Norman Vernon, after almost drowning in a rafting accident at age 15, was led to think of eternity and his future. He still lived a wayward life until he was led to Christ at an evangelistic meeting.)

I DESIRE ONLY TO BE HIS SERVANT

What to me is the title 'well-born,' when I have been born again in Christ? What to me is the title 'lord,' when I desire only to be a servant of the Lord Christ? What is it to me to be called, 'Your Grace,' when I have need of God's grace, help, and succor? All these vanities I will away with, and all else I will lay at the feet of Jesus, my dearest Lord, that I may have no hindrance in serving Him aright.

(Baron von Welz, renouncing his title and wealth to become a missionary in Dutch Guiana and there give his life in service.)

THE DAWN

One morn I rose and looked upon the world.
"Have I been blind until this hour?" I said.
On every trembling leaf the sun had spread,
And was like golden tapestry unfurled;
And as the moments passed more light was hurled
Upon the drinking earth athirst for light;
And I, beholding all this wondrous sight,
Cried out aloud, "O God, I love Thy world!"
And since that waking, often I drink deep
The joy of dawn, and peace abides with me;
And though I know that I again shall see
Dark fear with withered hand approach my sleep,
More sure am I when lonely night shall flee,
At dawn the sun will bring good cheer to me.

(Author Unknown)

COULD SUCH PERFECTION JUST HAPPEN TO BE?

How beautiful in form! How perfect in design! How symmetrical in construction! The main ribs were the same in each leaf, while the smaller being all had the same graceful slant and number! Such perfection of design could never just happen to be! Surely, there must be a Designer somewhere behind these leaves!

(Commenting one day when he found two four-leaf clovers)

There must be a Great Designer behind the lives of men in history! Verily, there must have been a Great Designer behind my life, and He must be interested in me personally!

(Samuel Smith, who had memorized Scripture to use in his debating tours to prove the fallacies of God's Word, now upon observing the four-leaf clovers, fell on his knees and begged for mercy.)

EVERYTHING HAS HAPPENED

Who are you, any one, who can remain unmoved when the Light breaks upon you?

Who can say it does not concern him?

Who can say it is just as well not to see as to see?

Who can ever be the same child or woman or man again after the Day has broken?

Who can admit there is anything else in the world; after this has come to the world?

I brushed all obstructions from my door sill and stepped into the road.

And though so many cried to me, I did not turn back;

And though I was very sorrowful having to leave so many friends behind, I did not turn back;

For when the soul is once started on the soul's journey, it can never turn back....

Can you now go on with your old life as if nothing had happened?

The whole universe has happened.

(Author Unknown)

THOUGHTS SHORTLY BEFORE EXECUTION

In a little while at five o'clock it is going to happen, we will be executed, and that is not so terrible....On the contrary, it is beautiful to be in God's strength. God has told us that he will not forsake us if only we pray to him for support. I feel so strongly my nearness to God. I am fully prepared to die....I have confessed all my sins to him and have become very quiet. Therefore do not mourn but trust in God and pray for strength....Give me a firm handshake. God's will be done....Greet everybody for the four of us....We are courageous. Be the same. They can only take our bodies. Our souls are in God's hands....May God bless you all. Have no hate. I die without hatred. God rules everything.

> (A twenty-two year old Dutch patriot in a letter to his parents before
> he was executed by a Nazi firing squad for the crime of trying to escape
> with his three companions to England and join the Dutch forces there.)

ONE STEP AT A TIME

Ten of us met in New York to sail. We were faith missionaries, with no board to take care of us. There was no home ready for us to go as far as we knew. No one was pledged to send us money. None of these things troubled me at first. I must have been half way across the Atlantic before I began seriously to wonder where I would go when I finally reached India. But it did come to me at last and then I began to pray about it. Then God gave me a dream. I saw myself standing on a tiny little plank which was floating in a vast ocean. Absolutely nothing in front of me, or behind me, or at the sides. But, as I lifted my foot as if to step, another little board appeared just in front, ready for me to step on it. So God comforted me and seemed to be telling me that I was to trust Him for one step at a time. And so I went happily on, always finding a plank in front ready to be stepped on when needed.

> (Mrs. W. K. Norton, from My Life, of the Pilgrim's Mission, Benares, India)

IF I HAVE NOT THE LOVE OF CHRIST

Though I have a scientific mind and a university degree in sociology and philosophy, and although I am an expert in social service and an authority on Browning, and though I use the language of the scientific laboratory so as to deceive the very elect into thinking I am a scholar, and have not a message of salvation and the love of Christ, I am a misfit in the pulpit and no preacher of the Gospel.

(Unknown Author)

ABOUT DYING

Really, I care not whether I am dying or not; for, if I die, I shall be with God; if I live, He will be with me.

(When asked by a friend during a man's last illness whether he thought himself dying.)

MY EDITORIALS MUST COINCIDE WITH THE BIBLE

On one side of that desk is a Bible and on the other side is a typewriter. I try to make the two sides of this desk speak the same thing. For I know that if what I write in my editorials coincides with what is in that book, it will live on; but if it is out of harmony with that book, it will perish.

(Editor of a large American newspaper)

A LIFE CHANGE

What I have in Christ is not an impression, but a life change; not an impression which might evaporate, but a faith of central personal change. I do not merely feel changes; I am changed. Another becomes my moral life. He has done more than deeply influence me. He has possessed me. I am not His loyal subject, but His absolute property.

(P. T. Forsyth, The Person and Place of Christ, Lecture xii.)

FROM THE BIBLE LEFT BEHIND BY PRISON VOLUNTEERS

I was not sufficiently impressed to have any special belief in what I was reading. I put the New Testament on the shelf. A little later when I was tired of doing nothing, I took down the book again and began to read. This time I saw how Jesus was handed over to Pilate and tried unjustly and put to death by crucifixion. As I read this I began to think. I went on, and my attention was next taken with these words: 'And Jesus said: Father, forgive them, for they know not what they do! I stopped.' I was stabbed to the heart as if by a five-inch nail. What did the verse reveal to me? Shall I call it the love of the heart of Christ? Shall I call it his compassion? I do not know what to call it. I only know that with an unspeakable grateful heart, I believed.

(Note left behind by a man who was executed. Two Japanese women had visited him, but found him unresponsive, so they left a copy of the New Testament on the table and left, as told by Henry Sloan Coffin's, 1877-1954, God Confronts Man in History)

❧ CLOSING THOUGHT ❧

It would be a profound mistake to assume that only one type of experience, and that a unique one, has the sole right to be called "a direct approach" to God. In John's vision of the New Jerusalem there were gates of entrance on all sides of the four-square city. So, too, when many persons stand on the shore of the sea in a moonlight night the path of light comes across the water straight in front of each beholder, and meets him where he stands as though he were the only one to be favored with the lane of light. It is somewhat so with the ways which lead to God. There are many in number, and they are adapted to the need and the aptitudes of the different wayfarers who are to make the pilgrimage. Any way which brings a person home is a good way.

(Rufus Jones)

❧ PART VIII ❧

Glimpses from 1951–2000
An Age of Turmoil and Scientific Advances,
but Hope for the Future

By the mid-60s religious enthusiasm had faded in the United States. It was a time of turmoil, including the Civil Rights movement, the Vietnam War, and the peace movement, followed by unprecedented prosperity, drug abuse, and controversies over the legalization of abortion and the constitutionality of school prayer. The Second Vatican Council led to an openness in relations between Catholics and Protestants. The late twentieth century saw increased complexities of life: unprecedented scientific and technological advances, including widespread use of computers and the proliferation of Internet usage; and fast paced medical and biogenetic advances, including "test tube" babies, cloning, and human gene decoding.

I am the bread of life. He who comes to me will never go hungry, and he who believes in me will never be thirsty.
JOHN 6:35

◢ ARCHIBALD RUTLEDGE ◣

(1883–1973)

Versatile and prolific American writer and poet who was chosen Poet Laureate of South Carolina in 1934. More than sixty of his poems have been set to music.

AS INFALLIBLE AS THE RISING SUN

Sunrise suggests to me not only the power of God grandly to continue what He has begun but it also conveys the reassurance of the Creator's love returning to us daily, bringing joy and forgiveness; and to many reflective heart it intimates that no night is final; for, since with God all things are possible, His almighty love has, I confidently believe, prepared for us a radiant future beyond the sundown of death. And if I meditate but momentarily upon what He has done and upon what He does do, confidence in immortality is natural, reasonable, and, to my way of believing, to be counted upon as infallible as the sunrise.

(Peace in the Heart)

SUSTAINED BY EVERLASTING ARMS

And when the time comes for our migration hence to a land unknown, through a misty darkness, He will not desert us. In the rainy night, in that cavernous and monstrous dark, the frailest abide secure. In that flight amid other spheres than ours I believe we shall know what it means to be sustained by Everlasting Arms.

("Children of Swamp and Wood", a nature story)

⊰ FRANK C. LAUBACH ⊱

(1884–1970)

American Congregational missionary to the Maros on the island of Mindanao in the Philippines. He came to them with a heart filled with love and a deep sense of God's presence. His literacy efforts enabled many to read and write. He was responsible for translating the Bible into many languages. In *Letters by a Modern Mystic,* letters written to his father while on the mission field, he relates his efforts to continually live in the presence of God.

THE MOST IMPORTANT THING

January 26, 1930

We used to sing a song in church in Benton which I liked, but which I never really practiced until now. It runs

Moment by moment I'm kept in His love;
Moment by moment I've life from above;
Looking to Jesus till glory doth shine;
Moment by moment, O Lord, I am Thine."

It is exactly that "moment by moment," every waking moment, surrender, responsiveness, obedience, sensitiveness, pliability, "lost in His love," that I now have the mind-bent to explore with all my might. I have two burning passions: First, to be like Jesus. Second, to respond to God as a violin responds to the bow of the master.....As for me I am convinced that this spiritual pilgrimage which I am making is infinitely worthwhile, the most important thing I know of to talk about. And talk I shall while there is anybody to listen. And I hunger—O how I hunger for others to tell me their soul adventures.

A CONTINUOUS DISCOVERY

May 24, 1930

A few months ago I was trying to write a chapter on the "discovering of God." Now that I have discovered Him, I find that it is a continuous discovery. Every day is rich with new aspects of Him and His working. As one makes new discoveries about his friends by being with them, so one discovers the individuality of God if one entertains him continuously. One thing I have seen this week is that God loves beauty. Everything he makes is lovely. The clouds, the tumbling river, the waving lake, the soaring eagle, the slender blade of grass, the whispering of the wind, the fluttering butterfly, this graceful transparent nameless child of the lake which clings to my window for an hour and vanishes forever. Beautiful craft of God!! And I know that He makes my thought-life beautiful when I am open all the day to Him. I throw these mind-windows apart and say, "God, what shall we think of now?" He answers always in some graceful, tender dream. And I know that God is love hungry, for He is constantly pointing me to some dull, dead soul which he has never reached and wistfully urges me to help Him reach that stolid, tight shut mind.... All day I see souls dead to God look sadly out of hungry eyes. I want them to know my discovery! That any man can have God! That every man does have God the moment he speaks to God, or listens for Him!

As I analyze myself I find several things happening to me as a result of the two months of strenuous effort to keep God in mind every minute. This concentration upon God is strenuous but everything else has ceased to be so, I think more clearly, I forget less frequently. Things which I did with a strain before, I now do easily and with no effort whatever, I worry about nothing, and lose no sleep. I walk on air a good part of the time. Even the mirror reveals a new light in my eyes and face. I no longer feel in a hurry about anything. Everything goes aright. Each minute I meet calmly as though it were not important. Nothing can go wrong excepting one thing. That is that God may slip from my mind if I do not keep on my guard. If He is there, the universe is with me. My task is simple and clear. I want to learn how to live so that to see someone is to pray for them.

✑ E. STANLEY JONES ✒

(1884–1973)

American pastor, counselor and religious writer who devoted his life to the subject of conversion. He was moved to be a missionary when he was eight. He saw a picture of a big tiger standing beside a small Indian boy, and underneath was the caption, "Who will tell me about Jesus?' And he said, "I will." His books have had a wide circulation and he has spoken to thousands from the platforms of almost every country in the world.

I FOUND THEE

Longing I sought Thy presence, Lord
With my whole heart did I call and pray,
And going out toward Thee, I found Thee,
Coming to me on the way.

MY CONVERSION

As soon as the burden rolled off and I became conscious that Jesus was my personal Saviour, I felt a sudden impulse and desire to throw my arms around the world and to share the experience with everybody else. A few minutes before I had no such desire, because I had nothing to share.

✿ ALBERT EDWARD DAY ✿

(1884–1973)

American Methodist minister and founder of The Disciplined Order of Christ. "One book that stirred me to the very depths was the story of some youths who had gone off to a summer camp. There they entered into a fellowship with God that lifted them out of the glooms of guilt, gave sparkle to their youth, and set a star in their sky...I began to feel, therefore, that I, too, might become a real Christian and end my half-and-half, in-and-out practice of religion, devoid of the power and gladness of religion." At age thirteen he determined to seek God with all his heart. In *An Autobiography of Prayer,* he relates these "authentic experiences."

I THEN WAS CERTAIN THAT IT WAS GOD

A simple, sincere act of as complete dedication of my whole self as I knew how to make, and a lifting of the soul Godward in quiet trust, was answered by an experience which no language can describe. It was like a flood of sunshine, "the light that never was on sea or land." It was like refining fire swiftly coursing through the whole physical being, cleansing but not consuming. It was an ecstasy that had no resemblance to the ordinary expansive emotions of adolescence, but was an inner gladness so intense as to be almost unendurable yet requiring no outer expression save one thrilling, "Alleluia." It was such a sense of being in the hands of God as one could never forget and never doubt....

There was nothing in my own past which would predict that the event of that momentous day would be what it was. I hardly knew myself as I became in that unforgettable hour. If ever an impact, from an objective source, was made on this life, it was then. And that impact was not mere circumstance, accidental or contrived. It was not identifiably human, specific or cumulative. I then was certain that it was God. Nothing in all the years of study and living since, has corroded that certainty.

GOD DID COME

God did come and let me know He had come. He did act as only God
can act, and achieve delivrances which were miraculous. He gave
a peace which passeth understanding while the necessarily slow
delivrance was being wrought. He imparted a strength which I never
could have commanded, to face the ardors and anxieties which
the days must still hold. That I know and did know all through the
uncomprehending years when this pilgrimage of prayer was making
its often dubious and desultory way.

Beyond all this, and to my way of thinking more significant than
all, were the many indubitable experiences of prayer as conscious fellowship with God. Here always was the strongest bastion of my faith,
and the most unfailingly persuasive witness to the significance of
prayer. Amid all the ups and downs of life, the vacillations of devotion, the intermittencies of prayer itself, and the scantiness of time
spent in "waiting upon God," this has been the one permanent possibility and most oft-repeated privilege—to have been aware of His
Presence and to have held conscious communion with Him.

OVERCOME WITH GOD'S PRESENCE

In the woods in May when the air was fragrant with the incense of
spring, soft winds were blowing, bird songs flooded the scene with
melody, and the sunshine laid its golden warmth over the whole
landscape. I have suddenly known that God was there. The woods
became a sanctuary, the stump where I had been sitting, an altar; the
bird songs were anthems echoing my heart's gladness and gratitude
to Him who once again was walking in an Eden His love had created.

GOD WAS MADE KNOWN

On crowded city streets and on the storm-swept deck of an army
transport making its dangerous way across the sea where subma-
rines lay in wait to destroy; in the humble chapels of my own faith
and under the vaulted arches where stately rituals sounded alien
to my Protestant ears; in little groups of serious souls waiting in
silence for the Divine manifestation and amid the multitudes who

sat scarcely hoping for anything more than a flight of rhetoric or a flash of wit—in these and many other places has the Presence made itself known in experiences, like nothing else that visits the mind and heart.

THE MOST INDISPENSABLE ASPECT

This half-century of pilgrimage has wrought deeply into my soul the conviction that the life of prayer is the most indispensable aspect of our career on earth. Without it, there cannot be either that personal holiness or social effectiveness for which earnest persons yearn, and in which alone is there hope for a desirable future for mankind.

GOD WAS IN THE AGONY

I have known the bitterness of death. There are some experiences of which one cannot speak or write save in veiled allusion. They are so terrible that only symbols can hint at their terror—so humiliating that others ought not to share the humiliation even of hearing them told. Everything that one prizes seems lost. Everything that one abhors seems to have taken possession of one's heart, one's career, one's future.

"This," one cries in agony, "is the end." No longer is there anything left to hope. It is an agony one cannot share with one's friends. One knows he must carry it in silence to the grave. One is helpless before the onslaught of sorrow. It hurts even now to remember the desolation and despair that laid hold upon mind and heart.

But God was in the agony. Though everything seemed lost, I knew I was not lost nor could be destroyed. The things that really mattered still remained—the chance to discover and declare the truth, to wait like a watcher for the glory of dawn and to feel the silent beauty of dying day, to practice the virtues which are their own reward, to love even when love was misunderstood and unrequited, to serve humanity in some humble way, and most of all to worship God and obey Him and know the holy awe of His ineffable comradship.

So there was a paradoxical peace even in the excruciating pain—a strange joy in the ravaging sorrow—a sustaining confidence amid the enveloping dread. Nothing "shall be able to separate us from the love of God, which is in Christ Jesus our Loud." This is the real security.

✑ ROBERT MCQUILKEN ✑
(FL. MID-1900'S)

American pastor who was President of Columbia International University, a center for missionary training. He was converted on August 15, 1911.

MY LORD AND I

When I finished (surrendering everything, his sins, his doubts, his loved ones, his fiancee, his past failures, his future), I had no special emotion, and I saw no vision. But it did seem for the first time consciously in my life that there were just two persons in the universe—my Lord and I, and nothing else mattered except the will of that other person.

MY LOVE FLAMED UP FROM THE DYING EMBERS

Life was heavy on me. My dearest friend and intimate companion, my delightful wife Muriel, was slipping away, one painful loss at a time, as Alzheimer's disease ravaged her brain. Just as the full impact of what was happening to us hit home, the life of Bob, our eldest son, was snuffed out in a diving accident.

Two years later, to care for Muriel, I left my life work at its peak. I was numb. Not bitter, let alone angry. Why should I be? That's the way life is, life in a broken world. But the passion in my love for God had evaporated, leaving a residue of resignation where once had been vibrant faith.

I knew that I was in deep trouble, and I did the only thing I knew to do—I went away to a mountain hideaway for prayer and fasting. It took about twenty-four hours to shake free of preoccupation with my own wounds and to focus on the excellencies of God. As I did, slowly love began to be rekindled. And with love come joy.

I wrote God a love letter, naming forty-one of his marvelous gifts to me, spotlighting eleven of his grandest acts in history, and exulting in ten of his characteristics that exceed my imagination. Surely he enjoyed my gratitude—who doesn't appreciate gratitude?

But I discovered something else. Something happened to me. I call it the reflex action of thanksgiving. My love flamed up from the dying embers, and my spirit soared. I discovered that ingratitude impoverishes—but that a heavy heart lifts on the wings of praise.

✄ RALPH W. SOCKMAN ✄

(1889–1970)

American Methodist pastor, chaplain, radio minister, professor, and prolific writer.

THE VALUE OF WORSHIP

I sit for six days a week like a weaver behind his loom busily fingering the threads of an intricate pattern. On the seventh day the church in its worship calls me around in front of the loom to look at the pattern on which I have been working. It bids me to compare the design of my days with the pattern shown me on Mount Sinai and the Mount of Olives. Some threads thereupon I have cut, others I pull more tightly, and most of all I renew my picture of the whole plan.

(In an interview with James B. Simpson)

ONE CROWDED HOUR OF GLORIOUS LIFE

When I look at Paul and beyond to the Christ himself, I get the feeling that their idea of eternal life is independent of time. I get a glimpse of experience which comes as Mozart said his musical compositions came. "My soul gets heated," said Mozart, "and if nothing disturbs me, the piece grows longer and brighter until however long it is, it is all finished at once in my mind so that I can see it at a glance as if it were a pretty picture or a pleasing person. Then I don't hear the notes one after another, as they are hereafter to be played, but it is as if in my fancy they were all at once."

May we not say that in such inspired moments Mozart was laying hold of life independent of time? And is not that what eternal life is? It is life that is not measured by the ticks of the clock or by the months in a calendar. It is existence where

One crowded hour of glorious life

Is worth an age without a name.

However ordinary our lives may be, have not most of us had some high moments of ecstasy or love when time was forgotten? At such moments we were touching the quality of what Paul and Christ call "eternal life." At such moments we were tasting "the powers of the age to come."

(Now to Live!, Abingdon-Cokesbury Press.)

⇜ CORRIE TEN BOOM ⇝

(1892–1983)

Holocaust survivor who was arrested by the Gestapo in Holland in February 1944 for harboring Jews and sent with her sister, Betsie, to Ravensbruck concentration camp. She stood with her sister, watching a guard beat a prisoner. 'Oh, the poor woman,' Corrie cried, meaning the prisoner. 'Yes, may God forgive her,' replied Betsie, meaning the guard. This attitude of forgiveness enabled Corrie to forgive her former persecutors. In a letter to the one who had exposed their work in Holland, she said, "The harm you planned was turned into good for me by God. I came nearer to Him…I have forgiven you everything." "Those who were able to forgive their former enemies were able also to return to the outside world and rebuild their lives, no matter what the physical scars. Those who nursed their bitterness remained invalids. It was as simple and as horrible as that." Corrie, after her release, spent the rest of her life traveling, speaking and writing about her experiences of God's goodness and faithfulness.

HAND IN HAND, WE WALKED ON

Behind the south wall the rattle of a machine gun broke the silence. Then everything was, again, terrifyingly quiet. It was 2 o'clock and it was as if everything around me were a ghost city and I the only one alive. I walked on and an uncontrollable homesickness surged up in my heart. Even in the garden there was only loneliness for the solitary ones (those sentenced to solitary confinement).

Suddenly I remembered Enoch. He was not filled with homesickness when he walked with God and so I was no longer alone either. God was with me. Hand in hand, we walked on, and saw the blue sky and the flowers and the flowering shrubs and I could see the yard as a part of a beautiful free world where I would be allowed to walk once again. In the same way, earth is a lonely garden and Heaven the Liberty where great joy awaits us children of the Light.

(Prison Letters)

GOD CAN USE EVEN LICE

When I was in a concentration camp during the war, the Bible was called the book of lies. It was a miracle that I still had my Bible. The room in which we lived with seven hundred women was so dirty that we were all full of lice. The guards and the other officials would never enter our room because they were afraid to get vermin from us. God can use even lice, for that is why I could bring a message from God's Word twice a day.

One day we got a new supervisor whose name was Lony. She was a prisoner, a cruel woman; she told the guard everything we did. One day I opened my Bible. A friend of mine said, "Don't do it today. Lony is sitting behind you. If she knows you have a Bible, she will see to it that you will be killed in a cruel way."

I prayed, "God give me the strength even now to bring our Word." He answered that prayer. I read the Bible, brought the message, prayed, and then we sang, "Commit thy ways unto the Lord." When the song had finished, we heard someone call, "Another song like that!" It was Lony; she had enjoyed the singing. Afterward I got a chance to explain the Gospel to her, to show her the way of salvation.

I am not a hero. When you know that what you are saying can mean a cruel death, then every word is as heavy as lead. But I have never had such joy and peace in my heart as when I gave that message, never before that time, nor afterward. God gave me grace to be a martyr. Now I know from experience that when God demands it of us, when He thinks we are worthy to be martyrs, He will also give us grace.

(the End Battle)

IN MY PRISON CELL

In my prison cell I gulped entire Gospels at a reading, seeing whole the magnificent drama of salvation. Was it possible that this war, Scheveningen prison, this very cell, none of it was unforeseen or accidental? Could it be part of the pattern first revealed in the Gospels? Hadn't Jesus been defeated as utterly and unarguably as our little underground group and our small plans had been? But if the Gospels were truly the pattern of God's activity, then defeat was only the beginning. I should look around at the bare little cell and wonder what conceivable victory could come from a place like this.

(The Hiding Place)

✍ F. C. HAPPOLD ✍
(1893–1971)

English schoolmaster and writer of books and articles on education, history, social studies, religion, and philosophy.

A DEEP SENSE OF PEACE AND SECURITY AND CERTAINTY

It happened in my room in Peterhouse on the evening of February 1, 1913, when I was an undergraduate at Cambridge. If I say that Christ came to me, I should be using conventional words which carry no precise meaning, for Christ comes to men and women in different ways. When I tried to record the experience at the time, I used the imagery of the vision of the Holy Grail; it seemed to me to be like that. There was, however, sensible vision. There was just the room, with its shabby furniture and the fire burning in the grate and the red-shaded lamp on the table. But the room was filled by a Presence, which in a strange way was both about me and within me, like light or warmth. I was overwhelmingly possessed by Someone who was not myself, and yet I felt I was more myself than I had ever been before. I was filled with an intense happiness, and almost unbearable joy, such as I had never known before and have never known since. And over all was a deep sense of peace and security and certainty.

❧ HOXIE N. FAIRCHILD ❧
(1894–1973)

Writer, poet, and college professor.

I HAVE NO WORDS IN WHICH TO DESCRIBE WHAT HAS HAPPENED
I tried my best, with rather complete lack of success, to live up to the ethical precepts of Christ. I thought much of God and of my relationship to him. I prayed and meditated. I studied the Bible and followed a homemade course of readings in the history and philosophy of religion. I went to church, not as a mere spectator but as a reverent worshiper. I fear that as a result I have become one of those irritating persons who say they know that Christianity is true. I have no words in which to describe what has happened. No mystical illumination has fallen to my lot, nor am I aware of any radical inward rebirth. But I think I know the truth of the text in the Epistle of St. James: 'Draw nigh to God and he will draw nigh to you.' The world looks different to me, and I feel myself in some measure a different man. I have gained a peace and a happiness which I could never have created by my own unaided powers, and I believe that I have found God in my prayers. Anyone who reads this Book can have the same experience if he seeks it. Until he seeks it, nothing that I could say of it would have any meaning for him

⚔ ARCHIBALD J. CRONIN ⚖
(1896–1981)

Scottish physician and novelist.

SURVEYING THE PAST

When a man surveys his past from middle age, he must surely ask himself what those bygone years have taught him. If I have learned anything in the swift unrolling of the web of time, it is the virtue of tolerance, of moderation in thought and deed, of forbearance towards one's fellowmen.

I have come also to acknowledge the great illusion which lies in the pursuit of a purely material goal. What slight satisfaction lies in temporal honor and worldly grandeur! All the material possessions for which I strove so strenuously mean less to me now than a glance of love from those who are dear to me.

Above all am I convinced of the need, irrevocable and inescapable, of every human heart for God. No matter how we try to escape, to lose ourselves in restless seeking, we cannot separate ourselves from our divine source. There is no substitute for God.

⚔ LEONARD WILSON ⚖
(1897–1970)

Prisoner during World War II.

BECAUSE I AM A FOLLOWER OF JESUS CHRIST

I speak to you this morning from personal experience of God's comfort and strength. I was interned by the Japanese; I was imprisoned by their military police for many months; I suffered many weary hours of beatings and tortures. Throughout that time I never turned to God in vain; always He helped and sustained. I wish to speak of these experiences, the key-note of which could be summed up in St. Paul's words, 'More than conquerors'.

....After my first beating I was almost afraid to pray for courage lest I should have another opportunity of exercising it; but my unspoken prayer was there.... They asked me why God did not save me. By the help of His Holy Spirit, I said, 'God does save me. He does not save me by freeing me from pain or punishment, but He saves me by giving me the spirit to bear it'; and when they asked me why I did not curse them, I told them that it was because I was a follower of Jesus Christ, who taught us that we were all brethren.

⊰ LAJOW ORDASS ⊱
(1901–1978)

Bishop of the Lutheran Church of Hungary who was imprisoned for protesting the Communist's confiscation of church schools.

SOLITARY CONFINEMENT

They placed me in solitary confinement. It was a tiny cell, perhaps six feet by eight feet, with no windows, and soundproofed. They hoped to break down my resistance by isolating me from all sensory perceptions. They thought I was alone. They were wrong. The risen Christ was present in that room, and in communion with him I was able to prevail.

⊰ HOWARD THURMAN ⊱
(1900–1981)

American educator, theologian, and the first full-time black professor at Boston University's School of Theology.

FISHING WITH GOD

As a child I was accustomed to spend many hours alone in my rowboat, fishing along the river, when there was no sound save the lapping of the waves against the boat. There were times when it seemed as if the earth and the river and the sky and I were one beat of the

same pulse. It was a time of watching and waiting for what I did
not know—yet I always knew. There would come a moment when
beyond the single pulse beat there was a sense of Presence which
seemed always to speak to me. My response to the sense of Presence
always had the quality of personal communion. There was no voice.
There was no image. There was no vision. There was God.

(Disciplines of the Spirit)

◈ VANCE HAVNER ◈

(1901–1986)

**American Baptist preacher, itinerant minister, and writer whose ministry
continued virtually until his death.**

IF I COULD STAND AT HIS VANTAGE POINT

If I could stand for five minutes at His vantage point and see the
entire scheme of things as He sees it, how absurd would be my dreads,
how ridiculous my fears and tears!

(Consider Jesus, *Baker Book House*)

I AM GLAD I GREW UP READING BOTH BOOKS

The story of my early years might well be called 'Two Books and a
Boy.' I grew up in the Carolina hills in an old-fashioned home with
a Bible at the heart of it. Father read the Scriptures each evening at
family devotions by the light of a kerosene lamp. I began to read
the Book early, memorized portions of it, fed upon the stories of its
heroes, Joseph and Moses and Samson and David and Daniel. Above
all, there was the story of Jesus.

Another book came into my life as a lad. Living as I did in the
country, I became interested in the bird life around me. We used to
buy boxes of baking soda, each of which contained a card with the
picture and description of a bird. I became fascinated with the subject and one day I secured a little bird guide. It opened a new world.

The Bible and the bird book did wonders for the boy. God has
written his message to us in two books, the revelation of nature and

the God-breathed Scriptures. The book of nature is not enough. By it we may know the art of God, but not the heart of God. We may know the garden but not the Gardener. So God sent His Son and gave us the account of it in a Book. I am glad that I grew up reading both books.

(Peace in the Valley, *Fleming Revell*)

✤ GLADYS AYLWARD ✤
(1902–1970)

Missionary to China who worked alone with no money or support, sharing the Gospel in the villages, prisons, and among lepers. She couldn't pass exams and had not been accepted by a missionary society, but still she knew God had called her to go, and she had to go. No one took her seriously. She read a magazine article about China that changed her life. She kept thinking of the millions in that distant land who had not yet heard of God's love. She is characterized by a humble dependence upon God in a steady stream of extreme circumstances, including suffering from typhus, pneumonia, relapsing fever and malnutrition.

HERE'S ME, GOD

O God, Here's my Bible! Here's my money! Here's me! Use me, God.

*(After being turned down by the missionary board, she returned to
her room, opened her purse and turned it upside down. Two pennies fell
onto her Bible. She then worked, scrimped, and saved up enough money
to travel by train across Europe and Asia all the way to China.)*

GOD LOOKED DOWN AND SAW GLADYS AYLWARD

I wasn't God's first choice for what I've done for China. There was somebody else—I don't know who it was—God's first choice. I don't know what happened. Perhaps he died. Perhaps he wasn't willing. And God looked down—and saw Gladys Aylward.

I HAVE PASSED THROUGH FIRE

I have two planks for a bed, two stools, two cups and a basin. On my broken wall is a small card which says, 'God hath chosen the weak things—I can do all things through Christ who strengthens me.' It is true I have passed through fire.

NOW THAT MY EARTHLY LIFE IS COMING TO AN END

My heart is full of praise that one so insignificant, uneducated, and ordinary in every way could be used to His glory for the blessing of His people in poor persecuted China.

⊰ ROSS J. S. HOFFMAN ⊱

(1902–)

American writer and professor of history. The main theme of his writings is the psychological and spiritual interpretation of history. He became a Christian through research in history.

GOD GRANTED ME THE GIFT OF FAITH

So there was left only one possible explanation of the riddle of Christ. He was what He claimed to be—the Incarnation of God, the Divine Word made flesh. When I added His divinity to His humanity the pieces of the puzzle fell into shape. I could find no escape from that conclusion and I felt that I must either banish it all from my mind as an insoluble enigma or accept this only possible solution. But that solution no longer warred with my philosophic outlook upon the universe; it no longer violated my experience of myself and of my fellow men. Moreover, I found myself coming under the imperious spell of this mighty and towering personality, found myself capable of loving Him. God granted me the gift of faith, and I confessed with Peter: "Thou art the Christ, the Son of the living God." He no longer seemed a remote figure out of the East two thousand years ago, but a timeless life as young and fresh today as ever. I had no sudden conversion. Faith came very slowly, and it was not easy to feel the reality of it after so many years of negation. As the new point of view was gradually gained, I had alternating moments of lively conviction and sluggish doubt. But grace was not wanting.

✍ Charles A. Lindbergh ✎
(1902–1974)

American pilot who made the first non-stop flight as a solo-pilot between New York and Paris.

THE INFINITE MAGNITUDE OF THE UNIVERSE

It's hard to be an agnostic here in the Spirit of St. Louis when I am so aware of the frailty of man's devices. If one dies, all God's creation goes on existing in a plan so perfectly balanced, so complex that it is beyond our comprehension. There's the infinite magnitude of the universe, the infinite detail, and man's consciousness of it all—a world audience to what, if not to God.

(Midway in his transatlantic flight, he began to think of the smallness of man and the deficiency of his devices and the greatness and marvels of God's universe.)

✍ Vaughn R. Shoemaker ✎
(1902–1991)

Pulitzer Prize winning cartoonist. For some years the *Chicago Daily News* printed on its front page each Christmas Eve a cartoon entitled "The Un-taken Gift," which showed beneath a beautifully decorated tree, an un-opened package labeled "Eternal Life." John 3:16 was quoted.

TO THIS DAY I HAVE NEVER BEEN SORRY

I was honest enough with myself back in 1922 to admit I was concerned about my soul. I was simple enough to accept the simple gospel and accepted Jesus Christ as my Saviour. To this day I have never been sorry. Having had little education or natural ability, for any success I have gained as a cartoonist I must give credit to God. I wouldn't dare start a day without first starting it on my knees, with God, beside my drawing-board. I gain wisdom from Him.

✺ MALCOLM MUGGERIDGE ✺

(1903–1990)

English author, journalist, once an atheist, who came to Christ at age 79, after a lifetime struggle between the world and spiritual longing, in part because of the life and witness of Mother Teresa.

RESPONDING TO A BELL THAT HAS LONG BEEN RINGING

(There was) a sense of homecoming, of picking up the threads of a lost life, of responding to a bell that has long been ringing, of finding a place at a table that has long been left vacant.

(Describing his coming to Christ, Time, Dec. 13, 1982, "People," p. 63)

I AM CONVINCED IN MY HEART

I am more convinced in my heart than I am in my experience that the view of life Christ came into the world to preach, and died to sanctify, remains as true and as valid as ever, and that all who care to, young and old, healthy and infirm, wise and foolish, educated and uneducated, may live thereby, finding in our troubled, confused world, as in all other circumstances and at all other times, an enlightenment and a serenity not otherwise attainable.

FOR ME, IT IS CHRIST OR NOTHING

So I come back to where I began, to that other King, one Jesus: to the Christian notion that man's efforts to make himself personally and collectively happy in earthly terms are doomed to failure. He must indeed, as Christ said, be born again, to a new man, or he is nothing. So at least I have concluded, having failed to find in past experience, present dilemmas, and future expectations any alternative proposition. So far as I am concerned, it is Christ or nothing.

A PARTICIPANT IN HIS PURPOSES

For me now the experience of living in this world is nearly over. My lines, such as they are, have been spoken, my remorse entrances and exits all made. It is a prospect, I am thankful to say, that I can face without panic, fear or undue remorse, confident that, as an infinitesimal part of God's creation, I am a participant in His purposes, which are loving, not malign; creative, not destructive; orderly, nor chaotic; and that, however somberly at times the darkness may hover and however men may seem at times to prefer the darkness, the Light that first came to Galilee 2,000 years ago, and through the succeeding centuries has illuminated all that was greatest in the work and lives of men, can never be put out.

THE LIVING WATER THAT CHRIST OFFERS

I may, I suppose, regard myself or pass for being a relatively successful man. People occasionally stare at me in the streets—that's fame. I can fairly easily earn enough to qualify for admission to the higher slopes of the Internal Revenue—that's success. Furnished with money and a little fame even the elderly, if they care to, may partake of trendy diversions—that's pleasure. It might happen once in a while that something I said or wrote was sufficiently heeded for me to persuade myself that it represented a serious impact on our time—that's fulfillment. Yet I say to you—and I beg you to believe me—multiply these tiny triumphs by a million, add them all together, and they are nothing—less than nothing, a positive impediment—measured against one draught of that living water Christ offers to the spiritually thirsty, irrespective of who they are.

(*Muggeridge's Obituary*, Christianity Today)

⚜ E. M. BLAIKLOCK ⚜

(1903– 1983)

Professor of classics at the University of Auckland in New Zealand.

WHY I AM STILL A CHRISTIAN

I met Christ as one might meet a friend, through another's introduction....an ardent manly minister of Christ commended his Master to me. I stopped, like one of the passing crowd, and looked. I was young, and life was opening before me in that time of exciting discovery. I found the poetry of Virgil that year; I found Racine and Shakespeare. And I found Christ. I was groping for some purpose in life, some loyalty, some basis for my feet. The man whose testimony I heeded called me only to experiment, to test the Christian faith by accepting it as a way of life. That was forty-nine years ago, and that is why the adverb in my title (still) is significant. The response of 1920 might be dismissed as a boy's idealism, youth's sudden rapture without relevance, were not that choice still the core of my experience after a lifetime in scholarship, authorship, journalism, travel, and public life. All that I value, through all those years, flows from that experience, that choice of a faith to live by.

(Why I Am Still a Christian, *Zondervan*, 1971)

⚜ KINGSLEY MORTIMER ⚜

Professor of anatomy, Salvation Army officer, and doctor in Rhodesia and Zambia, in India, and later in Indonesia. He had a lifelong interest in the interrelationship of medicine and religion.

AFTER FORTY YEARS OF FAITH

As an anatomist, I see structure in the spiritual world, just as I see it in the human body. As a doctor, I see in Christ the Source of Life which, never fully satisfied, generates its own horizons. I see a first 'original' chaos yield to order, the inharmonious transmuted to the disciplined. I see beyond law, certainly beyond natural law, into the spiritual world. If at times I see more questions than I do answers, I am still satisfied. After all, it is through life that I am working. When I die, all will be clear. I shall need no more dark mirrors. I shall see face to face, and the other questions I would like to ask can wait until then. I am still a Christian, after more than forty years of conscious faith, because I have found the answer to life's problems, and to the death which is always near me in my profession—and which I have met in person face to face—in the living Christ and the daily reality of knowing Him.

(Why I Am Still a Christian, p. 146, Zondervan, 1971)

◢ MARIA VON TRAPP ◣
(1905–1987)

Austrian baroness. The musical, "The Sound of Music," was based upon her family story.

IT'S LIKE A BEACON

I grew up in Austria and took the Bible for granted, except I didn't read it. It was there, and I was there, but I didn't have any real connection with it. I don't remember why, but I do remember how one day when I was in my late twenties, I opened the Bible and was just amazed, I couldn't stop reading. I started in the New Testament, and then went back to the Old, and there I found with growing excitement the answers to all the questions—how it all started, what is the most important thing in life. It is all there. It's like a beacon to get your connections from.

⚜ HERSCHELL H. HOBBS ⚜

(1906–1995)

American Southern Baptist minister and author of 125 books.

THE TRUE AND LASTING VALUES ARE SPIRITUAL IN NATURE

I have lived long enough to be convinced that the value of spiritual matters far outweighs the value of material things. From youth through the middle years of life, the temptation is to place emphasis on material values: making money, having what money will buy, and enjoying physical things. Those who become addicted to this life-style may find themselves trapped in it even through declining years. Whether or not they admit it, they will find they have settled for an empty and lesser goal. The true and lasting values are spiritual in nature.

⚜ GERALD KENNEDY ⚜

(1907–1980)

American pastor, bishop of the Methodist Church, contributor to many national religious magazines, and author of several books.

ONCE EXPERIENCED, IT CAN NEVER BE DOUBTED

To me, one of the most amazing things about religion is my inability to define it. No matter what the anthropologists or the philosophers may say about it, their words never even come close to saying what I know religion to be. Its reality is unseen but once experienced can never be doubted. It deals with matters of the future, yet strikes at this contemporary situation. It drives one to service for his brethren, but it sends a man away from the crowd to contemplate his separate soul. It is, in a word, the absolute and there is nothing else in our experience to measure it by.

(These Found the Way, *Westminster Press*)

A SERVANT OF JESUS CHRIST

But I discovered something else after a short time in the ministry. It was that the greatest examples and authorities are not enough. A man must know in himself and experience in his own heart. There comes a time when a man, and especially a preacher, knows that the examples of his brethren are not sufficient. God must come to him directly. He has to be able to proclaim that he has found the gospel. He needs to feel that he has experienced in his heart that which created the lives of the great men he has admired. This, I think, is the witness of the spirit, which is the truly transforming experience in life.

I made this discovery ultimately out of sheer necessity. The first year of my ministry after seminary was a year of desperate unhappiness. The stimulus of the classroom was gone, and the discipline of a schedule was missing. Things did not move and dull struggle stretched hopeless ahead. The pettiness of a discouraged, defeated church is beyond comprehension. I did not seem to have anything worth saying. I considered a dozen schemes to escape from my dilemma, ranging from suicide to teaching. Then it came to me that, if God had truly called me to the ministry, he would encourage people to come and hear me preach his Word. He had a responsibility which I was trying to carry alone. In as complete a surrender as I knew how to make, I turned everything over to him. With a sense of all or nothing, I took the leap of faith. And it worked!

Suddenly, I felt that a decisive word had been given me to deliver. I have never lost that feeling. There has not been a Sunday morning in my pulpit since that time when I did not feel that the Christian message was all-important for every person in the congregation. I knew every man needed it because it was all-important to me and it had changed my life. Living would be unbearable without Christ, so far as I am concerned, and my high calling is to bring men to a decision for him which will mean life for them. I am utterly convinced of the truth and power of Jesus Christ, whose servant I am.

(These Found the Way, p. 113–4, Ed. David Wesley Soper,
Westminster Press, 1951, David Wesley Soper)

This luminous experience took away much of the worry which used
to haunt me. This is not to say that I am never troubled, irritable or
anxious. But since this "conversion" I have been given more grace
to leave things in God hands and trust his way. I have accepted Jesus'
invitation: "Come to me, all who labor and are heavy-laden, and I
will give you rest. Take my yoke upon you, and learn from me; for I
am gentle and lowly in heart, and you will find rest for your souls.
For my yoke is easy, and my burden is light" (Matt. 11:28–30). I have
not found life by giving way to my whims, any more than any man,
but the discovery that there is available to Christians power enough
to live by has become my assurance.

With ever increasing clearness there has come to me the certainty that Jesus is the truth of life and the clue to God. It is a fine
thing when a man is delivered from his groping. I no longer take the
time to argue with men about the deity or divinity of Jesus. Those
terms mean many things to many men. But I turn to the New Testament for the testimonies of John and Paul: "And the Word became
flesh and dwelt among us" (John 1:14). "God was in Christ reconciling
the world to himself" (II Cor. 5:19). Here is the whole tremendous
truth expressed simply and briefly, and it gives us all the light and
understanding we need. It takes us beyond controversy.

I have had an increasing sense of God's unique action in Christ.
When I think of the shallow liberalism that I tried to preach and nur-
ture my soul with, I wonder that it took so long to be converted to
the depth and reality of orthodox Christianity. Sinful creature that I
am, of what use are mere moral homilies? But when at least the majesty of God's sacrifice in the event of the incarnation breaks upon
my spirit, I can be redeemed. And this comes with the sense of being
inevitable and beyond argument.

Well, I must stop now, though there is much more to be said.
There are experiences of salvation that await me in the future. I am
sure. Conversion is never static. It is a beginning—a launching out
into the deep. The sign of its happening is a singing in the heart, and

hardly ever a spirit of controversy. I am a debtor to so many people who prepared the way and surrounded me with Christian concern. But most of all I am a debtor to God, for "to me, though I am the very least of all the saints, this grace was given, to preach—the unsearchable riches of Christ" (Eph. 3:8)

(*Eph. 3:8; These Found the Way, ed. David Wesley Soper, p. 114-5, Westminster Press, 1951*)

THE BEGINNING OF LIFE'S GREAT ADVENTURE

I believe in God because he has faced me and laid his claims upon me. Just as a man knows it when he falls in love, or knows it when he thrills to the beauty of nature, so he knows it when God places his demand upon him. Maybe he cannot be as precise as John Wesley and say that it happened about a quarter of nine. But he knows that once he was lost and now he is found, and all his life is changed. The experience makes him humble. He may have learned enough about God to live by, but he now finds the ruling passion of his life is to learn more about him.

That is the hope of every Christian. It is the worthiest goal for any man's life. When we have gone far enough to be able to say, "I believe in God," we stand at the beginning of life's great adventure.

(*I Believe, Abingdon, 1958*)

❧ MILDRED E. WHITCOMB ❧
(1908–1967)

American journalist who was deeply influenced by Augustine, Thomas Aquinas and Lecomte du Nouy's *Human Destiny*.

THE MOST EXCITING THING THAT EVER HAPPENED TO ME

About 2 p.m. on Easter Sunday it suddenly came to me that I believed the whole Christian story. It was fantastic, certainly, yet I believed it just the same. And believing was the most exciting thing that had ever happened to me. It was like falling in love, only on a cosmic scale. Now that I had faith, I saw that emotion had been hand in hand with reason to lead me to faith....

When once I took fright at the very mention of God's name, I now understand why there are people who stand on street corners shouting the good news about God and his Son. Maybe all of us Christians should be shouting on street corners—shouting for peace, shouting for racial friendship, shouting for one world, shouting for true brotherhood in Christ.

The Church calls it conversion. The Bible calls it being born again. Now the author of that college term paper with the big, borrowed words calls it a miracle, this that has happened to her.

(Taken from "My Journey Through Doubt", Presbyterian Life, 1948)

✒ NELS F. S. FERRE ✐
(1908–1971)

Swedish-born American Congregational minister, professor of theology and philosophical theology, writer, and lecturer.

GOD KNEW THAT I NEEDED TO SUFFER LONG AND HARD

Without sentimentality he took away my health and gave me years of pain, of constant physical handicap. Its intensity and duration cannot be known outside the family; in pain dulled by medicine and with an irrepressible drive to be used, I appeared at the line of duty. I dared tell no one how much I was suffering, lest I lose my chance of participation. My wife and family are the heroes of those strange years. My wife cared for a baby daughter who was slowly dying during one of my hardest periods. Never can I stop thanking God for the purgatorial fire of those years. In them God's severity became personally accepted as goodness, and part of the process of conversion was actually effected.

To pain and death was added the chill of discouragement. I could not die or become a useless invalid because I had a commission from God. My mission and message were certain: that the sovereign Lord is saving Love; that herein is the needed clue to history and experience—cutting across literalism, naturalism, and liberalism to the absolute primacy of the eternal purpose and to God's activity within all process and history as the unsentimental user of earthquakes and cancer for man's ultimate good.

(These found the Way)

⊰ DAVID WESLEY SOPER ⊱
(1910–1965)

American pastor of Dutch Reformed and Methodist parishes, professor of Bible and philosophy, writer and lecturer who delivered, on average, two hundred addresses each year.

HAPPINESS AND FRUSTRATION

It seems to me that Christ has used two instruments in the endeavor to shape my soul in his likeness—happiness and frustration. Happiness and success and achievement and well-being (in the usual sense) are gifts of God. What is often overlooked is in that happiness, defeat, failure, and frustration are also necessary to our development. There was much ridicule of foxhole religion during the war, but I have never met a soul who did not pray more in trouble than in tranquillity.

(These found the Way)

⊰ ROBERT BOYD MUNGER ⊱
(1910–)

American Presbyterian pastor and writer.

I HAVE NEVER REGRETTED IT

One evening I invited Him into my heart. What an entrance he made! It was not a spectacular, emotional thing, but very real. Something happened at the very center of my life. He came into the darkness of my heart and turned on the light. He built a fire on the hearth

and banished the chill. He started music where there had been stillness, and he filled the emptiness with His own loving, wonderful
fellowship. I have never regretted opening the door to Christ and I
never will—not into eternity.

(What Jesus Says, 1955),

✍ RONALD REAGAN ✎
(1911-)

Fortieth President of the United States.

THE HAND OF GOD
God's miracles are to be found in nature itself, the wind and waves,
the wood that becomes a tree—all of these are explained biologically,
but behind them is the hand of God, and I believe that is true of creation itself.

✍ WERNHER VON BRAUN ✎
(1912–1977)

**German-born American rocket scientist who dreamed of developing rock-
ets from an early age. He designed the first ballistic missile and led the
team which put the first American satellite into orbit.**

MUST WE LIGHT A CANDLE TO SEE THE SUN?
The public has a deep respect for the amazing scientific advances
made within our lifetime. There is admiration for the scientific process of observation, experimentation of testing every concept to measure its validity. But it still bothers some people that we cannot prove
scientifically that God exists. Must we light a candle to see the sun?

NOTHING DISAPPEARS WITHOUT A TRACE
Many people seem to feel that science has somehow made "religious
ideas" untimely or old-fashioned. But I think science has a real surprise for the skeptics. Science, for instance, tells us that nothing in

nature, not even in the tiniest particle, can disappear without a trace. Nature does not know extinction. All it knows is transformation. Now if God applies this fundamental principle of indestructibility to the most minute and insignificant parts of his universe, does it not make sense to assume that He applies it also to the human soul? I think it does. And everything science has taught me and continues to teach me strengthens my belief in the continuity of our spiritual existence after death. Nothing disappears without a trace.

(Reader's Digest, *June 1960, cited in Ravenhill, Tried and Transfigured, 86.)*

✥ CHARLES L. ALLEN ✥

(1913-)

American Methodist minister and writer of devotional literature.

I WAS FIVE YEARS OLD

I was five years old when I went forward on the invitation to join the church. Some say that is too young. I can only answer it was not too young for me. Because I then wanted to live like Jesus as nearly as I could. According to some definitions of salvation, I was not saved, but if you consider one saved who is dedicated tot he best he knows then I was saved, and so is every other person who has made a like decision.

ᴈᴠ EDITH SCHAEFFER ᴠᴈ

(1914–)

**Author and speaker, who along with her husband Francis, began as over-
seas evangelists and soon were attracting many students to their chalet
in the Swiss Alps. From this came L'Abri Fellowship in 1955, a study center
and refuge for students seeking answers to the great philosophical questions of life.**

THE WORDS WERE SURGING THROUGH MY HEAD

I awakened yesterday morning with music and words surging
through my head: "Great is thy faithfulness, great is thy faithfulness,
morning by morning new mercies I see..." It was as if a full orchestra
and choir were in my room; yet not a sound could be heard by anyone else. What a fantastic detail of God's creation—people can sing
aloud, and can sing within....We don't need to awaken the whole
household by bursting forth in song; we can rejoice in song in our
heads at night, or start the day or the year that way.

("Christians Are Singing People," Christianity Today, *Jan. 7, 1977, p. 24.)*

ᴈᴠ CHAD WALSH ᴠᴈ

(1914–1991)

Episcopal priest, college teacher, and writer.

THE LIVING PARADOX

Reason and experience can carry the seeker very far, but it is only
after the final leap of faith—a leap into what is largely an unknown
country—that real certainty begins to take root. One of the many
paradoxes of Christianity is that you cannot be sure of its truth until
after you accept its truth.

The daily world and my own life appear very different to me
today from what they did five years ago. Overwhelming vistas open
both up and down; meaning is everywhere and inexorable. But at
the center of it all is the living paradox who is the heart of Christian

faith: the Incarnate God who did the unthinkable for no other reason than love.

(These Found the Way)

≈ HAROLD E. KOHN ≈
(1914–1996)

American writer who studied and wrote meditations using natural history.

AS IF GOD WERE HANGING OUT SIGNALS

One of the barest essentials for understanding nature is to know that everything has a purpose. Nothing merely exists. Everything exists for a reason, and to know the reason is the beginning of natural wisdom. And in nature, so in life, everywhere I go I see signs of hope as if God were hanging out signals that say, "I will not abandon you."

(Thoughts Afield)

≈ JOY DAVIDMAN ≈
(1915–1960)

High school English teacher who later pursued her lifelong interests of writing novels and poetry.

AND GOD CAME IN

When I was fourteen I went walking in the park on a Sunday afternoon, in clean, cold, luminous air. The trees tinkled with sleet; the city noises were muffled by the snow. Winter sunset, with a line of young maples sheathed in ice between me and the sun—as I looked up they burned unimaginably golden—burned and were not consumed.

I heard the voice in the burning tree; the meaning of all things was revealed and the sacrament at the heart of all beauty lay bare; time and space fell away, and for a moment the world was only a door swinging ajar....

A young poet like myself could be seized and shaken by spiritual powers a dozen times a day, and still take it for granted that there was no such thing as spirit. What happened to me was easily explained away....And yet if ever a human life was haunted, Christ haunted me.

Francis Thompson symbolized God as the "Hound of Haven," pursuing on relentless feet. With me, God was more like a cat. He had been stalking me for a very long time, waiting for his moment; he crept nearer so silently that I never knew he was here. Then, all at once, he sprang.

My husband had been overworking. One day he telephoned me from his New York office—I was at home in Westchester with the children—to tell me that he was having a nervous breakdown. He felt his mind going: he couldn't stay where he was and he couldn't bring himself to come home....Then he rang off.

There followed a day of frantic and vain telephoning. By nightfall there was nothing left to do but wait and see if he turned up, alive or dead. I put the babies to sleep and waited. For the first time in my life I felt helpless; for the first time my pride was forced to admit that I was not, after all, "the master of my fate" and "the captain of my soul." All my defenses—the walls of arrogance and cocksureness and self-love behind which I had hid from God—went down momentarily. And God came in .

(These Found the Way)

It was like waking from sleep

How can one describe the direct perception of God? It is infinite, unique; there are no words, there are no comparisons. Can one scoop up the sea in a teacup? Those who have known God will understand me; the others, I find, can neither listen nor understand. There was a Person with me in the room, directly present to my consciousness—a Person so real that all my previous life was by comparison mere shadow play. And I myself was more alive than I had ever been; it was like waking from sleep. So intense a life cannot be endured for long by flesh and blood; we must ordinarily take our life watered down, diluted as it were, by time and space and matter. My perception of God lasted perhaps half a minute.

In that time, however, many things happened. I forgave some of my enemies. I understood that God had always been there, and that, since childhood, I had been pouring half my energy into the task of keeping him out. I saw myself as I really was, with dismay and repentance; and, seeing, I changed. I have been turning into a different person since that half minute, everyone tells me.

When it was over I found myself on my knees, praying. I think I must have been the world's most astonished atheist. My surprise was so great that for a moment it distracted me from my fear; only for a moment, however. My awareness of God was no comforting illusion, conjured up to reassure me about my husband's safety. I was just as worried afterward as before. No; it was terror and ecstasy, repentance and rebirth.

(These Found the Way)

IT WENT RIGHT ON HAPPENING TO ME

I could not doubt the truth of my experience. It was so much the realest thing that had ever happened to me! And, in a gentler, less overwhelming form, it went right on happening. So my previous reasoning was at fault, and I must somehow find the error. I snatched at books I had despised before; reread *The Hound of Haven*, which I had ridiculed as a piece of phony rhetoric—and, understanding it, suddenly burst into tears. (Also a new thing; I had seldom previously cried except with rage.) I went back to C. S. Lewis and learned from him, slowly, how I had gone wrong. Without his works, I wonder if I and many others might not still be infants "crying in the night."

(These Found the Way)

A HAPPINESS SUCH AS I HAD NEVER DREAMED POSSIBLE

My present hope is twofold. I want to go deeper into the mystical knowledge of God, and I want that knowledge to govern my daily life. I had a good deal of pride and anger to overcome, and at times my progress is heartbreakingly slow—yet I think that I am going somewhere, by God's grace, according to plan. My present tasks are to look after my children and my husband and my garden and my house—and, perhaps, to serve God in books and letters as best I can. And my reward is a happiness such as I never dreamed possible. "In His will is our peace."

(These Found the Way)

ᴥ DOMINIC ZAPPA ᴥ

(-1962)

American artist who sculpted a life-size replica of Leonardo da Vinci's famous fresco of "The Last Supper." For each of the thirteen figures he used a five hundred–pound block of wood from a linden tree. It captures the dramatic moment after Jesus says to his disciples, "One of you shall betray me."

I HAVE FELT GOD'S HAND ON MY SHOULDER

Somehow for the last four years I have felt God's hand was on my shoulder. All the time I was working on the Apostles and Christ, I seemed to get encouragement, inspiration. I have never been happier than when I was doing this work.

(Comments made after sculpting

"The Last Supper" which took four years. It is 17 feet long and weighs more than 3,000 pounds.)

⚜ THOMAS MERTON ❧

(1915–1968)

American Trappist monk and writer who had a difficult childhood. He wandered aimlessly until he had a deep conversion experience while a student at Columbia University. He is known for his journal writing and meditations which promote a relationship with God through Jesus Christ, striking a delicate balance between the inner and outer life.

WHY?

Why should I worry about losing a bodily life that I must inevitably lose anyway, as long as I possess a spiritual life and identity that cannot be lost against my desire? Why should I fear to cease to be what I am not when I have already become something of what I am? Why should I go to great labor to possess satisfactions that cannot last an hour, and which bring misery after them when I already own God in His eternity of joy?

(Seeds of Contemplation)

GOD'S LOVE SPEAKS

If I were looking for God, every event and every moment would sow, in my will, grains of His life, that would spring up one day in a tremendous harvest.

For it is God's love that warms me in the sun and God's love that sends the cold rain. It is God's love that feeds me in the bread I eat and God that feeds me also by hunger and fasting. It is the love of God that sends the winter days when I am cold and sick, and the hot summer when I labor and my clothes are full of sweat; but it is God who breathes on me with light winds off the river and in the breezes out of the woods. His love spreads the shade of the sycamore over my head and sends the water-boy along the edge of the wheat field with a bucket from the spring, while the laborers are resting and the mules stand under the tree.

It is God's love that speaks to me in the birds and streams, but also behind the clamor of the city. God speaks to me in His judgment, and all these things are seeds sent to me from His will.

(Seeds of Contemplation)

IT WILL BE ALL RIGHT

If I didn't have spiritual faith, I would be a pessimist. But I'm an optimist. I've read the last page in the Bible. It's all going to turn out all right.

⚞ EDITH MARGARET CLARKSON ⚟

(1915–)

Poet and hymn writer. As a twenty-three year old teacher in a gold-mining town in northern Canada, far from friends and family, God spoke to her through John 20:21 in the phrase, "So send I you." She realized that this lonely area was her mission field.

THE OCEAN OF GOD'S LOVE

How good it is to know that deep within our being, the mighty, resistless current of God's Spirit is sweeping silently but surely homeward, carrying us securely in His sure embrace! Only the surface of our lives is ruffled by winds that blow in the wrong direction. The deep mainstream is moving steadily toward the ocean of God's love and purpose, there in His own good time to lose itself eternally in Him.

(All Nature Sings)

⚞ C. EVERETT KOOP ⚟
(1916–)

Pediatric surgeon who pioneered in developing pediatric surgery into a sophisticated life-saving science. He was appointed the U.S. Surgeon General in 1981.

WE FEEL PRIVILEGED

We've had so many little evidences of the things that God has accomplished in His world by taking our son that we feel, in a sense, privileged in God's planning for the kind of thing that we have seen happen. My wife and I have shared with our Christian friends in the form of a book titled, *Sometimes Mountains Move*. It is nothing more than an expression of the graciousness of God to us at the time of our greatest tragedy.

(Speaking of the death of a son in an avalanche while mountain climbing.)

⚞ JAMES H. SHAW ⚟
(1918–)

American professor of biological chemistry.

THE ONLY ANSWER

No standards for morals, no universal concern for one's neighbor, no satisfaction for the yearning human heart can spring from any amoral, impersonal body of knowledge. Science has no answer to man's dilemma. For me, the answer is a personal relationship with God freely given by Him in response to faith in and commitment to the claims of Jesus Christ. Science can never displace Jehovah God of the Bible and Lawgiver and Jesus Christ, His Son, as Saviour and Mediator between God and sinful man.

(Knight's Illustrations for Today, *Moody*.)

⋙ HAROLD J. BERMAN ⋘

(1918–)

American professor of law and author of twenty-five books and over three hundred articles.

THE TRUTH THAT SET ME FREE

To be a scholar is to search for truth. And to search for truth is to be open to the possibility that some discovered truth will lay claim to one's allegiance.

In my own case, the truth that "set me free" first appeared to me at the outbreak of World War II when I was twenty-one years old. I was in Europe, where I had been studying European history for a year. While I visited Germany, Hitler announced on the radio that Germany had invaded Poland. It was literally the outbreak of the world war, and many of us fled for France. The stations were crowded with peasants carrying potatoes and animals and personal effects. The earliest train I could catch left at midnight.

I thought that Hitler's invasion of Poland would lead to the total destruction of human civilization. I felt as one would feel today if all the major powers were to become involved in a full-scale nuclear war. I was shattered—in total despair. There, alone on that train, Jesus Christ appeared to me in a vision. His face reminded me of one of the Russian icons that I would later see—heavily scarred and tragic—not suffering but bearing the marks of having suffered. I suddenly realized that I was not entitled to such despair, that it was not I, but another, God himself, who bore the burden of human destiny, and that it was rather for me to believe in him even though human history was at an end.

And so this experience of "amazing grace" not only made me a Christian believer—against my heritage (Judaism)—but also freed me from that pride and illusion of intellect which is the besetting sin of academic scholarship.

WILLIAM FRANKLIN
❧ (BILLY) GRAHAM ❧
(1918–)

American evangelist who has spent much of his adult life, even in his seventies, holding crusades around the world. He has been highly respected by people of all denominations.

GOD HAS RENEWED MY STRENGTH

As an evangelist, I have often felt too far spent to minister from the pulpit to men and women who have filled stadiums to hear a message from the Lord. Yet again and again my weakness has vanished, and my strength has been renewed. I have been filled with God's power and not only in my soul but physically. On many occasions, God has become especially real, and has sent his unseen angelic visitors to touch my body to let me be His messenger for heaven, speaking as a dying man to dying men.

I CAME AWAY WITH CHRIST

I went to the meeting armed with a camera and a light meter. But I didn't come away with pictures. I came away with Christ. When I entered the arena, I had a set of beliefs, a moral standard, and a lifetime of religious forms and externals. I came away with a Person pervading me and living in me—Christ!

(David Rowlands attended a Billy Graham meeting in London
with no thought of being converted. Having been reared in a church,
he felt no need of anything more, but a miracle happened.)

❧ RUTH BELL GRAHAM ❦

(1920–)

Deeply religious American woman. She has been an inspiration to those whose lives she has touched through her life and her writing, including her husband, evangelist Billy Graham.

NOT ANSWERED IN THE WAY I WANTED

God has not always answered my prayers. If He had, I would have married the wrong man—several times.

❧ JOHN McINTYRE ❦

(1920–)

American professor of physics.

NO CONTRADICTION

As a scientist who discovered the Christian message when an adult, I can testify to the profundity and appeal of the Christian explanation of these facts that man is estranged from God and that his life is empty and incomplete until he returns to God through His son, Jesus Christ. Further, I know of no scientific facts which contradict this view.

(Knight's Illustrations for Today, *Moody*)

✍ GORDON J. VAN WYLEN ✎

(1920–)

American professor of mechanical engineering.

HE IS MY SAVIOUR

I can find nothing that prevents me from believing that Jesus Christ is the son of God or that He is my Saviour and the Saviour of the world. When one knows God and has experienced faith in Christ, all the world is open to him. I am thankful that God has made Himself known to me in Christ, and that He has given me His grace to live in this world as a Christian. "Let the redeemed of the Lord say so, whom he hath redeemed from the hand of the enemy" (Ps. 107:2)

(Knights Illustrations for Today, *Moody*)

✍ WARREN WEAVER ✎

(1921–)

American mathematician and author.

A HIGHLY PERSONAL AFFAIR

My relationship to God is a highly personal affair. When I am troubled or afraid; when I am deeply concerned for those I love, when I listen to the hymns that go back to the best memories of my childhood, then God is to me a directly comforting God, a protecting Father. And when I am trying to work out within myself a problem of right and wrong, then God is a clear and unambiguous voice, an unfailing source of moral guidance. I cannot think of a single instance in my life when I asked what was the right thing to do and the answer was not forthcoming.

(Knight's Illustrations for Today, *Moody*)

❧ WILLIAM P. ALSTON ❧

(1921–)

American philosopher, professor of philosophy, and author.

MY ATTEMPT TO LIVE WITHOUT GOD

For about fifteen years I led what seemed to be a purely secular life, though I now believe that things were going on under the surface of which I was not clearly aware at the time. Then in a year of leave, 1974–75, most of which was spent in Oxford, these things began to surface. I had never been completely at ease in my attempt to live without God. I was never an enthusiastic atheist. By the mid-1900's, the sense that I was missing out on something of fundamental importance was beginning to crystallize. Furthermore, I was rather a different person from the dropout of the late 1950's. For one thing, I had had a lot of psychotherapy, and with some of the internal tensions resolved, I was in a better position to make a realistic assessment of the problems. Moreover I was able to hear the gospel message straight or more nearly straight, at least in a position to hear it and not distort it into something wildly different. You may resist the idea that God should have had to wait until I had gone through a variety of life experiences and profited in various ways from psychotherapy before He could get His message across to me. Can't God deliver His message to anyone at any time and make sure they get it right? Of course He can. But quite clearly, He doesn't do this with everyone all the time. Why He doesn't, I don't presume to say. In any event, one thing He does instead is to make use of various indirect ways of preparing the ground, and I believe that my experience is a case in point.

(God and the Philosophers, *Oxford*)

✄ HAROLD E. HUGHES ✄

(1922–1996)

U. S. Senator form Iowa. In his autobiography, he confesses that in his earlier years he had been "a drunk, a liar, and a cheat." Before trying to kill himself, he felt he had to tell God why. In his distress, something miraculous happened. "Like a stricken child lost in the storm, I had suddenly stumbled into the warm arms of my Father."

EVERYTHING OF ANY VALUE IN MY LIFE IS TIED UP IN JESUS CHRIST

He is a personal Christ to me. He lives in me; and the way He walked, the way He lived, and the way He taught is a perfect example of the way I should walk, live and teach. I think the power He displayed on this earth can and will be displayed through those who have complete unity with Christ through the Holy Spirit. I believe that Jesus Christ is the Son of Man who came to earth to reconcile men to the Father. He is the Word, the answer to salvation, and the door to the Kingdom. Everything of any value in my life is surrounded by and tied up in Jesus Christ. The material things in life are valuable for a while, I guess, but that's not the value I'm looking for. I'm looking for the value of eternity and eternal life and salvation.

(The Man from Ida Grove, A Senator's Personal Story, *Chosen Books*, 1979)

✄ J. M. HOUSTON ✄

(1922–)

Scottish lecturer in geography, lay preacher, and writer in "The Witness," an English Christian periodical of geography and psychiatry.

AN ABUNDANT LIFE

It is a risk to be a Christian, to believe in the intrinsic values of righteousness and truth, to accept the eternal dimension of Christ's revelation to man, to believe in the intrinsic value of personal relations. Nevertheless, I would echo Paul's confession: "I look upon everything as loss compared with the overwhelming gain of knowing Christ Jesus my Lord....How changed are my ambitions! Now I long to know Christ and the power shown by His resurrection" (Phil. 3:8,10, J. B. Phillips). Often in moments of temptation, and they come in academic life, I need to be reminded that this is so, but when the heat of false desires subsides once more, I know it is true that Christ is life, an abundant life. Unlike the humanist who accepts that the ultimate reality is impersonal, the Christian believes it is personal—God Himself. I am still a Christian, amid all the turbulence and stress of life in a great university, because, increasingly, I hold this truth.

(Why I Am Still a Christian, Zondervan, 1971)

D. A. BLAIKLOCK

(1903–)

Medical doctor. His medicine became the framework for his Christian evangelism.

I KNEW CHRIST AT A VERY YOUNG AGE

Christ and all He stands for has been real to me for over twenty-five years. When I was very young, I grasped clearly what an allegiance to Him meant, with a clarity indeed which in some ways was brighter than the perception of many adult Christians. The simple and undefiled mind of a child, who comes from a home where Christ is honored and revered, is far more capable of understanding and feeling spiritual concepts than many sophisticated and entangled adults would be prepared to acknowledge. We must not despise another soul's youth, for it was childlike faith that Christ commended most.

(Why I Am Still a Christian, Zondervan, 1971)

MY FAITH HAS WITHSTOOD ASSAULTS

I, like many others, was vulnerable at this point in my later teens. The testing which came was sudden, violent, recurrent, prolonged, and almost overwhelming. My faith has withstood this assault of unbelief and in the process its ramifications have been worked out personally in considerable detail. This is inevitable in the case of all whose spiritual life survives such crises.

Let me say emphatically that I have found Christianity intellectually satisfying. It appeals to my reason as well as to my heart. My faith has withstood both the assaults of secular atheism and materialism, and the same ideology in its disguised and much more subtle form—the various types of "Christian atheism" and "new theology" which are so eroding the visible church today.

(Why I Am Still a Christian, *Zondervan*, 1971)

⚜ W. E. ANDERSEN ⚜

(1923–)

Australian lecturer in education and prolific writer.

I RECOGNIZED THAT I HAD ALREADY DECIDED

At the age of thirteen, in my first year at high school, arriving at the stage of puberty, a long, thin, unathletic adolescent, I found myself confronted in Scripture class with a teacher who expounded to us week by week the early chapters of John's Gospel....What was fresh and meaningful to me was the story of God at work powerfully with people, and particularly, as I remember, with Nicodemus and the Samaritan woman. Neither of these would seem obvious identifying figures for a thirteen-year-old, but this they proved to be! In addition, I was beginning to form, on the basis of the record, my own conception of Jesus Christ as a person and was conscious of the fact that He spoke, that He was the Word. I took particular note of John's statement: "But to all who did receive him, to those who have yielded him their allegiance, he gave the right to become children of God" (John 1:13, NEB).

(Why I Am Still a Christian, *Zondervan*, 1971)

THE TRUE GOD HAD KNOCKED AT MY DOOR

I was never one for lightning revelations or personal cataclysms, though I do not disparage those whose experiences of God are dramatic. Over a period of about six months I continued growing in the conviction that Jesus Christ was light and that He could be powerful in illuminating and energizing those who received Him. I commenced reading the Bible and went once or twice to the tiny interdenominational Christian group at school during the lunch hour. And then one day it was not so much that I decided, as that I recognized that I had already decided, and was already committed. I had, at some time in recent weeks or months, received the one whom I had been coming to know in the Gospels.

It was then that I began to be conscious of sin. It was not that I now remembered all manner of malpractices which had previously been repressed, for they had never existed. What I came to recognize was that my whole world had centered around my good self. I was in the strictest sense of the word egocentric, and though I would not have thought of the term then, this had been idolatry. The true God had knocked at my door; I had come to His light so that what I was might be clearly seen.

(Why I Am Still a Christian, Zondervan, 1971)

⊰ DONNA HUBER MIESBACH ⊱
(1924–)

Inspirational speaker, workshop presenter, editor of "Gleanings: A Bi-Monthly Discussion of Life Issues," and writer of inspirational poems and articles.

I KNEW MY SON WAS IN GOD'S HANDS

I have believed for a long time that all things come bearing a gift. It may take a while before we find out what that gift is, but if we are faithful to the task, it will be revealed. I've seen it happen too many times to ever doubt the truth of it. Knowing that enabled me to persevere after my husband died. I was convinced that something good would come of it, and I would not—could not—give up until I found it.

It was that way, too, many years ago when my son got hit broad-side and was sent flying 50 feet before coming down head first in a parking lot....I knew that God could use even this for some good pur-pose, and that was enough to sustain me. It kept my center intact. It fortified my courage so that no matter what—I knew my son was in God's hands. We all were in God's hands.....

Often I have asked myself, "Where does confidence such as this come from?"....In pondering this question over the years, I have come to the conclusion that this kind of deep, unshakable trust begins much like a child's simple faith. We trust because we believe. After a while that belief becomes a knowing. At first we may not know why we know, but we know just the same. Eventually that knowing and that trust begin to work themselves out in our daily affairs, and as they do, they grow into a conviction that cannot be shaken. We have seen it at work in our life, and we know. It is this kind of conviction that ploughs deep into our souls, that allows us to reach into the deepest part of our being and cling to what we find there. It enables us to meet even the most difficult of circumstances in the knowledge that there is good to be found—God to be found—even in this.

⊰ JOHN COMPTON BALL ⊱
(1924–)

American Baptist pastor.

I KNOW IT FROM EXPERIENCE

In a church in Philadelphia, a boy of fourteen rises in response to the invitation of the minister. As the meeting continues the lad sits and sobs. An arm goes around his shoulders and a voice says: "My boy, I'm a stranger to you and to the church, just a traveling sales-man, leaving at midnight for the West, but I want to say that the step you have taken you will never regret. I know it from experience, and if you are honestly committing yourself to Jesus He has already received you, and will never leave you. Trust Him, my boy, all the way. Good-night, God bless you."

He was gone, and the boy out under the stars walking home found the peace that passeth all understanding. For fifty-four years the Jesus Who came into his heart that night has traveled with him. The unknown salesman friend little knows, and some day, he who is now a preacher, will see him and thank him.

✑ WALTER R. HEARN ✐

(1926–)

American professor of biochemistry.

AN EXCITING HUMAN ADVENTURE

Science is like trying to follow God's thoughts or participate in the Creator's plan. It is an exciting human adventure. There are many practical human problems that science helps to solve. I like to see Christians have a part in solving them. I'm better at science than preaching. My work puts me in a position to witness where I couldn't as a preacher.

In my life, ultimate personal questions find their solution in my relationship to God through the person of Jesus Christ. We Christians believe that we can come into such direct contact with our Maker and Redeemer that his wisdom can be applied to our deepest problems and His love can be applied to our deepest problems and flow through us to touch others as well.

(Knight's Illustrations for Today, *Moody*)

✢ FREDERICK BUECHNER ✢

(1926–)

American novelist and autobiographical writer who used his theological training "with every hope being as much a minister in the books I wrote as in the classes I taught." After listening to one of George Buttrick's sermons in a nearby Presbyterian church in 1953, Buechner was converted.

LIKE FRESH WATER IN THE DESERT

It was only a glimpse, but it was like stumbling on fresh water in the desert, like remembering something so huge and extraordinary that memory had been unable to contain it. Though God was nowhere to be clearly seen, nowhere to be clearly heard, I had to be near him...the first time in my life, there in that wilderness, I caught what it must be like to love God truly, for his own sake, to love him no matter what. If I loved him with less than all my heart, soul, might, I loved him with at least as much of them as I had left for loving anything.

(A Room Called Remember)

GOD WAS PRESENT IN WHAT HAPPENED TO MY FATHER

God did not will what happened that early November morning in Essex Falls, New Jersey, but I believe that God was present in what happened. I cannot guess how he was present with my father—I can guess much better how utterly abandoned by God my father must have felt if he thought about God at all—but my faith as well as my prayer is that he was and continues to be present with him in ways beyond my guessing. I can speak with some assurance only of how God was present in that dark time for me in the sense that I was not destroyed by it, but came out of it with scars that I bear to this day, to be sure, but also somehow the wiser and the stronger for it. Who knows how I might have turned out if my father had lived, but through the loss of him all those long years ago I think that I learned something about how even tragedy can even be a means of grace that I might never have come to any other way. As I see it, in other words, God acts in history and in your and my brief histories not as the puppeteer who sets the scene and works the strings but rather as the great director who no matter what role fate casts us in conveys to us somehow from the wings, if we have our eyes, ears, hearts open and sometimes even if we don't, how we can play those roles in a way to enrich and ennoble and hallow the whole vast drama of things including our own small but crucial parts in it.

......To see how God's mercy was for me buried deep even in my father's death was not just to be able to forgive my father for dying and God for letting him die so young and without hope and all the people like my mother who were involved in his death but also to be able to forgive myself for all those years I had failed to air my crippling secret so that then, however slowly and uncertainly, I could start to find healing. It is in the experience of such healing that I believe we experience also God's loving forgiveness of us, and insofar as memory is the doorway to both experiences, it becomes not just therapeutic but sacred.

(Telling Secrets, 1991, *talking about the pain he suffered all these years from his father's suicide when he was just a young boy.*)

ALL MOMENTS ARE KEY MOMENTS

By examining as closely and candidly as I could the life that had come to seem to me in many ways a kind of trap or dead-end street, I discovered that it really wasn't that at all. I discovered that if you really keep your eye peeled to it and your ears open, if you really pay attention to it, even such a limited and limiting life as the one I was living on Rupert Mountain opened up onto extraordinary vistas. Taking your children to school and kissing your wife goodbye. Eating lunch with a friend. Trying to do a decent day's work. Hearing the rain patter against the window. There is no event so commonplace but that God is present within it, always hiddenly, always leaving you room to recognize him, or not to recognize him, but all the more fascinatingly because of that, all the more compellingly and hauntingly. In writing those lectures and the book they later turned into, it came to seem to me that if I were called upon to state in a few words the essence of everything I was trying to say both as a novelist and as a preacher, it would be something like this: Listen to your life. See it for the fathomless mystery it is. In the boredom and pain of it no less than in the excitement and gladness: touch, taste, smell your way to the holy and hidden heart of it because in the last analysis all moments are key moments, and life itself is grace.

(Now and Then, 1983 by the author. Permission by author)

⟨ BONNIDELL CLOUSE ⟩
(1928–)

American professor of educational and school psychology, author.

GOD KNEW THE PLANS HE HAD FOR ME
Dedication to God's service surely means different things to different people. Each of us is unique and God calls us in a variety of ways. Going in front of the church after a service may be all right for some people, but it never appealed to me....God's call to Jeremiah was different. This was One-on-one. No altar calls. No singing of twelve verses of "Just As I Am." This was just the Lord and Jeremiah getting it all sorted out. Regardless of the circumstances and regardless of the consequences, Jeremiah knew he had to serve the Lord. He had to do what God had called him to do. And then there was the wonderful promise given to Jeremiah: "For I know the thoughts that I think toward you," saith the Lord, "thoughts of peace, and not of evil, to give you an expected end."

The New International Version puts it even more beautifully. "For I know the plans I have for you." declares the lord, "plans to prosper you and not to harm you, plans to give you hope an a future: (Jer. 29:11) HOPE AND A FUTURE. What could be more exhilarating? Seeking to know God's will, and to do it, brings with it a promise that is better than anything offered by anyone or anything else. Jeremiah's doubts had been my doubts, his hesitation my hesitation, his feeling of fire in the bones when he heard the word of the Lord, my feeling of fire when I read the prophets, his decision to obey the Lord my decision to seek God's will and do it, his promise of hope and a future my promise of the best God had in store or me. Whatever the future would bring it would be a part of the divine plan. I knew God had spoken to me and I was satisfied......

When I claimed God's promise four decades ago that his thoughts toward me "were thoughts of peace, and not of evil," I did not know the extent to which this would be fulfilled. I marvel that God has been so good. His plans were truly "plans to give...hope and a future." And I know that the plans will remain intact for as long as he sees fit.

(Storying Ourselves: a Narrative Perspective

on Christian Psychology, *Baker Book House*)

✍ JOHN M. DRESCHER ✍

(1928–)

American pastor, author, and editor of *The Gospel Herald*.

GOD WAS SEEKING ME

I met God! It was not because I was searching for Him. He was seeking me. It did not take long. The first time I saw myself a sinner, and Christ mighty to save, I stood to my feet as a symbol of my response to His loving call. I met God in a personal way. He placed His hand of love and lordship on me, and somehow I knew I could trust the One who died for me.

I easily recall the time. The sermon was finished. In the quietness of the opening verse of the first invitation hymn the Holy Spirit spoke to me. I remember the time, not because I experienced a spectacular conversion, but because I saw a supernatural Saviour. And yet it was a spectacular conversion, since every conversion is that. Jesus, who died to save me, now as living Lord deserved all I was and hoped to be....simply trusting myself to my Father's love through the merits of Christ, I found peace, resting in His mercy and grace.

⚘ MARTIN LUTHER KING, JR. ⚘
(1929–1968)

American civil rights leader and Baptist pastor, who was assassinated. He was a staunch believer in Christ and in the human dignity of all people. He led the Montgomery bus boycott against racial segregation in 1955 and submitted himself to physical abuse and imprisonment in order to dramatize the racial oppression and discrimination of the black people in America. He believed that violence was immoral and self-defeating and could best be counteracted by love. His leadership in the heroic struggle for social justice made a significant impact on American society.

I'VE BEEN ON THE MOUNTAIN TOP

I don't know what will happen now, we've got some difficult days ahead. It really doesn't matter with me now, because I've been on the mountain top. I won't mind. Like anybody I would like to live a long life. Longevity has its place. But I'm not concerned about that just now. I want to do God's will and he's allowed me to go up the mountain and I've looked over and I've seen the Promised Land. I may not get there with you, but I want you to know tonight that we as a people will get to the Promised Land. Well, I'm happy tonight. I'm not worried about anything. I'm not fearing any man. Mine eyes have seen the glory of the coming of the Lord!

(Quoted in "The N. Y. Times", 1968)

INFINITE LOVE

My religion has come to mean more to me than ever before. I have come to believe more and more in a personal God—not a process, but a person, a creative power with infinite love who answers prayers.

(Quoted in "Redbook", September 1961)

THE GREATEST THING IN THE WORLD

I still believe that standing up for the truth of God is the greatest thing in the world. This is the end of life. The end of life is not to be happy. The end of life is not to achieve pleasure and avoid pain. The end of life is to do the will of God, come what may.

(Quoted in You Say You're Depressed!, *Donald Deffner, Abingdon, 1976, p. 80)*

✍ JAMES B. IRWIN ✍
(1930–1991)

American astronaut, pilot of the Lunar Module on the Apollo 15 mission to the moon in July, 1971. He later founded the High Flight Foundation, an organization of astronauts who tell both of their adventure as astronauts and their experiences as Christians.

I FELT A SENSE OF INSPIRATION ON THE MOON

I have encountered nothing on Apollo 15 or in this age of space and science that dilutes my faith in God. While I was on the moon, in fact, I felt a sense of inspiration, a feeling that someone was with me and watching over me, protecting me. There were several times when tasks seemed to be impossible—but they worked out all right every time.

(As quoted in The New York Times, *August 13, 1971)*

A SPECIAL CLOSENESS OF GOD

As we were fulfilling our scientific mission, I felt a special closeness of God in everything and I prayed to Him often. We had our difficulties, but the Lord helped us to overcome all of them. I sensed a kind of direct communication with God and felt His presence more than I had ever felt it on Earth. That was a real spiritual awakening for me. Since that time, God has given me a strong desire and compulsion to share my faith with others.

⊰ HENRY BLACKABY ⊱
(CONTEMPORARY)

Baptist pastor, teacher, and author committed to helping people know and experience God through revival and spiritual awakening.

CREATED TO BE GOD'S FRIEND

I was seventeen years old, a high-school student attending a youth rally, when suddenly I knew I was face-to-Face with God. He was making His rightful claim on my life. I felt as though no one else was present, only God and me. I did know an opportunity to respond to God's right to my life was given, and I was compelled by the strong hand of God to acknowledge God's call. That was the time I surrendered to His call. Others responded also. Some of them still speak to me with great tenderness about that moment. Since that encounter of God's initiative I have never been the same. I have never looked back. I have never struggled with any other direction for my life. God settled at that moment the direction for the rest of my life.—I was His alone.

Like Abram, I "went out, not knowing" anything of God's particulars. I only knew conclusively I was His and He was mine as Lord of all. Questioning the relationship has never been an issue. He has revealed His direction for my life one day at a time. Like Abram, I can now look back and see how God's Hand and Presence faithfully guided, protected, and provided for me. God's pattern and purpose are much clearer today than ever before. Each step with God was a huge moment of faith, and continues to be so to this very day.

(Created to be God's Friend Workbook)

HE MADE HIMSELF REAL AND PERSONAL

I have often heard my wife say that she believed God moved us to Saskatoon so we could live out, in real life, all we said we believed about God. Everything we said we believed about God would now be tested and made into character in us by the Loving Hand of God. I had always told God's people to trust God to provide all their needs.

Now we were where only God could provide for us. God would have to provide everything for our family, for there were only twenty people now in our church. We did trust Him, and He did become "our Provider" for the twelve years that we were pastoring there. He was also our Protector. We came to know this in real life when we traveled to our missions with the wind chill temperature at -110 degrees as the blizzards blew across the roads. He did protect us, and we never were stranded in twelve years of traveling to our missions (more than 500,000 miles). He said He was our Healer, but never did He become so real as Healer than during those early days, especially when my wife almost died, and in the times when He healed our broken hearts. We saw Him shape our very character as He made Himself real and personal. But He always did this in very real-life situations.

(Created to be God's Friend Workbook)

◈ CHARLES COLSON ◈

(1931–)

Prison minister. Colson was known as the "hatchet man" of the Nixon White House. He was converted to Christ while awaiting trial for his part in the Watergate break-in. The change had come when he first faced up to God through reading on the subject of pride in C. S. Lewis' *Mere Christianity*. If Christianity is true, he realized, every individual matters. Less than a week after his release from prison Colson was back visiting those who had been his fellow prisoners.

I HAD FOUND MY PURPOSE

All my life I labored for success, wealth, acceptance and power. The more I obtained, the less I discovered I had. Surrendering everything in absolute brokenness, however, was the beginning of finding the identity and purpose for which I had battled so hard. In giving up my life to Christ, I had found it. The same thing happened with the prison work. For nine months I struggled to control it, though in our fellowship we never wanted our real desires to appear that obvious.

Yet the harder I reached for the reins, the more elusive they were to grasp. When I stepped aside, gave it all up in honest relinquishment, the Lord gave it back.

(Loving God)

MY BIGGEST FAILURE

The real legacy of my life was my biggest failure—that I was an ex-convict. My greatest humiliation—being sent to prison—was the beginning of God's greatest use of my life; He chose the one experience in which I could not glory for His glory.

(Loving God)

OUT OF TRAGEDY CAME GREAT BLESSINGS

Out of tragedy and adversity came great blessings. I shudder to think of what I would have been if I had not gone to prison.

(Comments made after receiving the Templeton Prize
for Progress in Religion, Houston Chronical, Feb. 20, 1993, p. 3E)

ALVIN PLANTINGA
(1932–)

American professor of philosophy who led the revival in Christian philosophy.

I HAVE FELT THE PRESENCE OF GOD VERY POWERFULLY

One gloomy evening (in January perhaps) I was returning from dinner.... It was very dark, windy, raining, nasty. But suddenly it was as if the heavens opened; I heard, so it seemed, music of overwhelming power and grandeur and sweetness; there was light of unimaginable splendor and beauty; it seemed I could see into heaven itself; and I suddenly saw or perhaps felt with great clarity and persuasion and conviction that the Lord was really there and was all I had thought. The effects of this experience lingered for a long time; I was still caught up in arguments about the existence of God, but they often seemed to me merely academic, of little existential concern, as if one were to argue about whether there has really been a past, for example, or whether there really were other people, as opposed to cleverly constructed robots.

Such events have not been common subsequently, and there has been only one other occasion on which I felt the presence of God with as much immediacy and strength. That was when I once foolishly went hiking alone off-trail in really rugged country south of Mt. Shuksan in the North Cascades, getting lost when rain, snow and fog obscured all the peaks and landmarks. That night, while shivering under a stunted tree in a cold mixture of snow and rain, I felt as close to God as I ever have, before or since. It wasn't clear as to his intentions for me, and I wasn't sure I approved of what I thought his intentions might be (the statistics on people lost alone in that area were not at all encouraging), but I felt very close to him; his presence was enormously palpable.

On many other occasions I have felt the presence of God, sometimes very powerfully; in the mountains (the overwhelming grandeur of the night sky from a slope at thirteen thousand feet), at prayer, in church, when reading the Bible, listening to music, seeing the beauty of the sunshine on the leaves of a tree or on a blade of grass, being in the woods on a snowy night, and on other kinds of occasions. In particular I have often been overwhelmed with a sense of gratitude—sometimes of something specific like a glorious morning, but often with no particular focus. What I ought to be most grateful for—the life and death and resurrection of Christ, with the accompanying offer of eternal life—is harder, simply because of its stupendous and incomprehensible magnitude. You can say "Thank you" for a glorious morning, and even for your children's turning out well; what do you say in response to the suffering and death and resurrection of the Son of God? Or to the offer of redemption from sin, and eternal life?

(Philosophers Who Believe, IV Press, 1993)

✑ NICOLAS WOLTERSTORFF ✐

(1932–)

American professor of theology, philosophy, and religion.

THOUGHTS UPON THE DEATH OF A TEENAGE SON

To love is to run the risk of suffering. Or rather, in our world, to love is to suffer, there's no escaping it. Augustine knew it well; so Augustine recommended playing it safe, loving only what could neither die nor change on one—God and the soul. My whole tradition had taught me to love the world, to love the world as a gift, to love God through and in the world—wife, children, art, plants, learning. It had set me up for suffering. But it didn't tell me this: it didn't tell me that the invitation to love is the invitation to suffering. It let me find that out for myself, when it happened. Possibly it's best that way.

Now everything was different. Who is this God, looming over me? Majesty? I see no majesty. Grace? Can this be grace? I see nothing at all: dark clouds hide the face of God. Slowly the clouds lift. What I saw then was tears, a weeping God, suffering over my suffering. I had not realized that if God loves this world, God suffers; I had thoughtlessly supposed that God loved without suffering. I knew that divine love was the key. But I had not realized that the love that is the key is suffering love.

I do not know what to make of this; it is for me a mystery. But I find I can live with that. The gospel had never been presented to me as best explanation, most complete account; the tradition had always encouraged me to live with unanswered questions. Life eternal doesn't depend on getting all the questions answered; God is often as much behind the questions as behind the answers. But never had the unanswered question been so painful. Can I live this question with integrity, and without stumbling?

(Philosophers Who Believe, IV Press, 1993)

♂ DAVID TONGE ♀

(CONTEMPORARY)

Applied mathematician and lecturer from Wales. He has done research in the fields of cognitive processes and artificial intelligence. He was converted in 1976.

ALL THE TRUTH OF THE UNIVERSE IS TO BE FOUND IN HIM

I have discovered that the love, joy, and peace that the spiritual life brings far surpass the fruits of mere physical existence. I have begun to understand what Jesus means when he said, "I have come that you might have life, and might have it more abundantly." (John 10:1)....

As a scientist, I look for scientific "truth" in my research, knowing that such truth is transitory. It may be superseded or refuted at any time. But, since I am a Christian, my life and work are now based on the most comprehensive and unequivocal statement ever made about truth: Jesus Christ once said, "I am the truth" (John 14:6). All the truth of the universe is to be found in Him.

The trouble with this truth is that it defies ordinary definition and discovery. It transcends the logic of the scientist, the persuasive speeches of the politician, and the deepest reasoning of the atheist or agnostic philosopher. The only way of access to it is through the "new birth," through faith in Jesus Christ. It was by trusting Him that I found the fulfillment I had previously lacked. Today I know that I have found eternal truth in Jesus Christ, who said to those around Him, "You shall know the truth, and the truth shall make you free" (John 8:32).

(Scientists who Believe, *Moody*)

⚞ Boris P. Dotsenko ⚟

(CONTEMPORARY)

Researcher and professor of physical and mathematical science. He was brought up in communist Ukraine where churches had been burned down or closed and Christian preaching had become a crime.

THREE TIMES IN DIFFERENT PLACES

No analogy can do justice to God's provision for men to enjoy spiritual union with Him. Paraphrasing Francis Bacon, one may say that superficial and egocentric knowledge leads to atheism, while genuine, deep, and objective study leads to faith in God. I thank Him for bringing to my attention three times, in different places and over many years, His book, the Bible. And I thank Him too for granting me the faith to know Him personally and to experience his love. As a professor, I want to train my students in science. But, more importantly, I want to help them to become people who realize their chief responsibilities to society, to the world around them, and—above all—to God Himself.

(Scientists Who Believe, *Moody*)

⚞ Randall J. Fisk ⚟

(CONTEMPORARY)

American nuclear physicist and university physics professor.

GOD'S DISPLAYED EXCELLENCE

When I stare into a clear, star-filled sky, or contemplate the subatomic world, or look at a beautiful sunset, I have to agree with the psalmist David, "The heavens are telling of the glory of God; And their expanse is declaring the work of his hands" (Psalm 19:1).....The nuclear particles that I have studied are just the building blocks that God used in making everything that exists. The beauty of our world reflects the excellence of Him who created these infinitesimal particles, and who then formed them into every thing we see around us. Indeed, no thought I have ever pondered in the thought-provoking field of physics has staggered me more than this. Looking at the multitude of stars on a clear night, I know that the Creator of it all knows and loves me!

Let me tell you a story. I've been talking about the excellence and care God took in creating the universe. But that isn't God's specialty; it is not his highest glory. God's excellence is best displayed in his love. As I have grown to appreciate the excellent way that God's universe is made, I have even more learned to appreciate the excellent elegance of His love.

God's display of excellence in love can be found in the person and mission of Jesus Christ—the ultimate in love. The more closely I have looked at the Bible, the more I have observed that every act of Jesus was motivated by undiluted love. Jesus Christ never had a selfish thought. His entire life was based on helping others. He willingly experienced a death more agonizing than we can ever know, so that we could have eternal life and a relationship with God like that of children with their loving father.

(Scientists Who Believe, *Moody*)

GOD WORKED FAITH IN MY HEART

For a long time I had been searching for the truth. I went into physics to see what truth was there. I was dissatisfied with the idea that there was no God. I simply could not believe that a world so beautiful was the result of chance occurrences. The idea that my own being could have been nothing more than a meaningless accident also sounded very unlikely.

I didn't understand why at the time, but I had a real hunger to read about Jesus in the Bible. I was having an intellectual battle. Logically and historically, the good news of Jesus seemed very probably true. But can we ever really know what is the truth? First Corinthians 2:14 says that the natural mind cannot understand the things of God; they must be discerned by spiritual perception. When I continued reading God's Word, something inside me resonated in response, telling me that what I was reading was true. I can't point to a specific moment of salvation; it probably occurred when God worked faith in my heart by telling me that what I was reading in the Bible was true.

(Scientists Who Believe, Moody)

⊱ ROBERT L. HERRMANN ⊰

(1934-)

American professor of mathematics and biochemistry.

A PART OF GOD'S MASTER PLAN

A person who has no comprehension that God is at work in the world has an urgency about living as long as he can—sometimes even a panicky desperation. I don't share that frenzy, because I understand that this life is not all that there is. Instead of the "un-faith" of some of my research colleagues, I have an eternal expectation—a heavenly home that I expect to inhabit for a far longer period than my earthly lifetime. We read that in God's house are many mansions, and Jesus said that He was going to prepare a place for us there....

I know I am a part of God's master plan. I am not here by chance or by accident, but by prescription. And my death will be a part of that same plan of a loving God who is ready to promote me to a better world.

(Scientists Who Believe, Moody)

✎ THELMA ROBINSON ✎

(1934-)

British teacher, writer, author of *God in My Corner,* and a cancer survivor who "testifies to the faithfulness of God and the way He has opened doors of opportunity through what seemed at the time a terrible situation."

REFLECTIONS ON THE TWENTY-THIRD PSALM

God, Creator of the world, is my shepherd. I can say with certainty born of experience that I shall never want. There have been times of enforced rest, sometimes for days and weeks, but God used those times of stillness to bring peace to my soul. Several times I have walked through a valley with the shadow of death around me. Each time God has drawn me close and allayed my fears. God has supplied comfort through the discipline (rod) of his word. Jesus, the Bread (staff) of life, has been with me.

Despite the presence of enemies such as sickness, doubt, and fear, God has always prepared a feast of good things, anointing my head with the oil of mercy and grace. Often it has overflowed enough to share.

As I shared the twenty-third psalm with a 90-year-old friend in the hospital in the quietness of the ward, I felt the blessing of God's presence with us. Wherever I wander, God's goodness and mercy will follow me all the days of my life.

This is God's promise.

✎ PAUL C. VITZ ✎

(1935-)

American professor of psychology.

BY CHANCE?

When was I aware of God, or even of the possibility of God's presence in my life? Only looking back does it seem clear that the first fleeting conscious experience occurred in Paris in the summer of 1967. Early the first morning after I arrived I slipped out of the hotel and began wandering through the streets of the Isle de la Cite. (Like so many people, I loved Paris from my first minutes there.) By chance (?) I happened to walk into the Sainte Chapelle. Not knowing its fame, I was totally unprepared for its great beauty—spiritual beauty. The early light streaming through its windows for a brief moment told me of someone else. Then it was gone, and to all appearances forgotten.

(Storying Ourselves, Baker)

FILLED WITH TRULY GREAT SURPRISES

Looking back on my life as a Christian, I can say that it has been filled with truly great surprises—the greatest being that I became a Christian at all: this is the first miracle. The second is that the same kind of conversion took place, at the same time, in Timmie (his wife) as well: ours has been, remains, a shared journey. Frequently in this journey my expectations and plans have been very painfully confounded, but the consequences of these "ego-strippings" have always been blessings. This Christian Odyssey is still far from over, and who knows what lies ahead? In spite of retrospectives such as this report, the prize lies ahead, and I pray, with St. Paul, to be able to finish the race.

(Storying Ourselves, Baker)

⚛ EMILIE GRIFFIN ⚛

(1936–)

Accomplished advertising executive in a major New York advertising firm. "The converts who influenced me the most were C. S. Lewis, Bede Griffiths, and Thomas Merton," all of whom "wove their way into my own conversion story, and in them all, I began to see a pattern emerge."

GOD WAS CALLING ME

When I first began to experience the power of God in my own life, I could hardly believe it. Something very real and discernible was happening to me, yet I felt it could not or should not be happening. God was speaking to me; God was calling me. He spoke no louder than a whisper, but I heard him. And each time that I heard him, and chose him, a change occurred, the opening of a door I had not guessed was there. Each step, each crossing of a doorway was made with great uncertainty, my doubts mingling with my faith. But with each step, my strength and my conviction grew. I felt myself on sounder ground. Something was happening in my life, which I could recognize but which I could not yet name. It was conversion.

(Turning: Reflections on the Experience of Conversion)

I WAS HELPED BY READING ACCOUNTS BY OTHER CONVERTS

For me, conversion—this turning over of one's life and energies to God—came about first through a slow and hesitant pilgrimage, both intuitive and intellectual. In my journey I was helped by reading first-person accounts by other converts, especially those who were contemporaries or near contemporaries of mine. In their experience I could see my own. The witness given by their stories, and by their willingness to write down their experiences and to publish them, was as persuasive to me as the lives of early Christian martyrs. The resemblance between their struggles and my own gave me the courage to trust my own experience more. I found it helpful, too, to see that these people were dealing, as I was, with the issues of the so-called scientific age; and they were people of learning, intellectuals. They had not thrown reason over in favor of God. Their commitments had been formed out of thought as well as feeling.

(Turning: Reflections on the Experience of Conversion)

MOMENTS OF GRACE

On one of these Sunday mornings when I was at home, doing ordinary things like making breakfast and cleaning the apartment, I found myself thinking about God and especially about Jesus Christ. Suddenly the words came into my mind very strongly, almost like a voice, which Jesus had spoken to the disciples when he found them asleep: "Could you not watch with me one hour?"

I know now that in the lives of Christians experiences such as those happen with some frequency. But at the time this prompting seemed to me extraordinary, as though someone or something—I dared not think it was God himself—had spoken to me. This is not to say that I dropped everything at once and began going to church. But I did begin to reflect, for the first time, on the possibility of going to church again, if not in the Christian Science church, then in some other one. And I knew then, more clearly than before, that it was Jesus Christ I was looking for. He had asked me to watch one hour with him. I began to want to find him and to listen to him, to know what message he wanted to convey.

This moment was, I think, for me, the golden string. And it led me by a very tortuous path, at first. For it was not only intellectual inquiry and study that brought me to where I now am. There were some accidents, some twists of circumstance, that had a part to play. Looking back, one might suppose that these, too, were moments of grace. I do in fact think they were. But on the surface there is nothing remarkable about them.

(Turning: Reflections on the Experience of Conversion)

⚜ BARBARA JOHNSON ⚜
(CONTEMPORARY)

Popular speaker and author of seven books. Barbara and her husband Bill are founders of Spatula Ministries, a personal ministry dedicated to helping families in trouble.

WHEN WE SEEK HIM WITH ALL OUR HEARTS

People who know my story ask me how I ever survived learning about Larry's (her son) homosexuality and then enduring the lonely estrangement that occurred because I lashed out at him with anger and even hatred. This happened after I'd already endured devastating injuries to my husband and the deaths of two sons just as they reached the threshold of adult life. All of these experiences squashed my heart, but out of that came a fragrance in my life that could never have happened without going through the crushing pain. One of my favorite bits of verse says it so well: "There is no oil without squeezing the olives, no wine without pressing the grapes, no fragrance without crushing the flowers, and no real joy without sorrow."

How did I survive? I tried a lot of things and I learned a lot, mostly by trial and error. And I'm still learning. I try to steer away from the pat answer and the hollow formula. I also avoid the instant solution, the microwave maturity, the quick fix, the heavenly Band-Aid without surgery. That just isn't the way God works. As Jesus said in John 15:2, we need to be pruned, and pruning can be painful.

The bottom line, however, is exactly what I told that desperate lady who called the radio station that night wanting to know how to unravel the mysteries of a life that had overwhelmed her. God only knows. The secret things do belong to Him. When the "gloomees" try to strike us down, He always has the answer. And when we seek Him with all our hearts, the "gloomees" don't have a chance.

❧ ROBIN STRATTON ☙
(1940–)

Member of the Carmelite community.

A GENTLE AND WONDERFUL EXPERIENCE OF GOD

When I was eight, I had a gentle and wonderful experience of God. Though at the time I had no name for it, the experience has remained with me all my life. It occurred as I sat on the warm grass by a spring runlet in a little ravine across the street from our government housing project in Charlestown, Indiana. I was lost in a sense of wonder, oneness, and goodness that held me for I don't know how long. My contemplative sense of life was established that day.

("What It Means to Me to Be a Carmelite",
in Spiritual Life, *Volume 47, Number 4, Winter 2001)*

❧ PAUL M. ANDERSON ☙
(1938–)

American biochemistry and molecular biology professor.

A GIFT FROM GOD

Coming into this relationship with God was not something I accomplished on my own—it was a gift that God gave me. I did not receive this gift all at once but over a period of several months, perhaps years. However, I do recall one evening reading a statement made by the nineteenth-century professor of natural sciences Henry Drummond: "Will-power does not change men. Time does not change men. Christ does." I was somewhat startled—and excited—to realize that I understood its meaning.

Subsequently I bought a New Testament and read most of it in about three weeks. It amazed me. Here was a blueprint for living and a description and explanation of the sense of separation from God that I had been experiencing. The consistency that exists between the Old and New Testaments spoke to the character, purposes and promises of God, particularly the promise of a plan for reconciling human beings to himself. I was particularly impressed by the vivid authenticity of the biblical stories. The dark side of the human race is recognized along with the good side. The struggles, failures and weaknesses of great leaders are evident, as well as obedience to God. I came to understand that one of the ways God communicates to us is through the writings of godly people as collected in the Bible and that understanding its message is also a gift.

(Professors Who Believe, *IV Press*, 1998)

❧ E. C. "Gene" Ashby ❧
(CONTEMPORARY)

American chemistry and biochemistry professor.

THROUGH IT ALL GOD HAD A PLAN FOR MY LIFE

In recalling my early life in particular, I see clearly how the hand of God has guided my life through an intricate web of circumstances. Now my incredible journey is almost over, and I can truly say that the most important lesson I have learned in life is that God is faithful. In spite of tough times, illnesses, parental rejection, the difficulties of raising seven children, the trauma of the Vietnam War, and other painful events and difficult relationships, I would not change anything about my life. In everything God was molding me and shaping me to become the person he wanted me to be. I would not know God today the way I do if I had not suffered through the unique circumstances of my life. Today my sensitivity to suffering enables me to help others.

(Professors Who Believe, *IV Press*)

R. BETTY HOPE-GITTENS

(1939–)

Canadian employment consultant who has an eleven word philosophy, "Rejoice always, pray without ceasing, and in all circumstances give thanks."

FEELING THE WIND IS LIKE FEELING GOD'S PRESENCE

My daily morning walk is my time to talk with God. I always start by giving thanks for the sight of this new day; then I give thanks for God's gifts of hearing, seeing, and touching.

For many months of the year I encounter strong north and west winds. As I walk along, I find myself smiling and thinking how much feeling the wind is like feeling God's presence. I can't see the wind, but it is definitely present. It makes me feel cool and refreshed; it has a calming, soothing effect that gives me needed energy and strength, which allow me to go even further. When the wind is at my back I feel a surge of power that propels me onward. How much this is like feeling God's presence in my life!

I can't see God, but I can definitely see the results of God's presence in my life. I can hear the wind as it sweeps through the trees, between the buildings, and across the open fields. Similarly, I can hear God's words and sense God's presence in the lives of people with whom I speak. Sensing God's presence in my life allows me to face calmly and without fear whatever the future holds, always confident that nothing can ever separate me from God's love.

❧ KIT LANE ❧

(1939–)

American newspaper editor. While she and her husband were running two weekly newspapers in Michigan, "Out of the clear blue sky my heart became interested in learning more of Jesus (about 9:20 a.m., April 23, 1979)". "I have come to have a deep affection for what John Wesley called 'prevenient grace,' that little bit of the Holy Spirit that is in all that leads us to question and eventually believe."

I KNEW IN MY HEART THAT GOD WAS REAL

I was nearly 40 when I knew in my heart that God was real. At first I felt it had been a sudden transformation, wrought by the Lord alone. But gradually it became apparent that for 39 years God had been revealing Himself in small things I had 'pondered in my heart.' Mostly God used people for this work.

There was a printer I worked with who kept his radio tuned to a Christian station; a five-year old neighbor whose vivid description of the crucifixion was another piece of the puzzle. There were others: a nun who was a nurse, delivering two of my children with calm assurance; a young college student whose faith permeated the term papers he paid me to type; and many more.

I wrote to as many of these people as I could remember and contact to thank them for their part in my spiritual growth. But there were many others, some whose names I did not know, some whose contribution I did not understand or remember.

This awareness of how God uses people as witnesses has made me approach with care all contacts with others, lest I miss the opportunity the Lord has given me.

⊰ ROBERT R. SELVENDRAN ⊱

(1939–)

Sri Lankan research plant biochemist, now a British citizen. He is a fellow of the Royal Society of Chemistry and recipient of its Senior Medal for Food Chemistry in 1994. He contends that science is essentially a religious activity, which plays its own special role in unfolding the nature and purpose of God.

THE GREATEST DISCOVERY I HAVE EVER MADE

To this day, nearly twenty-five years after I first asked Christ to come into my life, I haven't found anything remotely comparable to the joy of knowing God through Christ Jesus, my Lord and Savior......I can claim that I have made several discoveries in my field, but none of them compares with the greatest discovery I have ever made. That happened in December 1958, when I discovered that Christ was indeed my Savior, Lord, and God—and not only my Savior, but the Savior of the whole world.

A DRAMATIC CHANGE

Before I became a Christian, I used to read the Bible occasionally, but somehow the characters seemed very distant to me. Jesus, at that time, was an historical person who did several charitable deeds, taught us about God and his love for us, and how best we could live in peace with one another. He also died a martyr's death, rose from the dead and ascended to heaven, which made me revere him, I must admit.

However, when I finally became a Christian, in December 1958, my whole attitude to the Bible changed dramatically, and for a few months after my conversion I literally could not put it down. This change in attitude can be best described by the following illustration: imagine entering a dark room full of treasures and trying to appreciate and estimate the value of the objects by touch alone. As it is difficult to do this, you get exasperated and try to find the exit door, but then your hand reaches the light switch and suddenly the whole room is flooded with light. With the room lit, exploring the

contents becomes a pleasure....In the Bible I find God's disclosures
to mankind: his plan for humanity and how he is bringing this about
without violating the free will he has given us.

(UBS Special Report 15, April 1997, p. 5)

THE UNIVERSE

The universe is still expanding, so large and well-ordered that it is
apparently beyond human comprehension. However, by a concerted
effort, the collective "scientific mind" is beginning not only to
comprehend it, but to put a meaningful construct on its origin and
progressive development. I find the whole enterprise so meaningful and awe-inspiring because it helps me to understand better the
Mind behind it all and the unfoldment of His purposes. It may be
said that the whole scientific endeavor is helping to put a "face" on
God, which can be understood by the inquiring natural mind of man.
Jesus said, "You will know the truth, and the truth shall set you free."
Better appreciation of the truth, from natural or spiritual phenomena, has a liberating and enriching influence on life and is a blessing
from God.

*(taken from "Concepts of God--An Enlarging View", a paper first
presented at the Christian Study Center, Norwich, England, 1995:
subsequently presented in Philadelphia and finally in Toronto, Canada.)*

A CHRISTIAN REFLECTING ON SCIENTIFIC TRUTH

I have been engaged in plant biochemical research for thirty
years. For an even longer period I have been a practicing Christian.
Throughout, I have been keen to share the excitement I find in science, which increases my awareness of the physical world about
us. I want to share also the joy and certainty of my new life in Christ
Jesus, which increases my awareness of God's purposes for humanity
and the world at large. Sharing these experiences ('verified truths')
has led to thought-provoking discussions with fellow-scientists and
with people from various walks of life in many parts of the world,
where my research has taken me over the years.

As a consequence, I have reflected long and hard on scientific and Christian views of the world. I have not found these to be mutually exclusive, but in fact complementary. Together they give a fuller and more meaningful picture of life, of the world and indeed of the universe.

("Analyst and Artist", Connect, Winter 1995, p. 14).

THE PATTERNS FIT TOGETHER
Within the great patterns of science smaller patterns fit together. The historical development of the Periodic Table of elements and of the structure of the atom are two examples of many such disclosures of science. Scientific truth may be said to lie in the coherence of the pattern(s) into meaningful constructs. This is where a Designing Hand seems to be revealed. For me—and there are many scientists who subscribe to the same view—the evidence points to the existence of an Intelligent Being.

The coherence of the pattern(s) may be compared to a man tracing out the various threads on the underside of an embroidery. He can tell us a great deal about the different courses, and their relationship to one another. However, as to why just those colours should have been brought together at all—on just that piece of canvas, so that when it is turned over it displays an exquisite pattern within which lie smaller patterns—he can say very little. The collocation of threads into that particular harmony is an inexplicable given, which the analyst cannot explain adequately, unless he invokes the artist whose creation it was in the first place. But no work of art, by itself, can convey to the viewer exactly what the artist knew and felt and tried to express. This disclosure can only be made by the artist himself.

Likewise, the world about us which displays orderliness, consistency, regularity and rationality calls for a Creator (God). The Creator, whose mind human beings can never fully fathom, inspired the writer of the first book of the Bible to begin with the words, 'In the beginning God created the heavens and the earth.'

("Analyst and Artist", Connect, Winter 1995, p.15.)

⚔ COLLEEN TOWNSEND EVANS ⚕

(CONTEMPORARY)

American writer of devotional books and articles, community leader.

THE REALITY OF GOD WAS MADE KNOWN

For me it began during my mid-teens when, without actually seeking it, I had an experience that was both mystical and profound. One
evening when I was alone, I went to my room—and found myself in
the presence of a blinding white light. It was all around me...over-
whelming, consuming. I was part of it and it was part of me. At the
core of my being—in my spirit—I felt free and peaceful. I was aware
of my oneness with all things, all people—especially with God.

Ever since that moment I have never doubted the reality of God
or His presence in our human lives. Although that experience wasn't
repeated, I still have the strength and assurance it gave me. That was
the beginning of my conscious spiritual journey.

For many years I didn't mention that evening to anyone except
my mother. In fact, even now I wonder about sharing such an
intensely personal incident, for I think we are in trouble when we
base our faith upon experience or feeling alone. And yet, what we
have seen and heard and touched is a valid part of ourselves. For me,
that moment was where my pilgrimage began.

*(She later went on to find a personal relationship with the living Christ. "He has given
me direction and a goal—and nothing has ever been quite the same for me." Excerpt from
A New Joy by Colleen Townsend Evans. Copyright 1973 by Fleming H. Revell Company)*

⪥ DELTON DEES ⪤

(1940–)

Evangelist who was led to speak on behalf of Christ's miraculous power to heal the broken hearted in over 12,000 crusades and to over five million young people in schools throughout the U. S.

I FOUND GOD BECAUSE OF A BET WITH SOME FRIENDS

When I was a four and a half year old baby I was rejected by my parents and left in an apartment to die. I had to go through the first grade four times because no one wanted me. At thirty years of age, I was a hardened atheist and only one phone call away from being a professional hit man for the syndicate. I wandered into a Baptist church on a bet with some close friends. I was going to prove how many hypocrites there were in the church. One hour later I was born again. Through bumps and curves and many battles, I have been rewarded beyond my wildest dreams and with God's help He has used me to tell the Gospel message.

⪥ JOHN F. WALKUP ⪤

(1941–)

American professor of electrical engineering.

A TREMENDOUS PRIVILEGE

As I get to know Jesus better, I understand more deeply that the truth I was seeking when I began college is fully embodied in a persona—Jesus Christ. God is calling out a people who are, by God's grace, forgiven and made new. He offers them a close relationship with him. I have learned that my inadequacy to meet life's challenges is not a handicap because God has designed me to find my adequacy in him. It has been a tremendous privilege and joy for me to be able to work with faculty and students searching for truth because I know that Jesus Christ himself is the ultimate source of truth.

(Professors Who Believe, *IV Press*, 1998)

≈ JOHN K. HOLMES ≈

(CONTEMPORARY)

American academic dean, lecturer on mathematics and physics.

WAS THERE ANY PURPOSE TO IT ALL?

As a college student, I was amazed by the order of the universe. Could all of this have come about by chance? How did life originate? And was there any purpose to it all? If there is no purpose to life, then our philosophy ought to be: "Eat, drink, and be merry; for tomorrow we die." But suppose, on the other hand, that there is a supreme Being who designed the universe and created man for His purposes. Then you and I must seek Him, and find His will for our lives.

It has been a great thrill for me to find that, at the other end of the bridge of faith, it isn't only God who wants to welcome us, but also a vast and varied company of other people who have crossed it, too.

(Scientists Who Believe)

≈ KENNETH G. ELZINGA ≈

(1941–)

American economics professor.

A FAITHFUL ANCHOR

Very few of my life's plans have worked out. I did not plan to remain on the faculty at UVA for over twenty-five years when I accepted its offer of employment; I did not plan to have my wife die of cancer at the age of thirty-three; I did not plan to have my best friends move away from Charlottesville. I never expected to publish, to enjoy the company of students, to overcome my fear of teaching or to be a co-author of mystery novels. But through it all I have found the Lord Jesus to be a faithful anchor. He gives me strength for today and hope for tomorrow.

(Professors Who Believe, IV Press, 1998)

✺ VERNA BENNER CARSON ✺

(CONTEMPORARY)

American professor of nursing.

HE PREPARES THOSE HE CALLS

When I accepted Jesus as my personal Savior in the fall of 1975, I never dreamed of the opportunities and challenges that lay ahead of me. Many of those opportunities came to me specifically as a professor of nursing in a large university setting. When I look at my own personal characteristics—somewhat shy, certainly not bold, a person who likes to please and tries to avoid rocking the boat—I marvel at the things that the Lord has allowed me to do. I have been privileged to teach nurses across the country the importance of spiritual care and the essential role that Jesus plays in that care, to boldly proclaim that Jesus is Lord in pubic forums, to write on the integration of spirituality and nursing and to take unpopular stands at the university based on my faith convictions. I was an unlikely candidate for these opportunities, yet I have never forgotten something a student told me years ago: "He doesn't call the prepared, he prepares those that he calls." The recognition of the Lord's role in what I accomplish keeps me humble and keeps me on my knees.

(Professors Who Believe, *IV Press*, 1998)

✺ RONALD D. ANDERSON ✺

(CONTEMPORARY)

American professor of education.

A DOUBLE SEARCH

An early writer described our search for God as the "double search," denoting our seeking for God and God's seeking for us. I find this image helpful. The search is not just a one-way search, and we are not limited to what can be gained from the human side of the search. As a Christian, I see God as having made the major move in the search; God has enabled me to search for him successfully, resulting in a relationship that is ongoing, personal and influential. Life does not have to be a continuing search for new insights from whatever source about how to find our way to God. It is no longer a search for God; it is a relationship with God in which the two of us jointly search out the path on which we are journeying together. It is a journey—sometimes through great difficulty and intense pain—that has direction and joy because of our relationship and because of the purpose and meaning that only God can give.

I am in awe of what God has created and what God continues to do in my life. The wonder is about who I am as compared to who I would be without this relationship with God, even though who I am still is less than society's or my ideal. It is about the freedom, contentment and peace that come with Jesus' "easy yoke." This wonder is part of my personal expression of faith.

(Professors Who Believe, IV Press, 1998)

ROBERT C. NEWMAN

(1941–)

A former astrophysicist who became a seminary professor after witnessing the death of a small child at a zoo. Could he have prevented that tragedy? "God used that event to convince me that I needed to focus my career plans on a pursuit that was higher than studying the stars."

HE GUIDES EACH ONE OF US

My scientific background helps me to understand God's power and wisdom, and it enlarges my ability to present a scientifically credible apologetic for His existence. I'm convinced that the God who made the stars uses His mighty wisdom and power to guide each one of us into the career that is the most satisfying and the most constructive way of life.

(Scientists Who Believe, Moody)

⟡ ROBERT C. ROBERTS ⟡
(1942–)

American professor of philosophy and author.

I EXPERIENCE GOD DAILY

I experience God each day, usually in undramatic ways that I may
not even notice unless I am attentive and well-attuned. I experience
Him in my interaction with students, be it pleasant or difficult; in
my relations with colleagues; in my intellectual labors, whether they
go smoothly or frustratingly; in my daily prayers; in the special work
that I do in the context of my congregation; and in my interactions
with my wife and children (perhaps especially these last). In the
background of all that I do and think is the sense that Jesus is there,
the Lord who commands, but also the Savior who has healed the rift
between us and the Father so that we human beings can live in confidence and hope despite our horrible, intractable sin.

(God and the Philosophers, *Oxford*)

⟡ CLARA M. MATHESON ⟡
(1943–)

**American teacher and writer. The following excerpts are taken from her
unpublished journal.**

WHEN MY DARKNESS BECAME LIGHT

The day in my life when my soul was awakened will always remain a
powerful memory. I did not know what had really happened to me,
but now after later reflection, I know that it was God's leading. I was
not more than 14 at the time when I was confronted with God's presence. I do not remember the exact day, probably because at the time
I dismissed the whole experience as too fantastic to be believable.
One summer Sunday as I was sitting in our little country church,
there came over me a joy, peace and bliss beyond anything I had
previously known. It was indeed a "peace of God which transcends

all understanding." The whole world appeared as a blaze of golden, inexpressible glory and light. When this "blaze" faded several hours later after returning home, I was left with something I have never forgotten and which constantly reminds me of the beauty locked up in everything around me. My first thought was of God, of seeing God. "You shall know that I am in my Father, and you in me, and I in you." If we want to see God, all we have to do is open our eyes and look. From that moment I knew that God was real and present and loved me with a tenderness beyond compare.

This event is, of course, special to me and always will remain so, but it is really not an unusual experience. Until my first years of teaching I had not realized that similar experiences do happen to people, and they testify to events very much like mine. And it was many years later that I realized that this type of experience is really quite common. I am continually amazed at His leading in every seemingly insignificant event of my life. Each event and circumstance, even those which seem harmful, are steppingstones to greater things He has in store for me. I praise His name for His power to change people's lives and to give a contentment and serenity which nothing of this world can give. And I rejoice because the experience in that little country church on that summer Sunday has sustained me and inspired me ever since.

TO LIVE IN GOD'S PRESENCE

I want to be constantly aware of the Lord's presence. To live in the presence of God means to live in such a way that all my thoughts and actions are being guided by Him. This is not an easy task. My humble prayer is that nothing will be undertaken without my being open to God's direction. This inner life must be continually nurtured or I will become ineffective and unproductive because my life will be separated from its sustenance. I am inspired by Frank Laubach's attempts to be constantly aware of God's presence. Will I be able to focus my thoughts on God all day long—in the mundane activities as well as in the special assignments? Will I be able to pray without ceasing? That is my goal.

IN THE FACE OF DEATH

The pursuit of success, of avoiding failure will seem of little importance in the face of death . What counts then is serenity and values that lie beyond success and failure. Death is a reality, but I do not need to fear it because Christ has conquered death through His resurrection. Since I am united with Him in faith, I know that death is only a doorway through which I will pass to eternal life with Him. I have caught a glimpse of God's working in my life and know I am a part of His great plan running through all eternity. This life on earth is just a speck on the glass of time, compared to the life within, eternal.

THE NEXT SYMPHONY

As the years pass, I become more tolerant and accepting of what God brings my way. I find a new peace and beauty as I grow older and begin to see more clearly what life is all about. The end of my earthly life's symphony represents a triumphant finale to what has preceded it, but, oh, the next symphony, what glory awaits me there!

ALL FEAR IS GONE

I will not fear, for God is always with me wherever I go and whatever I do. He will not allow me to face my trials alone.

❧ GLAPHRE GILLILAND ❧

(1943–)

Author and teacher, who in 1974 was called to a life of prayer, trusting God completely for the direction and provision of her life. What began as a private ministry of prayer and counseling developed into a teaching ministry called PRAYERLIFE.

I ALMOST MISSED IT

I almost missed all of that! The privilege of loving dirty-faced kids until I didn't notice those things as much as their hurts and hearts.

I almost missed it.

During my three years at that school, I prayed with all my production casts and crews before our performances—over one thousand different kids. Since many students were in numerous productions, I prayed with most of them several times. There was never one complaint.

I almost missed it.

I almost missed the opportunity for personal growth—all because I looked at my plan...and initially said no to a job I didn't think suited me.

Looking back on those three years, I have to wonder how much I crippled God's purpose for that time because I kept resisting his direction. Kept hanging on to my own perception of what was right for me.

But...whatever it wasn't...one thing it was...it was the beginning of a crucial lesson.

It's not a plan we create that determines our fulfillment.

It's what we let God do in the plan of His choosing.

(*Glaphre Guilliland*, When the Pieces don't Fit, God Makes the Difference, *Zondervan, pp. 297-8, 1984 by author.*)

↬ JAMES FINLEY ↫
(1943–)

American clinical psychologist, teacher, writer, and speaker. The following was taken from *The Awakening Call*, a prayer journal of reflections of Finley's own journey.

A GIFTED AWAKENING

If we look back to the first beginning of our spiritual journey we invariably come upon moments of spiritual awakening. Sometimes these moments (which appear and reappear throughout our lives) come to us while we are praying. But often they simply rise up out of life itself. We live out our lives seeing only the tip of the iceberg, and all that does appear above the surface does so fleetingly as a brief manifestation of some unseen abyss that endows the smallest of things and events with a value beyond comprehension.

Perhaps as a child lying alone at night listening to a summer rain, or in the wake of some unforgivable act when the one we wronged embraced us, or in holding a piece of chipped crystal up to the sun, there was given to us a gift of awareness. (Did we dare even mention it to anyone? Did we dare, even for a moment, to doubt the touch of we-know-not-what that was given there?) Before we did anything to earn it (we can never earn it), before we were ready to receive it (we are never ready), we were granted a gifted awakening.

⨳ BILL TAMMEUS ⨳
(1945–)

Editorial writer for *The Kansas City Star*. His writings often impart a sense of the spiritual. Used by permission of *The Kansas City Star*.

"IN THE DESERT WAYS I SING"
It was when the choir of which I was a part sang the gently moving phrase, "In the desert ways I sing" that the poignant music resonated with some deep place in my spirit and filled my eyes with unbidden tears.

My voice caught and I had to let the rest of the bass section carry on for a bar or two without me. Somehow I regrouped for the second part of the repeated last phrase: "Spring, O Living Water, spring!"

And I wondered anew just how music is able to touch us and change us, reveal us and shape us. Music, indeed, is one of the best arguments I know that humans are not just physical beings but also have an equally real spiritual dimension.

Music quickens our passive souls, offering testimony that we are not merely corporeal products of evolving cells. Rather, in some mysterious way, we are receivers of divine messages mediated to us through many means. None of those means is more persuasive than music, which essayist and poet Joseph Addison, 300 years ago, described as "the greatest good that mortals know/ And all of heaven we have below."

⚜ DUKE TUFTY ⚜

(1945–)

American minister who said, "God is all that we can know, all that we don't know and more. A paradox indeed."

MY GREATEST HOPE IN TIME OF NEED

God can be known in many ways by moving beyond the thinking mind to our deeper, spiritual, intuitive feelings. I was sitting on a park bench next to an elderly woman who looked very forlorn. Sitting with her was a 3- or 4-year-old child who reached up, put his hand on the woman's face and said, "It's going to be OK." In that moment I knew God as the loving tenderness of a young child. Standing before the Grand Canyon and gazing out at the wonder before me, I knew God as the awesome creator.

Marveling at the incredible technological advances of our day, I have come to know God as the unlimited intelligence of the universe. When in doubt and worry, I rise above my troubles and know God as my greatest hope in time of need. Thinking God into existence through definition and detail will always leave us short of satisfaction. Feeling God's existence in all that is around us leads to a realm of satisfaction that words cannot convey.

✍ VARIA ✑

(WRITTEN AT AGE 18 IN THE 1960's)

Eighteen year old who was imprisoned in the USSR for talking about the love of Jesus at a Communist meeting. After the meeting they took her away. Months passed and finally her friend Maria, who had led her to Christ, received this letter from her.

I CANNOT BE SILENT

My heart praises and thanks God, that, through you, He showed me the way to salvation. Now, being on this way, my life has a purpose and I know where to go and for whom to suffer. I feel the desire to tell and witness to everybody about the great joy of salvation that I have in my heart. Who can separate us from the love of God in Christ? Nobody and nothing. Neither prison nor suffering. The suffering that God sends us only strengthens us more and more in the faith in Him. My heart is so full that the grace of God overflows.

At work, they curse and punish me, giving me extra work because I cannot be silent. I must tell everyone what the Lord has done for me. He has made me a new being, a new creation, of me who was on the way of perdition. Can I be silent after this? No, never! As long as my lips can speak, I will witness to every one about His great love.

Here there are many who believe in Christ as their personal Savior. More than half of the prisoners are believers. We have among us great singers and good preachers of the Gospel. In the evening, when we gather after heavy work, how wonderful it is to pass at least some time together in prayer at the feet of our Savior. With Christ there is freedom everywhere. I learned here many beautiful hymns and every day God gives me more and more of His Word.

All our brethren greet you and are glad that your faith in God is so powerful and that you praise Him in your sufferings unceasingly.

(Jesus Freaks, dc Talk and the Voice of the Martyrs, *Asbury Publications, Tulsa, OK*)

❧ ANONYMOUS ❧

Taken from *Journal of an Ordinary Pilgrim*, 1954.

SHAPED TO A PURPOSE

I think that my whole life, from childhood until now, has been shaped to a purpose. The disappointments, the frustrations, the wrong turnings have all shown me what is not good enough and are leading me to what is best. I had to be shown everything I thought I wanted in order to be convinced of what I truly wanted. I had to be humbled and straightened out by unfortunate events, by confusion and despair, by failure, before I could follow God's way.

If only I could be patient enough to see the larger picture of what is happening to me and my relationships with my environment! If I could really see from God's point of view, I should know that, as long as I persist in following my own will, I shall be stopped short, shaken down to a mere nothing, and sent forth again on my pilgrimage with further directions. As long as I want to be important, I get confused and lose the way. Then I'm sent right back to the beginning of this journal, back to Despair and Hopelessness.

Why don't I see that to be sent back is so much more the evidence of God's love than to be allowed to go on in my own way? I don't see because I'm a small-minded person likely to be all wound up in each little event.

When something I achieve is disappointing, when something I want is withheld, and when something I do must be done over in another way, I must remember that all these things are shaping me to a greater use.

Evil, temptation, failure—beloved enemies, all of them. They're the real friends, and friends sometimes are the real enemies. How mean it would be of God to allow an eager person to succeed at some small thing and stay there forever! When no further effort is required, there's no further joy in living.

We forget about the steady guiding light of God's will, plunge frantically around with a variety of selfish motives, and find ourselves in a dead-end street. That's failure. But to fail and to go humbly back, patiently wait for guidance, and to go on wiser, calmer, and more confident—that is greatness.

SIMPLE AND DIRECT

My religion has become more simple and direct. It almost seems as though there were nothing to it but serenity and honesty, a confidence in the divine right, and the effort to do justly. But there's more to it than that. There's what St. Exupery called "becoming," an increasing knowledge of mankind, and, an increasing humility, a smaller, homelier vision of what service is (I don't think I'll change the world today; I'll just rearrange my kitchen cabinets). There's more than doing justly; there's also loving mercy and walking humbly with God. There's more than faith and hope: there's also love.

ᴇᴥ JAMES P. KEENER ᴥᴇ
(1946–)

American professor of mathematics.

I HAVE NEVER HEARD OF AN EFFECT THAT HAD NO CAUSE

I find it impossible to believe that there is no Creator. In all of my experience, in all of science, I have never heard of an effect that had no cause. I have never seen a design that had no designer, a law that had no lawgiver, an order that had not been ordered, information that had no informer. Chance produces nothing. Saying that something happened by chance merely begs the question of the causes that produced the effect. "It just happened" is simply not an acceptable answer. It is an open admission of ignorance.

(Professors who Believe, IV Press)

⊰ LINDA TRINKAUS ZAGZEBSKI ⊱

(1946–)

American author and professor of philosophy.

GOD COMES THROUGH DIFFERENT PATHS

Christianity is presented as the religion of the dispossessed—the poor, the powerless, the downtrodden, the friendless—in short, the unlucky. This is bad news for those of us who are all too vividly aware of our good fortune. I have been treated gently by life for the most part, but nonetheless I believe that everybody suffers, just not all in the same way. Everyone needs God, but that need comes to consciousness through different paths. The experience of being depraved or treated unjustly is one of them, but the experience of being exceptionally blessed is another.

(Philosophers Who Believe, IV Press, 1993)

⊰ MICHAEL B. YANG ⊱

American doctor of medicine.

I GREW UP AN ATHEIST

During my first semester at Harvard Medical School, at the suggestion of Christian friends and acquaintances, I began to examine the Bible and to investigate the Christian faith. It was a reasonable request; I had never before read the Bible, but only what others had said about it. At the very least, I thought, after reading their book, I would be able to tell Christians more accurately why they were wrong. Unfortunately, or rather fortunately for me, "The word of God is living and active, sharper than any two-edged sword" (Hebrews 4:12 RSV). As I examined the Bible in detail for the very first time, my mind began to change. I saw the distortions and misquotations of those who had argued against the Christian faith, and I saw the philosophical and historical evidences for Christianity. And in the Scriptures I also found a God who worked miracles.

As I read Jesus' works, what C. S. Lewis wrote in *Mere Christianity* echoed in some of my thoughts.

"A man who was merely a man who said the sort of things Jesus said would not be a great moral teacher....Either this man was, and is, the Son of God; or else a madman or something worse. You can shut Him up for a fool, you can spit at Him and kill Him as a demon; or you can fall at His feet and call Him Lord and God. But let us not come with any patronizing nonsense about His being a great human teacher. He has not left that open to us. He did not intend to.

I am one who fell at his feet in worship and experienced the fullness of his grace and truth.

(Finding God at Harvard)

⚜ GLENN C. LOURY ⚜

(1948–)

American professor of economics and author.

ON THE BASIS OF WHAT I HAVE WITNESSED IN MY LIFE
There was no one particular moment when the skies opened up and God came wafting down. Rather, over the mouths as I began to study the Bible, as I went to church, as I learned to pray, as I began to reflect honestly on my life, and as I began to open myself up to the Spirit of God to minister to me and to move me, I came to realize that there was something dramatic missing in my life. I realized that there was an explanation for the low condition of my life. The many things that seemed out of line were all connected to the spiritual vacancy that I was becoming aware of.

How do I know that the resurrection and the whole gospel are real? I know not only because of my acquaintance with the primary sources from the first century A.D., or even because of the words of Scripture. I know primarily, and I affirm to you this truth, on the basis of what I have witnessed in my own life. This knowledge of God's unconditional love for humankind provides moral grounding for my work in cultural and racial reconciliation, economics, and justice. Jesus Christ provides a basis for hope and for the most profound personal satisfaction.

(Finding God at Harvard)

✍ LOUISA (SUE) HULETT ✍

(1949–)

American political science professor.

HE CALLED ME AND SPOKE TO MY HEART

How wonderful of God to give us his word in Scripture—to tell us how much he loves us despite our inevitable failures, to encourage us, to forgive and redeem us and to draw us to him. Sometimes I think he is shouting at a deaf person, or maybe I'm not always listening. On the other hand, I know that the soul-searching and prayer that accompany each crisis help me in my walk with Jesus. He called me and spoke to my heart, and he is faithful. I may not always feel his presence, but I remember vividly the miracle of his touch ten years ago. The reality of that memory sustains me in dry times.

(Professors Who Believe, IV Press)

✍ J. GARY EDEN ✍

(1950–)

American university professor of electrical and computer engineering.

"THESE ARE BUT THE OUTER FRINGE OF HIS WORKS"

My own experience in science had convinced me that a greater reality does indeed lie beyond the physical existence with which each of us is familiar. After years of experimental research I continue to be amazed by the intricacies, for example, of the structure of atoms and diatomic molecules. As we gain successively deeper levels of understanding, new patterns and phenomena emerge, even in areas that were once considered well-understood. Particularly intriguing

to me, however, is the contrast that exists between the simplicity
and elegance of the underlying physical laws and principles. The
overwhelming complexity and beauty of the physical processes and
biological organisms that have been studied thus far—to say nothing of worlds yet to be explored—provide a glimpse of a being whose
intellect and creativity dwarf our own. The apostle Paul stresses this
connection when he states, "From the creation of the world (God's)
invisible qualities, such as His eternal power and divine nature, have
been made visible and have been understood through His handiwork
(Romans 1:20 New Berkeley Version). Commenting on the wonders of
the physical world, Job declares that "these are but the outer fringe
of His works; how faint the whisper we hear of Him! Who then can
understand the thunder of His power?" (Job 26:14 New Berkeley Version).

(Professors Who Believe, *IV Press*)

I AM PERSUADED BY TWO TRUTHS
First, the physical world—which displays a level of complexity and
beauty that we can only begin to fathom (much less duplicate)—
bears the unmistakable signature of a superior intellect. Second,
Christianity provides a rational explanation for life on this planet
as it really is, not as we would wish it to be. In light of these truths, I
accept the testimony of the apostle Peter, who states emphatically
that "when we made known to you the power and coming of our
Lord Jesus Christ, we were not following cleverly devised fables. On
the contrary, we were eyewitnesses of his majesty" (2 Peter 1:16 New
Berkeley Version).

(Professors Who Believe, *IV Press*)

⇜ C. Stephen Layman ⇝
(1950–)

American philosopher and author who had an interest in religion as a young child but struggled with doubt.

The wonder of creation and life

I read most of the works of C. S. Lewis, and through them I caught a glimpse of the vast sweep and richness of Christian theology. Through the lens of Lewis's theological works, something of the wonder of creation and life came through to me in a way it never had before. Looking back, I think this experience is one of the deep roots of my love of philosophy. For since my college years, it has been theology and philosophy that have again and again renewed my sense of the extraordinariness of existence.

⇜ Patricia H. Reiff ⇝
(1950–)

American space physicist and astronomer. "If you could in fact prove scientifically the existence of God, then there would not be any free choice, and God created us to be able to choose."

"Aha!"

I am both a scientist and a Christian. God has called me to understand his world and gives me the insight to do it. and yes, I ascribe many of my best ideas to divine inspiration—the "Aha! insight" that Martin Gardner discusses often comes to me in quiet times and dreams. I have felt the Lord leading me, both in my choice of career and in my everyday life. I have rested on a promise found in the Bible: "Trust in the Lord with all thine heart; and lean not unto thine own understanding. In all thy ways acknowledge him, and he shall direct thy paths" (Proverbs 3:5–6 KJV).

(Professors Who Believe, IV Press, 1998)

Science cannot prove that God exists. If it could, then only scientists could know him. Jesus came to the children and the poor, scorning the haughty intellectuals of his day. He came to show us what God living in you really looks like. He taught with simple parables that all can understand. He died a Lamb for our sins and forever opened the throne of God to human kind. My faith is based on God's Word and on the eyewitness accounts of men and women who were willing to die for their faith, not on cleverly crafted fables (2 Peter 1:6). The Dead Sea Scrolls demonstrate that today's Scripture manuscripts differ little from manuscripts that are two thousand years old. Archaeological discoveries continue to furnish new evidence of the veracity of the places and people spoken of in the Bible. God preserves his Word, and his Word is what speaks of Jesus. The Bible is very old, yet always new. Like an onion, it has many layers. Each time I read it, I go a layer deeper without ever coming to the end. Bible reading is challenging enough for an intellectual but simple enough for a child.

(Professors Who Believe, IV Press, 1998)

✑ C. STEPHEN EVANS ✑

American professor of philosophy and author.

A PRIVILEGED CALLING

How grateful to God I feel for the privilege of the calling I have had. Truly, for me "the lines have fallen out in pleasant places." I have been blessed in abilities, career, family, and church experiences. None of this strikes me as deserved. I would say that I experience my life as a journey that is a calling, a privileged calling in the sense that the vocation I have been assigned is one that corresponds to my most cherished desires. I do not know whether this is God's normal mode of operation, or whether he sometimes calls us to go against all our fondest hopes and desires. I suspect that he sometimes does do this, and that it is a mark of spiritual maturity to be able to do this. I know others have walked more difficult roads, and of course I do not know where my own road will take me in the future. Still, up till now, my own paths have generally been level and straight. Perhaps the gratifying character of my own life is a kind of concession to my weakness, a sign that I was not up to sterner, more challenging tasks. But I cannot in my humanness refrain from thanking God for what he has given me, even if this is so.

(Storying Ourselves, Baker)

ஃ SIANG-YANG TAN ஃ
(1954–)

American professor of psychology.

How writing this autobiography affected me

First, I have been blessed afresh, with deep thanksgiving from my heart, by the sovereignty and gracious providence of a loving and faithful God who has guided my life in such amazing ways. Truly, great is his faithfulness!

Second, the uniqueness of Jesus Christ as Lord and Savior and the ultimate Answer to the deepest needs of human beings and the problem of sin, has rung out loud and clear. He has changed my life dramatically since my conversion on August 12, 1968, and continues to transform my life as well as many other lives. I am deeply thankful for his salvation, and for his love and grace that motivate me with compassion and caring to minister as a "wounded healer" to broken lives in a fallen world.

Third, the power and spiritual gifts of the Holy Spirit have touched my life and ministry in deeper ways in recent years. I am not only very grateful for such anointing and blessing, but I have been reminded to be faithful in using whatever spiritual gifts and power he graciously bestows on me for more effective ministry, for his Glory. I am motivated afresh to spend more time in solitude for prayer and deeper communion with the Lord and his Word, and to

continue to practice the spiritual disciplines with joy and celebration!

(Storying Ourselves, Baker Book House)

❧ ANNE LAMOTT ❧
(1954–)

Christian writer of novels and other books.

MY COMING TO FAITH

My coming to faith did not start with a leap but rather a series of
staggers from what seemed one sage place to another. Like lily pads,
round and green, these places summoned and then held me up while
I grew...I can see how flimsy and indirect a path they made. Yet each
step brought me closer to the verdant pad of faith on which I somehow stay afloat today.

We in our faith work...stumble along toward where we think
we're supposed to go, bumbling along, and here is what's so amazing—we end up getting exactly where we're supposed to be.

(Traveling Mercies: Some Thoughts on Faith)

❧ ZAHID ❧
(FL. 1986)

**Pakistani Muslim who, until his conversion, was a leader of a mob who
attacked Christians. Then when he began sharing Jesus with everyone he
knew, he was imprisoned for two years, beaten and tortured. His captors
pulled out his fingernails and tied him to a ceiling fan by his hair.**

I KNEW HE WAS THE TRUTH

I was reading the Bible looking for contradictions I could use against
the Christian faith. All of a sudden a great light appeared in my
room and I heard a voice call my name. The light was bright, it lit
the entire room. "Zahid, why do you persecute me?" I was scared. I

didn't know what to do. I thought I was dreaming. I asked "Who are you?"

I heard, "I am the way, the truth, and the life.!"

For the next three nights the light and the voice returned. Finally, on the fourth night, I knelt down and I accepted Jesus as my Savior. I could not deny Jesus. Mohammed had never visited me; Jesus had. I knew He was the truth. (The court had unexpectedly issued an order to release Zahid because there was not enough evidence to execute him.)

I live in a land ruled by the false teaching of Islam. My people are blinded, and I was chosen by God to be His voice. I count all that I have suffered nothing compared to the endless joy of knowing Jesus, the way, the truth and the life.

> (Jesus Freaks, dc Talk and the Voice
> Martyrs, *Asbury Publications*)

❧ MAX LUCADO ❧

(1955–)

American pastor, missionary, writer of best sellers in the evangelical Christian market.

MY CHOICE

I am a spiritual being. After this body is dead, my spirit will soar. I refuse to let what will rot, rule the eternal. I choose self-control. I will be drunk only by joy. I will be impassioned only by my faith. I will be influenced only by God. I will be taught only by Christ.

> (When God Whispers Your Name, *Word*)

ᴥ CRAIG BRELSFORD ᴥ
(CONTEMPORARY)

Editor of the Hickory, N. C. *Daily Record*. After speaking with Chinese Pastor Lin, he commented, "I'd never before been in a church in a country where Christians risk persecution. The visits affected me deeply."

A TURNING POINT IN MY FAITH

After spending 17 years in prison for his Christian beliefs, Pastor Lin Xiangao of Canton, China, was offered a choice by the Communist authorities. Renounce Christ and go free, or continue doing hard labor. The pastor refused and remained in prison three more years.

"I knew if I denied Christ, the previous 17 years would have been in vain," Pastor Lin, a leader in China's "house church" movement, told me. "Now I thank God every day for these 20 years."

That conversation marked a turning point in my faith. To me the unfailing love of God had been a concept I believed. To Pastor Lin, that love was an experience he lived. God has turned pastor Lin's difficult life into a living testimony of divine reconciliation with humankind through Jesus Christ.

ᴥ HOLLY McKISSICK ᴥ
(CONTEMPORARY)

Pastor of St. Andrew Christian Church in Olathe, Kansas and a regular contributor to the Kansas City Star.

I EXPERIENCE GOD IN THE JOY AND SUFFERING ALL AROUND ME

Once it happened to me in a hogarcito, a "little home," in a slum of San Salvador. In the midst of a million people suffering the brutality of poverty and civil war, there was a little house with seven women and their small children, all of whom had been abused in the war, who were re-creating their lives and, bit by bit, their community. Two times I have held my newborn baby and felt the waters of birth, like the gift of creation, like the waters of baptism, wash over me.

And once, through an unbelievable twist of events, I bumped into an estranged friend at a restaurant, and I was forgiven and embraced.

(In response to a reader's question about experiencing
God, in The Kansas City Star, *January 14, 2000)*

ᘓᕽ Merry Stanford ᕽᘓ

(1950–)

Reported in the January, 2000 issue of "Friends Journal."

THE GRACE THAT AMAZINGLY ENTERED MY LIFE

On one blustery March some years ago I was sitting in meditation, trying to find some peace of mind. I struggled with the pain of my self-hatred and my memories, and I threw my anguish angrily back in the face of God who had, I believed, forsaken me as a child to my tormentors and was now forsaking me to social isolation. How could a loving God abandon me in that way?! I cried it out to the heavens.

Then, very suddenly and very tangibly, in every way but the visual, there was present with me the person of Jesus. He knelt before me, reached out to me tenderly. I broke into sobs, calling spontaneously to him, "Where were you? How could you have left me like that?! And then I was given to know something that is hard to explain. I saw the stream of humanity, flowing from an early and violent beginning, through decreasingly violent stages, toward the light that is the peace and love of God. And I knew that in order to traverse that vast distance, human beings had to grow, had to reach toward the light. And that, in reaching, they would step upon each other, would violate each other, would hurt and maim and kill each other. And they would do all these things to their children, as well as to each other. So, for their emotional protection, children are born with the ability to dissociate, to forget violence that occurred at the hands of their caretakers, so they can survive to adulthood, when they can finally remember in safety. This had been a gift, my dissociation: not a weakness, but a gift! And then I was given to see that this Jesus who was present now with me had stayed with my body when I left it, had even stood with me in sorrow as I perpetrated the violence that broke my heart.

It was then that I really accepted Jesus in my core. How could I refuse him? He was the one who held my hand through the depths of my despair, the only one who had been able to be there with me in the worst of the pain. Even my beloved husband, present for so much of my distress during my recovery, had not been able to bear the pain that Jesus bore for me that day. Perhaps the difference was in me. I knew from reading the Gospels that Jesus of Nazareth had been tortured. I knew that he understood that level of physical pain and emotional degradation. I was able to let him bear it, because I knew that he knew what he was getting into! It was as if I were a war survivor, unable to really talk about the war except with my war buddies. Jesus was, and is, the quintessential war buddy—one who knew the horrors of my private war, was able to transcend it, and helped me do likewise.

So that's my story of the grace that amazingly entered my life and propelled it forward. I write it because I can no longer keep quiet about it. I give thanks for simultaneously having been given the strength to face the self-hatred that lives within me and for having been saved from the destruction that could have proceeded from it. There may be some among you who will read this story, will recognize some likeness to yourself, and will hunger for the peace of Christ. If you ask, it will come to you. Even if you don't, but yearn for it in the privacy of your heart, it will come to you. But it will come faster if you ask, without reserve. There is no requirement to bear the pain alone. There is no need to be as stubborn as I was. There is one, even Christ Jesus, who can speak to thy condition.

(Used by permission of "Friends Journal")

✠ EINAR INGVI MAGNUSSON ✠

(1958–)

Teacher and author of three books and hundreds of testimonies in newspapers in Iceland where he now lives. "God provides so generously for his children. I have so much to thank Him for."

GOD PREPARES US FOR A TASK HE HAS IN MIND FOR US

A friend of mine, who lives in Slovakia in eastern Europe, told me that when she was young she loved to go walking for hours in the hills. She said that sometimes she would disappear the whole day. Her grandmother would tell her, "You have the shoes of a wanderer." I believe that God prepares each of us for a task that we will come to do later in life. I am certain that God prepared my friend when she was a child. Today my friend is a missionary for the Lord. As a child she had wandering shoes, and today she has the shoes of a missionary. What a glorious task!

(The little girl later became the author's wife. "Receiving her to become my wife after my most difficult period in my life, was an answer to my prayers.")

✠ JOYCE C. DAY ✠

(1959–)

American United Methodist pastor who faced many barriers in her efforts to go to seminary and get through the other requirements for ordained ministry. "It was and is wonderful to see how God can and did overcome these barriers."

THE FREEDOM GOD HAS PREPARED

It was a beautiful spring day, and I was headed home from work. As I walked down the stairs to the parking deck, I discovered a brightly colored butterfly trapped inside the glass-enclosed stairwell. The butterfly kept flying against the glass unable to escape into the outside world that was easily visible from its prison.

I put my hand down, hoping the butterfly would perch on it so
I could carry it out. It landed for a brief moment but fluttered away
again when I moved. I tried to shoo it through the doorway, but it
only continued to hit the window. Finally, I cupped my hands gently
around its wings and carried it safely to freedom.

As I opened my hands to let the butterfly go, I thought of
the times God has tried to help me. In my fear and impatience, I
often fight God's guidance and waste my effort on useless activity.
Although I may see something wonderful out in front of me, alone
I am unable to overcome the barriers standing between me and the
goal. But if I quiet myself and stand still, I will feel God's hands holding me close. Then those loving hands carry me beyond the barriers
and into the freedom God has prepared.

❧ JONI EARECKSON TADA ☙
(1960–)

**Accomplished artist, writer, and speaker for the cause of Christ. She was
paralyzed from a diving accident. She has developed a line of greeting
cards and does her drawings by holding a pen between her teeth. Beneath
each drawing she adds the letters PTL, "Praise the Lord!"**

ONLY GOD KNOWS WHY

In the Psalms we're told that God does not deal with us according to
our sins and iniquities. My accident was not a punishment for my
wrongdoing—whether or not I deserved it. Only God knows why
I was paralyzed. Maybe He knew I'd be ultimately happier serving
Him. If I were still on my feet, it's hard to say how things might have
gone. I probably would have drifted through life—marriage, maybe
even divorce—dissatisfied and disillusioned. When I was in high
school, I lived selfishly and never built on any longlasting values. I
lived simply for each day and the pleasure I wanted—and almost
always at the expense of others.

(Joni)

⚜ BRENT FOSTER ⚜

(1968-1995)

American student who was successful in high school and college and was admired by all. He died of inoperable bone cancer.

REAL LIFE BEGINS WITH GOD

Although my illness will appear a tragedy to the world around me, those who know God will understand the truth which he brought to us himself by entering human history in the person of Jesus Christ. As recorded in his Word, all good gifts are from above, and all the good I will miss in an extended earthly life are but shadows of the real thing. Real life begins with God. This is not the end for me but just the beginning. I find the concluding words of C. S. Lewis' *Chronicles of Narnia* very fitting: "Now at last they were beginning Chapter One of the Great Story which no one on earth has read: which goes on forever in which every chapter is better than the one before."

(Finding God at Harvard, Zondervan, 1996)

⚜ RESHMA ARORA SAMUEL ⚜

(1972–)

Indian author and lecturer who works with Management for Human Resources.

A TIME OF PLOWING AND HARROWING

I went through a time of great pain and agony when a series of troubles and heartaches caused me immense distress. Often I felt very lonely and forsaken. All I could say was, "Lord, you know how frail I am. I am only dust, Lord!" Many times I could not express my deep anguish to anyone.

But after enduring my trial and testing period, I came to see the struggles as a time of plowing and harrowing. Though this process was painful, God used it. The areas in my life that had been plowed were sown with new life and direction. The change brought about in my life is proof to me of God's perfect love. Attempting to make a stand for the truths of the gospel of Jesus Christ often led to losses in various areas, but the moment of triumph and blessing came when I realized that those were only momentary losses because whatever we give up for Christ is restored manifold through the glory He bestows (Romans 8:18).

❧ CONNIE SEMY P. MELLA ❧

(1973–)

College professor in the Philippines.

I AM FILLED WITH WONDER

Every time I see a rainbow, I am filled with wonder and I praise God. Each rainbow reminds me of God's promise. In spite of the floods of hardship and loss, we see that God values us and offers us life. Standing in God's covenant, I can face challenges with hope and assurance.

❧ CASSIE BERNALL ❧

(1982–1999)

American high school student. This was her response about 11 a.m. on April 20, 1999, during the Columbine High School rampage when confronted by one of the gunmen who saw her praying. Angered, the attacker pointed a shotgun at her and sarcastically asked her if she believed in God. He asked her why, but before she had time to answer she was shot to death. At her funeral service over seventy-five young people made first-time commitments to Christ.

DO YOU BELIEVE IN GOD?

Yes!

✃ OTHER CONTEMPORARY WRITERS ✄

THE KNOWLEDGE OF GOD'S PRESENCE HAS SHAKEN ME

I cannot remember a time when I doubted God as real and as a person, when I was not aware of him. This has at certain times been an awareness that has shaken me in soul and body and with the utmost profundity, with love, yes, but even more with the mere fact of this superhumanly real person who confronts me.

(Author Unknown)

IT HAPPENED AGAIN THIS MORNING

I sat in my "prayer place" and watched dawn defeat the darkness of night. It happens every morning, a miracle of light that renews our existence. This morning the sky's gray, pre-dawn glow was replaced by sunlight dancing over the wall and window sill. Soon the room was filled with glorious light.

Almost 30 years ago I lost much of the light when disease robbed me of more than half of my ability to see. I lost some of my physical eyesight, but God has given me the ability to see more clearly the spiritual light. Each morning I wait for the dawn of a new day, and the new opportunities, joys, and responsibilities it brings.

Today I will see beauty in the faces of my loved ones, the bloom of a flower, a bird in flight, and more things than I can count. I give thanks to God for each of them. This afternoon I will watch the sun set behind the western horizon, knowing that it will rise again tomorrow. It has always been this way, regardless of the date we assign to the day in which it happens; and it will always be this way until the final sunrise that ushers us into the light of God's eternity.

(Ray Sobrette)

AN ENCOUNTER THAT CHANGED MY LIFE

One day I had a brief encounter with someone which changed my whole life. I was in my late teens, an airman in the Royal Air Force serving in Palestine. Walking along the road one afternoon, I noticed ahead of me the tall figure of a man dressed in Arabic clothing. His back was towards me, but as I got closer he turned and faced me. As our eyes met, I felt a sensation that I had not known before and have not known since.

The features of the man were much the same as those in paintings I have seen of our Savior, the lean face and small beard. But what attracted my attention were the searching eyes which seemed to draw me out spiritually and say to my soul, "Don't fight me, follow me." I believe I stood still, as if transfixed, for a few moments. No words were spoken, no sign made. Then he turned away, and I continued on my way.

That radiant face is still imprinted on my memory though twenty-eight years have passed; but I cherish more an inner glow from the spirit of Christ which dwells within me since that day when I decided to let Christ into my life and follow Him.

(K. D. Coombes)

IT WAS PART OF GOD'S PLAN

I am a young black woman who lives in a small town. The population of our area is equally divided between black and white, though there is very little interaction between us. Some years go, I was diagnosed with thyroid cancer. During that period in my life, I felt uncertain and fearful about my health. My family was very supportive, but I needed a friend who could relate to my situation. A year later, a pleasant young white woman was employed where I work. Our spirits connected instantly. Later I discovered she had breast cancer. During that period in our lives, we prayed, laughed, and cried together. Today, eight years later, we are both cancer free. Just as God bonded Jonathan and David from different worlds, it was part of God's plan that this woman and I be friends. God understands all our needs, even the need for a loving friend.

(Sharon Ward, 1962-)

SUFFERING DREW ME TO GOD

I have known more of God since I came to this bed than through all my life.

(Ralph Erskine, speaking while his body was racked with pain)

A PERSONAL THING

One summer I spent some time at Mount Robson, British Columbia, where I camped and lived with fellow mountaineers of the Alpine Club of Canada. On a rainy day a group of us were drinking tea in a tent, when a discussion arose about religion. A young scientist turned to me with a patronizing air and said, "But you don't really believe, do you, that Jesus is the Son of God?" he said. "How do you know it is true?"

I shall never forget what followed. I simply did what any other convinced man would have done: I looked him straight in the eye and said: "How do I know that Jesus is the Son of God? I know it because I know Him personally." For at least a half minute our eyes locked. Then he turned away. The argument was over.

(Author unknown)

IT WAS ALL PART OF A PURPOSE

I came into an anatomy room to study. The dead body meant nothing at all to me. I could not visualize the man or woman it might have been. Life left few records on these immobile faces. For weeks I worked and each day the wonder grew; and then, one day, I was working on an arm and hand, studying the perfect mechanical arrangements of the muscles and tendons—how the sheaths of certain muscles are split to let tendons of other muscles through, that the hand may be delicate and small and yet powerful. I was all alone in the laboratory when the overwhelming belief came; a thing like this is not just a chance, but a part of a plan, a plan so big that only God could have conceived it. Religion had been a matter of form, a thinking without convictions, and now everything was an evidence of God; the tendons of the hand, the patterns of the little blue butterfly's wings—it was all part of a purpose.

(A woman physician, in The Altantic Monthly*)*

IT CAME TO ME THEN

Though I had loving friends and activities to keep me busy, as a widow I was lonely and depressed. It seemed that my mind was filled with sad memories. Then I went to spend some time at a little house on the edge of a beautiful lake in the mountains. As I rested on the porch, I listened to the wind whispering in the treetops. Birds were chirping, and there was the sound of water lapping against stones. All was peaceful. The world is beautiful, I thought, and I thanked God for the beauty of creation.

During my time at that mountain house, I felt a growing sense of indescribable joy that filled my soul and lifted my heart. I no longer felt lonely and bereft. It came to me then that the presence of Jesus was there. His spirit filled my little mountain retreat, and I realized that he desired communion with me. Jesus Christ became real to me in a deeper way than I ever thought possible. His constant nearness continues to fill my heart with peace.

(Martha P. Giles)

THANK YOU FOR THE BEATING

"Sir, let me explain how I see this issue. Your supreme weapon is killing. My supreme weapon is dying. Here is how it works. You know that my sermons on tape have spread all over the country. If you kill me, those sermons will be sprinkled with my blood. Everyone will know I died for my preaching. And everyone who has a tape will pick it up and say, 'I'd better listen again to what this man preached, because he really meant it; he sealed it with his life.' So, Sir, my sermons will speak ten times louder than before. I will actually rejoice in this supreme victory if you kill me."

(Josef Tson, the evangelical dissident in Communist Romania, was often summoned before government officers who used every tactic to break his faith in Christ. Once, being interrogated at Ploiesti, an officer threatened to kill him. After Tson's remarks, the officer sent him home; taken from "Thank You for the Beating," Christian Herald, April 1988)

GOD'S GIFT

Whatever came to me I looked upon as God's gift for some special purpose. If it were a difficulty, He gave it to me to struggle with, to strengthen my mind and faith; if it were a helpless invalid cast on me for support, or even a beggar, I thought, God has given me another chance to do His work. The idea has sweetened and helped me all my life.

(Author Unknown)

When I was 5 years old, I was in a coma for three weeks. The doctors kept saying I wouldn't live. The nurse who attended me threatened to resign every day because she couldn't bear the thought of being in the room when I died. The doctors begged my mother, "Please don't pray for Marilynn anymore because she won't have a mind left if she does live. Let her go." Well, my mother ignored that, never left my bedside night or day, and she prayed. Oh, how she prayed. I opened my eyes to the sound of my mother's voice saying to me, "Marilynn, the Lord has a purpose for your life. He saved your life for a special purpose, and you need to do whatever He asks you to do."

Even as a 5–year-old that made a huge impression on me. I'm so thankful my mom told me God had a special purpose for my life because from that point on I always talked to Jesus, and every day I asked Him what I should do. He always told me. He still does today.

(Marilynn Blackaby, wife of Henry Blackaby, Home Life, February 2001. 2000 LifeWay Christian Resources of the Southern Baptist Convention. All rights reserved. Used by permission.)

ぶ CLOSING THOUGHT ぷ

If we look back to the beginning of our spiritual journey, we invariably come upon moments of spiritual awakening. Sometimes these
moments, which appear and reappear throughout our lives, come
to us while we are praying. But more often they simply rise up out
of life itself. We live out our lives seeing only the tip of the iceberg,
and all that does appear above the surface does so fleetingly as a brief
manifestation of some unseen reality that endows the smallest of
things and events with a value beyond comprehension.

ACKNOWLEDGMENTS

I AM DEEPLY INDEBTED to those who have contributed to making this endeavor a reality; working with all of them has been a privilege.

Many people have provided assistance by reviewing selections, and by offering encouragement, insightful suggestions, and inspiration. My thanks goes to Harold Hosler, who reviewed all of the selections and provided excellent input. Glen Carls, Lois Forsythe, and Stan Baldwin each provided insightful suggestions. My sister, Ruth Werries, was an inspiration. It has been particularly gratifying to work with my editor, Shannon Bernier of Hendrickson Publishers. Her confidence in my project, her professional competence, and her creativity stand out. I wish to thank my husband, Joe, who encouraged me and tirelessly kept me from becoming too narrowly involved in this huge project by providing balance in my daily life. I am also grateful to the writers whose inspiring quotations are included in this anthology.

Others were instrumental in giving me access to much of the vast quantity of written works on religion. Ten years ago, my brother, Glen Carls, provided me with hundreds of books on religious topics. These books were the foundation and impetus for my research. Dorothy Weedin was gracious in lending me helpful material from her collection. Aaron Andrews obtained numerous library books for me. Grover Stuart of Steel's Used Christian Books in Kansas City, Missouri searched out pertinent written works from the store's stacks. Carol Schroeder and Elisabeth Ross of the Missouri Statewide Reference Center were of immense help in researching dates and biographical information. Charline Spangler of the Carrollton Public Library of Carrollton, Missouri patiently obtained many books for me via interlibrary loan, and I visited many a Missouri library rich in materials relevant to this writing. In particular, the libraries of William Jewell College, Midwestern Baptist Theological Seminary, Conception Abbey Seminary, Calvary Bible College, St. Paul's School of Theology, Concordia Seminary, and Nazarene Theological Seminary provided an abundance of resources.

My deepest thanks goes to these many individuals and libraries, without which this endeavor would not have been possible. My hope is that these expressions of faith of people throughout history will continue to serve God's purpose and bring glory to His name.

NOTES

Part I

11. Ignatius of Antioch, introductory quote in *A Treasury of Sermon Illustrations*, ed. Charles L. Wallis, 57; *Epistle of Ignatius to the Ephesians*, Ch 1 & 2, in *Roots of Faith*, ed. Robert Van de Weyer, 22; *Epistle of Ignatius to the Trallians*, Ch. 4 &5, in *Roots of Faith*, ed. Robert Van de Weyer, 26; *Epistle of Ignatius to the Romans*, Ch. 3, in *Roots of Faith*, ed. Robert Van de Weyer, 27; *Epistle of Ignatius to the Romans*, Ch. 5 & 6, in *Roots of Faith*, ed. Robert Van de Weyer, 28; *Fox's Book of the Martyrs*, ed. John Fox, 14. All *Roots of Faith* quotes used by permission of John Hunt Publishers.

13. Barnabas, *The Epistle of Barnabas*, Ch. 1; in *Roots of Faith*, ed. Robert Van de Weyer, 42

13. Calconis, in *Selection from Latter Testimonies and Dying Words*, ed. A. H. Gottshall, 39

14. Epictetus, *Discourses of Epictetus*, trans. P. E. Matheson, 1916.

14. Polycarp, "Martyrdom of Polycarp"; in, *Apostolic Fathers*, ed. Bishop Lightfoot, 963; in *An Anthology of Jesus*, comp. James Marchant, 273. All *Anthology of Jesus* quotes used by permission of Kregel Publications, Grand Rapids, Mich.

15. Justin Martyr, *Justin's Apology*, Ch. 4; in *Roots of Faith*, ed. Robert Van de Weyer, 92

15. Sanctus, in *Selections from Latter Testimonies and Dying Words*, ed. A. H. Gottshall, 177.

16. Athenagoras, *Athenagora's Apology*, Ch. 1, in *Roots of Faith*, ed. Robert Van de Weyer, 102.

16. Thecla, in *Doubleday Christian Quotation Collection*, comp. Hannah Ward.

17. Clement of Alexandria, *Exhortation to the Greeks*, in *The Christian Reader*, ed. Stanley I. Stuber, 31.

17. Perpetua, in *Fox's Book of the Martyrs*, ed. John Fox, 20.

18. Genesius of Rome, in *Early Christian Prayers*, ed. A. Hamman, in *Doubleday Christian Quotation Collection*, comp. Hannah Ward, 9.

18. Tertullian, *Tertullian on Prayer*, Ch. 2, in *Roots of Faith*, ed. Robert Van de Weyer, 121.

19. Cyprian, in The *Early Christian Fathers*, Henry Bettenson, ed., in *Doubleday Christian Quotation Collection*, comp. Hannah Ward, 8; in 1001 *Illustrations for Preaching and Teaching*, ed. G. Curtis Jones. All *1000 Illustrations for Preaching and Teaching* quotes used by permission of Broadman & Holman, Nashville, Tenn.; *A Field of Diamonds*, ed. Joseph S. Johnson, 125. All of *A Field of Diamonds* quotes used by permission of the editor.

20. Andronicus, in *Selections from Latter Testimonies and Dying Words*, ed. A. H. Gottshall, 12.

20. Eusebius of Caesarea, "Life and Writings of Eusebius of Caearea"; in *The Christian Classics Ethereal Library*

21. Ambrose, in *Doubleday Christian Quotation Collection*, comp. Hannah Ward, 12; in *On This Day*, ed. Robert J. Morgan, April 3; in *A Field of Diamonds*, ed. Joseph S. Johnson, 168

21. Jerome, *Epistle 99*

22. John Chrysostom, in *The Late Christian Fathers*, ed. Henry Bettenson, Oxford University Press; 1970, in *A Treasury of Sermon Illustrations*, ed. Charles L. Wallis, 222.

23. Augustine, 1-3. *Confessions*, Book X, Sect. 38; 4. *Little Book of Prayers*.

26. Paulinus of Nola, in *Early Christian Prayers*, in *Doubleday Christian Quotation Collection*, comp. Hannah Ward, 36.

26. Patrick, in *On This Day*, ed. Robert J. Morgan, March 17; in *Doubleday Christian Quotation Collection*, comp. Hannah Ward, 35; in *The New Encyclopedia of Christian Quotations*, ed. Mark Water, 592; *Doubleday Christian Quotation Collection*, comp. Hannah Ward, 35; in *On*

This Day, ed. Robert J. Morgan, March 17; Saint Patrick's breastplate, "Christ with me, Christ before me." All Robert J. Morgan quotes used by permission of Thomas Nelson, Inc.

Part II

33. Anselm, *Proslogium*

33. Bernard of Clairvaux, *St. Bernard's Sermons on the Song of Songs;* in *Mysticism: A Study and an Anthology*, ed. F. C. Happold, © by the Estate of F. C. Happold, 1963, 1964, 1970.

34. Hildegard of Bingen, *Meditations*, in *Quotable Saints*, comp. Ronda De Sola Chervin, 93. All *Quotable Saints* quotes used by permission of the compiler.

34. Hugh of St. Victor, in *The Soul Afire*, ed. H. A. Reinhold, 238.

35. Thomas a Becket, in *Doubleday Christian Quotation Collection*, comp. Hannah Ward, 57.

35. Dante Alighieri, *The Divine Comedy*

36. Richard Rolle of Hempole, *The Fire of Love*

36. Unknown Bishop of the Early Church, in *6000 Sermon Illustrations*, ed. Elon Foster, 135

37. Margaret Ebner, *Revelations*

38. *Theologia Germanica, Theologica Germanica*, (New York: Macmillan, 1913).

38. John Wycliff, *The English Works of Wycliffe*, (London: Trubner & Co., 1880).

39. John Huss, in *Knight's Illustrations for Today*, ed. Walter B. Knight, 75-76. All Walter B. Knight quotes used by permission of the Knight Estate.

39. Girolano Savanarola, in *Jesus Freaks*, ed. dc Talk and The Voice of the Martyrs, 223. All *Jesus Freaks* quotes used by permission of Albury Publications, Tulsa, Okla.

40. Catherine of Genoa, *Life and Teachings;* in *Quotable Saints*, comp. Ronda De Sola Chervin, 164, 76.

40. Sir Thomas More, *A Dialog of Comfort Against Tribulation: The Life and Illustrious Martyrdom of Sir Thomas More.*

41. Michael Sattler, in *On This Day*, ed. Robert J. Morgan, May 20, May 2.

42. Martin Luther, in *Joy in His Presence*, ed. Joan Winmill Brown, May 28; in *Joy in His Presence*, July 6; *Here I Stand: A Life of Martin Luther*, Roland H. Bainton; *Here I Stand; A Life of Martin Luther;* in *A Treasury of Sermon Illustrations*, ed. Charles L. Wallis, 110; in *Knight's Illustrations for Today*, ed. Walter B. Knight, 78; Luther's Prayer, in *1000 New Illustrations*, ed. G. Curtis Jones. All *Joy in His Presence* quotes used by permission of compiler.

44. William Tyndale, introductory quote in *Latter Testimonies and Dying Words*, comp. A. H. Gottschall, 201; website: williamtyndale.com; Prologue from *Pathway to the Holy Scriptures.*

45. Hans Denck, *On the Law of God*, in *A Second Reader's Notebook*, comp. Gerald Kennedy, 152.

45. Thomas Bilney, in *Doubleday Christian Quotation Collection*, comp. Hannah Ward, 88.

45. Nicolas Caren, in *Jesus Freaks*, ed. dc Talk and the Voice of the Martyrs, 249.

46. Anne Askew, *Latter Apprehension and Examination.*

47. Ignatius of Loyola, in *Doubleday Christian Quotation Collection*, comp. Hannah Ward, 95-6.

47. Katherine von Bora, in *Doubleday Christian Quotation Collection*, comp. Hannah Ward, 89.

48. Nicolas Ridley, in *Fox's Book of the Martyrs*, ed. John Fox, in *Jesus Freaks*, ed. dc Talk and Voice of the Martyrs, 270.

48. Francis Borgia, in *Doubleday Christian Quotation Collection*, comp. Hannah Ward, 88.

49. Lady Jane Grey, written in her New Testament which she gave to her sister shortly before her death.

49. Christopher Burton, in *Doubleday Christian Quotation Collection*, comp. Hannah Ward, 89.

49. Teresa of Avila in *OmniRead Treasuries*, comp. Peter Sumner. All *OmniRead Treasuries* quotes used by permission of compiler.

50. William Shakespeare, *Henry VI*, Part 2, the king speaking; in *Knight's Master Book of New Illustrations*, ed. Walter B. Knight, 13.

PART III
55. Galileo, in *Words of Life*, ed. Charles L. Wallis, 4; "Dialog on the Great World System", 1632.
55. Johannes Kepler, in *Forty Thousand Sublime and Beautiful Thoughts*, ed. Charles Noel Douglas, Vol. I, 845.
56. John Donne, in *Encyclopedia of Religious Quotations*, ed. Frank S. Mead, 269.
56. Thomas Heywood, from "The Search for God."
57. Jakob Boehm, 1,2. *Confessions*; 3. *Latter Testimonies and Dying Words*, ed. A. H. Gottshall, 28.
57. Thomas Wentworth, in *Latter Testimonies and Dying Words*, A. H. Gottshall, 209.
58. Edward Herbert, in *Encyclopedia of Religious Quotations*, ed. Frank S. Mead, 292.
58. John Selden, in *New Dictionary of Thoughts*, ed. Tryon Edwards, 561.
59. Oliver Cromwell, introductory quote in *A Treasury of Sermon Illustrations*, ed. Charles L Wallis, 96.
60. Charles I of England, in *Encyclopedia of Religious Quotations*, ed. Frank S. Mead, 99.
60. Samuel Rutherford, *An Apololgy for Divine Grace; The Letters of Samuel Rutherford.*
61. Jean Eudes, in *Doubleday Christian Quotation Collection*, comp. Hannah Ward, 119.
61. Roger Williams, from "God Makes a Path"; in *A Field of Diamonds*, comp. Joseph S. Johnson, 180.
62. Sir Thomas Browne, *Religio Medici*, in *You Can say that Again*, comp. R. E. O. White, 210. All *You Can Say That Again* quotes used by permission of Zondervan Publishing House, Grand Rapids, Mich.
62. Obadiah Holmes, in *On This Day*, ed. Robert J. Morgan, Sept 6.
63. Joseph Eliot, in *Joy and Strength*, comp. Mary W. Tileston, 66.
64. John Milton, from "Sonnet on His Blindness."
64. Robert Leighton, in *Joy and Strength*, comp. Mary Tileston Wilder, 341.
65. Brother Lawrence, *The Practice of the Presence of God.*
66. Jeremy Taylor, *Holy Living and Dying.*
66. Henry More, in *Letters of the Scattered Brotherhood*, ed. Mary Strong, 155.
67. Isaac Penington, in *Selections from the Works of Isaac Penington.*
67. John Bulwer, in *6000 Sermon Illustrations*, ed. Elon Foster, 370.
68. William Dewsbury, in *Quaker Faith and Practice*; in *Doubleday Christian Quotation Collection*, comp. Hannah Ward, 117. All *Quaker Faith and Practice* quotes used by permission of Quakers in Britain.
68. James Guthrie, in *On This Day*, ed. Robert J. Morgan, February 19.
69. Blaise Pascal, Pensees (Thoughts); in *Selections from The Thoughts*, 121; words found in the lining of Pascal's cloak after his death; in *OmniRead Treasuries*, comp. Peter Sumner.
71. George Fox, *A Journal or Historical Account of the Life of George Fox.*
72. John Bunyan, *Grace Abounding to the Chief of Sinners; Pilgrim's Progress*, Mr. Steadfast speaking; in *A Treasury of Sermon Illustrations*, comp. Charles L. Wallis, 46; in *A Treasury of Sermon Illustrations.*
73. Thomas Traherne, *Centuries of Meditation.*
73. Isaac Newton, in *You Can Say That Again*, comp. R. E. O. White, 319; in *A Treasury of Sermon Illustrations*, ed. Charles L. Wallis, 64-5; in *Encyclopedia of 7700 Illustrations*, comp. Paul Lee Tan, 1056.
74. Marie Guyon, *Autobiography of Marie Guyon*, © 1897 by Trench, Trubner & Co., 1817; *Autobiography*, in *6000 Sermon Illustrations*, ed. Elon Foster, 636.
75. Robert Barclay, in *Quaker Faith and Practice*, in *Treasury of the Christian Faith*, ed. Stanley I. Stuber, 411.
76. Francois Fenclon, *Spiritual Letters of Archbishop Fenelon.*
77. Donald Cargill, Walter Smith, James Boig, William Cuthill, and William Thomson, in *On This Day*, ed. Robert J. Morgan, July 27.

Part IV

81. August Hermann Francke, *The Autobiography, 1692*, in *God's Glory, Neighbor's Good: a brief introduction to the life and writings of August Hermann Francke*, Gary R. Sattler; in *Pietists—Selected Writings*, ed. Peter C. Erb.

82. Joseph Addison, in *The Golden Book of Immortality*, comp. Thomas Curtis Clark, 198.

82. Johann S. Bach, in *Knight's Illustrations for Today*, ed. Walter B. Knight, 160.

83. George Handel, in "Messiah: Behind the Scenes of Handel's Masterpiece," Richard D. Dinwiddle, in *Christianity Today* (December 18, 1982): 12.

83. Nicolas Zinzendorf, in "Call in the Witnesses," Calvin Miller, in Proclaim! (Spring, 1999); 7; quote in explanation in *New Sermon Illustrations for All Occasions*, ed. G. B. F. Hallock, 163; in *Count Zinzendorf*, J. R. Weinlick; in *More Fascinating Conversion Stories*, comp. Samuel Fisk, 167. All *New Sermon Illustrations* used by permission of Baker Book House. All *40 Fascinating Conversion Stories* and *More Conversion Stories* quotes used by permission of Kregel Publications, Grand Rapids, Mich..

85. Jonathan Edwards, 1,2. in *The Life and Character of Jonathan Edwards*, ed. S. Hopkins, 24-35; 3. in *The Life and Character of Jonathan Edwards*; in *A Treasury of Sermon Illustrations*, ed. Charles Wallis, 137.

86. John Wesley, *The Journal of John Wesley*, ed. Nehemial Curnock, 465-477, May 24, 1738; in *Deeper Experiences of Famous Christians*, ed. J. Gilchrist Lawson, 161; *The Journal of John Wesley*; "The Dawn", in *3000 Illustrations for Christian Service*, ed. Walter B. Knight, 306; *The Journal of John Wesley*; in *1000 New Illustrations*, comp. and ed. Al Bryant, 80. All *1000 New Illustrations* quotes used by permission of Zondervan Publishing House, Grand Rapids, Mich.

88. Benjamin Franklin, in *A Treasury of Sermon Illustrations*, ed. Charles L. Wallis, 228.

89. Charles Wesley, from a hymn describing an event on Whitsunday, May 21, 1738.

90. Ludwig von Beethoven, in *OmniRead Treasuries*, comp. Peter Sumner.

90. George Whitefield, *The Life of God in the Soul of Man*, Henry Scougal, 12, 13.

91. David Brainerd, in Jesse Page's biography of David Brainerd, 1901, in *More Fascinating Stories*, ed. Samuel Fisk, 25; 2, 4, 6. in *Life of Brainerd*, by Jonathan Edwards and S. E. Dwight; 3. in *Knight's Treasury of Illustrations*, ed. Walter B. Knight, 57; 5. in *Joy and Strength*, comp. Mary Wilder Tileston, 342.

93. John Woolman, *The Journal and Essays of John Woolman*.

93. John Newton, in *On This Day*, ed. Robert J. Morgan, March 10; in *OmniRead Treasuries*, comp. Peter Sumner; in *The New Dictionary of Thoughts*, ed. Tryon Edwards, 560; from Newton's epitaph, in *OmniRead Treasuries*, comp. Peter Sumner; in *A Treasury of Sermon Illustrations*, ed. Charles L. Wallis, 83.

95. William Cowper, in *You Can Say That Again*, comp. R. E. O. White, 61; from the poem, "I, too, have been with Jesus."

96. Joseph Hadyn, in *The Spiritual Lives of Great Composers*, Patrick Kavanaugh, 21; in *Knight's Treasury of Illustrations*, ed. Walter B. Knight, 173-4; *The Spiritual Lives of Great Composers*, 21.

97. John Adams, in *Treasury of the Christian Faith*, comp. Stanley I. Stuber, 48.

97. Patrick Henry, *The New Dictionary of Thoughts*, ed. Tryon Edwards; in *Greatest Thoughts about Jesus Christ*, ed. J. Gilchrist Lawson.

98. Sir William Jones, in *6000 Sermon Illustrations*, ed. Elon Foster, 57.

98. Richard Cecil, *Memoir*, in *One Thousand New Illustrations*, ed. Aquilla Webb; *Memoir*, in *Forty Thousand Sublime and Beautiful Thoughts*, ed. Charles Noel Douglas, Vol. I, 176.

99. Johann Wolfgang von Goethe, introductory quote from the Easter Hymn in *Faust*; 1. in *OmniRead Treasuries*, comp. Peter Sumner; 2, 3. conversations of Goethe with Eckermann, in *The Golden Book of Immortality*, ed. Thomas Curtis Clark, 196.

100. Thomas Erskine, in *Joy and Strength*, comp. Mary W. Tileston, 62, 246.

101. Unknown, as recorded by Leslie D. Weatherhead.

101. Comments by a poor Methodist woman, in *Daily Strength for Daily Needs*, comp. Mary W. Tileston, 19.

101. Thomas Rutherford, in *The Lunn Log*, comp. The Lunn Family, 19.

Part V

105. William Blake, in *A Treasury of the Kingdom*, comp. E. A. Blackburn, 132.

105. William Carey, 1-3. *William Carey: A Biography*, William Drewey, 74. Copyright © 1979.Used by permission of Zondervan Publishing House, Grand Rapids, Mich.; 4. in *On This Day*, ed. Robert J. Morgan, March 12.

107. Christmas Evans, in *Deeper Experiences of Famous Christians*, ed. J. Gilchrist Lawson, 205-6.

108. John Quincy Adams, in *Encyclopedia of 7700 Illustrations*, comp. Paul Lee Tan, 189; in *A Treasury of Wisdom and Inspiration*, ed. David St. Leger, 34.

109. William Wordsworth, from "Lines Composed a Few Miles Above Tintern Abbey on Revisiting the Banks of Wye during a Tour," in *The Viking Book of Poetry of the English Speaking World*, ed. Richard Aldington (New York: Viking, 1941) 662-667; from "The Solitary Reaper."

109. Samuel Taylor Coleridge, in *I Quote*, comp. Virginia Ely, 64, 27.

110. Sir Humphrey Davy, in *Knight's Illustrations for Today*, ed. Walter B. Knight, 110.

111. William Ellery Channing, *Works*, Boston edition, 1848, Vol. IV.

112. Elizabeth Fry, in *Quaker Faith and Practice*, by the Religious Society of Friends in Britain.

112. Henry Martyn, in *Journal and Letters of the Rev. Henry Martyn*, (M. W. Dodd, 1851); in *On This day*, ed. Robert J. Morgan, May 16.

113. Daniel Webster, in *3000 Illustrations for Christian Service*, ed. Walter B. Knight, 249.

114. John James Audubon, in *OmniRead Treasuries*, comp. Peter Sumner.

114. Peter Cartwright, in *Deeper Experiences of Famous Christians*, ed. J. Gilchrist Lawson, 230-1.

115. Adoniram Judson, *How Christ Came to Church*, with the life story by A. T. Pierson. (Philadelphai: American Baptist Pub. Society, 1896); in *Encyclopedia of 7700 Illustrations*, comp. Paul Lee Tan, 1508; in *Latter Testimonies and Dying Words*, ed. A. H. Gottshall, 120.

116. Ann Heseltine Judson, from her journal; in *A Treasury of Sermon Illustrations*, ed. Charles L. Wallis, 207; Nancy Judson, "Letter to Miss Carleton," Massachusetts Baptist Missionary, 1990, 166-7.

117. Michael Faraday, in "Gospel Trumpet", in *Knight's Master Book of New Quotations*, ed. Walter B. Knight, 566; in *The New Encyclopedia of Christian Quotations*, comp. Mark Water.

118. Charles Finney, *Memoirs of Rev. Charles G. Finney*, 12-17.

119. Allen Gardiner, in *A Treasury of Sermon Illustrations*, ed. Charles Wallis, 206-7.

120. Merle D'Aubigne, in *1001 Illustrations for Pulpit and Platform*, ed. Aquilla Webb, 106.

121. William Cullen Bryant, from "To a Waterfowl" and "A Forest Hymn."

121. Thomas Arnold, *Doubleday Christian Quotation Collection*, comp. Hannah Ward, 161.

122. Thomas Carlyle, *A Treasury of Sermon Illustrations*, ed. Charles L. Wallis, 133; *The Collected Letters of Thomas and Jane Welsh Carlyle*.

122. Robert Moffat, in *Knight's Master Book of New Illustrations*, ed. Walter B. Knight, 120.

123. Soren Kierkegaard, *Prayers of Kierkegaard*, ed. by Perry D.LeFevre. Reprinted by permission of the University of Chicago Press, © 1956.

124. Emily Bronte, from "And first an hour of mournful musing" and "Last Lines."

124. Christian Karl von Bunsen, in *Joy and Strength*, comp. Mary W. Tileston, 332.

125. The Negro Singer's own Book, 1841, in *Encyclopedia of Religious Quotations*, ed. Frank S. Mead, 250.

125. Sarah Wood, in *The Pilgrim Path: Interesting Incidents in the Experience of Christians*, Am. Tract Society.

125. Edward Payson, in *6000 Sermon Illustrations*, ed. Elon Foster, 252.

Part VI

129. John Todd, in *Nelson's Complete Book*, ed. Robert J. Morgan, 191.

130. John Henry Newman, 1. *Apologia pro Vita Sua*; 2, 3. *Meditations and Devotions*, 400-1, 308. (London: Longmans & Green).

131. Victor Hugo, in *Treasury of Courage and Confidence*, ed. Norman Vincent Peale, 285.

132. Horace Bushnell, reported by George W. Truett, in *1000 Evangelistic Illustrations*, ed, Aquilla Webb, 80.

133. Ralph Waldo Emerson, *Journal*, in *The Christian Reader*, ed. Stanley I Stuber, 376; common quote found in many sources; untitled poem, Poetry Database of Kansas City Public Library; in *Encyclopedia of Religious Quotations*, comp. Frank S. Mead, 132.

134. George Mueller, introductory quote in *Latter Testimonies and Dying Words*, ed. A. H. Gottshall, 35; *Autobiography of George Mueller* (London: Pickering & Inglis, 1929), 1-10; in *Deeper Experiences of Famous Christians*, ed. J. Gilchrist Lawson, 289-290; in *Doubleday Christian Quotation Collection*, comp. Hannah Ward, 184; in *Encyclopedia of 7700 Illustrations*, comp. Paul Lee Tan, 1366; in *On This Day*, ed. Robert J. Morgan, July 3; in *Knight's Illustrations For Today*, ed. Walter B. Knight, 31.

136. Elizabeth B. Browning, from "Round Our Restlessness" and "De Profundis."

137. Louis Agassiz, in *Treasury of Christian Faith*, ed. Stanley I. Stuber, 290-1.

138. Anthony Mary Claret, in *Doubleday Christian Quotation Collection*, comp. Hannah Ward, 168.

138. Henry Wadsworth Longfellow, from "Him Evermore I Behold"; *The Encyclopedia of Religious Quotations*, comp. Frank S. Mead, 122.

139. John Greenleaf Whittier, from "The Eternal Goodness," "The Meeting," and "Barclay of Ury."

140. George Osborn, in *Knight's Treasury Of Illustrations*, ed. Walter B. Knight, 185.

141. Abraham Lincoln, 1. in *Treasury of the Christian Faith*, ed. Stanley I. Stuber, 291; 2, 5. In *Encyclopedia Of Religious Quotations*, comp. Frank S. Mead, 177; 3. in *Knight's Illustrations for Today*, ed. Walter B. Knight, 226; 4. in *Knight's Treasury Of Illustrations*, ed. Walter B. Knight, 370; 6. common quote.

143. Alfred, Lord Tennyson, in *A Treasury of Sermon Illustrations*, ed. Charles L. Wallis, 46; from "Crossing the Bar," in *One Thousand New Illustrations*, ed. Aquilla Webb, 194.

144. William E. Gladstone, in *Cyclopedia of Bible Illustrations*, comp. Paul E. Holdcraft, 37; in *Knight's Illustrations for Today*, ed. Walter B. Knight, 133.

144. Theodore Parker, in *Encyclopedia of Religious Quotations*, comp. Frank S. Mead, 251.

145. James F. Clarke, *Autobiography, Diary and Correspondence*.

145. Sir James Simpson, in *A Treasury of Sermon Illustrations*, ed. Charles L. Wallis, 54.

146. Harriet Beecher Stowe, in *Treasury of Confidence and Courage*, ed. Norman Vincent Peale, 222-223.

147. Robert Browning, from "Paracelsus," "A Death in the Desert," and "Paraelsus."

148. Robert McCheyne, in *Knight's Treasury of Illustrations*, ed. Walter B. Knight, 268.

148. David Livingstone, introductory quote in *Knight's Master Book of New Illustrations*, ed. Walter B. Knight, 622; in *Forty Fascinating Conversion Stories*, comp. Samuel Fisk, 82; in *Encyclopedia of Religious Quotations*, comp. Frank S. Mead, 55; in *A Treasury of Sermon Illustrations*, ed. Charles L. Wallis, 53; in *Anthology of Jesus*, comp. James Marchant, 223-4; in *Encyclopedia of 7700 Illustrations*, comp. Paul Lee Tan, 523.

150. Henry Ward Beecher, 1-3. *Autobiographical Reminiscences*, Henry Ward Beecher; 4-6. in *A Treasury of Illustrations*, Henry Ward Beecher; 7. in *Thirty Thousand Thoughts*, ed. H. D. M. Spence-Jones, Vol. I, 134; 8. in *Treasury of Sermon Illustrations*, ed. Charles L. Wallis, 119.

154. James Calvert, introductory quote in *Life Sentence*, Charles Colson, (Minneapolis: World Wide Publications, 1979) 154; *My Favorite Illustrations of Herschell Hobbs*, ed. Ronald K. Brown. Copyright © 1999. Used by permission of Broadman & Holman, Nashville, Tenn.

154. Thomas H. Hill, *Christ As Savior*.

155. George Eliot, in *Joy In His Presence*, ed. Joan Winmill Brown, July 2; in *3000 Illustrations for Christian Service*, ed. Walter B. Knight, 262.

156. James Russell Lowell, from "The Sail's Horizon."

156. Walt Whitman, from "Song of Myself."

157. John Ruskin, in *Treasury of the Christian World*, comp. A. Gordon Nasby, 69; in *Knight's Treasury of Illustrations*, ed. Walter B. Knight, 10.

158. Queen Victoria, in *Doubleday Christian Quotation Collection*, comp. Hannah Ward, 198.

158. Florence Nightingale, in *Joy in His Presence*, ed. Joan Winmill Brown, July 29.

159. Fanny Crosby, in *Encyclopedia of 7700 Illustrations*, comp. Paul Lee Tan, 310.

159. John Caird, *University Sermons*.

160. B. F. Crary, in *Pioneer Experiences*, ed. Phoebe Palmer.

161. Feodor Dostoevsky, *The Brothers Karamozov*; in *Treasury of the Christian World*, comp. A. Gordon Nasby; in *Treasury of Courage and Confidence*, ed. Norman Vincent Peale, 215-216.

162. Henri-Frederic Amiel, *Amiel's Journal*, trans. Mrs. Humphrey Ward.

163. Frederick Max Mueller, in *New Sermon Illustrations for All Occasions*, ed. G. B. F. Hallock, 22.

164. Thomas Jonathan (Stonewall), in *Knight's Illustrations for Today*, ed. Walter B. Knight, 23, 239.

165. George MacDonald, in *Daily Strength for Daily Needs*, comp. Mary W. Tileston, 216; "Within and Without," Part I, Sc. 1; in *Encyclopedia of Religious Quotations*, ed. Frank S. Mead, 317; from "Mary Marston, ch 57; in *Encyclopedia Of Religious Quotations*, ed. Frank S. Mead, 250; in *Doubleday Christian Quotation Collection*, comp. Hannah Ward, 181; in *The Poetical Works of George MacDonald*.

166. Annie Keary, in *Daily Strength for Daily Needs*, comp. Mary W. Tileston, 224.

166. Edward Bickersteth, "The Fountain", in *Leaves of Gold*, ed. Clyde Francis Lytle, 40.

167. Theophane Venard, in *Quotable Saints*, comp. Ronda De Sola Chervin, 50.

167. Mrs. John Mason Turner, in "The Congregationalist," a newspaper from the 1880s.

168. General Lew Wallace, in *Treasury of the Christian Faith*, ed. Charles L. Wallis, 414.

169. Elizabeth Rundle Charles, in *Joy and Strength*, comp. Mary W. Tileston, 3; in *Daily Strength for Daily Needs*, comp. Mary W. Tileston, 152.

170. Leo Tolstoy, "What I Believe", introduction, *Count Leo Tolstoy*, trans. Aylmer Maude; "Thoughts on God", in *Lift Up Your Eyes* with an introduction by Stanley R. Hopper (New York: The Julian Press, Inc. 1960) 385, taken from notes or jottings; in *Treasury of the Christian Faith*, comp. Stanley I. Stuber, 282.

172. Andrew Murray, 1. in *The Life of Andrew Murray of South Africa*, J. DuPlessis, 66; 2,3. in *The Lunn Log*, comp. the Lunn Family.

173. William Booth, by F. S. Wicks, in *One Thousand Evangelistic Illustrations*, ed. Aquilla Webb, 188.

173. John Paton, "The Story of John G. Paton," in *3000 Illustrations for Christian Service*, ed. Walter B. Knight; in *A Frank Foreham Treasury*, ed. Frank Foreham, Ch. 16.

174. Shang-mo Hsi, in *You Can Say That Again*, comp. R. E. O. White, 61.

175. Robert Arthur Gascoyne-Cecil, in *3000 Illustrations for Christian Service*, ed. Walter B. Knight, 558.

175. Joseph Parker, in *Greatest Thoughts about Jesus Christ*, ed. J. Gilchrist Lawson, 47; *The Inner Life of Christ: as revealed in the Gospel of Matthew*, Vol. II, 320-321.

177. James A. Garfield, in *500 Gospel Incidents, Illustrations and Testimonies*, ed. John Ritchie, 44; in *Greatest Thoughts about Jesus Christ*, ed. J. Gilchrist Lawson, 136.

178. Thomas DeWitt Talmage, in *The Authentic Life of T. DeWitt Talmage*, John Rusk, 374, 323.

179. J. Hudson Taylor, in *A Treasury of Sermon Illustrations*, ed. Charles L. Wallis, 153; *J. Hudson Taylor, A Retrospect*, 8-10.

180. Hannah Whitall Smith, 1-3. *The Unselfishness of God*, 131-9, from her diary; 5. A letter from Mrs. Pearsall Smith, from *A Religious Rebel*, edited by Logan Pearsall Smith (1948), 156 f.; in *Diary of Readings*, ed. John Baillie, Day 40.

184. Charles H. Spurgeon, *Conversion: The Great Change*, 15-21; "Meditations for This Morning," February 1, 2001, in Christian Classics Ethereal Library; *Daily Meditations for Prayer*; "How Spurgeon Found Christ," a leaflet; in *Daily Meditations for Prayer*; *Spurgeon's Sermons*, vol. 2, 6; in *Nelson's Complete Book*, ed. Robert J. Morgan, 358.

187. Phillips Brooks, common quote found on a bookmark; in *The New Encyclopedia of Christian Quotations*, comp. Mark Water, 608; *The Influence of Jesus.*

188. George Congreve, in *Doubleday Christian Quotation Collection*, comp. Hannah Ward, 208.

189. Lyman Abbott, "What Christianity Means to Me," in *Reminiscences* (Boston: Houghton Mifflin, 1913); *Light from Many Lamps*, comp. Lillian Eichler Watson, 57.

190. Frances Havergal, in *Latter Testimonies and Dying Words*, comp. A. H. Gottshall; in *Doubleday Christian Quotation Collection*, comp. Hannah Ward, 175.

190. John Clifford, "Looking Back," from his diary; in *Anthology of Jesus*, comp. James Marchant, 334.

191. Dwight L. Moody, in *A Treasury of Sermon Illustrations*, ed. Charles L. Wallis, 116; *The Life of Dwight L. Moody*, William R. Moody (New York: Fleming H. Revell, 1900); in *Nelson's Complete Book*, ed. Robert J. Morgan, 789; common quote; in *Deeper Experiences of Famous Christians*, ed. J. Gilchrist Lawson, 339; *Because He Lives*, Walter K. Knight; in *Knight's Master Book of New Illustrations*, 559; *The Faith That Satisfies*, William M. Anderson (New York: Loizeaux Brothers, 1948) 165; in *Greatest Thoughts about Jesus Christ*, ed. J. Gilchrist Lawson, 196.

194. John Pierpont Morgan, in *The Cream Book: Sentence Sermons*, comp. Keith L. Brooks, 21.

194. J. R. Miller, in *A Treasury of Sermon Illustrations*, ed. Charles L. Wallis, 243; *Glimpses through Life's Windows: Selections from the Writings of J. R. Miller.*

195. James Chalmers, in *A Treasury of Sermon Illustrations*, ed. Charles L. Wallis, 207.

196. Henry M. Stanley, in "The Australian Baptist", in *1001 Illustrations for Pulpit & Platform*, ed. Aquilla Webb, 180; in *A Field of Diamonds*, comp. Joseph S. Johnson, 289.

197. Handley C. G. Moule, *Jesus and the Resurrection: expository studies on St. John XXI*, Ch. 1., 8.

197. Sidney Lanier, from "The Marshes of Glynn."

198. John Fiske, in *The Golden Book of Immortality*, comp. Thomas Curtis Clark, 193.

198. Heinrich Hoffmann, in *Cyclopedia of Bible Illustrations*, comp. Paul E. Holdcraft, 38.

198. George Matheson, *My Aspirations*; by Betty Zimmerman; in *1000 New Illustrations*, comp. Al Bryant, 224; "Voices of the Spirit," Ch. XI, 28.

199. Samuel H. Hadley, by Charles K. Hutchinson in *Treasury of the Christian Faith*, ed. Stanley I. Stuber, 248-9; "Home Department" (Baptist Bulletin).

200. Isabella Gilmore, in *Doubleday Christian Quotation Collection*, comp. Hannah Ward.

201. William McKinley, "The Illustrator", in *Treasury of the Christian Faith*, ed. Stanley I. Stuber, 414.

201. Newman Smyth, from "The Religious Feeling"; in *Greatest Thoughts about Jesus Christ*, ed. J. Gilchrist Lawson, 93.

202. A. B. Simpson, in *The Life of A. B. Simpson*, A. E. Thompson, 11-17.

203. Russell Conwell, in *Knight's Illustrations for Today*, ed. Walter B. Knight, 326.

203. Joseph Estlin Carpenter, in *Joseph Estlin Carpenter*, C. H. Herford; in *From Darkness to Light*, ed. Victor Gollancz, 390. Used by permission of Victor Gollancz Ltd., London.

204. Henry J. Heinz, in *Knight's Master Book of New Illustrations*, ed. Walter B. Knight, 736.

205. James Huntington, in *You Can Say That Again*, comp. R. E. O. White, 61.

205. Frederich B. Meyer, in "The Illustrator."

206. Thomas A. Edison, in *Treasury of the Christian Faith*, ed. Stanley I. Stuber, 322.

207. Sir William Osler, in *Treasury of the Christian Faith*, ed. Stanley I. Stuber, 716.

207. Robert Louis Stevenson, introductory quote in *Knight's Illustrations for Today*, ed. Walter B. Knight, 289.; from "The stars shall last for a million years."

207. Henry Drummond, *The Greatest Thing in the World*; in *Encyclopedia of Religious Quotations*, comp. Frank S. Mead, 306.

208. Forbes Robinson, in *Forbes Robinson, Disciple of Love: Selections from his letters and addresses*, ed. M. R. J. Manktelow.

208. F. E. Marsten, in *Sunshine for Shut-Ins.*

209. Unknown, by J. C. Mitchell, in *A Treasury of Sermon Illustrations*, ed. Walter B. Knight, 212.

209. Wendell Phillips, in *Knight's Treasury of Illustrations*, ed. Walter B. Knight, 76.

209. John L. Lincoln, in *The Encyclopedia of Religious Quotations*, comp. Frank S. Mead, 89.
210. Frances Angermayer, from "The Great Gardener."
210. Herbert Shipman, in *A Field of Diamonds*, comp. Joseph S. Johnson, 11.
211. John Wilhelm Rowntree, in *Varieties of Religious Experience*, William James.
211. B. H. Carroll, taken from a book of his messages, 1898, with an introduction by J. B. Cranfell.
212. David T. Robertson, in *I was Born Again*, Norman A. Wingate.

Part VII

215. Sir Oliver Lodge, in *Treasury of the Christian World*, comp. A. Gordon Nasby, 200.
215. Henry van Dyke, in *Knight's Up-to-the-Minute Illustrations*, ed. Walter B. Knight, 141.
215. Edwin Markham, from "The Place of Peace."
216. John Trevor, *My Quest for God*.
217. Charles M. Sheldon, in *Treasury of the Christian Faith*, ed. Stanley I. Stuber, 433.
218. Charles de Foucauld, *The Spiritual Autobiography of Charles de Foucauld*, trans. J. Holland Smith (New York: Kennedy, 1964); in *Quotable Saints*, comp. Ronda De Sola Chervin, 88.
218. Theodore Roosevelt, in "The Illustrator", in *Knight's Treasury of Illustrations*, ed. Walter B. Knight.
219. Michael Pupin, introductory quote in *New Sermon Illustrations for All Occasions*, ed. G. B. F. Hallock, 27; *Immigrant to Inventor*.
220. William J. Bryan, in *The Life of William Jennings Bryan*, Genevieve Forbes Herrick; in *Encyclopedia of 7700 Illustrations*, ed. Paul Lee Tan, 1552; in *Knight's Master Book of NEW Illustrations*, ed. Walter B. Knight, 554.
221. William A. Quayle, "The Christ of Christmas", in *A Treasury of Wisdom and Inspiration*, ed. David St. Leger, 328; in *5000 Best Modern Sermon Illustrations*, ed. G. B. D. Hallock, 227.
221. Samuel Chadwick, in "Gospel Banner", in *Knight's Treasury of Illustrations*, ed. Walter B. Knight, 423.
222. Samuel Logan Brengle, in *Portrait of a Prophet*, Clarence W. Hall. Reprinted by permission of The Salvation Army National Headquarters.
223. Rodney "Gypsy" Smith, *Autobiography*; in *40 Conversion Stories*, comp. Samuel Fisk, 133; in *On This Day*, ed. Robert J. Morgan, June 25.
224. William R. Inge, in *Treasury of the Christian Faith*, ed. Stanley I. Stuber, 107.
224. Walter Rauschenbusch, from "The Postern Gate"; in *Encyclopedia of Religious Quotations*, ed. Frank S. Mead, 114.
225. Rabindranath Tagore, *Gitanjali*.
226. Walter B. Hinson, *A Grain of Wheat and Other Sermons*.
227. Billy Sunday, from an account in *The Boston Herald*, as told in many of his sermons; also in *Knight's Master Book of New Illustrations*, ed. Walter B. Knight, 121-2.
228. Charles R. Brown, in *New Sermon Illustrations for All Occasions*, ed. G. B. F. Hallock, 153.
229. Charles T. Studd, in *Doubleday Christian Quotation Collection*, comp. Hannah Ward, 222; *C. T. Studd*, Norman Grubb, in *40 Fascinating Conversion Stories*, ed. Samuel Fisk, 139-40.
229. Sir Francis Younghusband, in *Watcher on the Hills*, Raynor C. Johnson..
230. Rufus Jones, "A Small Town Boy" in the *Quaker Reader*, selected and introduced by Jessamyn West; *Inner Life; The Luminous Trail*, 165; *My Idea of God; American Spiritual Autobiographies*, ed. Louis Finkelstein, 124. Used by permission of Mary Hoxie Jones.
233. Alfred C. Lane, in *The Faith of Great Scientists*, The American Weekly, 1948, © by Hearst Pub. Co., 39.
233. John H. Jowett, in *Knight's Illustrations for Today*, ed. Walter B. Knight, 340
234. Miguel de Unamuno, *Prosa Diversa*; in *Encyclopedia of Religious Quotations*, ed. Frank S. Mead, 243.

235. Sir Wilfred Grenfell of Labrador, *What Life Means to me.* Copyright © 1927. Used by permission of Houghton Mifflin; in *Knight's Treasury of Illustrations*, ed. Walter B. Knight, 66; in *Treasury of Sermon Illustrations*, ed. Charles L. Wallis, 228; *Knight's Treasury of Illustrations*, ed. Walter B. Knight, 19; *A Labrador Doctor* (his autobiography), in *A Treasury of Sermon Illustrations*, ed. Charles L. Wallis, 207.

237. William Lyon Phelps, in *A Field of Diamonds*, comp. Joseph S. Johnson, 80.

237. William Adams Brown, in *Treasury of the Christian Faith*, comp. Stanley I. Stuber, 89, 283.

238. N. McGee Waters, in *5000 Best Modern Sermon Illustrations*, ed. G. B. F. Hallock, 231.

238. H. G. Wells, *God the Invisible King*; in *A Treasury of Sermon Illustrations*, ed. Charles L. Wallis, 139.

240. Robert E. Speer, by Christian R. Reisner, in *A Treasury of the Christian Faith*, comp. Stanley I. Stuber, 701; in *A Treasury of Sermon Illustrations*, ed. Charles L. Wallis, 39-40.

241. Amy Carmichael, letter written in the Old Forest House, 1922; letter written to one of her "children" that she worked with; in *Nelson's Complete Book*, ed. Robert J. Morgan, 696.

242. Mary Austin, introductory quote in *Treasury of the Christian Faith*, comp. Stanley I. Stuber, 518; *Experiences Facing Death.*

243. Hugh Black, in *New Sermon Illustrations for All Occasions*, ed. G. B. F. Hallock, 99.

244. Charles Scoville, in *A Field of Diamonds*, comp. Joseph S. Johnson, 76.

244. Melvin Trotter, in *Knight's Treasury of Illustrations*, ed. Walter B. Knight, 339.

245. Alice Hegan Rice, *My Pillow Book*, 4. Reprinted by permission of Ameron Ltd., Mattituck, N.Y.

245. David Grayson, 1,2. *Great Possessions; Adventures in Friendship.*

246. Mrs Charles E. (Lettie) Cowman, in *Knight's Treasury of Illustrations*, ed. Walter B. Knight, 268; in *Joy in His Presence*, ed. Joan Winmill Brown, November 22.

247. C. F. Andrews, *Letters to a Friend*, 25.

248. Francis J. McConnell, in *The Golden Book of Immortality*, comp. Thomas Curtis Clark, 196.

249. Elizabeth Elliott, in *The Dynamics of Religious Conversion*, V. Bailey Gillespie.

249. Phillip Cabot, *Except Ye Be Born Again.*

250. Anne Douglas Sedgwick, writing to a friend from the sickbed about what trust in Christ meant to her.

250. George Moore, writing in his diary after a severe attack of pleurisy.

251. Robert Norwood, in *A Treasury of the Christian Faith*, comp. Stanley I. Stuber, 629.

251. Gilbert K. Chesterton, *The Collected Poems of G. K. Chesterton.*

252. Johannes Anker-Larsen, *With the Door Open.*

253. Emily Herman, *Creative Prayer*, 117, 114.

254. Mary McLeod Bethune, in *American Spiritual Autobiographies*, 182-3, 186. Used by permission of Cookman-Bethune College Library.

255. Carl G. Jung, *Memories, Dreams, Reflections* (New York: Vantage Books, 1965). Used by permission of Random House.

256. Albert Schweitzer, in *Daily Celebration*, William Barclay.

256. J. C. Penney, reported by John Fitts, in *Illustrations Unlimited*, ed. James S. Hewitt, 49; *How To Stop Worrying and Start Living*, Dale Carnegie, 253-254.

257. Harry A. Ironside, in *Ordained By the Lord*, Schuyler English © Loizeaux Brothers, Inc.

258. Ancilla (pseud. of Grace A. Wood), *The Following Feet.*

259. John E. Brown, *John Brown of Arkansas.*

259. Joseph Fort Newton, in *The Golden Book of Immortality*, comp. Thomas Curtis Clark, 27.

260. Upton Sinclair, *What God Means to Me.*

261. Harry Bissiker, in *Treasury of the Christian World*, comp. A. Gordon Nasby, 340.

262. Harry Emerson Fosdick, 1. *On Being a Real Person*; describing his call to the ministry; 2, 3. in *Treasury of the Christian Faith*, comp. Stanley I. Stuber, 227, 326.

263. Clarence McCartney, in *McCartney's Illustrations*, ed. Clarence McCartney, 145.

264. Ralph S. Cushman, from "Sundown" and "Why" in *More Hilltop Verses and Prayers*, Ralph Cushman and Robert Earl Cushman.

265. Helen Keller, "A Flame of Fire"; *Midstream: My Later Life*; in *OmniRead Treasuries*, ed. Peter Sumner; in *Light from Many Lamps*, comp. Lillian Eichler Watson, 93; Donald Davidson, in *Treasury of the Christian World*, comp. A. Gordon Nasby, 132; common quote; in *Treasury Of the Christian Faith*, comp. Stanley I. Stuber, 42; *Midstream: My Later Life*; common quote.

267. W. Cosby Bell, by D. A. MacLennan, in *Treasury of the Christian Faith*, comp. Stanley I. Stuber, 432.

268. Alexander Yelchaninov, *Diary*.

268. William Temple, *The New Encyclopedia of Christian Quotations*, ed. Mark Walter, 773.

268. Walter Wilson, *Let's Go Fishing with the Doctor*.

269. Raissa Maritain, *Raissa's Journal*. Used by permission of Donald P. Ford, Jr., executor.

270. Victor F. Hess, "The Faith of Great Scientists," *The American Weekly*, © 1948 by the Hearst Pub. Co., 11.

271. Hugh Walpole, in *Greatest Thoughts about Jesus Christ*, ed. J. Gilchrist Lawson.

271. Thomas A. Lambie, in *Knight's Illustrations for Today*, ed. Walter B. Knight, 260-261.

272. Oswald W. S. McCall, *The Hand of God*.

273. Teunis E. Gouwens, in *New Sermon Illustrations for All Occasions*, ed. G. B. F. Hallock, 348.

273. Sister Eva of Friedenshort, in *You Can Say That Again*, ed. R. E. O. White, 61.

273. Martha Snell Nicholson, *His Banner Over Me*. Used by permission of Moody Press, Chicago; in *40 Fascinating Conversion Stories*, comp. Samuel Fisk, 112-113.

274. John Baillie, in *Joy in His Presence*, ed. Joan Winmill Brown, November 24.

275. Charles E. Fuller, in "The People's Magazine," in *Knight's Master Book of New Illustrations*, ed. Walter B. Knight, 118-9; in *Encyclopedia Of 7700 Illustrations*, comp. Paul Lee Tan, 545-6.

277. Toyohiko Kagawa, in *OmniRead Treasuries*, comp. Peter Sumner.

277. Robert G. LeTourneau, *Mover of Men and Mountains* (Upper Saddle River, N.J.: Prentice Hall, 1960). Used by permission of Richard LeTourneau.

279. Sadhu Sundar Singh, in *The Sadhu*, B. H. Streeter and A. J. Appasamy; in *Anthology of Jesus*, comp. James Marchant, ed. Warren B. Wiersbe, 233; *With and Without Christ*.

280. Oswald J. Smith, in *I Was Born Again*, Norman A. Wingate, 105.

281. Katharine Butler Hathaway, *The Journals and Letters of the Little Locksmith*. Used by permission of F. Anthony Butler, Trustee.

281. Christopher Morley, *Inward Ho!* Copyright 1923, 1950 by Christopher Morley.

282. Dwight D. Eisenhower, in *Wings of Joy*, comp. Joan Winmill Brown, 53; in *The New Encyclopedia of Christian Quotations*, ed. Mark Water, 1072.

282. Edith Stein, in *Doubleday Christian Quotation Collection*, comp. Hannah Ward, 221.

283. Edna St. Vincent Millay, from "Renascence"; *Renascence and other Poems by Edna St. Vincent Millay*.

283. Arthur H. Compton, in *Knight's Illustrations for Today*, ed. Walter B. Knight, 322.

284. William Faulkner, in *Chemical & Engineering News*, Dec. 24, 2001, 3.

284. A. W. Tozer, *Renewed Day By Day* © 1980, vol. 1; *The Root of the Righteous* © 1955, 1986. Both excerpts reprinted with permission of Christian Publications, Camp Hill, Pa.

285. C. S. Lewis, *Mere Christianity*. Copyright © C. S. Lewis Pte. Ltd. 1942, 1943, 1944, 1952, reprinted by permission; *Til We Have Faces*; *Weight of Glory*, "Is Theology Poetry?" copyright © C. S. Lewis Pte. Ltd. 1949, reprinted by permission; *Mere Christianity*, 106; in *New Life*, the Disciplined Order of Christ newsletter; from *Surprised by Joy: The Shape of My Early Life* by C. S. Lewis, copyright © by C. S. Lewis Pte. Ltd. and renewed 1984 by Arthur Owen Barfield, reprinted by permission of Harcourt, Inc.

288. Edwin P. Booth, *From Experience to Faith*, 93.

288. Whittaker Chambers, *Witness* (New York: Random House, 1953). Used by permission.

289. Peter Marshall, from "Tap on the Shoulder" a sermon published in *Mr. Jones, Meet the Master: Sermons and Prayers of Peter Marshall*.

290. Greta Palmer, "Escaping from an Atheist's Cell", originally published as, "Why I Am a Catholic" by Gretta Palmer, copyright ©1947 by The Sign; in *The Road to Damascus*.

290. Dawson Trotman, *Born to Reproduce*.

291. Dietrich Bonhoeffer, introductory comments to two Nazi guards who were taking him to be executed, in *Conversion: A Spiritual Journey by Malcolm Muggeridge* (London: William Collins Sons, 1988), 146; *Letters and Papers from Prison*. Reprinted with permission of Scribner, an imprint of Simon & Schuster Adult Publishing Group from *Letters and Papers from Prison* by Dietrich Bonhoeffer, copyright © 1953, 1967, 1971 by SCM Press, Ltd.

292. John Stam, in *Wings of Joy*, comp. Joan Winmill Brown.

292. Etty Hillesum, from *An Interrupted Life: Diaries of Etty Hillesum, 1941-1943* by Etty Hillesum, translated by Arno Pomerans, Translation copyright © 1983 by Jonathan Cape Ltd. Copyright © 1981 by De Haan/uniboek b. v. Bussem. Used by permission of Pantheon Books, a div. of Random House, Inc.

293. *The Shaker Manifesto*, XII, 3, 1882.

293. Paul Elmer More, *Pages from an Oxford Diary*, Chapter XXVII and XXXII.

293. Merton S. Rice, in *Treasury of the Christian Faith*, ed. Stanley I. Stuber, 275.

294. Perry J. Stackhouse, in *Lamplight: Illustrations and Quotations for Pulpit and Forum*, ed. Perry J. Stackhouse, 1989. All *Lamplight* quotes used by permission of Baker Book House.

295. John R. Ewers, in *Treasury of the Christian Faith*, comp. Stanley I. Stuber, 412.

295. Arthur Wentworth Hewitt, in *New Sermon Illustrations for All Occasion*, ed. G. B. F. Hallock, 99-100.

296. Samuel Moor Shoemaker, in *Illustrations Unlimited*, ed. James S. Hewitt, 150. All *Illustrations Unlimited* used by permission of Tyndale House Publishers, Wheaton, Ill.

297. D. R. Davies, *In Search of Myself*.

298. Author unknown, in *2500 Best Modern Illustrations*, ed. G. B. F. Hallock, 322.

299. M. Louise Haskins, from "The Gate of the Year."

299. Unknown soldier, killed in W. W. I; poem found after his death, "If it Be All for Naught".

299. Norman Vernon, in *I was Born Again*, Norman A. Wingate.

300. Baron von Welz, in "The Pilgrim", in *Knight's Master Book of New Illustrations*, ed. Walter B. Knight, 106.

301. Samuel Smith, in *I Was Born Again*, Norman Wingate.

302. 22 Year old Dutch patriot, "This Week", in *A Treasury of Sermon Illustrations*, ed. Charles L Wallis, 95.

302. Mrs. W. K. Norton, *My Life*, The Pilgrim's Mission, Benares, India.

303. Author Unknown, in *Knight's Treasury of Illustrations*, ed. Walter B. Knight, 217l.

303. Author Unknown, in *Christian Life*, 1957.

303. Editor of a newspaper, in *New Sermon Illustrations for all Occasions*, ed. G. B. F. Hallock, 100.

303. P. (Peter) T. Forsyth, *The Person and Places of Christ*, Lecture XII.

304. Author unknown, as told by Henry Sloan Coffin in 1877 in *God Confronts Man In History*.

PART VIII

307. Archibald Rutledge, *Peace in the Heart;* "Children of the Swamp and Wood," in *Knight's Master Book of New Illustrations*, ed. Walter B. Knight, 556.

308. Frank Laubach, *Letters From a Modern Mystic*, Laubach Literacy, 1937, excerpts from Jan. 26, 1930; May 24, 1930. Used by permission of Laubach Literacy.

310. E. Stanley Jones, "Longing I Sought Thee," from the pamphlet, "How to Pray," in *The Christian Advocate*; in *A Treasury of Sermons Illustrations*, ed. Charles L. Wallis, 83.

311. Albert E. Day, *An Autobiography of Prayer*, p. 23-24 31, 30, 177, 17. Used by permission of The Disciplined Order of Christ Ashland, Ohio.

314. Robert McQuilkin, in *On This Day*, ed. Robert J. Morgan, August 15; in *Nelson's Complete Book*, ed. Robert J. Morgan, 814.

315. Ralph Sockman, interview with James A. Simpson; in *Contemporary Quotations*, ed. James Beesley Simpson, 1961; *Now to Live!* Used by permission of Abingdon Press, Nashville, Tenn.

317. Corrie ten Boom, *Prison Letters*, 1975. Used by permission of Baker Book House; *The End Battle*, 1997. Used by permission of Baker Book House; *The Hiding Place*, 1973, with John & Elizabeth Sherrill. Used by permission of Chosen Books and John & Elizabeth Sherrill.

319. F. C. Happold, *Adventures in Search of a Creed*, in *Mysticism: A Study and An Anthology*, 133-135.

320. Hoxie Fairchild, *Toward Belief*, 140. Used by permission of Simon & Schuster.

320. A. J. Cronin, "Adventures In Two Worlds," in Thomas S. Kepler, *Leaves From a Spiritual Notebook*.

322. Lajow Ordass, by Andrew Wyerman, in *Illustrations Unlimited*, ed. James S. Hewitt, 165.

322. Howard Thurman, *Disciplines of the Spirit*, 1963. Used by permission of Friends United Press.

323. Vance Havner, *Consider Him* © 1983. Used by permission of Baker Book House; *Peace in the Valley*, © 1962. Used by permission of Baker Book House.

324. Gladys Aylward, in *Nelson's Complete Book*, ed. Robert J. Morgan, 460; in *Doubleday Christian Quotation Collection*, comp. Hannah Ward, 231; in *Nelson's Complete Book*, ed. Robert J. Morgan, 460.

325. Ross J. S. Hoffman, *Restoration*, copyright ©1934 by Sheed & Ward.

326. Charles Lindbergh, in *Encyclopedia of 7700 Illustrations*, comp. Paul Lee Tan, 484.

326. Vaughn R. Shoemaker, in *Encyclopedia of 7700 Illustrations,* comp. Paul Lee Tan, 1058.

327. Malcolm Muggeridge, in *Time*, Dec 13, 1982, "People," 63; *The Lunn Log*, comp. The Lunn Family, 18; The Lunn Log, 67; Muggeridge's obituary, *Christianity Today*.

329. E. M. Blaiklock, from an address given at the University of Auckland, in July 1965, titled "Why I Am Still a Christian", in *Why I Am Still a Christian*, ed. E. M. Blaiklock, 11-12. All quotes from *Why I am Still a Christian* used by permission of Zondervan Publishing House, Grand Rapids, Mich.

329. Kingsley Mortimer, "Medicine of Faith", 1971; in *Why I am Still a Christian*, ed. E. M. Blaiklock, 146.

330. Maria von Trapp, in *Books That Made the Difference: What People Told Us*, Gordon & Patricia Sabine, Copyright © 1983. Used by permission of Library Professional Publications, an imprint of The Shoe String Press.

331. Hershell Hobbs, in *My Favorite Illustrations of Hershell Hobbs*, ed. Ronald G. Brown, 216. Used by permission of Broadman & Holamn Publishers, Nashville, Tenn.

331. Gerald Kennedy, in *A Second Reader's Notebook*, ed. Gerald Kennedy, 286; "Beyond Controversy," in *These Found the Way*, ed. David Wesley Soper, 113-114; in *These Found the Way*, 114-115; *I Believe* by Gerald Kennedy, 18. Copyright © 1958. Used by permission of Abingdon Press, Nashville, Tenn.

334. Mildred E. Whitcomb, "My Journey through Doubt", *Presbyterian Life*, 1948.

335. Nels S. Ferre, "The Third Conversion Never Fails," in *These Found the Way*, ed. David Wesley Soper, 136-137.

336. David Wesley Soper, "Unfinished Business," in *These Found the Way*, ed. David Wesley Soper, 171.

336. Robert Boyd Munger, *What Jesus Says*.

337. Werhner von Braun, in *Encyclopedia of 7700 Illustrations*, comp. Paul Lee Tan, 485; *Reader's Digest*, June 1960.

338. Charles l. Allen, in *Charles L. Allen Treasury*, ed. Charles L. Wallis. Copyright © 1970. Used by permission of Baker Book House.

339. Edith Schaeffer, "Christians Are Singing People," *Christianity Today* (January 7, 1977): 24.

339. Chad Walsh, "Several Roads Lead to Jerusalem," in *These Found the Way*, ed. David Wesley Soper, 128.

340. Harold E. Kohn, *Thoughts Afield*. Copyright © 1959. Used by permission of Wm. B. Eerdmans Publishing, Grand Rapids, Mich.

340. Joy Davidman, "The Longest Way Round," in *These Found the Way*, ed. David Wesley Soper, 13-23, 24, 26.

343. Dominic Zappa, in *The Kansas City Star*.

343. Thomas Merton, *New Seeds of Contemplation*. Copyright ©1961 by the Abbey of Gethsemani, Inc. Reprinted by permission of New Directions Publishing Corp.

345. Edith Margaret Clarkson, *All Nature Sings*. Copyright ©1968. Used by permission of Wm. B. Eerdmans Publishing Co., Grand Rapids, Mich.

346. James H. Shaw, in *Knight's Illustrations for Today*, ed. Walter B. Knight, 324.

346. Harold J. Berman, in *Finding God at Harvard*, ed. Kelly Monroe, 295. All quotes from *Finding God at Harvard* used by permission of Zondervan Publishing House, Grand Rapids, Mich.

347. Billy Graham, in *Encyclopedia of 7700 Illustrations*, ed. Paul Lee Tan,129; David Rowlands, in *Knight's Illustrations for Today*, ed. Walter B. Knight, 71.

348. Ruth Bell Graham, in *Wings of Joy*, comp. Joan Winmill Brown, 52.

348. John McIntyre, in *Knight's Illustrations for Today*, ed. Walter B. Knight, 323.

349. Gordon J. Van Wylen, in *Knight's Illustrations for Today*, ed. Walter B. Knight, 323.

349. Warren Weaver, *Knight's Illustration for Today*, ed. Walter B. Knight, 322.

350. William P. Alston, in *God and the Philosophers*, ed. Thomas V. Morris. Copyright © 1994. All *God and the Philosophers* quotes used by permission of Oxford University Press, London.

351. Harold E. Hughes, *The Man from Ida Grove: A Senator's Personal Story*. Copyright © 1979. Used by permission of Eva M. Hughes.

351. J. M. Houston, "A God-Centered Personality," in *Why I Am Still a Christian*, ed. E. M. Blaiklock, 92-3.

352. D. A. Blaiklock, "A Medical Doctor's View," in *Why I Am Still a Christian*, ed. E. M. Blaiklock, 39.

353. W. E. Anderson, "A Philosopher Examines the Question," in *Why I Am Still a Christian*, ed. E. M. Blaiklock, 25, 26.

354. Donna Huber Miesbach, in "Gleanings: A Bimonthy Discussion of Life." Used by permission.

355. John Compton Ball, *God's Message*, 127.

356. Walter R. Hearn, in *Knight's Illustrations for Today*, ed. Walter B. Knight, 323.

357. Frederick Buechner, *A Room Called Remember: Meditations Through the Seasons* (New York: Harper 1984); *Telling Secrets: Uncollected Pieces* (San Francisco: Harper, 1991); *Now and Then* (New York: Harper, 1983), 120. Used by permission of the author.

359. Bonnidell Clouse, in *Storying Ourselves*, ed. D. John Lee, 93. Copyright © 1993. All *Storying Ourselves* quotes used by permission of Baker Book House.

360. John M. Drescher, *Testimony of Triumph*. Copyright © 1980. Used by permission of Zondervan Publishing House, Grand Rapids, Mich.

361. Martin Luther King, Jr., "The New York Times," 1968; "Redbook," September 1961; In *You Say You're Depressed!*, by Donald Deffner, Abingdon, 1976, 80.

362. James B. Irwin, "The New York Times," August 13, 1971.

363. Henry Blackaby, *Created to Be God's Friend Workbook*, 37, 61. Copyright © 2000. Used by permission of Thomas Nelson, Inc., Nashville, Tenn.

364. Charles Colson, *Loving God*. Copyright © 1983. Used by permission of Zondervan Publishing House, Grand Rapids, Mich; *Houston Chronicle*, February 20, 1993; 3E.

365. Alvin Plantinga, in *Philosophers Who Believe*, ed. Kelly James Clark, 52, 51-2. Copyright © 1993. All quotes from *Philosophers Who Believe* used by permission of InterVarsity Press, Downers Grove, Ill.

367. Nicolas Wolterstorff, in *Philosophers Who Believe*, ed. Kelly James Clark, 273-275.

368. David Tonge, "The Search of Truth," in *Scientists Who Believe*, ed. Eric C. Barrett, 80-82. All quotes from *Scientists Who Believe* used by permission of Moody Press, Chicago.

369. Boris P. Dotsenko, "Flight to Faith," in *Scientists Who Believe*, ed. Eric C. Barrett, 9.

369. Randall J. Fisk, "Beyond Einstein," in *Scientists Who Believe*, ed. Eric C. Barrett, 85-87, 88.

371. Robert L. Hermann, "Searching for Longer Youth", in *Scientists Who Believe*, ed. Eric C. Barrett, 170.

371. Thelma Robinson, personal account. Used by permission.

372. Paul C. Vitz, in *Storying Ourselves*, ed. D. John Lee, 121, 129.

373. Emilie Griffin, *Turning: Reflections on the Experience of Conversion*. Copyright © 1980. Used by permission of Doubleday, Inc, N.Y.

375. Barbara Johnson, *Pack Up Your Gloomees in a Great Big Box, Then Sit on the Lid and Laugh!* © by Barbara Johnson, from the introduction (Dallas: Word Publishing Co., 1993). Used by permission of the author.

376. Robin Stratton, "What It Means to be a Carmelite," in *Spiritual Life*, Vol. 97, Number 4, Winter 2001. Used by permission of *Spiritual Life*.

377. Paul M. Anderson, "A Common Thread," in *Professors Who Believe*, ed. Paul M. Anderson, 21.

378. E. C. "Gene" Ashby, "God is Faithful," in *Professors Who Believe*, ed. Paul M. Anderson, 54.

378 .R. Betty Hope-Gitens, personal account. Used by permission of the author.

379. Kit Lane, personal account, originally appeared in *The Upper Room*, Oct., 1990. Used by permission.

380. Robert Selvendran, "Seeing Things Differently"; *UBS Special Report 15*, April 1997, 5; *Connect*, Winter 1995, 14-15. Used by permission of the author.

383. Colleen Townsend Evans, *A New Joy*, p. 44-46. Copyright © 1978. Used by permission of Baker Book House, Grand Rapids, Mich.

384. Delton Dees, in *The Carrollton Democrat*, Carrollton, Mo., March 10, 2000. Used by permission.

384. John F. Walkup, "From Religion to Relationship," in *Professors Who Believe*, ed. Paul Anderson, 85.

385. John K. Holmes, "Crossing Bridges," in *Scientists Who Believe*, ed. Eric C. Barrett, 139.

385. Kenneth G. Elzinga, "Christ the Anchor, Christ the Servant," in *Professors Who Believe*, ed. Paul M. Anderson, 108-9.

386. Verna Benner Carson, "A Life Journey with Jesus," in *Professors Who Believe*, ed. Paul M. Anderson, 103-104.

386. Ronald D. Anderson, "Hard Questions, Easy Yoke," in *Professors Who Believe*, ed. Paul M. Anderson, 113.

387. Robert C. Newman, "From One Heavenly Subject to Another," an interview with the Radio Academy of Science, August, 1981; in *Scientists Who Believe*, ed. Eric C. Barrett, 130.

388. Robert C. Roberts, in *God and the Philosophers*, ed. Thomas V. Morris, 127.

390. Glaphre Guilliland, *When the Pieces Don't Fit, God Makes the Difference* (Grand Rapids: Zondervan, 1984). 297-298. Used by permission of the author.

391. James Finley, *The Awakening Call: Fostering Intimacy with God*, 57. Used by permission of the author.

392. Bill Tammeus, in *The Kansas City Star*. Used by permission of *The Kansas City Star*.

393. Duke Tufty, personal account in *The Kansas City Star*, September 16, 2000.

394. Varia, in *Jesus Freaks: Stories of Those Who Stood Up for Jesus*, dc Talk and the Voice of the Martyrs.

396. Anonymous, *Journal of An Ordinary Pilgrim*, 1954.

397. James P. Keener, "Confessions of a Weird Mathematician," in *Professors Who Believe*, ed. Paul M. Anderson, 91.

397. Linda Trinkaus Zagzebski, in *Philosophers Who Believe*, ed. Kelly James Clark, 254.

397 Michael B. Yang, in *Finding God at Harvard*, ed. Kelly Monroe, 122-3.

398. Glen C. Loury, in *Finding God at Harvard*, ed. Kelly Monroe, 73.

399. Luisa (Sue) Hulett, "A Prodigal Child Finds Faith," in *Professors Who Believe*, ed. Paul M. Anderson, 135.

399. J. Gary Eden, "Unseen Realities," in *Professors Who Believe*, ed. Paul M. Anderson, 77.

401. C. Stephen Layman, in *God and the Philosophers*, ed. Thomas V. Morris, 89.

401. Patricia Reiff, "Three Heavens—Our Home," in *Professors Who Believe*, ed. Paul M. Anderson, 61, 64.

402. C. Stephen Evans, in *Storying Ourselves*, ed. D. John Lee, 207-208.

403. Sing-Yang Tan, in *Storying Ourselves*, ed. D. John Lee, 52-53.

404. Anne Lamott, *Traveling Mercies: Some Thoughts on Faith*. Copyright © 1999. Used by permission of Random House, New York, N. Y.

404. Zahid, in *Jesus Freaks: Stories of Those Who Stood Up for Jesus*, dc Talk and Voice of the Martyrs.

405. Max Lucado, *When God Whispers Your Name.* Copyright © 1994. Reprinted by permission of Thomas Nelson Publishing, Nashville, Tenn..

406. Craig Brelsford, in *The Upper Room,* June 9, 1999. Used by permission of author.

406. Holly McKissick, personal account in *The Kansas City Star,* Jan. 14, 2000. Used by permission.

407. Merry Stanford, in *Friends Journal,* January 2000. Used by permission of *Friends Journal.*

409. Einar Ingvi Magnusson, in *The Upper Room,* April 25, 1998. Used by permission.

409. Joyce C. Day, in *The Upper Room,* June 11, 1997. Used by permission.

410. Joni Eareckson Tada, from the introduction to *Joni* by Joni Earickson Tada. Copyright © 1996. Used by permission of Zondervan Publishing House, Grand Rapids, Mich.

411. Brent Foster, in *Finding God at Harvard,* ed. Kelly Monroe.

411. Reshma Arora Samuel, in *The Upper Room.* Used by permission.

412. Connie Semy P. Mella, in *The Upper Room,* Aug. 3, 1999. Used by permission.

412. Cassie Bernall, in *The Kansas City Star,* April 21, 1999.

413. Ray Sobrette, in *The Upper Room,* Jan 12, 2000. Used by permission.

413. K. D. Coombes, in *The Upper Room,* Jan 27, 1977. Used by permission.

414. Sharon Ward, in *The Upper Room.* Used by permission.

414. Ralph Erskine, in *A Treasury of Sermon Illustrations,* ed. Charles L. Wallis, 269.

415. Author Unknown, in "Christianity Today", in *Knight's Treasury of Illustrations,* ed. Walter B. Knight, 3.

415. Martha P. Giles, in *The Upper Room.* Used by permission.

416. Josef Tson. "Thank You for the Beating," *Christian Herald* (April 1988).

417. Author Unknown. *Sunshine For Shut-Ins,* 128.

417. Woman physician, in "The Atlantic Monthly," in *Knight's Illustrations for Today,* ed. Walter B. Knight, 135.

417. Marilyn Blackaby. *Home Life,* February 2001, © LifeWay Christian Resources of the Southern Baptist Convention. All rights reserved. Used by permission.

BIBLIOGRAPHY

(These are anthologies, most having several citations.)

Anderson, Paul, ed., *Professors Who Believe: The Spiritual Journeys of Christian Faculty*. Downers Grove IL: InterVarsity Press, 1998.

Baillie, John, ed., *Diary of Readings*. New York: Charles Scribner's Sons, 1955.

Barrett, Eric C. and David Fisher, eds., *Scientists Who Believe: 21 Tell Their Own Stories*. Chicago: Moody Press, 1984.

Blackburn, E. A., comp., *A Treasury of the Kingdom*. New York and London: Oxford University Press, 1954.

Blaiklock, E. M., comp. and ed., *Why I Am Still a Christian*. Grand Rapids MI: Zondervan Publishing Hose, 1971.

Brown, Joan Winmill, comp. and ed. *Wings of Joy*. Old Tappan NJ: F. H. Revell, 1977.

Brown, Joan Winmill, ed., *Joy in His Presence*. Minneapolis MN: World Wide Publications, 1982.

Bryant, Al, comp. and ed., *1000 New Illustrations*. Grand Rapids MI: Zondervan Publishing House, 1957.

Catrevas, C. N., *New Dictionary of Thoughts*, originally *A Cyclopedia of Quotations*, ed., Tryon Edwards, revised by C. N. Catrevas. U. S. A: Standard Book Company, 1961.

Chervin, Ronda De Sola, comp., *Quotable Saints*. Ann Arbor, MI: Servant Publications, 1992.

Clark, Kelly James, ed., *Philosophers Who Believe: The Spiritual Journeys of 11 Leading Thinkers*. Downers Grove IL: InterVarsity Press, 1993.

Clark, Thomas Curtis, and Hazel Davis Clark, comps. and eds., *The Golden Book of Immortality*. New York: Association Press, 1954.

Copeland, Lewis, ed., *Popular Quotations for All Uses*. Garden City NJ: Garden City Pulishig Co., 1942.

Douglas, Charles Noel, comp., *Forty Thousand Sublime and Beautiful Thoughts*. New York: The Christian Herald, 1904.

Ely, Virginia. *I Quote: A Collection of Ancient & Modern Wisdom & Inspiration*. George W. Stewart, Publisher, Inc., 1947.

Fisk, Samuel, comp., *40 Fascinating Conversion Stories*. Grand Rapids MI: Kregel Publications, 1993.

Fisk, Samuel, comp., *More Fascinating Conversion Stories*. Grand Rapids MI: Kregel Publications, 1994.

Foster, Elon, ed., *6000 Sermon Illustrations*. Grand Rapids MI: Baker Books, 1952.

Fox, John, ed., updated by Harold J. Chadwick, *Fox's Book of the Martyrs*. Gainesville FL: Bridge Logos Publishers, 2001.

Freeman, Bill, ed., *How They found Christ*. Scottsdale, Arizona: Ministry Publications, 1983.

Fremantle, Anne, ed. with an introduction by W. H. Auden, *The Protestant Mystics: An Anthology of Spiritual Experience from Martin Luther to T. S. Eliot*. New York: The New American Library, 1964.

Gottschall, A. H., comp., *Selections from Latter Testimonies and Dying Words of Saints and sinners: Being the Closing Expressions of Nearly Seventeen Hundred Persons, Believers and Unbelievers*. Harrisburg PA: "The Old Path", 1900.

Hallock, G. B. F., comp and ed., *New Sermon Illustrations for All Occasions*. Westwood NJ: Fleming H. Revell Company, 1957.

Hallock, G. B. F., ed., *2500 Best Modern Illustrations*. New York & London: Harper & Brothers, 1935.

Hallock, G. B. F., ed., *Five Thousand Best Modern Illustrations*. New York: George H. Doran Company, 1927.

Happold, F. C., *Mysticism: A Study and an Anthology*. Middlesex, England and Baltimore MD: Penguin Books, 1963. © estate of F. C. Happold, 1963, 1964, 1970.

Hart, William J., ed., *600 Sermon Illustrations*. Baker Book House, 1969.

Hewett, James S. , ed., *Illustrations Unlimited: A Topical Collection of Hundreds of Stories, Quotations, and Humor for Speakers, Writers, Pastors and Teachers.* Wheaton IL: Tyndale House Publishers, Inc., 1988.

Hewitt, James S., ed., *Illustrations Unlimited.* Wheaton IL: Tyndale House Publishers, 1988.

Hobbs, Herschell. *My Favorite Illustrations of Herschell Hobbs.* Compiled by Ronald K. Brown. Nashville TN: Broadman and Holman, 1999.

Holdcraft, Paul E., comp., *Cyclopedia of Bible Illustrations.* New York and Nashville TN: Abingdon-Cokesbury Press, 1947.

Jesus Freaks, dc Talk and the Voice of the Martyrs. Albury Publications, Tulsa, OK: 1999.

Johnson, Joseph S., comp., *A Field of Diamonds.* Nashville TN: Broadman Press, 1974.

Jones, G. Curtis, ed., *1000 Illustrations for Preaching and Teaching.* Nashville TN: Broadman Press, 1986.

Kenndy, Gerald, comp., *A Second Reader's Notebook.* New York: Harper & Brother, 1959.

Knight, Walter B. Knight, ed., *Knight's Treasury of Illustrations.* Grand Rapids, MI: Wm. B. Eerdmans Publishing Co., 1963.

Knight, Walter B., ed., *3000 Illustrations for Christian Service.* Grand Rapids MI: Wm. B. Eerdmans Publishing Co., 1947.

Knight, Walter B., ed., *Knight's Illustrations for Today.* Chicago: The Moody Bible Institute of Chicago, 1970.

Knight, Walter B., ed., *Knight's Master Book of NEW Illustrations;* Grand Rapids MI: Wm. B. Eerdmans Publishing Co., 1956.

Knight, Walter B., ed., *Knight's Up-to-the Minute Illustrations.* Chicago: Moody Press, 1974.

Lawson, J. Gilchrist, ed., *Greatest Thoughts about Jesus Christ.* New York: Richard Smith, 1930.

Lawson, James Gilchrist, ed., *Deeper Experiences of Famous Christians.* Anderson, Indiana: The Warner Press, 1911.

Lee, D. John, ed., *Storying Ourselves: A Narrative Perspective on Christians in Psychology.* Grand Rapids MI: Baker Book House, 1993.

Luccock, Halford E., and Frances Brentano, eds., *The Questing Spirit: Religion in the Literature of Our Times*. New York: Coward-McCann, Inc., 1947.

Lunn Family, comps., *The Lunn Log*. Kansas City: Beacon Hill Press of Kansas City, 1974.

Lytle, Clyde Francis, ed., *Leaves of Gold*. Williamsport PA: The Coslett Publishing Co., 1938.

Macartney, Clarence E., *Macartney's Illustrations: Illustrations from the Sermons of Clarence E. Macartney*. New York and Nashville TN, 1945.

Marchant, Sir James, arranged and selected by. *Anthology of Jesus*. London: Cassell & Co., © 1921. Reprinted: Wiersbe, Warren W. ed., *Anthology of Jesus*. Grand Rapids MI: Kregel Publications, 1981.

Mead, Frank S., ed. and comp., *Encyclopedia of Religious Quotations*. Westwood NJ: Fleming H. Revell Company, 1965.

Monroe, Kelly, ed., *Finding God at Harvard*. Grand Rapids MI: Zondervan, 1996.

Morgan, Robert J., ed., *Nelson's Complete Book of Stories, Illustrations & Quotes*. Nashville TN Thomas Nelson, Inc., 2000.

Morgan, Robert J., *On This Day: 365 Amazing and Inspiring Stories about Saints, Martyrs and Heroes*. Nashville TN: Thomas Nelson Publishers, 1997.

Morris, Thomas V, ed., *God and the Philosophers: The Reconciliation of Faith and Reason*. New York: Oxford University Press, 1994.

Nasby, A. Gordon, comp. and ed., *Treasury of the Christian World*. New York: Harper & Brothers, 1953.

Peale, Norman Vincent, ed., *Treasury of Courage and Confidence*. Pauling NY: Foundation for Christian Living, in association with Doubleday & Co., 1970.

Pepper, Margaret, comp. and ed., *A Dictionary of Religious Quotations*. London: Andre Deutsch Ltd., 1989.

Reinhold, H. A. , ed., *The Soul Afire: Revelations of the Mystics*. New York: Meridian Books, © 1944 Pantheon Books.

Ritchie, John, ed., *500 Gospel Incidents Illustrations and Testimonies*. London: Alfred Holness, 1912.

Simpson, James Beesley, ed., *Contemporary Quotations*. New York: Crowell, 1964.

Soper, David Wesley, ed., *These Found the Way: Thirteen Converts to Protestant Christianity*. Philadelphia: Westminster Press, 1951.

Spence-Jones, H. D. M., ed, *Thirty Thousand Thoughts*, vol. 1. New York: Funk Wagnalls, 1889.

St. Leger, David, ed., *A Treasury of Wisdom and Inspiration*. New York: The New American Library of World Literature, 1954.

Stackhouse, Perry J., ed., *Lamplight: Illustrations and Quotations for Pulpit and Platform*. New York: Fleming Revell Company, 1939.

Stuber, Stanley I., and Thomas Curtis Clark, eds., *Treasury of the Christian Faith*. New York: Association Press, 1949.

Stuber, Stanley I., ed., *The Christian Reader*. Association Press, 1952.

Sumner, Peter Stafford, comp., *OmniRead Treasuries*. Found on the internet at peterspearls.com.

Sunshine for Shut-Ins, comp. by a "shut-in". New York: Thomas Y. Crowell & Co. Publishers, 1895.

Tan, Paul Lee, comp. and ed. *Encyclopedia of 7700 Illustrations: Signs of the Times*. Rockville MD: Assurance Publishers, 1982.

Tileston, Mary W., comp., *Daily Strength for Daily Needs*. Old Tappan NJ: Fleming H. Revell Company, 1966. © 1886 by Mary W. Tileston.

Tileston, Mary Wilder, comp., *Joy and Strength*. Minneapolis, MN: World Wide Publications, 1986. © 1901, 1929 by Mary Wilder Tileston.

Van de Weyer, Robert, ed., *Roots of Faith: An Anthology of Early Christian Spirituality to Contemplate and Treasure*. Grand Rapids MI: Wm. B. Eerdmans Publishing Co., 1997.

Wallis, Charles L., ed., *The Treasure Chest*. New York and London: Harper & Row Publishers, 1965.

Wallis, Charles L., ed., *A Treasury of Sermon Illustrations*. Nashville TN: Abingdon Press, ©1950 by Pierce & Smith.

Wallis, Charles, L. ed., *Words of Life*. New York: Harper & Row, 1966.

Ward, Hannah, and Jennifer Ward, comps., *The Doubleday Christian Quotation Collection*. (New York: Doubleday Dell Publishers, 1997.

Water, Mark, comp., *The New Encyclopedia of Christian Quotations*. Grand Rapids MI: Baker Book Publishers, 1973.

Watson, Lillian Eichler, selected and commentary by, *Light From Many Lamps*. New York: Simon & Schuster, 1951.

Webb, Aquilla, *1001 Illustrations for Pulpit and Platform*. New York and London: Harper & Brothers, Publishers, 1926.

Webb, Aquilla, ed., *One Thousand Evangelistic Illustrations*. New York: George H. Doran Company, 1921.

Webb, Aquilla. Ed., with an introduction by James A. Backley. *One Thousand New Illustrations*. New York and London: Harper & Brothers, 1931.

White, R. E. O., comp. and arranger, *You Can say That Again: An Anthology of Words Fitly Spoken*. Grand Rapids, MI: Zondervan Publishing House: 1991.

Wingate, Norman A., *I Was Born Again*. Mechanicsburg PA: The Lighthouse Press, 1946.

Author Index

Abbott, Lyman	1835-1922
Adams, John	1735-1826
Adams, John Quincy	1767-1848
Addison, Joseph	1672-1719
Agassiz, Louis	1807-1873
Allen, Charles L.	1913-
Alston, William P.	1921-
Ambrose	c.340-397
Amiel, Henri-Frederic	1821-1881
Andersen, W. E.	1923-
Anderson, Paul M.	1938-
Anderson, Ronald D.	contemporary
Andrews, C. F.	1871-1940
Andronicus	(martyred 303)
Angermayer, Frances, poet	
Anker-Larsen, Johannes	1874-1957
Anselm	1033-1109
Arnold, Thomas	1795-1842
Ashby, E. C. "Gene"	1930-
Askew, Anne	d. 1546
Athenagoras	2nd cent.
Audubon, John James	1785-1851
Augustine of Hippo	354-430
Austin, Mary	1868-1934
Aylward, Gladys	(1904 or a few years earlier-1970)
Bach, Johann Sebastian	1685-1750
Baille, John	1886-1960
Ball, John Compton	1924
Barclay, Robert	1648-1690
Barnabas (the apostle)	(lived during parts of the 1st and 2nd centuries)
Becket, Thomas a	1118-1170
Beecher, Henry Ward	813-1887
Beethoven, Ludwig von	1712-1773
Bell, W. Cosby	1881-1933
Berman, Harold J.	1918-
Bernall, Cassie	1982-1999
Bernard of Clairvaux	1090-1153
Bethune, Mary McLeod	1875-1953
Bickersteth, Edward H.	1825-1906
Bilney, Thomas	-1531
Bisseker, Harry	1878-
Black, Hugh	1868-1953
Blackaby, Henry	contemporary
Blackaby, Marilyn	contemporary
Blaiklock, D. A.	contemporary